MEDIA ECONOMICS
Theory and Practice

Second Edition

LEA's COMMUNICATION SERIES
Jennings Bryant/Dolf Zillmann, General Editors

Selected titles in Mass Communication (Alan Rubin, Advisory Editor) include:

Alexander/Owers/Carveth • *Media Economics Theory and Practice, Second Edition*

Lacy/Sohn/Wicks • *Media Management: A Casebook Approach*

Moore/Farrar/Collins • *Advertising and Public Relations Law*

Moore • *Mass Communication Law and Ethics*

Sterling/Bracken/Hill • *Mass Communications Research Resources: An Annotated Guide*

Warner • *Media Management Review*

For a complete list of other titles in LEA's Communication Series, please contact Lawrence Erlbaum Associates, Publishers

MEDIA ECONOMICS
Theory and Practice

Second Edition

Edited by

Alison Alexander
University of Georgia

James Owers
Georgia State University

Rod Carveth
University of Bridgeport

 LAWRENCE ERLBAUM ASSOCIATES, PUBLISHERS
1998   Mahwah, New Jersey   London

Lawrence Erlbaum Associates, Inc., Publishers
10 Industrial Avenue
Mahwah, New Jersey 07430

Cover Design by Kathryn Houghtaling Lacey

Library of Congress Cataloging-in-Publication Data

Media economics : theory and practice / edited by Alison
Alexander, James Owers, Rod Carveth. — 2nd ed.
        p. cm.
    Includes bibliographical references and indexes.
    ISBN 0-8058-1842-1 (paper : alk. paper)
    1. Mass media—Economic aspects.   I. Alexander,
Alison, 1949–   . II. Owers, James. III. Carveth, Rod.
    P96.E25M4   1998
    338.4'730223—dc21   97-11806
                                                CIP

Books published by Lawrence Erlbaum Associates are printed
on acid-free paper, and their bindings are chosen for strength
and durability.

Printed in the United States of America
10 9 8 7 6 5 4 3 2

Contents

Preface

The importance of media economics became apparent in the massive business reorganizations of the 1980s and 1990s. Due to regulatory, technological, and financial changes, media became the target of takeovers, breakups, mergers, and acquisitions. Media economics became much more than understanding cash flow within a single business organization. This book is designed to focus on the principle of economics in the business sector and to apply it to specific media industries.

This volume examines the process of media economics decision making through an exploration of such topics as industrial restructuring, regulatory constraints on media operations, and changing economic value. Because the structure and value of media industries have changed so rapidly over the last decade, it is important to understand the mechanics of such change so as to provide insight into the processes reproducing contemporary trends in media economics, rather than simply documenting historical patterns.

Part I of this book focuses on the concerns of media economics, the techniques of economic and business analysis, and overall characteristics of the rapidly changing media environments. Chapter 1, by James Owers, Rod Carveth, and Alison Alexander, is designed to provide a framework of reference in economics and business. This chapter should enable the reader without a background in these areas to appreciate the overall structure, conceptual content, and application of economics to media business. For the reader with a strong background in economic and business studies, this chapter serves as a brief review and introduction to the application of these disciplines to media firms.

Chapter 2, by Douglas Gomery, outlines the concepts of economic structure, media conduct, and media performance as basic dimensions that should allow for the full study of media as business and social institutions. He asks the reader to consider the standards by which the structure and conduct of media firms can be evaluated.

Chapter 3, by Robert Corn-Revere and Rod Carveth, provides a context for understanding the recent regulatory changes for media industries, particularly the Telecommunications Act of 1996. From the vantage point of Corn-Revere, a communications lawyer for over a decade, the authors produce a view of the legal structures that guide public policy toward electronic media.

In chapter 4, Benjamin Bates looks at the details involved in the valuation of media properties. He reviews the economic concepts and principles of value for the noneconomist and reflects the generally accepted practices in valuation. Bates also reviews how these concepts of value are applied in examining the worth of particular firms in the communication industries. The role of valuation is critical for the management of media properties, and the technical and conceptual complexities of valuation are considered in this chapter.

The final chapter of Part I by Gary Ozanich and Michael Wirth (chapter 5) considers business combinations in the media industries through an analysis of the amount and types of restructuring within the communications industries and as related to the whole of the U.S. economy. The authors closely detail those transactions of the 1980s and 1990s to consider thoroughly how mergers and acquisitions are employed in changing the structure of media firms.

Part II examines economic practice within specific media industries. Chapter 6 (Robert Picard), chapter 7 (Barry Litman), chapter 8 (Sydney Carroll and Herbert Howard), chapter 9 (Douglas Gomery), chapter 10 (Jonathan Tankel and Wenmouth Williams), and chapter 11 (Eric Rothenbuhler and John Streck) illustrate contemporary business practices in the newspaper, television, cable, movie, radio, and music industries. Picard predicts that despite a decline in readership, newspaper companies will remain healthy by adopting technological innovations in adapting to the lifestyle changes of its readers. Litman argues that if the current television networks are to remain financially viable, they are going to have to find a market niche with their programming rather than continuing their present strategy of attempting to reach a mass market. Carroll and Howard note that the cable industry is at a crossroads, with impending competition creating new opportunities and new dangers. By contrast, Gomery sees no end to the domination of the movie industry by the current Hollywood oligopoly, noting that the industry has successfully adapted to recent changes. Tankel and Williams explore the interdependence of media economic resources, noting the changes that have occurred historically with the advent of new technologies, and their implications for the contemporary radio industry. Rothenbuhler and Streck, in an important addition to this edition, overview the recorded music industry, with particular attention to the structure of the industry and the strategic decision-making techniques that record companies use to address the characteristic uncertainty in the music business.

The final chapters review changes in international economic practices and in the economics of online media. Adapting a theoretical framework provided by economist Michael Porter (*The Competitive Advantage of Nations*), the authors argue that the 1990s are a decade of globalization as coventures and global integration of media industries become the norm. The authors examine the economics of the burgeoning online world. What will be profitable and how the major players will emerge is discussed.

For those who wish to pursue issues, further, suggested readings are provided at the end of each chapter. A glossary is also provided, as are two appendices for those interested in financial media management.

ACKNOWLEDGMENTS

A project such as this would not be possible without the efforts of many people. We particularly thank our authors for their patience and expertise. We also acknowledge the editors of this series and the reviewers and readers of the previous edition who have given us helpful feedback. In addition, we thank our families: Claudette and Alana Soucy-Carveth, and Katie, Jaime, and Torie Owers.

—*Alison Alexander*
—*James Owers*
—*Rod Carveth*

Part I

Economic Value and Structure

1

An Introduction to Media Economics Theory and Practice

James Owers
Georgia State University

Rod Carveth
University of Bridgeport

Alison Alexander
University of Georgia

MEDIA ECONOMICS AS A FIELD OF STUDY

At the end of 1995, many politically conservative critics and politicians attacked daytime television talk shows for lowering the cultural standards of society by presenting "degrading" content. Realizing that daytime talk shows are generally lucrative for their producers, the critics recommended that advertisers of these shows be persuaded to withdraw their sponsorship. Should persuasion fail, the critics suggested that consumers boycott the products of the offending sponsors. What is important about this example is not that a group of citizens wanted to ban a form of media content (that has been happening since the development of the mass media), but that the only effective way to control such content was through economic means.

The field of media economics is often seen as a subspecialty of both media studies and economics. However, as events over the last 15 years have indicated, media economics has become a new field, combining principles of both the study of communication media and the study of economics.

The study of media concerns itself with issues of freedom of speech, access to the media, the social impact of media content, and the effects of new communication technology. All these areas involve a discussion of economic principles to some degree. Daytime television talk shows have proliferated in the 1990s because they

1

are relatively inexpensive to produce and advertisers have supported them. Violent television shows and movies are produced not only because they are popular in the United States, but also because they do extremely well in the international syndication marketplace. Whether all citizens will enjoy universal access to the new telecommunications technologies will depend on how information service providers are able to recover their costs and make a profit. A. J. Leibling once said, "Freedom of the press belongs to whomever owns one." Although this may be a cynical quote, ownership of a mass-media vehicle requires substantial capital investment, linking economic means to the information in the media environment.

Similarly, the field of economics is informed by the study of the media. In his popular introductory text, Samuelson (1976) defined economics as

> The study of how people and society end up choosing, with or without the use of money, to employ scarce productive resources that could have alternative uses, to produce various commodities and distribute them for consumption, now or in the future, among various persons and groups in society. (p. 3)

Thus, economics is concerned with *what* is produced, the technology and organization of *how* it is produced, and *for whom* it is produced. For example, a firm produces outputs it expects will sell to its target client groups (what) and it will employ the most efficient technology and effective organization as possible (how). The proceeds of selling the output will be distributed to employees, suppliers, and (if there remains a profit) owners/shareholders (for whom).

Media economics is a term employed to refer to the business operations and financial activities of firms producing and selling output into the various media industries.[1] Firms in particular industries have obvious similarities, and when an industry reaches sufficient scale it typically spawns a field of study focusing on the unique operating and financial attributes of firms in that industry. There are fields of study examining the unique attributes of banking, real estate, airlines, and almost all major lines of business. It is within this context that media economics reflects an industry that has long since reached the scale where it has its own field of specialized industry analysis and knowledge—media economics—examining firms operating in the various media industries. The operations of these firms are undertaken in the context of given market conditions, technological alternatives, and their anticipated financial implications. Media economics is concerned with how the media industries allocate resources to create information and entertainment content to meet the needs of audiences, advertisers, and other societal institutions (Picard, 1990).

---

[1]Media industries can be classified in a number of ways based on product (print, broadcast, film, recorded music, etc.), regulation, technology, and sequence in the product chain (production, distribution, exhibition). Although all systems of classification involve overlap, the most widely used categorization uses the Standard Industrial Classification (SIC) code. Most media industries fall into the 4800 and 2700 categories of SIC codes.

The context of scarce resources, technological and organizational constraints, responses to preferences of consumers, and the distributional aspects of whose tastes and preferences will dominate is pervasive in all economic analysis. Media economics focuses on the consideration of the genre of goods and services comprising the media segment of the economy.

The media industries are generally very visible segments of the economy. The major firms in these industries are known to almost all adults as a result of their pervasive products. CBS, Disney, Gannett, and Turner Broadcasting are examples of well-known media firms. Although the general nature of prominent firms is familiar, structurally the media industries are complex. Many media firms have interests in several major media industries. For example, the 1996 merger of Turner Broadcasting with Time Warner resulted in a company with major interests in film and television production, magazine and book publishing, pay-cable programming, and cable TV system ownership. In addition, some firms not usually categorized as involved in media industries nevertheless have major media interests (e.g., General Electric, the corporate owner of the NBC television network, and Westinghouse and CBS). These attributes are not unique to the media industries—they are longstanding features of industrial organization in most well-established industries. Questions related to "who owns the media" are substantially complicated by this ubiquitous characteristic of industrial organization.

The chapters of this book address basic principles of micro- and macroeconomics and apply them to the media industries. Without considering the detailed particular focus of specific types of media firms, the overall relationship of each function to media operations is outlined. Two appendices are provided at the end of the volume for those interested in accounting and financial management in the media industries. It is the role of this chapter to develop the economic and corporate contexts within which media economics is practiced. The first section considers *macroeconomics*—the overall functioning of the economy as a context for all industries and firms. The second section considers the specific economic functions and behaviors of firms and individuals, an analysis known as *microeconomics*. The functional dimensions of all firms are identified and described in the third section, and the dynamics of how firms change is the subject of the final section.

The remaining chapters in Part I of this book explore in more detail important economic elements such as structure, value, resources, utility, and regulation. Part II considers the application of media economic principles to particular media industries.

MACROECONOMICS

As indicated previously, macroeconomics refers to *aggregates* in the economy and how the economy works as a system. An important macroeconomic aggregate is gross domestic product (GDP). This refers to the total output of goods and services (in a particular year). The components of GDP are consumption (C), investment (I), and government expenditures (G).[2] Hence

$$GDP = C + I + G$$

Consumption

Not surprisingly, the consideration of what influences the amount of consumption of a particular product or service is labeled *demand analysis*. Such factors are analyzed under microeconomics. In macroeconomics, the primary influences on aggregate consumption are the level of income, growth in income, the inclination ("propensity") to save, and expectations regarding the future course of the economy. The "marginal propensity to save" refers to how much of an *extra* dollar of

---

[2] The business operations and financial affairs of media firms refer to the complete set of activities encompassed in the production and distribution of media products and services. In all nations, business activities are undertaken within the overall structures and constraints set by society. The result is that meia industries vary considerably from one country to another. The context for media firms is set by the political, social, and legal environment of the society within which the business is conducted.

The overall nature of a country's political organization is clearly a fundamental factor in the determination of the media industries and business practices of media firms. The political extremes are "communist-totalitarian" and "laissez-faire," respectively. This volume concentrates on the media industries in the United States. The primary focus is on the point in the political economy continuum often referred to by economists as the "mixed capitalist society." This refers to an industrialized station in which the property rights are primarily, although not exclusively, in the hands of private citizens, but where there are also regulatory and other constraints on permissible business conduct. Overall economic control is held by both public and private institutions. Yet most of the means of production are operated by private sector corporations, as distinct from government corporations owned by the government.

Examples of mixed capitalist economics include the United States, Canada, and the major Western European countries. Casual familiarity with these economies makes it apparent that they have important structural differences. For example, in Western Europe the primary utilities (electricity, gas, water, etc.) are typically provided by government corporations where there are direct controls over monopolistic-type, "exploitative" practices. In contrast, in the United States, these services are typically provided by private sector companies whose conduct is prescribed by regulations (e.g., public utility commissions or PUCOs) designed to protect consumers from unfair practices. The ownership of broadcast media also differs considerably between Western Europe and the United States.

Despite the differences encompassed by the expression mixed capitalist economy, its generality means that although the focus of this book is on media industries and firms in the United States, much of the material has applicability to other industrialized societies. This is particularly the case given recent trends. The recent deregulation, global integration, and privatization trends that are now influencing many Western (and other) economies will likely make the respective media industries more similar to the United States than previously.

Given the mixed-capitalist economic context, our consideration of the economic context for media firms can be partitioned into microeconomic and macroeconomic issues. This is perhaps the most important distinction in economics. Microeconomics focuses on the decision-making processes of individuals and firms, and the supply, demand, and price of particular goods and services. Macroeconomics refers to aggregates in the economy and how the economy works as a system. It is difficult to have substantial insights in economics unless there is familiarity with the different perspectives of macroeconomics and microeconomics.

income will be saved. Consumption expenditures are those outlays for which there is little realizable (saleable) remnant at the end of the year. In contrast to the macroeconomic use of the term *investment* considered in the following section, consumption is an intuitively straightforward concept. Some income goes toward meeting nondiscretionary expenses such as income taxes and social security taxes. The component of our income that is not subject to legal disposition by way of charges such as taxes is known as disposable income (DI). An important aspect of total consumption expenditure is the division of disposable income into consumption and saving (S):

$$DI = C + S$$

The consumption expenditures of *households* (a term that includes any domestic unit, regardless of the nature or size of the "family") on media products and services is part of consumption expenditures. In an overall manner, the proportion of consumption dollars going to media expenditures has increased. In 1920, the percentage of DI spent on broadcast media was zero. The relationship between technology, product development, and patterns of consumption expenditures is important. When a new media product or service becomes technologically feasible, it competes with other potential uses of consumer purchasing power. The outcome of such a competition turns on whether the new products are substitutes or complements for existing products in the marketplace. TV has significantly reduced the market potential for radio (they are partially substitutes), whereas the availability of VCRs has increased the potential for film studios (they are complementary products in the marketplace).

The contribution of the media industries to GDP is substantial. In 1982, the contribution of these industries to GDP was 2.6%. By 1986, it had grown to be 2.9% of GDP. The increasing role continued into the late 1980s. Although the economy as a whole grew at an average compound rate of 7.4% in the 1981–1986 interval, media industry spending grew at an average rate of 11.2%. It should be noted that these growth rates are high relative to historical growth rates. The interval covered by these statistics includes some of the most rapid growth in the 1980s, and begins with recession-year base figures. On average, the economy grows at a rate much less than 7.4%. Moreover, the share of the media industries will not necessarily continue to grow. Growth patterns in the media industries in 1989 and 1990 were much lower for most segments, supporting the contention that the 1981–1988 interval was something of a "golden age" for media industries, at least financially. The recession that began in 1990 had a major impact for many segments of the media industries. For example, this recession led to a marked decline in retail and classified advertising for newspapers. By June 1991, in a survey of publishers, general managers, and advertising executives, the advertising slump then being experienced was considered the worst in 20 years.

One of the most important factors affecting consumption (C) is demography. From the period of 1946–1964, the United States underwent a major demographic shift commonly referred to as the "baby boom," the oldest members of which are now turning 50. During this period, live births in this country reached 4 million per year. Following 1964, the birth rate leveled off to slightly more than 2 million births per year, with a moderate rise during the early 1980s. Hence, although the youth market drove marketing and media decisions during the 1970s, the 1980s witnessed a dramatic decline in that cohort group. For example, the number of teenagers amounted to almost 21 million in 1980, and declined to about 16.5 million in 1995. This decline in the youth market meant changes in terms of program content (*Happy Days* replaced by *thirtysomething*) and media consumption (teens represent about 50% of theatrical box-office receipts).

The baby boomers, however, will affect directly and indirectly many of the media decisions for the next 40 years (until the year 2039, when the youngest "boomer" will be 75). If currents trends hold, entertainment expenditures will continue to remain at the same levels until after the year 2000. People aged 35 to 44 spend 50% above average on entertainment, and twice the average for video accessories and audio equipment. If the slightly larger 25- to 34-year-old cohort group spends in a similar manner, then entertainment expenditures will continue to be high. Entertainment purchases will decline by the year 2000, however, due to the twin impacts of older cohort groups spending less on entertainment coupled with a dramatic drop off in the number of 25- to 34-year-olds.

As the number of teens in the United States declines, statistics show that the fastest growing age group in the United States are the elderly. From 13% of the population in 1980, people over the age of 55 will constitute 20% of the U.S. population by the year 2005. Put another way, between 1990 and 2020 the number of people over the age of 50 will increase by 74%, whereas the number of those under 50 will grow by 1%. This shift will be meaningful in terms of media content and marketing, as older people tend to read more and consume television more than other age groups.

In addition, an increasing number of women continued to enter the workforce. By the year 2000, more than 80% of women aged 25 to 54 will be in the labor force, and most of the rest will be out of the workforce only temporarily. At the same time, decisions to have children are being put off to a later date, and the number of households with married couples are declining (in fact, by 2010 married couples will no longer be a majority of households). For television, this means a decreasing number of viewers for daytime television, both for adult shows (soap operas) and children's program (such as *Sesame Street* and cartoons).

The demographics also show that society will become more multicultural. Immigration is growing at a greater rate than the "natural increase" (growth defined as the number of births minus the number of deaths). Currently, 1 in 10 baby boomers were born outside the United States. By the year 2000, one employee in four will come from a minority group. The Hispanic market has already become increasingly important to advertisers, as close to 29.6 million Americans could be considered to belong to this ethnic group. This growing market has significant implications for advertisers, Hispanic broadcast and cable services, and print media. One media firm that took notice of the growing Hispanic market is the *Miami Herald*, which serves Dade County (FL) Hispanics with *El Nuevo Herald*, a free daily Spanish-language supplement. As of 1990, *El Nuevo* had a news staff of 60, and a circulation of 100,000. In addition, Spanish-language Univision and Telemundo are two of the fastest growing U.S. cable services. Recognizing the demographic composition of markets is an important macroeconomic consideration.

Investment

Investment in the context of macroeconomics refers to the acquisition of capital goods—those with a life of several years. In contrast to the intuitively appealing definition of consumption, the economic definition of investment in the context of GDP is more complex. It refers to *new* investment in "real" assets—new plants and equipment, the creation of new businesses, additional inventory, and new construction. This provides a good example of the difference between the *real* and *financial* aspects of the economy. When a household buys a new bond issued by a (media) firm, it is a financial investment (typically possible because of savings) for the household, but it is not an investment that becomes part of GDP. Only real-asset expenditures are considered investment for the sake of GDP. Thus, if the media firm uses the money from the bond to develop a new product (e.g., a new movie) or build a new studio, that expenditure is investment in the macroeconomic context.

Investment plays a very important role in influencing fluctuations in the business cycle. Later coverage on valuation and investment decisions (see chapters 4 and 5, this volume) formalize the well-founded intuition that both households and firms are more likely to make investments if they have relatively optimistic expectations regarding the future. Real-asset investment expenditures such as new houses, autos, and appliances by households and new studios, equipment, and products by firms have a *multiplier effect* in the economy (GDP). For each dollar spent on investment items, there is a multiple increase in GDP. This is a double-edged sword. It tends to add to the momentum on upward swings in the economy, but the failure to spend on investment exacerbates a recession.

As an illustration of the multiplier effect, consider the case of a production studio deciding to invest in a new film. If it spends, for example, $20 million on the movie production, then that is a direct increase of the same amount in the "I" component of GDP. However, the $20 million it invests is paid to actors, other employees, and other business firms supplying necessary inputs. In turn, the employees will consume some of their wages and salaries (i.e., increase the "C" component of GDP) and the other business firms will pay (most of) their receipts out to their employees or make other business expenditures. Clearly the $20 million invested in the new film increases the GDP by an amount greater than the expenditure itself. Investment has a multiplied effect. Economists have examined the multiplier in great detail and estimates of its numerical value are made. Numerical estimates of the multiplier often fall in the range of three to five. If it is, say, four, then the incremental investment (I) of $20 million in the film would increase the GDP by $80 million after all the incremental cycles had worked their way through the economy.

The multiplier effect makes the level of investment a critical factor in determining the level of economic activity (GDP). The motivation for states and cities to have films shot in their locales is apparent from this consideration of the multiplier effect. Economists have long been aware of the multiplier effect and government policy frequently seeks to influence the level of investment.

Government Expenditure (G), Monetary Policy, and Regulation

The two primary economic functions of government policy are *fiscal policy* and *monetary policy*. Fiscal policy deals with the raising of revenues by government and the level and type of government expenditures. The raising of revenues by government is generally conceived of as coming from taxes. However, in addition to income and business taxes, most Western European governments receive revenues from the Value Added Tax (VAT).

Debate on fiscal policy is inevitable. Regardless of personal perspectives on taxes and government expenditures, the important economic consequences of different policies should not be overlooked. For example, increasing taxes reduces disposable income (DI) and this typically reduces consumption (C). If the taxes do not result in increased government expenditure (G), then, all other things being equal, GDP will decline. The 1980s saw a lowering of the marginal tax rates in the United States and Great Britain. The "supply-side" perspective proposes that there is an optimal tax rate that maximizes tax revenues. This rate is conceived of as being "relatively" low and there is thus strong incentive to be productive. The perspective was widely emulated in the policies of other economies.

Analysis of the levels and types of taxes and government expenditures requires a consideration of both economic policy and issues of political philosophy. The different perspectives of tax rates and level of government expenditure reflect varying interpretations of the role of government in society and these are manifested in party affiliation and other political activity. For example, considerable debate in the United States concerns the impact of running large domestic deficits. Some critics call for a constitutional amendment to require that the federal budget be balanced; other critics see the deficits as unfortunate, but not critical for the economy.[3]

---

[3]Given that the 1996 U.S. GDP was approximately $6 trillion and the federal governmental deficit was $120 billion, some interpret the small relative size to diminish the importance of the deficit.

For media managers, understanding the economic motivation for, and consequences of, government fiscal policy further improves management in that the impact of present conditions on future fiscal policy can be better anticipated. The importance of fiscal policy is reflected in the substantial lobbying efforts that are brought to bear in attempts to influence tax codes and fiscal policy. For example, broadcasters have long lobbied Congress not to impose spectrum fees for ownership of broadcast licenses.

Fiscal policy, governmental revenue, and expenditure decision making, is part of the total economic environment affecting firms. Awareness of such policy is essential for both understanding what is occurring in the broad economic environment and determining normative strategies for viable and proactive media management. A widely admired quality in effective managers is the ability to prosper regardless of what party is in political power. This ability is critically contingent on an understanding of particular politicians and parties and the associated economic policies.

Monetary policy refers to the government's influence over the banking system, money supply and the level of interest rates. Countries with dynamic media industries all have central banks that serve important functions. In the United States, the Federal Reserve Bank System (the "Fed") is the central bank. In the United Kingdom, it is the Bank of England. These banks are the instruments of government monetary policy via several mechanisms.

Although the modern system of banking with one central banking system functions quite similarly in the various mixed-capitalist economies, the details of the banking systems vary considerably. In the United States, there are approximately 10,400 commercial banks, whereas in the United Kingdom and Canada there are approximately 10 to 12 large banks with many branches throughout the respective countries.

Although there is debate on just how powerful the Fed is, most economists and financial practitioners consider its capabilities to be extensive. For example, the Fed, under the chairmanship of Paul Volker (who came into the position in October 1979), placed an emphasis on reducing inflation. The Fed did this by maintaining "tight money" conditions, which manifest themselves in scarce credit, high interest rates, and lower levels of economic activity (GDP). This confluence of factors often come together late in an expansion cycle. The Fed can slow down an "overheated" economy.

By contrast, when the economy is in a recession, the Fed typically increases the supply of money (through government bond transactions in the financial markets and discount rate changes) and this reduces interest rates (as it did in the early 1990s under the leadership of Fed chairman Alan Greenspan). A reduced cost of borrowing typically increases investment (I) and economic activity so long as business confidence has not dropped too far. If business confidence is below a certain threshold, then even an increase in the money supply may not be effective—"The Fed cannot push on a string."

Because of the importance of matters affected by central bank policy, following the course of monetary policy is necessary for the proficient management of any firm. In international comparative analyses of economics of long-term growth and low inflation rates, the Fed gets very high ratings. The strong growth of the U.S. economy in 1994–1997, and the concurrent low inflation and interest rates is a reflection of this.

Beyond fiscal and monetary policy, there are other means by which the government can affect business. The political philosophy governing such policy is a critical issue. The shift from the Carter administration to the Reagan–Bush administration was more than just a matter of Republicans replacing Democrats in the Oval Office. Ideologically, the shift signaled that Americans were tired of "big" government, and wanted government to be less intrusive in matters of the business. Thus, the Reagan–Bush years resulted in fewer restrictions on the media industries. In broadcasting, practices such as audience ascertainment, programming logs, commercial time restrictions, and even the Fairness Doctrine were eliminated. In addition, the number of broadcast stations an individual or company could own increased from 7 per class (AM, FM, or TV) to 12, and the 3-year mandatory period for owning a station was eliminated. With FCC chairman Mark Fowler leading the way, the marketplace rather than regulation became the operating principle for media operations.[4]

Additionally, the concept of what constituted antitrust was shifted from a within-industry perspective to an interindustry perspective. Hence, the rationale for eliminating the Fairness Doctrine was that with so many media outlets, the unfairness of one outlet would be more than offset by the fairness of others. This is a direct reflection of the impact of technology and competing delivery systems on industry structure and competitive concerns.

In addition, the Cable Act of 1984 signaled that the federal government would relax restrictions on the cable industry, such as control over rates. Although cable franchises exist as local monopolies, the Act specified that cable systems would be exempt from municipal regulation if there was effective competition in the market. In 1985, the FCC defined effective competition as the existence of three over-the-air broadcast signals. As a result, costs increased for consumers and cable franchises became more profitable. Cable companies also began to created tiers of service, splitting basic cable service into two or more levels to subscribe to, with each level costing a bit more per month. As cable became more attractive as an investment, the number of services proliferated.[5]

---

[4]Curiously, there were increasing calls for restrictions on some content (leading to an expansion of the prohibition of indecent content), and some restrictions on media business practices (such as the Financial Interest and Syndication Rule) that were left intact. These apparent anomalies were clearly not philosophically in line with the Administration.

[5]However, as rates for basic cable and pay channels continued to increase, the public became more dissatisfied, and called for more regulation on the local, state, and federal level. Although no new cable legislation was approved in 1990, the FCC expanded local regulatory control to more systems.

The hands-off approach taken by the government during the 1980s also affected the newspaper industry. Newspapers continued to dwindle during the decade, declining from 1,745 dailies in 1980 to 1,626 in July 1990. Only 21 cities had competing daily newspapers. There were attempts to introduce new papers in such cities as New York, Atlanta, and Washington, but these papers quickly died. A typical experience was that suffered by Ingersoll Publications, which tried to launch the *St. Louis Sun* in September 1989. The *Sun* was born in an era of decline for the newspaper industry, and suffered from, ironically, strong competition from competing suburban papers—some of which Ingersoll owned. Seven months and $30 million later, Ingersoll closed the *Sun,* and quit the U.S. newspaper business.

One way to combat the decline of competing daily newspapers is the use of the Joint Operating Agreement (JOA). The JOA allows competing newspapers in financial trouble to combine some of their operations, so long as they keep separate editorial identities. These agreements must be approved by the Justice Department. However, many critics charge that the JOA has been used inappropriately, allowing competing newspapers to set noncompetitive advertising and subscription rates. During the 1980s, the wisdom of the JOA came under question. Despite a great deal of criticism that the request was merely designed to keep costs down, the then-Edwin-Meese-led Justice Department approved the combining of operation of the *Detroit News* and the *Detroit Free Press*, thereby further reducing the number of cities with competitive daily newspapers.

Finally, in an attempt to promote economic growth, the government began to loosen the strings on the various financial markets to increase the level of investment and trigger the multiplier effect. Although the changes were generally welcomed by the business community, there were some unintended negative consequences. A prominent example from recent economic experience in the United States is the so-called Savings and Loan Crisis. In 1982, Congress passed major deregulatory legislation that, among other things, made it possible for savings and loan institutions (S&Ls) to invest in assets (such as high-yield "junk bonds"—many issued by media firms—and real estate development projects) outside their traditional fields of experience and expertise. However, the regulation kept in place federally guaranteed insurance (up to $100,000) for S&L depositors. The resulting incentive structure motivated S&Ls to take on high-risk projects. If such investments played out as hoped, the gains would go to S&L stockholders and managers. If the investments failed, the insurance functions of the federal government would meet most of the losses. Ultimately, many of these investments failed, and the insurance of deposits is meeting the economic losses despite the insolvency of many S&L institutions.[6]

---

[6]The consequences of the S&L crisis were administratively handled by the Resolution Trust Corporation (RTC). The problems were such that in July 1995 a bill was introduced in Congress to end the S & L industry as a separate category. By 1996, the S&L crisis was substantially resolved and the RTC closed down.

The key point is that the high-risk projects undertaken by many S&Ls were, in fact, rational activity by S&L managers and owners given the incentive structure created by government policy and regulation. A dysfunctional structure had been created. This illustrates the potential for a "fallacy of composition"[7] if the economic environment and incentive structures are not aligned.

In addition, the government also took a hands-off approach to the changing financial practices in mergers and acquisitions, especially the leveraged buyout (LBO) deals financed with junk bonds. The development of the junk bond market provided financing for many transactions that could not be financed by traditional sources. Although junk bonds came to be associated with the illegal and unethical activities of their prime proponents (such as Michael Milken and the firm Drexel Burnham Lambert), there is a legitimate debate regarding their role in increasing efficiency by transferring assets to the control of more aggressive, higher producing managers. The relaxation of regulations on the financing of media deals meant that the psychology of the market could hold. What happened next was that some investors overpaid for media properties. Some deals were done at prices that reflected an exaggerated perception of what the target company was worth.

Despite the government actions in response to the junk bond and S&L crises, the financial markets remain relatively free of controls in the mid-1990s. Market forces remain the primary determinant of trends and transactions, and the lack of aggressive antitrust actions in response to transactions such as the Captial Cities/ABC/Disney and Time Warner/Turner Broadcasting mergers illustrate that there has not been a substantial revision of government policy on such matters under the Clinton administration. In the mid-1990s it was the joint forces of (a) the market and (b) the ongoing evolution of industrial organization (illustrated by the formation of the film and TV production company DreamWorks SKG), rather than government policy, that determined major developments in the media (and most other) industries.

The Telecommunications Act of 1996 (see chapter 3, this volume) had a significant impact on the shape of the electronic media industry. For example, the virtual elimination of ownership limits in the radio industry has created an unprecedented wave of mergers (e.g., Westinghouse and Infinity). However, it has also created problems for radio advertisers, such as predatory pricing.

A primary advantage for advertising on the $11.5 billion radio medium is low cost. But mergers such as Westinghouse and Infinity mean that more than 30% of radio ad revenues in 6 of the top 10 markets could be controlled by one radio group. In the immediate aftermath of the merger, ad agency media buyers reported no substantial increases in ad rates, but feared such effects as limited control of certain demographics and formats. Price hikes, they feared, would be only a matter of time.

---

[7]Economists use the term *fallacy of composition* to refer to situations where the optimization by individuals or firms does not lead to overall best outcomes for society.

Such concerns may mean the government will have to decide what concentration means in the radio marketplace. The radio industry has argued that radio is not a separate market and the federal review should include TV and newspapers. Antitrust enforcement will need to balance the share of domination in media acquisition behaviors and the effect on voices in the marketplace.

International Economics

There are two overall "balances" that are of particular significance for an economy. The first is the internal government budget–government revenues minus expenditures. The other balance is the difference between imports and exports—the *external accounts.* Consideration of the external accounts introduces complex issues of international economics, substantial coverage of which is outside the scope of this book. Government policy is critical for the practice of foreign trade and commerce. Although there are some notable instances of protectionism, tariffs, and quotas, in recent years, U.S. policies have been to maintain open markets for foreign goods. The generally well-reasoned motivation for this set of policies is that it will make goods available on the domestic market at competitive prices and keep domestic producers efficient. In the theory of Ricardo, if all countries have free trade, then *comparative advantage* will see each country specializing in the production of goods and services for which it is best suited and most competitive. This creates the optimal outcome—Pareto optimality—the state where no economic unit can be made better off as a result of reallocation of production and distribution without another unit becoming worse off.

When international trade is taken into consideration, the basic model of GDP needs to be modified. Interpreting consumption (C), investment (I) and government (G) to be purely domestic expenditures, then exports (X) and imports (M) must be accounted for. Thus:

$$GDP = C + I + G + (X - M)$$

The current account balance is what is referred to as all exports minus all imports (X – M). Both exports and imports include physical trade, as well as "invisibles" such as interest and insurance premiums from transactions with nonresidents ("foreigners").

Exports have been increasing in recent years. 1995 was a particularly strong year, in part due to the "weak dollar," that made U.S. exports less expensive for foreign buyers in terms of their currency.

In the case of the United States, media products are a major export. Media exports greatly exceed media imports, making a substantial net positive contribution to the balance of payments. As is frequently the case, exports are good for both the individual exporting company, and the country's economy. Export sales play a major role in the success of many U.S. movies that are not major box-office successes in the domestic marketplace.

MICROECONOMICS—CONSUMERS, FIRMS, AND MARKETS

Microeconomics deals with how individual economic units (households and firms) make decisions regarding their economic activity. As discussed at the beginning of this chapter, each society must address the economic questions of (a) *what* goods and services will be produced (scarcity choices); (b) *how* they will be produced (technology and industrial organization issues); and (c) *for whom* they will be produced (income distribution). There is a close relationship between macro- and microeconomics. The macroeconomic environment is the context within which microeconomic decisions are made, and government policy also influences micro-economic issues. For example, income distribution is substantially influenced by taxation policies and distributional policies such as welfare and unemployment programs.

Economic analysis typically assumes that individual economic units (house-holds and firms) make their respective economic decisions in a "rational" manner. The "rational economic unit" is presumed to maximize its goal or "objective function" (utility or satisfaction for households, profits and value for firms) within the constraints of their resources, and the economic and legal environment. This stresses the important responsibility of the government to create economic and legal environments, and incentive systems whereby the pursuit of individual economic goals is also conducive to the maximization of aggregate economic well-being (generally equivalent to maximizing GDP). For example, if I can maximize profits by using an inexpensive but polluting technology, then my maximization will not be conducive to society's maximization if I am not forced to incur the costs associated with my polluting. When the correlation between individual maximiza-tion and aggregate, societal maximization is not present, the notion of *fallacy of composition* is employed to refer to economic activity that maximizes the goal attainment of individual economic units but does not maximize overall social welfare. When government policies have the effect of creating such a divergence, serious misallocation of scarce economic resources can, and often does, result.

One application of the fallacy of composition to the media industries is the issue of violent media content. Many successful (e.g., profitable) films and television programs are action-oriented and contain a significant amount of violent portrayals. Critics, backed by a substantial amount of social science research evidence, contend that although media firms maximize profit potential with this form of media content, such content may lead to unfavorable societal consequences, such as antisocial behavior on the part of its audiences. Only when "activists" took direct action did Time Warner divest its interests in its "gangsta rap" music operations in 1995.

Given that individual households and firms maximize within an existing economic context and related incentive structure, we now turn to a consideration of the decision-making processes of households/individuals and firms, and the economic mechanisms by which their economic activities are coordinated.

Households and Individuals—"Consumers"

Economists assume that individuals maximize utility. *Utility* refers to satisfaction and enjoyment from the consumption (today or in the future) of a particular good or service. The economic analysis of utility examines why particular choices are made. For example, declining network viewership is readily explained in terms of microeconomic theory of consumer choice, and the increasing range of choices.

Consumer choice is a broader consideration than comparison of substitutes. Not only does it consider such questions as "Why do I purchase CDs instead of audiocassettes?" but also "Why do I not buy a large-screen TV even if I can afford one?" There are two key attributes to answering questions relating to choice and demand for particular items—*resources* and *individual preferences*.

Resources generally refer to purchasing power. Individuals generate purchasing power from their assets—marketable skill sets produce wages and salaries, financial assets yield interest and dividends, and other assets such as real estate and businesses yield profits (or losses). The returns from our various assets are determined in the labor and financial markets and in the fortunes of businesses directly owned.

As defined, resources include the *stock* of assets owned and the *flow* of income they generate. This means that an individual's purchasing power includes the possibility of spending all financial and business assets (and possibly borrowing against future earnings) in any one period, and having only wages and salary income in future periods. That possibility is present, and, given a presumption of free choice, should be. The key point is that *preferences* are the province of individuals. This is not inconsistent with "rational-person" economic behaviors. In the full and rigorous development of the economics of choice, rational behavior requires only decisions consistent with economic scarcity, not a particular set of preferences. Rational economic behavior has individuals always preferring more income to less, and not paying higher prices than necessary for pure substitute packages of goods and services.

Economists have an equilibrium condition for the optimal outcome of individual purchase decisions whereby the last (i.e., marginal) dollar spent on each different type of good and service ("i," "j," "k," etc.) generates the same "marginal utility." Expressed formally, with each MUi indicating the marginal utility from the consumption of an additional unit of good "i," and Pi indicating the price of that unit:

$$\frac{MU_i}{P_i} = \frac{MU_j}{P_j} = \frac{MU_k}{P_k} = \text{ for all consumption choices (i, j, k, etc.)}$$

Given that the marginal utility from the last unit of a particular good or service declines as more units are purchased, typically additional units will be purchased only if the price declines. Given the equilibrium condition expressed in the equation just given, for *individual* consumers there will be a "downward-sloping" demand curve for any particular good or service. Starting from a given optimal position, more will be purchased only if the price declines. This relationship is depicted in Fig. 1.1.

Although preferences vary from one individual consumer to another, the "law" of diminishing marginal utility applies to all consumers and the *aggregate* demand relationship for a particular good or service at a particular point in time will also be downward sloping. It will have the same general shape as the *individual* demand curve in Fig. 1.2 although the units on the X-axis will be different—perhaps thousands or millions rather than single-digit numbers.

As in all areas of marketing, the downward sloping demand curve relationship provides many insights into the operation of media industries. Although we have couched the discussion in terms of consumer demand, the cost analysis relating to firms' maximizing decisions means that the demand for inputs into the production and marketing process is also downward sloping. For example, in the softening market for advertising in late 1990, the networks were able to place "floaters" (advertisements that can be, within limits, aired at a time of the network's choice) only by substantially reducing the rate. In the mid-1990s, some print advertisers are beginning to face competition from Internet advertisers (see chap. 13, this volume).

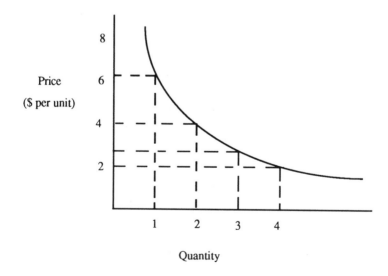

FIG. 1.1. Individual consumer's downward sloping demand curve.

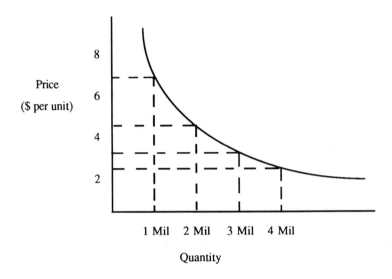

FIG. 1.2. Aggregate market's downward sloping demand curve.

Firms' Decisions—"Producers"

Firms purchase inputs (land, labor, and capital) in resource markets, and transform these inputs into outputs (products and services), employing the technological and industrial organizational choices considered to be the most efficient of those available. Marketing and distribution costs are incurred in attaining the final sale of the output. Generally, the goal is the maximizing of economic profits.[8]

The "theory of the firm" is a large and complex body of knowledge that is important for a full examination of the coverage of supply of goods and services. Here we take an overview of decisions made by firms and leave the interested reader to seek further coverage in the referenced materials (cf. Picard, 1990).

Firms have varying degrees of influence in their input markets as far as affecting prices is concerned. For example, a small firm seeking to purchase less than 1% of the offering in a particular market will have little opportunity to influence the price by exercising its option (or threatening to do so) to not make a purchase at the going price. By contrast, a large firm will have considerable potential in this arena. In summary, some firms will be "price takers" in the inputs/factor-of-production markets, whereas others will be "price influencers."

Just how input prices relate to the cost of production will be significantly influenced by the production process and form of organization employed in the

---

[8]"Economic profits" are different in important ways from "accounting profits" defined in Appendix A of this volume. Economic profit is calculated after the cost of owner's equity is subtracted and is similar to the contemporary uses of "value creation."

transformation of inputs into outputs. These issues are referred to by economists as the "production function." Technology clearly plays a key role in determining potential production techniques and their relative efficiency. A prominent media example is the role of electronic typesetting in the newspaper industry. Although many workers were understandably resistant to this technology, fearing loss of jobs, the potential of electronic typesetting to make the newspaper industry more efficient is clear.

For a given price and volume, maximizing profits requires minimum production cost. Total costs of production include both *fixed costs* and *variable costs*. Examples of fixed costs include depreciation on the plant and the wages of staff employees (as contrasted to production-line employees). Variable costs include the materials directly used in producing output and the wages of production line employees. The fixed/variable cost relationships are depicted in Fig. 1.3.

Some costs are neither purely fixed or variable in nature. In particular, several costs have a "step-function" nature—they take discrete steps up, but do not vary in direct proportion to units of output. For example, a plant may have the capacity to produce 250,000 newspapers per day. When circulation demand requires that a second plant be built, the introduction of the second plant would significantly increase fixed costs at the 250,000 level of production in a step-like manner.

These cost structures will vary considerably from one type of media industry to another. Once a decision to make a film is taken, most costs become fixed. By contrast, for a publishing firm printing a book that does not have a large advance, a significant portion of its costs will be variable, determined largely by the number of books produced. The cost relationships depicted in Fig. 1.3 are the simplest; in practice, complexities such as nonlinearities are encountered. Recent refinements in cost measurement systems such as Activity Based Costing (ABC) have provided critical additional information to managers.

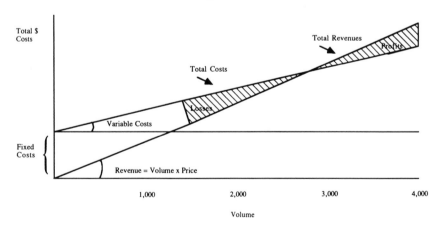

FIG. 1.3. Cost and revenue relationships.

A key factor in determining the competitive structure of industries in terms of the number of competitors and relative efficiency is what happens to the average cost of production as volume increases. The average cost of a unit of production for a given level of production is:

$$\frac{\text{Fixed costs} + (\text{Variable Cost Per Unit} \times \text{Number of Units Produced})}{\text{Number of Units Produced}}$$

The simplest models of production assume that initially the average cost of production decreases as scale economies are realized. However, after some (relatively low) level of output, average costs of production begin to increase, typically because of some limited resource that makes other factors/inputs less productive. The scarce factor can be as clear-cut as the physically limited size of a key location site (such as a production studio) or as complex as the ability (or lack thereof) of a particular management team to efficiently manage an increasingly large enterprise. If there is managerial limitation in terms of span of control, then doubling all inputs may result in an increase in production that is less than double. If a doubling of inputs results in more than a doubling of units of output, then generally economies of scale are still being realized.

In the first analysis, the "theory of the firm" assumes that firms' costs of producing units increase, as a result of having exhausted opportunities for economies of scale and encountering nonreplicable resources. Economists capture these inclinations in an upward sloping supply curve, as in Fig. 1.4. Because firms are operating at levels of output such that units costs are increasing as volume increases, they can supply more to a market only at the higher prices necessary to meet their increasing unit cost of production.

The competitive structure of media industries reflects different levels of efficiency, economies of scale, and industrial organization. For example, the broadcast television industry has relatively few firms, reflecting both the technology of production (channel/license availability) and the scale of operations necessary to achieve most efficient cost relationships. By contrast, the book and magazine publishing industries have literally thousands of firms, albeit dominated by a few major companies. The technology of print publishing is such that the fixed costs of physical production are typically not the major factor in the overall cost structure. Perhaps the critical factor in the profitable operation of smaller scale publishing houses is the availability of an efficient and effective distribution channel. *Effective* refers to getting the task accomplished, whereas *efficiency* refers to the cost effectiveness of doing so. As introductory business texts often note, "killing a housefly with a sledgehammer is effective, but not efficient."

Markets

For a given good or service, the superimposition of demand and supply curves on the same diagram leads to an analysis as depicted in Fig. 1.4. The "theory of the

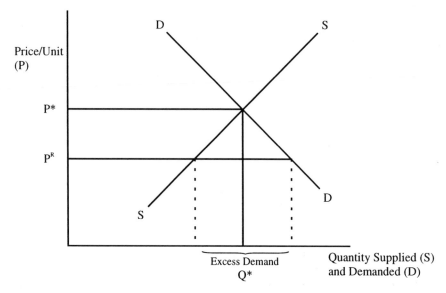

FIG. 1.4. Supply and demand relationships and market outcomes.

consumer" sustains the downward sloping demand "curve," which can take the shape of either a curve or a line, and the "theory of the firm" the upward sloping demand curve. What will be the outcome in the marketplace?

At point P*, Q* in Fig. 1.4, the curves coincide. This indicates the "marketing clearing" price (P*), and corresponding quantity (Q*) transacted. If this intersection of supply and demand is resolved in this manner, the market is said to be in "equilibrium." Buyers will want to demand Q* units, and firms will want to supply Q* units. As economists say, "there will be a coincidence of wants, not a want of coincidence."

The depiction of "the Market" as in Fig. 1.4 is a powerful analytical framework. For example, if a regulatory authority sets a price P^R less than the market clearning P*, then at that regulatory price quantity demanded will exceed the quantity firms choose to supply at that price, and there will "excess demand"—leading to nonprice allocation, such as queuing and "rationing coupons."

The impact of additional suppliers in a market will move the supply curve "out/down," generally with the impact of a decrease in price. The relevance of this to media markets is direct. For example, the Telecommunications Act of 1996 (see chapter 3, this volume) has the potential to radically change the supply structure in telecommunications, with potential decreases in price and heightened competition among suppliers.

Supply and demand curves are not easily measured for any given market. Firms often try to determine the "shape" of the demand curve they "face" (or supply) by such techniques as market surveys and experimenting with the impact of price changes. And of key relevance to the media industries is the fact that advertising is motivated by the potential to influence demand curves. Advertising attempts to "raise" the demand curves.

Conditions of Supply and Demand—Elasticity

As before, the familiar upward-sloping supply curve reflects hypothetical combinations of price and quantity supplied. As price increases, producers make a higher profit and wish to place more product on the market. When one or more of the factors previously held constant changes, this shifts the supply curve outward (increase in supply) or inward (decrease in supply), depending on which factor changed and its positive or negative relationship to supply. The shape of the supply curve is known as its *elasticity* and reflects the relative responsiveness of quantity supplied to changes in prices. Elasticity depends primarily on the closeness of substitutes in production and the amount of time available for producers to respond.

If a supplier faces a "steep" (inelastic) demand curve, then a price increase imposed by the supplier (being a jump in the supply curve) will lead to a large price increase, and a little decrease in market-clearing quantities. Conversely, if a supplier facing elastic demand curves increases prices, that supplier will lose a large part of the demand, and the price increase will be only partly "passed on." Again, numerous applications of these relationship can be observed in the media markets. These considerations are also of direct relevance to government policy. If a tax is added to a good or service, the effect is equivalent to raising the supply curve. Who really "absorbs" the tax? In the formal terminology of tax theory, what is the "incidence" of the tax? It is determined by the relative elasticities of demand and supply. In the extreme case of a completely inelastic demand curve (i.e., a price has no impact on quantity demanded), all the burden (incidence) is borne by buyers. The price goes up by the full amount of the tax per unit.

However, a discussion of elasticity highlights a feature of demand curves—they change over time. Although a demand curve may look very inelastic, the availability of substitutes will have an impact over time; so will the impact of technology. For example, the increase in automobile fuel efficiency significantly reduced the demand curve for gasoline, although the gas lines of 1974 and 1979 indicated clearly the short-run inelasticity of demand.

Market Imperfections

The ideal case depicted earlier is a reflection of the conditions economists call "perfect markets." This assumes knowledgeable consumers, many competing suppliers, and an upward-sloping supply curve. There are many instances where such ideal conditions are not met, and many of these are encountered in the media industries.

For example, if there is only one supplier, there is the potential for monopolist behaviors (see chapter 2, this volume). Duopolies are two-competitor markets, as are sometimes the case in large-city newspapers. These are examples of market conditions that provide the potential for strategies and behaviors that are to the detriment of consumers. A "pure" monopolist can change very high prices, at least in the short run before substitutes get established. This explains the regulations on cable-TV rates, in order to prevent a single supplier from "acting like a monopolist."

Another market condition that can have related implications is where the per-unit cost continues to decrease as volume increases, which is different from the assumptions underlying the upward-sloping supply curve in the preceding analysis. An efficient large-scale producer will be able to drive out other competitors, or prevent them reaching profitability, and become a monopolist. The announcements in late 1995 of plans by NBC and News Corporation to establish competition to CNN may provide an example of these factors in practice, if the currently dominant position of CNN prevents new competitors from being established.

This ideal notion of the marketplace is closely tied to the wide dispersal of market power associated with the perfectly competitive market structure. When firms become large and command significant market control, the supply, demand, and price functions of the market are disrupted and consumer sovereignty is diminished. On a local market level, this is what has happened with the newspaper and cable industries, as most people have only one local newspaper and one local cable system. Similarly, when the market fails to adequately provide public goods or take account of products with harmful byproducts (externalities), then the government may have to step in and play a role as well. The 1995 debate over violent content in television shows is an excellent example of such issues.

THE FUNCTIONAL DIMENSIONS OF MEDIA FIRMS

Awareness of microeconomic principles provides a conceptual framework for understanding the operations of media firms. These principles directly apply to such dimensions as industrial organization, production and distribution, technology use, marketing and promotion, accounting and information systems, financial management, and transactions in the financial system. These are now considered in turn.

Organization

Business firms of any substantial size are what sociologists term *complex organizations*. The sophistication of contemporary technology and the size of operation necessary to release the economies of scale often associated with its implementation mean that many business firms are indeed complex organizations. Certainly many media firms fit this profile. It is difficult to envisage the functions of a television network being accomplished without a large and complex structure.

An organization can be defined as two or more people working together to achieve a common goal, and most media and other business organizations require the coordination of many individuals and activities. The coordination of activities requires a structured interrelationship between the various functions and subtasks that are required to achieve the overall organizational goals. The primary representation of this in the typical business firm is the organization chart. The organization chart formalizes the grouping of tasks, areas of responsibility, and reporting channels. A typical organization chart of a U.S. media corporation is shown in the following illustration.

An Illustrative Organization Chart for a Publicly Owned U.S. Media Corporation

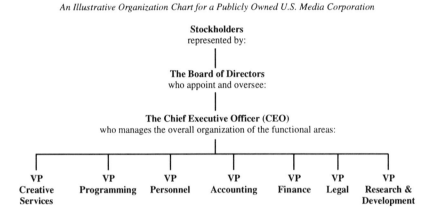

Organizational Structure

A typical organization chart reflects the legal and functional structure of the corporation in the mixed capitalist economy. Members of the board of directors are appointed (at least technically and legally) by the stockholders. The chief executive officer (CEO) is responsible for the ongoing operations across all the functional areas within the policy guidelines provided by the Board of Directors. Primary functional areas range from production (e.g., movie) to financial (e.g., raising monies for movie production). In addition to these primary functional areas, there is an increasing role of international operations.

Just how the responsibility for each functional area is allocated is a function of the type of organizational structure employed. The type reflected earlier is a combination of *line* and *staff* organizational format. Line refers to the actual production of the goods and services that the firm primarily exists to produce, whereas staff describes those functions that do not directly produce the primary good or service, but which are necessary for the overall functioning of the firm.

The functional areas of accounting and personnel are typical of staff functions in media firms.

The matrix form of organization has both vertical and horizontal (in the context of the organization chart shown earlier) areas of responsibility. Quite often the organization of international operations employs the matrix arrangement. The manager of a foreign branch will often have responsibility for all the functional areas in his territory, but will work closely with the home office functional vice presidents in each area for major decisions in the respective arena. For example, the marketing of television programs in multiple foreign markets is handled by one vice president of international programming who coordinates her activities with other relevant vice presidents within the network.

Production

In the terminology of economics, *production* refers to the creation of the good or service being provided by the firm. In the media industries, the production varies from the physical products of print media (e.g., newspapers, magazines) to the transient products of broadcast media (e.g., broadcast news and entertainment programs). Much of this book is devoted to consideration of the specifics of the production undertakings of various media industries. This line function receives more general attention here.

The process of creating a product to distribute to market varies widely across the media industries. In the case of newspapers, for example, production is by necessity compressed into a few hours. Most processes—assembling newsworthy items from reporters and wire services, layout and typesetting, the physical availability of the product for distribution—must take place in a compressed time frame. In contrast, the time frame for a book may be months or years.

Within particular segments of the industry, there have been some notable changes in the production process in recent years. For example, few book and magazine publishers now physically undertake their own printing, as major commercial printers such as R.R. Donnolley do the majority of book and magazine printing. Technological developments have facilitated efficient operations for firms that require geographically dispersed facilities locations. For example, the availability of satellite communications improves the efficiency of the production process for publications where there is a standard product that is printed (with minor variations reflecting regional editions) in several locations. Prominent examples include *The Wall Street Journal* and *USA Today*.

One media industry that has become increasingly dependent on technology has been the newspaper industry. Although household growth has risen substantially since World War II, newspaper circulation has been flat since 1945. In 1970, 95 daily newspapers were delivered for every 100 households. As of 1990, that figure was down to 65 newspapers for every 100 households (Fost,

1990). In order to financially survive in an information industry that includes such rivals as television, radio, and computers, news management has employed many technologically driven changes to make their news operations more attractive to consumers.

Technological innovations prompted the newspaper industry to enter into a newspaper design "revolution" during the 1980s. During that time, newspapers began to make a commitment to Run-of-Press (ROP) color. This move to ROP color came about in part because of the success of *USA Today*, which was not only the first newspaper to use color on a continuous basis, but also the first to make widespread use of satellite technology for distribution. Leading papers such as *The New York Times* and *The Los Angeles Times* invested in ROP to position themselves for the future. Newspapers are also investing in high-quality engraving scanners for color separations, and computer systems for their graphics. Services, such as AP Access Graphics—a cooperative that allows its members to select from a daily menu of charts, graphs, and maps from a host computer—emerged to meet the demand for information graphics.

The 1980s saw a major advance in the use of computer software, especially in the broadcast industry. Broadcasting and cable companies are already using PC- or Macintosh-based paint systems (such as Adobe Systems' Illustrator and Photoshop, Aldus Freehand and Letraset's Colorstudio) for computer graphics, photo retouching, and image manipulation. Other computer software applications have been developed for scriptwriting, and for use in program syndication services. The role of Pixar's technology in the production of the Disney film *Toy Story* is a prominent example of recent developments.

Innovations in camera technology have also been important. Cameras used in sports, documentaries, and undercover newsgathering, such as the Panasonic CD1 cameras, are 2 inches long and a ½ inch in diameter, and cost only $3,000.

The technological development of online computer services, the Internet and the World Wide Web (WWW) has forced traditional media to adapt. For example, major book publishers Bantam Doubleday Dell (BDD), Wiley, and Houghton Mifflin were among the first to establish presences on the WWW. BDD's web site, described by the company as a "new book community," features a different author each week, with author profiles, photographs, jacket graphics, and free access to complete first chapters. Wiley's web site includes access to Wiley imprints worldwide, plus online versions of selected technical journals. Users can also access Wiley's college and trade book titles, video clips, sample chapters, downloadable software, and manuscript submission guidelines. Houghton Mifflin redesigned the trade and reference home pages at its web site in response to user requests to enhance the pages' usefulness and interactivity. Additional features were added, such as author forums, demos, catalogues, and marketing tips for bookstores. By 1997, nearly all major book publishers had established a significant presence on the WWW.

Newspapers and magazines are also embracing the new online services. Knight-Ridder and Landmark Communications, two leading newspaper publishers, formed a joint venture to bring more newspapers online. As part of the agreement, Knight-Ridder bought a stake in Landmark's InfiNet service, which helps papers get on the Internet while allowing them to offer Internet access services to their subscribers. Among the papers available online through InfiMet are Landmark's *Norfolk Virginian-Pilot, Roanoke Times,* and *Greensboro News & Record* as well as Knight-Ridder's 26 dailies.

In addition to online versions of their hard copy newspapers, some newspapers are offering value-added options as a way of generating additional revenue streams. For example, *Wall Street Journal* publisher Dow Jones created Money & Investing Update, a subscription-based web site offering financial news, stock quotes, and market information updated throughout the day. A second site is an Internet directory coinciding with a directory of advertisers in the print version of the *Journal,* including links to the advertisers' home pages.

Distribution

The channels of distribution, market coverage, use of intermediaries, and techniques of physical distribution clearly vary according to the specific media industry being considered, and the significance of distribution management varies. For the TV networks, the pattern of owned and affiliated stations provides a relatively stable pattern and distribution is not perceived to be an area of that business requiring continual attention. In contrast, for small-scale book publishers, channels of marketing and distribution generate repetitive problems and the search for a "better" solution is in some ways ongoing.

Probably the most revolutionary change in distribution that occurred as a result of technology was the growth of the number of homes that have VCRs and remote controls. The number of homes with VCRs increased from 1% in 1980 to more than 65% in 1989.

The impact of VCRs is twofold. First, VCRs led to a whole new "ancillary" market for theatrical films. Motion picture companies now derive revenues from video sales to either video rental outlets or direct sales ("sell through") to consumers. Film companies now obtain greater profits from home video sales than from box-office receipts. Home video viewing—which has an earlier "release window" than pay cable or broadcast TV—has also had an impact on pay-cable viewership, broadcast TV viewership, and (ironically) theatrical moviegoing.

Second, VCRs have resulted in a whole new way for people to view television. Viewers can now "time shift," that is, tape programs to watch at another time, rather than at the time a broadcast or cable network airs its programs. The most popular type of program that is recorded is the daytime soap opera, a direct result of the increasing number of working women in this country. Viewers can also "graze," or sample programs across the dial at any one time. More importantly for advertisers, viewers can zip through commercials by fastforwarding or zap them by not recording them.

The expansion of fiber optics in the cable industry during the 1980s resulted in consumers having the potential of receiving hundreds of channels. Even more importantly, the development of the addressable converter meant that cable companies could more easily implement pay-per-view (PPV) services. So far, PPV has been used for major events types of broadcasts (heavyweight championship fights, concerts) and as movie services. The expansion of fiber optics also means there is the potential for more narrowly targeted cable services. In the future, sports fans may be able to view electronic media channels dedicated to football, basketball, or baseball. The narrowness of the market will only be limited by the potential revenue (either through advertising or by subscription) of that market.

Future Technological Developments

The media industries devote substantial research and development resources to develop technological innovations designed to help improve the production and distribution of their media products. This section reviews a few such innovations just beginning to take hold in the 1990s.

The early efforts of radio stations to transmit audio material via the Internet were hampered by the need for long download times. Two relatively recent software innovations—Progressive Networks' RealAudio and Xing Technology's Stream-Works—have changed all of that. RealAudio, which allows programmers to store audio material and listeners to call it up when they want it, has won dozens of adherents, including ABC News, National Public Radio (NPR), C-SPAN, KPIG in Monterey Bay, CA, WKSU-FM at Kent State University, WWOZ in New Orleans, and the Korean Broadcasting System as well as web sites Rock Radio, Adam Curry's Metaverse, and Radio HK, which is believed to be the first to make 24-hour-a-day programming available via "cybercasting."

As Progressive Networks worked to add real-time transmission capabilities to RealAudio, Xing Technology jumped ahead with its StreamWorks software, making live cybercasting possible for a number of radio stations across the United States and Canada. KPIG Radio of Monterey Bay, CA, an early user of RealAudio, began using StreamWorks to offer what it calls the first 24-hour broadcast over the Internet.

The global scope of the Net allows stations to reach out beyond their local audiences, creating new opportunities for niche programming and advertising sales. They can also supplement their audio material with text, graphics, hyperlinks, and more. Using one service, North American Network's RadioSpace, stations can download broadcast-ready soundbites on a variety of subjects via the WWW.

One of the most exciting technological developments of 1996 was the launch of WebTV Networks Inc. (http://www.webtv.net), a privately held start-up founded in June 1995 by three former Apple Computer employees. The company announced that Sony and Philips had licensed its set-top box, which hooks up to the television, and would begin deploying it in Fall 1996. Although there have been other attempts at marrying personal computers and television, WebTV makes the graphic Web pages look good on a television.

There are two components to WebTV: a design for making set-top boxes and an actual online service. The boxes are equipped with a 33.6-Kbps modem, software that eliminates flicker on the TV screen, digital-quality audio and video output, and an ISO Smart Card reader that will read credit and ATM cards. Cable modem functionality is planned for the future. Users of WebTV are able to browse the Net with WebTV's remote control.

The online service portion will support up to five users, and each user will have an Internet e-mail address, a favorites list, and customized settings. E-mail can be typed with a virtual on-screen keyboard or with a planned optional full remote keyboard. The design of the box calls is equipped so that software enhancements and updates can be made automatically over the network.

In addition to licensees Sony and Philips Consumer Electronics, WebTV has partnered with Concentric Networks (for the Net connection), Excite (which will provide a specialized version of Excite for WebTV subscribers), Progressive Networks (RealAudio), Spyglass (for its SurfWatch child-protection software), HeadSpace (music and audio effects), and Integrated Device Technology (MIPS RISC microprocessor). WebTV plans a significant amount of content for its online service, especially local content.

Less than 20% of homes in the United States use an online service. A WebTV set-top box, if priced inexpensively enough, could go a long way toward getting into the 80% of homes that don't have access. The set-top box price will initially be less than $500. The service should work with any Internet provider offering TCP/IP connections, though the ease of configurations for other network providers remains an unknown.

Another service that tries to marry the PC and TV is Intel's Intercast. Intercast links TV and the Web by transmitting HTML on a part of the broadcast signal known as the Vertical Blanking Interval (VBI), currently used to transmit services such as closed captioning. With Intercasting, one window would display normal television broadcasts while another window would display a Web page of information related to the broadcast. NBC and CNN also plan to use Intercast technology. MTV's 1996 launch of its M2 channel would take advantage of Intercast on a 24-hour basis. One example of how MTV will use the service is that it will "Intercast" tour dates for an artist while the artist's video is playing.

Marketing/Promotion

Marketing is an inclusive term involving market identification and research, evaluation and standardization of products and services, and the promotion and selling of the product/service. Over time and frequently in a cyclical manner, most of the media industries both benefit and suffer from changes in the markets served and changes brought about by technological developments. For example, the beeper industry grew as a result of the technological developments facilitating its operation, and now faces challenging competition from the cellular telephone technology and industry. Clearly broadcast TV is exposed to new competitive challenges with the pervasive availability of cable television, direct broadcast satellite services, and high-definition television technology.

The nature of the competitive arena varies widely within the media industries. Book publishing includes literally thousands of firms in the United States and there are few barriers to entry. Although structural challenges such as distribution channels explain why the industry is dominated by a relatively small number of firms, nevertheless many small, specialized firms continue to prosper. For example, the Ten-Speed Press has had considerable success with its *What Color is Your Parachute?* By contrast, until the widespread availability of cable television, the networks operated under approximately oligopolistic market conditions, under which a small number of firms dominate and control the market. Now, however, the technological and distributional developments mean that many TV consumers see numerous substitutes to network TV available. Reflecting full awareness of these trends, there is now considerable investment by networks in those additional services (e.g., ABC and ESPN) although such investment is closely monitored by the FCC.

Accounting and Information Systems

Some familiarity with the essentials of financial accounting is necessary for a full awareness of what is involved in media management. Accounting must process many types of data as a functional area of activity. While the general presentation of accounting focuses on the types of accounting data found in financial statements, a broader interpretation of the role of accounting is to perceive the accounting function as part of the total information system within the firm.

Accounting as a profession has two primary branches—financial accounting, and cost and management accounting. They are considered in Appendix A. After identifying the main concerns of cost and management accounting, this appendix focuses on financial accounting.

Financial Management of Media Operations

Many of the numbers reported in the balance sheet are primarily the result of financial decisions made by the firm. For example, the level of debt is typically determined at least partly by management's interpretation of what is an optimal level of debt. The results of the firm's operations also has an impact on the firm financial statements. Clearly whether sales are profitable will have a major impact on the overall financial performance. Analysis and interpretation of accounting statements thus includes an examination of the consequences of the firm's operating and financial decisions.

Financial Decisions

Modern financial management perceives the challenges of this functional responsibility to be selecting worthwhile investments in media assets and managing existing assets, acquiring the necessary funds to finance the assets, and providing returns to the sources of funds (interest to lenders, dividends and capital gains to stockholders). These investment, financing and distribution decisions are considered in turn in Appendix B.

Rate of Return

The rate of return (ROR) is a primary metric in finance. It is a generally simple concept, and can be introduced by way of a numerical example. If a security was purchased a year ago for $100, today it is worth $110, and the security paid a $5 dividend throughout the year, then an intuitively appealing (and correct) rate of return is 15% over the year. Formally:

$$ROR = \frac{PRICEend - PRICEbeginning}{PRICEbeginning} + \frac{INCOMEduring}{PRICEbeginning}$$

$$= \frac{110-100}{100} + \frac{5}{100} = \frac{15}{100} = 15\%$$

or

$$ROR = \text{Capital Gain component of ROR} + \text{Income component of ROR}$$

Risk and Return

Rate of return is a central focus for both managers and investors, and there is a fundamental relationship between *risk* and Required Rate of Return (RROR). Without going through the intricate mathematical derivation of the relevant models from economics and finance, it is intuitively appealing that the higher the perceived risk, the greater the required return. In compensation for a greater potential downside, investors must be paid (in the form of higher expected return) for taking on more risk.

The formal model of risk/return most widely used in finance is the Capital Asset Pricing Model (CAPM).[9] Verbally, the required ROR on security "j" is the sum of a risk-free rate of return (the price of time) plus a return for risk bearing. Risk compensation depends on the price of risk per unit of time and the amount of risk. Reflecting this, the return for risk is the product of two components:

- The *Market Premium*, or the price per unit of risk. It is the amount by which the average return on the overall stock market exceeds the risk free rate earned by Treasury bills. The market premium typically falls in the range of 6% to 9%.
- The risk measure *beta*, or the *variation relative to a portfolio* of well-diversified stocks (the market portfolio). The metric for beta is such that investments for which the ROR varies more than the market have a beta of more than 1. Those that vary less than the market have betas of less than 1.

Media firms exhibit a variety of beta coefficients. Large, diversified media firms typically have beta coefficients in the range of 1.05 to 1.25, whereas the stocks of small specialty media firms can exhibit beta coefficients in the 1.5 to 2.0 range. These beta coefficients are widely used in the practice of media management and investments.

The Financial System

Financial decisions are made within the context of the overall financial system. The financial system includes: (a) financial markets (such as the New York Stock Exchange); (b) financial instruments (such as stock and bonds); (c) financial institutions and intermediaries (such as banks); (d) financial practices and procedures; and (e) financial laws and regulations. The primary functions of the financial system are to transfer savings to productive investments, provide efficient means of making payments, retain confidence in the currency, and enable law-abiding economic units to acquire such necessary financial services as risk management (via the insurance industry) in cost-efficient ways. Confidence in the integrity of the financial system is critical for its effective functioning. We concentrate here on the financial markets.

---

[9]This model specifies the risk/return relationship for a (any) particular asset "j" as follows:

Expected ROR = A risk - free rate + a premium for risk.

$Ex(ROR_j) = R_f + [(R_m) - R_f)]$ times $Beta_j$

$R_j = R_f + [(R_m) - R_f)] \cdot B_j$

Where:

R_f = the risk - free ROR, proxied by the T - Bill rate,

R_m = the return on the overall stock market, proxied by the average return of the Standard and Poors 500 stocks, for example.

$Beta_j$ = The Covariance of returns of security "j" and the return on the market, standardized by dividing the variance of the market return (R_m)

$Beta_j = \frac{COV(R_j R_m)}{VAR(R_m)}$

Financial Markets

The fundamental partition in stock markets is between *primary markets* and *secondary markets*. Primary markets are where new securities are issued, whereas secondary markets are where existing ("used") securities are traded.

Primary Markets

These are the various markets and processes by which new securities are issued by firms (stocks and bonds), government and government agencies (bonds), and households (e.g., mortgages). This category includes many segments and market processes. For firms, investment banking plays a critical role in the primary markets. The prices paid when new securities are issued reflect current interest rates and required rates of return.

Firms issue new stocks in one of two ways: (a) the first public offering of a firm's stock (Initial Public Offerings—IPOs); and (b) additional issue of an already publicly traded firm (secondary offerings). This market involves the marketing and distribution functions of investment bankers. The volume of trading in the primary markets is but a small fraction of that in secondary markets. The media have produced some of the more closely followed recent IPOs, such as Netscape's (where the issue price of $28 rose to $75 within 3 hours of trading) and Pixar's.

Secondary Markets

In these markets, existing ("used") financial securities are traded. The transactions in these markets do not directly provide new capital to firms although prices in secondary markets are important because they affect the rates of return firms must pay when they do make new security issues in the primary markets. These markets include the well-known stock markets—the New York Stock Exchange (NYSE) and the American Stock Exchange (ASE). In addition to these exchange markets, the secondary markets also include the over-the-counter (OTC) market. The OTC stock market uses the National Association of Securities Dealers Automatic Quotation (NASDAQ) system to make markets for securities. The securities traded OTC are typically those of smaller public companies, although some of the companies traded OTC on the National Market System (NMS) segment of that market are sufficiently large to trade on the NYSE and ASE if they choose. Examples of such firms include Apple Computer, Microsoft, and MCI. The OTC market is a major market for the trading of bonds.

There are many other financial markets, including those for options, forward and futures contracts, foreign exchange, and such specialized securities as commercial paper. A media manager who comes to be involved in the financial management of a firm will require formal courses in both corporate financial management and the processes and practices of the financial markets.

THE DYNAMICS OF MEDIA ECONOMICS

Corporate Goals

In the corporate form the shareholders are legally considered the constituents with the ultimate authority for the conduct of the corporate affairs within the given legal context. The goal assumed for corporate management is "the maximization of shareholder wealth," equivalent to pursuing the goal of maximizing the stock price—the market value" of a firm. This goal of maximizing shareholder wealth has prompted a significant number of U.S. firms to adopt measures to trim costs (downsize), increase revenues (expand) or both. These measures tend to fall into two categories, incremental changes and corporate restructuring.[10]

Incremental Changes

Companies engaging in incremental changes are attempt to become more effective and efficient firms without massive modifications of their structure, function and culture. Among the more common type of incremental changes are discussed here.

Creating Cost Efficiencies

The increasing demands of corporate shareholders in the last 15 years to wanted continued improvement in their returns on investment have forced companies to operate as efficiently as possible, that is, control costs. Achieving these efficiencies can take on a variety of forms. For example, one such way may be a shift in accounting practices to Activity-Based Costing (ABC), a method created by Robert S. Kaplan of Harvard Business School (along with others). Traditional accounting practices identify costs according to the category of expense (i.e., salaries, fringe benefits, fixed costs, etc.). Activity-based costing spreads costs over the tasks that are performed (i.e., processing orders, buying component parts, assembling parts, etc.). This type of accounting provides a more accurate assessment of costs, and allows companies to analyze "cost drivers." For example, when Advanced Micro

---

[10]Does maximizing stock price imply insensitivity to other parties with a legitimate interest in the affairs of the firm? In recent years, the notion that there are numerous parties interested in and affected by the conduct of any firm's business has been formalized in the concept of "stakeholders." There are several categories of stakeholders, shareholders being just one such party. Although appropriate and useful for a consideration of the role of firms overall, for the purposes of managerial decision making there is a need for an unambiguous goal. Maximizing the value of the firm to its stockholders reflects the legal structure of the limited liability corporation and provides management with an unambiguous goal. Clearly this goal is contentious, but the logical implications of trying to simultaneously maximize the worth of the firm to all its stakeholders generates inconsistencies and no viable framework for decision making. In addition, stockholders are typically the predominant stakeholders. When firms are not performing well, it is often cost cutting and other measures that are taken to protect the interests of stockholders, perhaps at cost to other parties (e.g., layoffs.)

Devices, a semiconductor manufacturer, used traditional accounting procedures, it overestimated the cost of high-volume chips and underestimated the cost of low-volume chips. By switching to activity-based costing, the company discovered that the low-volume chips were 75% more costly than they had estimated. AMD was then able to alter its product mix.

One of the problems facing entertainment companies, however, is that success in the marketplace tends to fluctuate more wildly than for other industries. For example, after a decade where situation comedies did well in the syndication marketplace, programmers discovered that public tastes shifted to more expensive hour-long adventure shows, such as *Highlander: The Series* and *Xena: Warrior Princess*. Such a shift is not only related to cost, but is a complete production changeover (situation comedies are generally videotaped using interior sets; dramatic shows are filmed using more exterior shots).

A second way of achieving efficiencies is to reduce the costs of production. During the 1980s, all three broadcast networks (CapCities/ABC, CBS and GE-NBC) changed their ownership structure, with a heavy amount of financing required to accomplish the deals. This was followed by a time when the advertising market began to slow down. Consequently, these networks have been forced to impose cost reduction measures, particularly in the areas of news and public affairs. Even previously "untouchable" programming, such as news coverage of national party political conventions, was curtailed during 1988. On the local level, network affiliates and independent stations alike are trying to hold the line on syndicated program prices. Prices appear to have peaked with *The Cosby Show* ($60,000 and up per episode in major markets). Many local stations felt they had enough program inventory to be selective in their new acquisitions. As a result, new offerings, such as off-network reruns of the *Golden Girls*, found relatively few takers until prices become more realistic. In addition, a supply of cheaper first-run programming (game shows, talk shows, and "infotainment" shows) began to drive prices down. On average, price per episode will continue to decline.

A third major area of cost reduction is through personnel layoffs. "Raiders" and other potential acquirers (domestic or foreign) can make offers for firms considered to be inefficiently operated. This puts considerable pressure on management teams for dramatic short-term improvement in the bottom-line. The associated striving for maximal profitability and cash flows was felt by both incumbents and those who wrested control of media firms from previous managers. The cuts in broadcast network employee ranks often associated with the restructuring of the 1980s has been widely documented. Further cuts may come from advances in the mechanization of media production, such as the replacement of camera operators at NBC News by robotic cameras. The 1990 *New York Daily News* management/labor struggle, and the 1995 to 1996 strike at the *Detroit Free Press* were very visible manifestations of the pressures that can build in the quest to hold down costs.

Pursuing Additional Revenue Streams

The Cable Act of 1984 freed cable systems from most local rate control. Cable systems raised pay cable prices, thereby increasing their earning potential. Municipalities, however, retained rate control over "basic" cable services. Consequently, many cable systems began to break their basic service into *tiers*, redefining "basic" as carriage of local over-the-air broadcast signals and low-profit cable networks. More popular cable networks were then carried on a "premium basic" or "basic plus" tier, not covered by local rate control. During the late 1980s, cable companies had their sale value pegged at $2,500 per subscriber, up from $1,000 per subscriber in 1980.

In 1992, Congress again passed legislation to control cable rates, especially basic cable rates. As a result, costs for tiers above basic cable rose dramatically. The Telecommunications Act of 1996 eliminated federal control over cable rates. However, because of slowing cable penetration rates, and potential competition from other technologies (such as direct broadcast satellite—DBS), key players in the cable industry (such as TCI) moved to raise revenue by providing Internet access and phone service.

Deferred Investment

Several media industries have delayed or canceled expansion plans. For example, one area of the film industry where there is beginning to be a retrenchment is in the movie theater business. At the end of 1990, General Cinema and American Multi-Cinema announced plans to cut back on the number of movie screens built. Film studios have generally taken advantage of the increase in screens by rolling out on a national basis. More screens, however, have meant more prints and advertising costs.

"Niche" Marketing

From the period of 1978 to 1997, broadcast network share of the audience dropped from 90% to just under 50%, thus raising the question of the role that networks will play in the future. From 1988 to 1992, CBS tried to carve an identity as a sports programming broadcast network. CBS Sports acquired rights to baseball, exclusivity to the NCAA college basketball tournament, and the 1992 Olympics, paying out some $2 billion. It billed 1990 as the "Dream Season" for sports. Although CBS' effort proved to be a costly ($1 billion+) failure, Fox, WB, and UPN have been more successful as youth-oriented and culturally diverse networks. In magazine publishing, many of the 11,000 titles available on newsstands are niche titles. The rapidly expanding Internet publishing is leading to further niche-pursuit, limited-interest titles.

Restructuring—Overall Motivations

Corporate organizations have been changing rapidly in recent years. Many attributes of the corporate formal organization involve trade-offs on issues such as span of control, economies of scale, and the bureaucratic structures often associated with large and complex organizations. In the 1980s, there emerged an increasing awareness of the potentially inefficient structure of some large corporate organizations. The associated "wave" of restructuring saw many firms reduce in size or substantially change the set of operations encompassed under the one corporate organization. Concurrently, other firms increased in size and added to their range of activities and operations. In many instances, the respective changes can be considered efficient in the given circumstances. The circumstances include the nature of the particular firms, current market conditions for both inputs and outputs, the technology involved in its operations, and the contracting arrangements necessary for its operations.

The primary motivation behind much of this activity is to achieve more efficient organizational forms. However, there are a variety of potential motivations for mergers, not all of which generate more efficient organizations. Managers may seek to maximize the size of their "empire" and acquire other firms even if is not an efficient process. They may engage in mergers that are unlikely to be efficient, even if their goal is profitability improvement. Although a controversial contention, some analysts suggest that this profile could be applied to the Time-Warner merger. In the summer of 1989, Paramount offered stockholders in Time, Inc. $175 (and then $200) per share, but the offer was rejected by Time, Inc. management and its board of directors. It was never put to a stockholder vote, a controversial attribute of some recent corporate control contests (Grundfest, 1990). In October 1990, Time-Warner shares sold for less than $70. For Time, Inc. shareholders this was approximately one third of what one party (Paramount) was willing to pay for the shares in the summer of 1989. Furthermore, in June 1991, in an effort to reduce the $11 billion debt resulting from the merger of Time and Warner, the company proposed to raise $3 billion through an offering of 34.5 million new shares of Time-Warner stock. Current shareholders, however, would be required to buy new shares to maintain their percentage ownership. Stock prices fell from $117 on June 4, 1991, down to $94.68 on June 7 following the announcement of the plan. The plan was subject to Securities and Exchange Commission (SEC) scrutiny and withdrawn by management in early July 1991.

A key attribute associated with restructuring is valuation. As noted in Bates (chap. 4, this volume), valuation combines scientific tools of analysis (e.g., present value mathematics) with estimates of future sales levels and cash flows. Clearly the estimation of future flows is an inexact process, and different sets of expectations and varying degrees of hubris will result in different individuals and firms having individual valuations for a given property or business. Typically, if a business is being transacted, it goes to the highest bidder. This is why businesses sell even their best divisions (sometimes called "cash cows" or "crown jewels"). If a business receives an offer for a good property and the bid reflects a valuation above what the firms considers to be the value of the division or unit, accepting the offer is rational.

It is different valuations (based on different sets of expectations of future sales, profits and cash flows) that generated much of the restructuring activity of the past decade. In this valuation process, the potential for a division to be worth different amounts to different corporate owners should be recognized. For example, a firm with international operations may be able to generate more incremental cash flows from the rights to publish the lines of a domestic publisher overseas than could the domestic publisher by establishing a new international division. Although this notion of *synergy* is particularly pleasing conceptually, empirical research often fails to identify material evidence that it is realized, particularly in domestic mergers. In fact, much of the restructuring activity in recent years has been the undoing of earlier mergers that did not work out. Some studies have indicated that as many as 50% of all mergers are (at least partially) reversed by divestitures in the following decade. The actual (in contrast to anticipated) synergies can be negative if dysfunctional bureaucracies become necessary to control very large corporate organizations. As in production, there can be both economies and, past a certain scale, diseconomies of organization.

Restructuring Strategies

Major restructuring involves the following categories of changes (Hite & Owers, 1983):

- Business combinations (mergers and acquisitions).
- Business separations (divestitures such as sell-offs and spin-offs).
- Substantial realignment of the financing and ownership of a given business (such as leveraged buyouts and recapitalizations).

Although the sell-off is the most frequently used form of restructuring, this section also describes the other forms that restructuring may take, in order to give the reader a broader perspective and familiarity with the terminology.

Business Combinations—Mergers, Acquisitions, and Joint Ventures

There have been five "waves" of business combination activity in the U.S. economy. The first occurred in the early years of the 20th century, the era of the large trusts; the second occurred in the 1920s, and the third in the late 1960s. However, all of these previous merger waves were overshadowed in magnitude by the combination and merger wave of the 1980s, which itself has been exceeded by the 1990s merger wave. Business combinations can be implemented by friendly mergers or contested changes in control such as hostile tender offers. There is a role for proxy contests in this process.

The term *business combination* typically conjures up notions of whole-firm combinations, such as mergers and acquisitions. A discussion of mergers and acquisitions is found in chapter 5, this volume. However, an important category of business combination occurs when two or more firms selectively combine parts of their operations and form joint ventures. Joint venture formation in the U.S. economy (and internationally) is extensive, and is playing a growing role in the media industries. Strategic alignments via joint ventures are increasingly a means of achieving improved results without formally merging firms. Formal mergers involve many complexities and raise sensitive issues such as who will manage the combined firm and how differing "corporate cultures" will be integrated. Joint ventures avoid many of these issues and are more readily undone if they are not successful. Moreover, by selectively combining only those parts of two firms where the potential for synergy is greatest, the likelihood of efficiency gains may be greatest. Research findings are generally supportive such as those of each of these hypotheses.

Business Separations and Recapitalizations

The process by which firms reduce their scale and scope of operations is generally termed *divestiture*. This term *divestiture*, however, is often used to refer to one specific strategy for separating out part of a firm's operations—the *sell-off*. Although the sell-off is the most frequently used form, we also describe the spin-off and liquidation strategies for business separation. Leverage increasing recapitalizations and realignments have become important techniques for changing corporate organization and ownership structure.

Sell-Offs (Divestitures).   The sell-off is the most widely used strategy for separating out operations. Conceptually it is not complex—an exchange of a subunit (product line, division, subsidiary, etc.) for an agreed amount. The consideration (means of payment) can be cash or securities in the acquiring firm, or some combination thereof. The sell-off by itself does not reduce the assets of the firm; it only changes their composition. An operating asset is exchanged for cash or securities. If there is an associated special dividend, the firm can be reduced in size. The motivations for sell-offs vary from a need for cash so that the corporation may survive to having received offers so attractive that even prime assets such as cash cows are sold.[11] A prominent media sell-off was the purchase of CBS Records by Sony Corporation.

---

[11] It has been shown that sell-offs result in increases in value to both divesting and acquiring firms. The findings of Hite, Owers, and Rogers (1987) showed that in completed transactions, sellers gained 4.05% in equity value and acquirers approximately 1.39% in the week of the initial announcement. These seemingly small percentage magnitudes should not be considered inconsequential—they can relate to equity securities (shares) with a value measured in billions of dollars. Indeed, they are significant both statistically and economically. The finding that acquirers of divested units increase in value is also

Spin-Offs.   Spin-offs are substantially more complex business separations than sell-offs. They involve separating out some operations from a firm, establishing them as a newly separate corporation, and distributing shares of ownership in that separated company as special dividends to stockholders of the parent corporation. The impact of spin-offs on the value of the divesting firm is substantial: The average percentage increase in stock price associated with spin-offs is approximately 7%.

Spin-offs have been used quite extensively by media firms. In some instances the use is entirely voluntary. For example, Columbia Pictures (under Sony ownership) spun-off Columbia Pictures Television from the rest of its entertainment operations. In others, the separating out of operations by spin-off follows antitrust action by the Justice Department or the Federal Trade Commission. The 1971 spin-off of Viacom by CBS is a prominent example of the latter. The 1984 breakup of AT&T was "forced," whereas the 1996 trivestiture was voluntary.

Liquidations.   As a voluntary restructuring strategy, the term *liquidation* does not necessarily imply financial distress. Firms might choose to liquidate for tax reasons, because of contests for control of the corporation such as tender offers, or because of some decline in the reputation of the organization that makes efficient transactions in the financial markets difficult. Voluntary liquidations can be *partial* or *complete*. In a partial liquidation, the process frequently involves the sell-off of a part of the firm, and paying a special dividend from proceeds. A total liquidation means that assets are sold piecemeal and liabilities are settled, the balance being distributed to stockholders, who are the residual claimants. Total liquidations are associated with major increases in the value of the liquidating firm's shares. On average, liquidating firms gain approximately 25% in value over the year ending with their liquidation announcement (Hite, Owers, & Rogers, 1987). The reasons for voluntary liquidations are varied, although before the Tax Reform Act of 1986, there were considerable tax motivations that could help make a firm worth more dead than alive. Reeves Telecom is an example of the voluntary liquidation by a media firm.

Leverage Increasing Restructurings and Realignments.   These re-structuring strategies come in several forms. In essence, they involve the partial

---

particularly noteworthy, given that the evidence on acquirers of whole firms in mergers and acquisitions suggests that typically acquirers do not substantially gain, and even experience small losses. Thus in whole-firm acquisitions, only the owners of target firms (i.e., those acquired) gain on a consistent basis when the immediate effect of the transaction on stock values is examined. The long-term impacts are more difficult to separate and measure. However, overall there is no strong evidence that acquirer firms (buyers) consistently gain from that activity.

The gains to both parties in sell-off divestitures and the formation of joint ventures, when contrasted with the evidence on whole-firm combinations, suggests that a key to mutually satisfactory business restructuring is the selectivity afforded by divestitures and joint ventures.

substitution of debt for equity and a realignment of operations. There are frequently associated sell-offs and spin-offs of part of the original operations. Such restructurings can occur without a change in management, and are often used as a preemptive measure by a firm facing a contest for its control (such as the treat of an unsolicited takeover offer). Alternatively, leverage-increasing restructurings can occur after a "raider" has taken control and attempts to increase the value of the firm. By many evaluations, CBS underwent a leverage-increasing restructuring in the mid-1980s when the Tisch Organization acquired a 25% interest in the firm.

This category of restructuring is often associated with the issue of large amounts of additional debt (sometimes including high-yield junk bonds). As a result, a debate has emerged regarding whether the later-issued junk bond debt securities have a negative effect on the value of investment-grade bonds previously issued by the firm. Investment grade bonds are generally those with ratings in the "A" and "B" ranges. The major rating agencies are Moodys and Standard and Poors. When firms issue large quantities of junk bonds, the total risk of firm default is increased. Thus, even though the junk bonds have a lower priority of claim than the earlier-issued, the outstanding investment grade bonds also become more risky. Increasingly, the evidence suggests that preexisting investment grade bonds do decrease in value in many transactions where there is a significant increase in the junk bonds issued by a firm.

The Impact of Restructuring and Other Recent Developments on Media Economic Practices

The decade of the 1980s was characterized by industrial "merger mania," and the media industry was certainly not immune to this phenomenon. News of the most recent spin-offs, sell-offs, LBOs, equity carveouts, and voluntary liquidations competed with movie, TV, and Broadway show reviews on newspaper entertainment pages.

Usually, restructuring activity takes place when the previous organizational form is perceived to be nonoptimal. For example, if a conglomerate has become too unwieldy as a result of bureaucratic considerations, then a breakup of the firm into smaller units may be efficient. However, the merger activity that took place in the 1980s was largely the result of a unique combination of factors.

Prior to 1984, tendencies to media restructuring activity were constrained by the regulatory limits on station ownership and antitrafficking rules. Those rules were lifted at a time when there was an abundance of available capital by which to do deals. Additionally, advertising rates continued to rise at 10% to 15% per year. The government also took a hands-off approach to antitrust enforcement and the changing financial practices in mergers and acquisitions, especially the high-cost LBO deals financed with junk bonds that left a number of companies to contend with huge debts.

Unfortunately, as the 1980s ended the advertising market experienced a major decline. Companies that based their financial decisions on multiples of 12 to 15 times earnings found that they had overpaid for their media properties. The downturn was especially painful for companies that financed their deals with junk bonds. Not only did they find that the earnings potential of their media properties was no longer there, but Congress, as part of the S&L bailout, forced the S&Ls to divest themselves of junk-bond portfolios. As a result, just as junk bond demand had dried up, there was a new supply. Some companies, such as Grant Broadcasting, folded, whereas others, such as Turner Broadcasting, undertook further restructuring to finance earlier deals.

It was not unusual during the 1980s for stations to be bought at between 12 and 20 times cash flow. Illustrative of the problems inherent in such expensive transactions was that of SCI-TV, owned by George Gillett. KravisKohlberggRoberts (KKR) and Gillett bought six stations from Storer Communications in 1985 for $1.3 billion. In order to finance the deal, they had to float expensive bond issues (at 15.5% to 17.5% interest). The deal did not turn out well. In 1988, Gillett tried to sell WJW-TV in Cleveland for $157 million (11 times cash flow) in order to pay down some of his acquired debt load. However, given that ad revenues had turned sour, the deal fell through. Gillett had to scramble to work out a deal with investors to postpone receiving interest on their bonds for several years.

The stock market crash of October 1987 slowed down the buying frenzy, but it did not stop it. As was observed during the stock market crash in 1929, media restructuring, once it begins, appears to be somewhat immune to conditions of severe market swings. In addition, whether this is a general business truism or one that applies only to media industries is uncertain. Nevertheless, the efficiencies caused by both economies of scale and by cost trimming left the media in a position to withstand the October 1987 shock wave. In fact, in the months after the October 1987 crash, media stocks not only survived, but, as a class, outperformed the Dow Jones index (Owers & Carveth, 1988).

For broadcast companies, a great deal of the restructuring occurred during a spate of mergers and acquisitions from 1984 to 1986. Restructuring activity slowed down due in large measure to a reevaluation of broadcast companies' value. During period of 1984 to 1986, ever-spiraling prices were paid for stations and station groups, with purchase prices being calculated at 13 to 15 times earnings. After the crash, the investment community began looking not at earnings, but at assets. Consequently, prices for broadcast companies declined to a level of 11 to 13 times earnings.

Much of the restructuring activity during the 1980s assumed ever-increasing levels of revenue generation. For most of the decade, revenues *did* increase. For example, in 1987 advertising accounted for 2.43% of GDP, up from 1.87% in the 1970s. As the decade ended, however, sources of media revenues flattened or declined. In addition, more media firms entered the marketplace to compete for revenues, thus slicing the advertising pie into smaller and smaller pieces. Media companies, especially those that acquired a substantial amount of debt, were forced to adopt one or more business practices to adapt to the new economic realities.

To the surprise of many, the level of restructuring has risen to new highs during the 1990s. Many large-scale transactions have received much attention—CapCities/ABC merging with Disney, CBS combining with Westinghouse, and Time Warner acquiring Turner Broadcasting. There have also been major divestitures, such as Sony divesting itself of Columbia Pictures, and AT&T's trivestiture. These are but a small portion of the total number and value of transactions. The ongoing high level of restructuring attests to the changing nature of the media industries, and the need for constant adaptation to maintain superior performance in light of changing competitive, technological, and regulatory environments. In economic terms, long-term equilibrium is a condition of ongoing change and evolution.

CONCLUSION

This chapter has established the economic and corporate frameworks for media economics. The economic framework consists of the guidelines and constraints imposed by societal choices (political economy), the specific decision-making processes of consumers and firms (microeconomics), and the overall, aggregate attributes of the economy (macroeconomics).

The corporate framework consists of the underpinnings of industrial organization, the respective functional areas of the firm's operations, and the impacts of globalization. The chapter also revealed how the economic and technological milieus generate ongoing forces for change and evolution in media firms. As we noted, these forces combined in the 1980s. The resulting restructuring dramatically altered the media industry landscape. The chapter also reviewed the restructuring strategies by which the resulting changes were implemented and identified specific implications of this process.

REFERENCES

Fost, D. (1990, September). Newspapers enter the age of information. *American Demographics,* pp. 14–16.
Garneau, G. (1995, June). Another way to go online. *Editor & Publisher*, p. 24.
Grundfest, J. (1990). Subordination of American capital. *Journal of Financial Economics, 27* 89–116.
Hite, G., Owers, J., & Rogers, R. (1987). The market for interfirm asset sales: Partial sell-offs and toal liquidations. *Journal of Financial Economics, 18,* 229–252.

Owers, J., & Carveth, R. (1988, November). *The party's over: Media acquisition activity after the "crash."* Paper presented at the Speech Communication Association Conference, New Orleans, LA.

Picard, R. (1990). *Media economics.* Beverly Hills, CA: Sage.

Samuelson, P. (1976). *Economics* (10th ed.). New York: McGraw-Hill.

2

Media Ownership: Concepts and Principles

Douglas Gomery
University of Maryland

The production, distribution, and presentation of broadcasting television, home video, cable television, newspapers, magazines, books, recorded music, and movies—the mass media—require great expense and frequently generate enormous profits. No research in mass communication can ignore questions of mass-media ownership and the economic implications of that control. Mass-media businesses routinely take in and spend vast sums of money. The mass media in the United States, and more and more of the world, seek to maximize profits, and thus can safely be studied as economic institutions. But how should one go about trying to make sense of the effects of mass-media industrial ownership and operation (Gomery, 1993)?

Media economics should move into the center of communications study by offering powerful and flexible methods by which to analyze mass-media industries in the context of core concerns of the communication process. Marxist "critical studies" and free-market empiricism lack appeal because they ask us to analyze a subject when we already "know" a predetermined answer. From critics from the left, the mass media assume an all-encompassing conspiracy by monopolists. Yet a cursory examination of the contemporary magazine and radio industries undercuts any such a monolithic image. By contrast, conservative free-market advocates assume that efficient operation represents the paramount and only goal for any enterprise, even ones so vital to democracy and quality of life as mass communication and mass entertainment. Studying the economics of mass communication as though one was simply trying to make toaster companies run "leaner and meaner" is far too narrow a perspective.

No research in public communication can hope to make its mark in the world of public policy unless it addresses questions of economic influence and effect. Critics from all sides have long found problems with the media and asserted a

45

plethora of corrective regulations by which to improve industry operation and content production. We should not restrict analysis of media economics only to today's problem industries; the complete range of media industries and institutions—including the Internet when and if it achieves mass status—needs to be regularly analyzed to establish a base from which to understand and evaluate the workings of the mass media.

This new emphasis on media economics needs to have at its core the study of changing conditions of quality, hereafter referred to as the study of performance. This perspective favors a model for media economic analysis that not only examines questions of "who owns the media" (economic structure) and "how the corporations operate in the real world" (media conduct), but also a methodology that looks directly in the end at how well the mass media perform in modern society. Based on the pioneering work found in industrial organization economics, the media economist first should establish and define the basic conditions of an industry, seek to establish its major players (structure), define the behavior dictated by this structure (conduct), and finally evaluate the core questions of industry performance (Gomery, 1989; Scherer & Ross, 1990).

Simply listing "who owns the media" is not enough. One needs to hypothesize and understand how a particular form of industrial structure leads to certain corporate conduct. We need a system for media economics analysis of the linkage among structure, conduct, and performance that leads to discussions of the need for public policy reformulations. Examining performance of media industries should be the ultimate step in media economics analysis.

It is at the level of performance analysis that all communication scholars should—and can—take interest in media economics. It is here where we need to foster a connection between media economics and the longtime concerns of our field, whether this deals with questions of how to best promote diversity or how best to foster freedom of speech and discussion. If we can link the study of the economics of ownership and corporate behavior to the communication qualities we desire, communication scholars can begin to make recommendations for policy change that the players in real-world public-policy discussion will take seriously (McQuail, 1992).

The study of economics is supposed to be objective and positive, not something dealing with normative issues. However, as issues of media freedom and audience choice, of proper news objectivity and depth, continue to swirl we should stop being afraid to combine empirical research and normative concerns. What defines good media performance has long assumed an outcome of competitive pressures and a plethora of voices, a flourishing marketplace of ideas. But this purely competitive (to use the economics term) ideal is rarely met in our modern world. We need to combine media economic analysis and normative analysis to see how we might deal with public policy concerns about the mass media. Economic analysis can best help us make more informed choices of appropriate government action and assess the range of policy influences and effects (Entman, 1985).

Before we grapple with the difficult questions of performance, however, we need to closely examine the economics of market structure and conduct. First, the analysis of economic structure seeks to establish the number of buyers and sellers in a market, to identify barriers to entry to potential new competitors, to isolate the effects of horizontal and vertical ownership patterns, and to study the consequences of conglomerate control (Gomery, 1989).

It may seem like we are approaching a world of "one media," yet in economic reality there exists defined collections of media businesses competing for customers. It is best to not take on the whole of media economics, but restrict examinations to an industry-by-industry basis and then sum up subgroups to look at the total picture.

Analysis of economic conduct can begin by noting that revenues for media businesses fall into two distinct classes. On the one hand there is direct payment. Books, popular music, movies, and pay-TV sell their wares directly to the public. On the other hand there is the world of indirect payment characterized by advertisers "buying" audiences. Over-the-air television, radio, magazines, and newspapers rely on advertising dollars to create the bulk of their revenues. These media may have a small initial charge (e.g., the subscription price of a newspaper), but advertising fees generate the bulk of the revenues (Picard, 1989).

The important difference here for the study of industrial conduct is that with direct payment customers are able to telegraph directly their preferences. For advertising supported media, the client is the advertiser, not the viewer or listener or reader. Advertisers seek out media that can best help sell products or services; advertisers desire placement in media that can persuade customers who can be convinced to change their buying behavior and have the means to execute new purchases.

Given this duality of revenue generation, the industrial organization economic model postulates that the structure of a media industry determines the particular characteristics of its economic behavior. Once a certain market structure is established, the media economist then looks for certain techniques of price setting and program production, for certain types of marketing and promotion. In short, a certain category of market structural leads to specific corporate conduct.

Market structure and conduct in the media world fall into three distinct categories: monopoly, oligopoly, and monopolistic competition. We need to examine these three forms of media ownership here.

MONOPOLY

In a media industrial monopoly, a single firm dominates. The basic-cable television franchise and the single-community daily newspaper provide two examples of media monopoly. To take advantage of this power and exploit economies of larger scale operation, cable-television and newspaper corporations collect their monopolies under one institutional umbrella. In the cable-TV world we call them *multiple system operators*; the industry leaders include Tele-Communications, Inc. and Time Warner. In the United States and elsewhere, newspaper owners form groups headed by Gannett, Times Mirror, and Knight-Ridder.

A monopoly fosters economic behavior familiar to any subscriber to cable television. In any local jurisdiction there is typically one cable television company. If one does not like the lone cable TV corporation's offerings and prices, then the choices are not to subscribe or to move. The monopoly cable company has little incentive to keep prices down, to add channels, or to offer high quality service. This is a product of being a monopolist and seeking to maximize profits with no effective competition.

OLIGOPOLY

In an oligopoly a handful of firms dominate, the most heralded example being the longtime three (now more) television networks. Other oligopolies can be found in the six major music record labels and the six commanding major Hollywood studios that offer up not only most of the movies we see, but also most prime-time television programs (Owen & Wildman, 1992; Vogel, 1995).

To maintain their positions of power in recent decades, media oligopolies have diversified. Typically, Disney not only owns and operates a famous movie studio and set of theme parks, but also a television network (ABC), a score of successful television and radio stations, two sports cable-TV networks (ESPN and ESPN2), a string of newspapers, a collection of highly profitable magazines, and more. Because of this diversification, Disney is not dependent on the business cycle of a single operation. Unprofitable subsidiaries can be reconstructed and repositioned with funds generated from other profitable ongoing businesses. This enables an oligopoly to offer a high barrier to entry; potential rivals lack this conglomerate protection.

An oligopoly sees its small number of firms operate in reaction to each other. The metaphor is a poker game with five or six players. Each player knows a great deal about what the other is up to, but does not possess perfect knowledge. Take the case of the four dominant over-the-air television networks. When NBC offers a new comedy at a particular time on a particular day, its rivals—ABC, CBS, and Fox—counterprogram. This leads to some experimentation, but all too often only means a numbing generic sameness where like programs (e.g., comedies, dramas, or soap operas) face off against each other.

Economists have a great deal of trouble modeling oligopolistic behavior. The outcomes of oligopolistic corporate interplay depend on how many firms there are, how big they are in relationship to each other, past corporate histories, and sometimes the whims of individual owners. Analyzing a purely competitive situation is easier. A firm then can only operate myopically in its best interest. Formulating corporate action in response to hundreds of other rivals is too costly and makes no sense in a world of profit maximization.

MONOPOLISTIC COMPETITION

Monopolistic competition denotes a marketplace where there are many sellers, but for any specific product or service there are but a few competing differentiable products. Today's magazine industry is monopolistically competitive; the radio industry was until the mid-1990s. For example, although there are thousands of magazines, they can be grouped by identifiable genres, from hobbyist quarterlies to scandal sheets to seriously monthlies. Within a single genre only a small number of publications compete for a reader's purchase and attention. The same "competition" can said to have been at work—in large media markets prior to the consolidation caused by the Communications Act of 1996—for radio broadcasting, with their range of familiar formats, from album oriented rock to country to all-news (Gomery, 1996; Husni, 1989; Owen, 1976).

PERFORMANCE

Analysis of economic structure and conduct initiates and logically leads to analysis of performance. Indeed, what media scholars and critics care most about are the economic linkages to media performance. Remedies are proposed when proper performance of the industry is not met. We need to select performance criteria that are precise, and that are operational. How well has a media industry functioned when compared to some ideal standard? If there is market failure, then is there a regulatory remedy (Litman & Bridges, 1986; McQuail, 1992)?

For example, a generation ago the FCC instituted the so-called Prime-Time Access Rule. The then three dominant over-the-air television networks were deemed to have too much power and were not operating in the public interest. To mitigate oligopoly power and lead to "better behavior," the FCC required that "local" programs be presented during 30 minutes of prime time. In short, the television station licensee affiliated with a network was required behave a certain way in exchange for the valuable franchise held. However, this policy was ill conceived and backfired; continual runs of *Wheel of Fortune*, or *Family Feud*, although selected by local stations, hardly make for what most observers judge as "quality local programming."

Prior to heralding a new regulation or filing an antitrust suit policymakers struggle with locating criteria by which to judge economic performance. What do we want out of a media industry? I suggest six media performance norms that encompass most judgments and take them up in order of ease of use. That is, the first criteria considered are easier to deal with than those further down on the list (McQuail, 1992).

1. Media industries should not waste resources; that is they should be as efficient as possible. Monopolists waste resources in order to maintain their position of power. However, what about control by a few firms? Many argue that

this is just as bad, acknowledging that these industries regularly cooperate through powerful trade associations and thus hardly represent "lean-and-mean" business operations. Watchers of the network television business are familiar with the excesses and waste aptly labeled the "Cadillac culture" operations of the 1960s and 1970s. However, while free-market economists focus on only this performance criterion, media economics ought to weigh at least five more.

2. Media industries should to facilitate free speech and political discussion. A democracy needs freedom of expression to make it work and the mass media should be open enough to promote debate of all points of view. For example, do the new reality-based television shows—tabloid TV—help the process of public debate? Should we citizens care and press for regulation? Most policy has been directed at limiting economic behavior, while permitting media to say what they wish. Indeed some have made the argument that monopolists, not competitors, have the security and additional resources to report and investigate lengthy stories. However, are they objective by criteria of factualness, accuracy, and completeness?

3. Media industries should facilitate public order. In times of war, violence, and crime, how should we regulate the media (if at all) to ensure differences? This is a growing area of concern as the media easily jump across national (and local) boundaries.

4. Media industries should protect and maintain cultural quality, offer some role of the media in education. Many regularly ask: Can advertising generated-revenue companies not simply dish up more sensationalism?

5. Media industries should bring new technologies as quickly as possible to the marketplace. It has long been known that monopolies and collusive oligopolies resist the innovation of new technologies in order to protect their highly profitable status quo positions.

6. Media industries should distribute their products and services to rich, poor, and all of those in between. The mass media, because of scale economies and underwriting by advertisers, have long been justifiably praised because they are so cheap to acquire. For example, broadcast television has long been widely available to even the poorest members of society. However, access is becoming more and more restrictive as a larger share of the mass media go to direct payment. Cable television charges run up into the hundreds and even thousands of dollars per annum. If television is an important link in our democracy, how will our process of government change as one third do not have access to cable television?

PUBLIC POLICY

The history of the mass media in the United States suggests that we will ever have to choose among media industry monopolies, oligopolies, or situations of monopolistic competition. That is we will ever have to choose among less than perfectly desirable market structures and conducts. Idealists speculate on a world of one media industry; realists know that in modern capitalism corporations will operate differently within industry market structures that are not purely competitive.

Once we understand media industry structure and conduct, we will need to be clear what performance criteria we wish to prioritize and work from there. The media economist can play a central role by evaluating proposals for regulation and analyze their effects on structure, conduct, and performance. However, the media economist should not seek to impose performance criteria. Media scholars can help specify what appropriate criteria might be. Communication scholars should seek to influence the public policies toward public communication rather than simply leave the field to lawyers. Only with media economics at the core of our field can we hope to effect public policy influence.

We should take this task of media economics, broadly defined, very seriously. Societies of the future will be dependent on complex electronic information networks offering information and communication. There will be globalization of distribution. We need to help judge proper performance and tender (if necessary) corrective public policy actions.

Should we offer strong countervailing governmental power? Should we let the free market tap the energies (and rewards) of technical innovation? Or should we, as we do at the present, seek to optimize the mixture of a regulated and unregulated media world?

We will have to, in the future, worry about many, many channels, with greater ease of access, and growing expense of use. We will have—for the media of the future—to worry more and more about bridging information and media gaps, about securing political involvement, about maintaining creativity, independence, and diversity, about social solidarity and minority rights, about cultural autonomy and identity. Media economics will be able to help us sort though these thorny public policy questions. Thus, it should move to the core of our field as we move into the new media environment.

We need to rationally adopt public policies to facilitate all citizens having access to many channels and sources, offering different content, alternative voices. We will need know how the common structures of message production and distribution and presentation effect audiences. Thus, in the future we need, on an industry-by-industry basis, to examine the structure, conduct, and performance of changing media economics.

FURTHER READINGS

Gomery, D. (1993). The centrality of media economics. *Journal of Communication, 43*(3), 190–198.
Gomery, D. (1996, December). Tune in: Radio's still a big player. *American Journalism Review*, 44.
Owen, B. M., & Wildman, S. S. (1992). *Video economics*. Cambridge, MA: Harvard University Press.
Picard, R. G. (1989). *Media economics: Concepts and issues*. Newbury Park, CA: Sage.
Vogel, H. L. (1995). *Entertainment industry analysis* (3rd ed.). New York: Cambridge University Press.

REFERENCES

Entman, R. M. (1985). Newspaper competition and first amendment ideals: Does monopoly matter? *Journal of Communication, 35*(3), 147–165.

Gomery, D. (1989). Media economics: Terms of analysis. *Critical Studies in Mass Communication, 6*(1), 43–60.

Gomery, D. (1992). *Shared pleasures.* Madison: University of Wisconsin Press.

Gomery, D. (1993). The centrality of media economics. *Journal of Communication, 43*(3), 190–198.

Gomery, D. (1996, December). Tune in: Radio's still a big player. *American Journalism Review,* 44.

Husni, S. A. (1989). Influences on the survival of new consumer magazines. *Journal of Media Economics, 1*(1), 39–50.

Litman, B., & Bridges, J. (1986). An economic analysis of daily newspaper performance. *Newspaper Research Journal, 7*(1), 9–26.

McQuail, D. (1992). *Media performance.* Newbury Park, CA: Sage.

Owen, B. M. (1976). Regulating diversity: The case of radio formats. *Journal of Broadcasting, 21*(3), 305–319.

Owen, B. M., & Wildman, S. S. (1992). *Video economics.* Cambridge, MA: Harvard University Press.

Picard, R. G. (1989). *Media economics: Concepts and issues.* Newbury Park, CA: Sage.

Scherer, F. M., & Ross, D. (1990). *Industrial market structure and economic performance* (3rd ed.). Boston: Houghton Mifflin.

Vogel, H. L. (1995). *Entertainment industry analysis* (3rd ed.). New York: Cambridge University Press.

3

Economics and Media Regulation

Robert Corn-Revere
Hogan and Hartson

Rod Carveth
University of Bridgeport

TELECOMMUNICATIONS ACT OF 1996

On February 1, 1996, after months of negotiations and political wrangling, Congress overwhelmingly passed the Telecommunications Act of 1996 (the Act). The Act is the first comprehensive rewrite of the Communications Act of 1934, and dramatically changes the ground rules for competition and regulation in virtually all sectors of the communications industry, from local and long-distance telephone services to cable television, broadcasting, and equipment manufacturing.

For decades, communications policy—including ownership and service restrictions that maintained protected monopolies at both the state and federal levels—has been set largely by the Federal Communications Commission (FCC), state public utility commissions (PUCs), and the federal courts' enforcement of the 1984 antitrust consent decree that dismantled the Bell System. However, the ambiguity inherent in enforcing a 62-year-old statute led to legal uncertainty and conflicting interpretations. With the 1996 Act, Congress clearly adopted *competition* as the basic charter for all telecommunications markets.

The Act eliminated most cross-market entry barriers, relaxed concentration and merger rules, and placed new implementation obligations on the FCC and state regulators. Surprisingly, restrictions were imposed on content areas such as television violence and "indecent" online communications, a Congressional action many critics saw as more to promote its views of appropriate social and moral behavior than to unleash competitive market forces.

The Act overruled all state restrictions on competition in local and long-distance telephone service. The Bell Operating Companies ("Baby Bells") were freed to provide long-distance service outside their regions, and inside their regions once completing a series of steps to remove entry barriers for local telephone competition.[1] New "universal service" rules continue subsidization of telephone service for rural and low-income subscribers, and assist schools, libraries, and other public institutions in becoming connected to sophisticated telecommunications services. The 1984 antitrust consent decrees are repealed, but their requirements for "equal access" ("1 +" dialing) to all long-distance carriers are maintained.

The Act relaxed the FCC's media concentration rules by allowing any single company or network to own TV stations that reach as many as 35% of the nation's television households (the previous limit was 25%). The FCC would be required to consider changing other limits on ownership in a single community. Networks would for the first time be allowed to own cable television systems, but no network could acquire another network. All nationwide limits on radio-station ownership were repealed, but local limits on concentration were maintained, although relaxed.

Television broadcasters would be allowed "spectrum flexibility" to use additional frequencies for high-definition for other purposes, but would have to return any additional spectrum allocated by the FCC and possibly pay auction fees. In April 1997, the FCC announced rules governing the transition of broadcasters from analog to digital broadcasting, phasing in the transition in a manner such that major market stations would have to switch to digital channels earlier than small market stations.

The Act substantially relaxed the rules governing cable television systems under the 1992 Cable Act, including rate deregulation. Ironically, the 1995 report on the competitiveness of the cable-TV industry concluded that although some progress has begun toward a competitive marketplace for the distribution of video programming, cable-television systems continue to enjoy market power in local markets. Overall subscribership for cable operators was over 91% of total multichannel video programming distribution (MVPD) subscribership, dwarfing subscribership to direct broadcast satellite (DBS) multichannel multipoint distribution (MMDS)

---

[1]The Act declares invalid all state rules that restrict entry or limit competition in telephone service, both local and long distance. It dismantles the AT&T and GTE antitrust consent decrees, including their controversial prohibitions on entry by the Bell Operating Companies (BOCs) into the interLATA telephone market. (LATAs, or Local Access and Transport Areas, are regional areas, similar to area codes, that divided the local and long-distance telephone markets under the AT&T consent decree.) Competitive safeguards, known as "separate affiliates" and a prohibition of cross-subsidization, are required to protect against anticompetitive behavior by local telephone companies.

The BOCs and GTE will be permitted to offer interLATA service once they have taken steps to remove entry barriers to competition for local exchange service, that is local telephone service. The Act requires the BOCs to implement a series of reforms known as the "competitive checklist" in order to qualify for providing long-distance service outside their regions. It also requires all local exchange carriers (LECs) to interconnect with new entrants, unbundle their networks and allow resale by competitors, provide number portability so customers can keep their phone numbers when switching local providers, and other steps to promote an effectively competitive local exchange market. State PUCs are charged with a major responsibility in implementing local telephone competition.

and satellite master antenna television (SMATV) systems ("Second Annual Report," 1995).

The Act also provided new content restrictions. Television equipment manufacturers are required to equip all new TVs with a so-called "V-chip" ("V" standing for violence) allowing parental blocking of violent, sexually explicit, or indecent programming. A voluntary system of ratings for broadcast and cable television programming is preferred, but the FCC is required to prescribe, with advice and recommendations from an advisory panel, a ratings code for television programming "that contains sexual, violent or other indecent material" if such a voluntary ratings system is not created by industry within 1 year.

An amendment to the bill originating in the Senate,[2] titled the Communications Decency Act (CDA), created criminal penalties for the "knowing" transmission over the Internet of material considered "indecent to minors." Those provisions also made it a crime to make any computer network transmission with the intent to "annoy" or "harass" the recipient, and extend a criminal ban on discussing abortion devices and procedures to computer network communications. Commercial online services that engage in voluntary blocking are protected from prosecution.[3]

The American Civil Liberties Union (ACLU) and a coalition of other civil-liberties groups filed suit to enjoin the Act's indecency sections within minutes of President Clinton's signing of the bill. In June 1996, the Circuit Court struck down the CDA. The Justice Department appealed the Circuit Court's decision to the Supreme Court. On June 26, 1997, the Supreme Court struck down the CDA by a vote of 7 to 2.

Justice John Paul Stevens, writing for the majority, ruled:

> The Government apparently assumes that the unregulated availability of "indecent" and "patently offensive" material on the Internet is driving countless citizens away from the medium because of the risk of exposing themselves or their children to harmful material.

---

[2] Originally, the House of Representatives took a different tack, passing HR 1978, the Internet Freedom and Family Empowerment Act, that encouraged the sale and use of parental empowerment tools, and prohibited the FCC from meddling in the business of providing Internet services. However, the CDA was included in the final compromise bill.

[3] The Supreme Court "indecency" is Constitutionally protected. In *Sable Communications v. FCC* (1989), a case involving dial-in phone-sex services, the U.S. Supreme Court held that, even though a ban on *obscenity* in "dial-a-porn" services is constitutional, a ban on *indecency* is not. Citing earlier holdings, the Court said that "[t]he government may not reduce the adult population to only what is fit for children."

Even if the federal government had the constitutional authority to regulate indecency in computer communications, it would be required by the First Amendment to employ only the "least restrictive means" in doing so. The computer industry has been working to design tools that individuals can use to filter offensive content and that parents can use to screen content for their children, which would likely qualify as a less restrictive means than banning the speech altogether.

We find this argument singularly unpersuasive. The dramatic expansion of this new marketplace of ideas contradicts the factual basis of this contention. The record demonstrates that the growth of the Internet has been and continues to be phenomenal. As a matter of constitutional tradition, in the absence of evidence to the contrary, we presume that governmental regulation of the content of speech is more likely to interfere with the free exchange of ideas than to encourage it. The interest in encouraging freedom of expression in a democratic society outweighs any theoretical but unproven benefit of censorship. (*Reno v. ACLU, 1997*).

FCC Reaction to the Act

Reaction by the FCC to the Act was swift. The day President Clinton signed the Telecom Act (February 8, 1996), the FCC granted several waivers to the Walt Disney Company to help facilitate its merger with Cap Cities/ABC.[4] Within a month, the Commission implemented new rules on TV and radio station ownership.[5] In April 1996, the Commission proposed rules that would extend the license terms for television and radio stations to 8 years. The Act provided that broadcast licenses may be granted for terms "not to exceed" 8 years for both television and radio stations. The Commission, arguing that the "lengthened license terms would reduce the burden to broadcasters seeking periodic renewal of their licenses, as well as reduce the associated burden on the Commission" adopted the maximum renewal period (Action, April 11, 1996).

---

[4] Action by the Commission February 8, 1996, by Memorandum Opinion and Order (FCC 96–48). The Commission granted (a) a permanent waiver of the duopoly rule to permit Disney to continue CC/ABC's common ownership of a television station in Philadelphia and in New York City; (b) six permanent waivers of the one-to-a-market rule involving television and radio stations commonly owned by CC/ABC in New York, Chicago, Detroit-Flint, Detroit-Toledo, Los Angeles, and San Francisco; (c) a 6-month wait Disney to control KCAL-TV and KABC-TV, both licensed to Los Angeles, with the provision Disney divest itself of one of the stations; and (d) two 18-month waivers of the newspaper-broadcast cross-ownership rule to permit Disney to continue CC/ABC's common ownership of radio stations in Detminder in Pontiac and its ownership of radio stations in Fort Worth and the *Fort Worth Star-Telegram.*

[5] Commercial radio ownership on a nationwide basis generally had been limited to no more than 20 AM stations and no more than 20 FM stations (an additional 3 AM and 3 FM stations were allowed if they were small business-controlled or minority-controlled.

1. In a radio market with 45 or more commercial radio stations, a party may own, operate, or control up to 8 commercial radio stations, not more than 5 of which are in the same service (AM or FM).

2. In a radio market with between 30 and 44 (inclusive) commercial radio stations, a party may own, operate, or control up to 7 commercial radio stations, not more than 4 of which are in the same service (AM or FM).

3. In a radio market with between 15 and 29 (inclusive) commercial radio stations, a party may own, operate, or control up to 6 commercial radio stations, not more than 4 of which are in the same service (AM or FM).

4. In a radio market with 14 or fewer commercial radio stations, a party may own, operate, or control up to 5 commercial radio stations, not more than 3 of which are in the same service (AM or FM), except that a party may not own, operate, or control more than 50% of the stations in such market.

The Act is yet another example of how the legal and economic characteristics of media industries are inextricably related. With the advent of electronic communications technologies, governmental control moved to a system of regulation. The regulatory structure was designed to be flexible and adaptive to the changing shape of the industry. As economic power shifts between various media players, or as developing technologies alter the playing field, the governing agencies—most prominently, the FCC—react to maintain their views of the public interest. As a result, virtually all significant economic developments among the regulated media industries provoke some kind of regulatory response. As a corollary to this premise, regulations have profound implications for the economic well-being of media corporations.

THE RISE OF FEDERAL REGULATION

Unlike newer communications technologies, broadcasting was born into an unregulated environment. Wireless communications had existed for almost a quarter of a century, but the first commercial broadcast did not occur until 1920. Consequently, existing law (the Wireless Ship Act of 1910 and the Radio Act of 1912) related principally to maritime uses of radio. With the November 2, 1920 transmission of election returns by station KDKA in Pittsburgh, commercial broadcasting began, and along with it, the justification for a whole new field of regulation.

Once initiated, commercial broadcasting grew quickly. By the beginning of 1922 the Department of Commerce had authorized 30 radio stations. That year, however, an additional 600 stations took to the air. In 1922, 1 in every 500 U.S. households was equipped with a radio receiver, but in 4 short years the number rose to 1 in every 6 households. The rapid proliferation of both transmitters and receivers led to a chaotic situation that prompted numerous calls for federal legislation. The growth of broadcasting (as well as the demand for regulation) accelerated in 1926, prompted in part by the decision in *United States v. Zenith Corporation* that the Secretary of Commerce lacked the authority to assign wavelengths or deny broadcast licenses.[6]

Congress responded by passing the Radio Act of 1927—the first attempt at establishing a comprehensive regulatory framework for radio, including broadcasting. The Act created the Federal Radio Commission (FRC) staffed with five commissioners were charged with general authority over radio broadcasting. The commissioners were charged with regulating the medium in ways that would promote the "public interest, convenience or necessity."

---

[6]12 F.2d 614 (N.D. Ill. 1926). *See also Hoover v. Intercity Radio Corp.*, 286 F 1002 (D.C. Cir. 1923), *appeal dismissed*, 266 U.S. 636 (1924). Some have theorized that the government induced interference between broadcast stations as a pretext to justify regulation. See, e.g., J. Emord, *Freedom, Technology and the First Amendment*, 153–157 (1991).

The public interest standard for broadcast regulation—a concept borrowed from the regulation of railroads—was not defined in the Radio Act. Rather, the FRC was mandated to perform its various tasks, including classifying radio stations, describing the type of service to be provided, assigning frequencies, making rules to prevent interference, establishing the power and location of transmitters, and establishing coverage areas in a way that maximized the public good. Of course, this begged the essential question of what constitutes "the public good." The FRC took the position that the Supreme Court eventually would define the public interest on a case-by-case basis. Nevertheless, the Commission outlined the primary attributes of the public interest in its policy statements and licensing decisions.

The Radio Act was superseded by passage of the Communications Act of 1934. In addition to consolidating the government's regulation of radio, the new law created the (FCC) to succeed the FRC. The Communications Act simply recodified many of the essential features of the Radio Act, including the public interest standard. Other than a few general directives, as noted later, the Communications Act continued to leave the term *public interest* undefined.

Congress purposefully left the regulatory standard open, with the details to be filled in by the FCC over time. This had much to do with the fact that radio was a new and complicated technology. The FCC's broad powers were based on the assumption that "Congress could neither foresee nor easily comprehend ... the highly complex and rapidly expanding nature of communications technology" (*National Association of Regulatory Utility Commissioners v. FCC*, 1976). This approach has not lacked critics. As one court noted, "the [Communications] Act provides virtually no specifics as to the nature of those public obligations inherent in the public interest standard" (*Office of Communication of the United Church of Christ v. FCC*, 1983). Some have taken the pragmatic view that the public interest means nothing more than what a majority of commissioners says it means at any given point in time.

Nevertheless, shortly after the Communications Act was adopted, the Supreme Court ruled that the open-ended public interest approach was sufficiently precise to withstand constitutional scrutiny. In *FCC v. Pottsville Broadcasting Co.* (1940), the Court called the public interest standard "as concrete as the complicated factors for judgment in such a field of delegated authority permit," and labeled the approach "a supple instrument for the exercise of discretion."

Despite the lack of a categorical definition of the public interest, various provisions of the Act operationally define what Congress intended. For example, the Act directs the FCC to provide, to the extent possible, rapid and efficient communication service; adequate facilities at reasonable charges; provision for national defense and safety of lives and property; and a fair, efficient and equitable distribution of radio service to each of the states and communities. In 1983, Congress added to this list of objectives by adopting a new section establishing "the policy of the United States to encourage the provision of new technologies and services to the public." This new provision created a presumption favoring increased competition in the communications marketplace.

This reliance on competition in the communications marketplace as a determinant of the public interest brought to the surface a notion that had always been implicit in the public interest standard: *Media economics help define the public good.* Although this is not quite the same as saying "what is good for NBC is good for the nation," one broadcaster summed up the industry outlook to one Commissioner by saying, "there's been a lot of [talk] about money. You guys like to talk about the public interest. To us it's the same thing." Or, as FCC Commissioner Sherrie Marshall explained to an audience at the 1990 National Association of Broadcasters Convention, there is often a "harmonic convergence" between the public interest and a given applicant's private interest.

Indeed, economic issues permeate virtually every category of FCC decision making. Under the Communications Act, the Commission is responsible for allocating radio spectrum to various services, assigning licenses to competing parties, and otherwise managing the usage of the assigned frequencies. It is essential that the agency take into account economic factors when choosing which service should receive an allocation of increasingly scarce and valuable spectrum. Similarly, marketplace phenomena can be important when deciding which applicant should receive a grant of a federal radio license. Moreover, regulatory choices, once made, are not necessarily permanent. Economic conditions often determine the shape of the public interest.

ECONOMICS AND CHANGING REGULATIONS

The changing fortunes of AM and FM radio provide a clear example of how market adjustments result in regulatory changes. Edwin Armstrong invented FM radio in the 1930s as a way of overcoming interference problems associated with AM service. FM (frequency modulation) is a means of encoding information on a carrier wave by varying the frequency. AM (amplitude modulation) encodes information by varying the strength of the carrier. AM is more susceptible to interference because outside sources of energy—atmospheric static, electric motors, or other devices—interact with the carrier wave to produce static. FM is not affected by such phenomena because the amplitude of the carrier remains constant and outside energy fluctuations do not affect the frequency. The net result of this technical difference is that FM made possible a system superior to the one that developed during the first decade of American broadcasting. AM broadcasting currently occupies 535–1705 kHz on the broadcast frequency spectrum and FM occupies 88–108 MHZ.

After Armstrong secured patents for his FM system in 1933, he was invited to test his invention at RCA's Empire State Building facilities. Once he proved the superiority of his system, Armstrong believed that his friend David Sarnoff, head of RCA, would use the new technology to revolutionize the radio industry. Although initial tests were even more successful than even Armstrong expected, RCA was slow in promoting the new system. In fact, Sarnoff opposed allocation of spectrum for FM broadcasting at FCC hearings in 1936. Instead, Sarnoff urged that the spectrum be reserved to test television.

The reasons underlying RCA's position were not difficult to understand. Promoting FM service would undermine its existing investment in AM facilities. Moreover, FM was in competition with television for spectrum allocation and RCA owned television patents. One historian has noted that "in almost every overt and covert action, it can be seen that RCA (and the majority of the AM industry) was trying to forestall something that would either cut down, or cut out, their operation" (Erickson, 1973).

The FCC finally allocated spectrum for commercial FM service in 1941. However, 4 years later the Commission moved FM service to another part of the frequency band. Justified as a means of avoiding interference caused by sunspots, the move was supported primarily by AM interests and adopted over the objections of the FCC's engineering staff. In a single order, all existing FM receivers were rendered obsolete. This action, along with several intervening regulatory measures, helped keep FM a second-class service for decades.

By 1964 FM radio still was not in good financial shape. Many of the 1,300 FM stations that existed were largely dependent on the revenues of more successful co-owned AM stations for their survival. As a result, the FCC initiated a rulemaking proceeding designed to promote FM as an independent service. This led to a rule prohibiting FM stations from duplicating more than 50% of the programming of co-owned AM stations in the same local area (*Report and Order,* 1964). The regulation was designed to serve two goals. First, it sought to strengthen FM service by forcing the creation of an independent programming service. Second, the Commission believed that a separate programming service would encourage consumers to buy and use FM receivers.

Ten years later, the FCC revisited the AM/FM duplication rules because the number of independent FM stations had increased, as had their revenues and the number of FM receivers. The economic advances of FM service led the Commission to strengthen the nonduplication prohibition. It limited the FM station of an AM/FM combination to not more than 25% duplication of either station in communities of 25,000 population or larger (*Report and Order,* 1976).

Further upheavals in the radio marketplace led to even more profound regulatory changes. In 1986, the FCC found that "FM service is now a fully competitive and viable component of the radio industry" and that FM had captured more than 70% of the radio audience (*Amendment,* 1986, p. 1613). The number of FM stations had tripled between 1964 and 1986, far eclipsing the growth of AM service. Indeed, the FCC determined that "many heretofore profitable AM stations are now experiencing economic difficulties as a result of the shift of listeners to FM stations" (p.

1614). After examining the "structure and market conditions that have occurred in the radio industry in recent years" the Commission concluded that "the program duplication rule no longer appears necessary or desirable" (p. 1612). Consequently, it eliminated the nonduplication rules because they were no longer necessary to foster independent FM service. The FCC also sought to help ailing AM operations.

In 1991, the FCC suggested that it might reimpose the nonduplication rule as part of an effort to save AM radio from economic demise. As part of a comprehensive package of changes, the Commission proposed weeding out marginal AM stations, in part by perhaps depriving stations their ability to cut programming costs by simulcasting the FM signal of co-owned stations (*Review of the Technical Assessment Criteria for the AM Broadcast Service,* 1991). The FCC subsequently eliminated the duopoly rule in 1994, to allow for an owner to have more than one AM station per market, and raised national ownership caps. With this proposal, the FCC came full circle with regulations originally adopted in 1964—suggesting changes born entirely of the economic state of the industry.

THE *CARROLL* DOCTRINE AND RELATED POLICIES

Many times economic considerations force the FCC to choose between applicants for the same broadcast service. The classic statement of this approach was presented in *Carroll Broadcasting Co. v. FCC*, decided by the United States Court of Appeals for the District of Columbia Circuit in 1958. In that case, Carroll Broadcasting Company had opposed the grant of a radio station license in a community 12 miles from Carrollton, GA, the location of the Carroll station. The station licensee alleged that authorization of another station in such close proximity would impair its ability to serve the public adequately. Although the Supreme Court had established in *Federal Communications Commission v. Sanders Brothers Radio Station* (1940) that economic injury to an existing radio station is not grounds for denying a new application, Carroll argued that its loss would be so significant as to deprive the public of service.

The Court of Appeals agreed, noting:

> [W]hether a station makes $5,000, or $10,000, or $50,000 is a matter in which the public has no interest so long as service is not adversely affected; service may well be improved by competition. But, if the situation in a given area is such that available revenue will not support good service in more than one station, the public interest may well be in the licensing of one rather than two stations. To license two stations where there is revenue for only one may result in no good service at all. So economic injury to an existing station, while not in and of itself a matter of moment, becomes important on the facts when it spells diminution or destruction of service. At that point the element of injury ceases to be a matter of purely private concern. (*Carroll Broadcasting v. FCC,* 1958)

This decision forced the FCC to adopt a procedure for assessing the economic harm from its new licensing decisions. Thus, under what became known as the *Carroll* doctrine, when an existing licensee offered proof of detrimental economic effect from a proposed new broadcasting station that ss of service to the public, the Commission was required to consider the issue, and, if sufficient evidence was presented, conduct a hearing and make findings on the issue. The petitioner in such cases had to provide sufficient statistical evidence "to enable the Commission to make an informed judgment as to the overall market revenue potential" (*WLVA, Inc. v. FCC,* 1972). The elements of such a showing typically included information concerning the number of businesses in the area, the total volume of retail sales, other advertising media and other data regarding the economics of broadcasting in the specific market.

As a direct result of the *Carroll* decision, the FCC was required to reconsider its decision regarding West Georgia Broadcasting Company—the potential competitor to Carroll Broadcasting. After examining the record and weighing the "speculative injury to the public interest," however, the FCC concluded that Carroll had not met its burden of proof on the economic injury issue and granted West Georgia's application.

Despite this inauspicious beginning, existing licensees routinely pleaded a *Carroll* issue when confronted with a new station applicant in its market. Although such tactics offered little chance of actually preventing competition, the required Commission review (and possible hearing) served to at least delay and drive up the cost of competition. Indeed, although the FCC applied the *Carroll* doctrine for a 30-year period, it never once denied a new license on the basis that a new station would result in a net loss of service.

The chronic futility of being forced to mount a *Carroll* review in licensing proceedings prompted the FCC to reevaluate the policy in 1988 (*Policies,* 1988). The Commission found that changes in the media marketplace undermined whatever validity had ever existed for the economic theories that supported the doctrine. For example, since the doctrine was first articulated, the FCC found that the number of radio stations increased by 144% and the number of commercial television stations by 152%. Additionally, newer communications technologies—including cable television—had proliferated. Finally, studies indicated that the advertising market was continuing to expand, and that new stations tended to draw their advertisers from new sources rather than take business from existing stations.

Given these findings, the Commission concluded it was silly to attempt to protect existing stations from competition created by the addition of a single new competitor. It thus held "that the underlying premise of the *Carroll* doctrine, the theory of ruinous competition, *i.e.,* that increased competition in broadcasting can be destructive to the public interest, is not valid in the broadcast field" (*Policies,* 1988, p. 640).

At the same time, the Commission eliminated a similar policy that related specifically to UHF television stations. The UHF impact policy, which the Commission established in 1960, protected UHF stations from economic loss associated with the licensing of new VHF television stations. In contrast to the *Carroll* doctrine, the UHF impact policy protected UHF stations as a class, and not just individual stations, and, at least for a time, was applied rigorously by the FCC. Because of economic changes, however, such as an increase in the number of UHF stations operating at a profit, the FCC held that they no longer needed special protection and eliminated the policy. Meanwhile, the Commission retained a similar policy governing the licensing of common carriers (e.g., telephone companies; *Washington Utilities and Transportation Commission v. FCC,* 1975).

THE IMPOSITION AND RELAXATION OF FINANCIAL INTEREST AND SYNDICATION RESTRICTIONS ON NETWORKS

As demonstrated by the struggle between AM and FM radio, economic considerations may define the motivations of the various industry participants in regulatory initiatives. Similarly, the changes in the *Carroll* Doctrine show that economic effects on a licensee may be the basis of the FCC's substantive policy. In addition to these examples, the FCC has based regulatory policy on the relative economic positions of various industry players, both inside and outside of broadcasting. The Commission's adoption and recent modification of Financial Interest and Syndication (finsyn) Rules is evidence of this phenomenon.

The Commission adopted the finsyn rules in 1970 to prevent the three television networks from restricting the market for television programming (*Competition and Responsibility,* 1970). The rules prevented the networks from acquiring financial interests in subsequent broadcasts of the programs aired on their stations, and prohibited them from engaging in the business of syndicating such programming. In other words, the rules permitted the networks merely to lease the shows they aired and left to others the lucrative business of selling the rights for reruns of popular network programming. The rules were predicated on the theory that programming diversity would be limited to the extent three large corporations owned or controlled the majority of television programming available to the viewing audience.

In the intervening years, and given vast changes in the media marketplace, the FCC considered altering or repealing the finsyn rules. In 1983, for example, the Commission tentatively decided to loosen the restrictions on the networks, but that decision was never implemented. Again in 1990, prompted by the emergence of a fourth national television network (Fox Broadcasting Network), the Commission reconsidered the continuing need for the rules. Not only had broadcasting changed during the two decades the rules were in place, but the development of cable television networks tended to undermine the theory that three networks could control the market for video programming.

After a protracted and contentious proceeding, the FCC decided by a vote of 3 to 2 to allow the networks to share in part in the program production and syndication business. The difference between the majority and minority views at the Commission lay principally in the Commissioners' differing beliefs about the economic conditions affecting the video marketplace. The two dissenting votes, cast by Chairman Sikes and Commissioner Quello, were based on the belief that markets had sufficiently changed to allow greater relaxation of the rules and that the economic viability of the networks was threatened without greater relief. The majority, on the other hand, suggested that the networks continued to exercise market power over program producers with respect to the acquisition of prime-time programming (*Evaluation*, 1991).

Putting aside the differences between the two perspectives, the majority and minority both agreed that economic changes warranted regulatory change; and there was a general acknowledgment that future evolution of the marketplace could lead to further loosening of the rules. The majority voted, for example, to review the rules again in 4 years to determine if further changes in the media environment might support elimination of the remaining regulations. The review process was accelerated, however, when the U.S. Court of Appeals reversed the majority decision and returned the matter to the FCC for further proceedings. The finsyn rules were finally abolished in 1995.

THE CONTINUING REGULATORY BATTLE BETWEEN BROADCASTING AND CABLE TELEVISION

The Commission's protection of existing services from prospective competitors has not been limited to those proposing to use the same transmission technology. Regulation also has been extended to new technologies in order to maintain a certain balance of power between competing media. This has been the history of broadcasting/cable-television relations. The Commission initially adopted rules to protect broadcasters from the new medium. Later, it freed cable television from restrictions in an effort to promote the new technology. Generally, the requirements changed over time as the relative fortunes of the various industries fluctuated.

Although the product of both broadcasting and cable is delivered through the same appliance—the television—the different transmission media are subject to radically different regulatory regimes. Broadcasters transmit signals over the air subject to a federal license that imposes a number of public trustee conditions on the licensee. Cable, on the other hand, involves the transmission of electrical signals over coaxial cables (and, in some systems, fiber-optic lines). Except for some auxiliary microwave authorizations, cable systems are not licensed by the federal government but are regulated by local franchise requirements.

This difference is the key to the contentious regulatory relationship between the two industries. Government rules that are applied to one medium generally are not applied to the other. Yet broadcasting and cable compete in the same marketplace for viewers. As a result, competition between broadcasting and cable has not been limited to the market, but has spilled over into the regulatory arena. Representatives of the regulated industries continuously implore the government to maintain a "level playing field." This is a shorthand way of calling on regulators to eliminate rules that, in one industry's view, unfairly favor its competition. More often, it merely is an attempt to manipulate the regulatory environment in ways that will have a positive effect on that industry's economic environment. As one lobbyist put it (half jokingly), "All I seek is a fair advantage." Over time, as the cable industry has grown, the regulatory "advantage" has shifted as if on a pendulum.

Development of Cable Television

In some respects, cable television is not a "new" technology. It originated in the late 1940s—about the same time as the advent of commercial television. The first systems were installed in 1948 as a means of delivering quality television signals to viewers in locations where terrain prevented adequate over-the-air reception. Typically, such systems involved placing antenna on a mountaintop to receive television signals and transmitting them via cable to the homes below. At the time the system was aptly called community antenna television, or CATV. The first cable system was installed not as a stand-alone business; rather, it was built by an appliance store owner who wished to demonstrate good reception so that he could sell more television sets. Despite this prosaic origin, there were 70 cable systems providing service to 14,000 subscribers by 1950.

This earliest incarnation of cable caused broadcasters little concern. Quite to the contrary, broadcasters welcomed measures that would improve reception, because it meant additional viewers. However, this harmonious relationship ended as cable systems expanded channel capacity and began to offer additional programming choices. In 1961 the cable operator serving San Diego began to import television signals from Los Angeles, which is more than 100 miles away. Although San Diego was already served by three VHF network affiliates, the cable system also provided four independent signals that otherwise would have been unavailable in the market. This competitive threat prompted broadcasters to seek FCC regulation of cable systems.

Economic Analysis and Cable Regulation

Although the Commission previously eschewed direct regulation of cable systems, in 1962 it began to deny permission for carriage of broadcast signals that might adversely affect local television stations (*Carter Mountain Transmission Corp.*, 1962). The FCC subsequently adopted formal rules banned the importation of distant signals into a top-100 market unless the cable operator could demonstrate that the transmission would not hurt UHF broadcasters in the affected market (*First Report and Order,* 1965). These rules were predicated on two assumptions. First, the Commission believed that importation of distant signals could fragment the audience for local stations, thus eroding their revenue bases, perhaps to the point of affecting their programming or driving them from the air. Second, the Commission considered the retransmission of broadcast programming—for which thing—to be an unfair competitive advantage over local broadcast stations. These conclusions were based on economic studies submitted to the FCC by the regulated industries.

As time passed and technology developed, however, the validity of economic analyses became questionable. Moreover, the Commission's assumptions regarding industry evolution began to shift. For example, when it first adopted distant signal and other protectionist rules, such as "must-carry" obligations, the FCC viewed cable television as merely an adjunct of broadcasting. The rules were designed to ensure that cable did not undermine the economic strength of television. But by 1975, the Commission began to seek ways "to assure the orderly development of this new technology into the national communications structure" (*Report and Order,* 1975, p. 863).

This subtle but significant shift in emphasis hailed a change in how the Commission assessed the economic data presented to it. Moreover, the Commission became increasingly dissatisfied with its previous "intuitive model" for predicting competitive effects of the development of cable television on broadcasting. Accordingly, in 1977 it initiated a Notice of Inquiry to reexamine the assumption that an unregulated cable industry would ravage existing broadcasters. This "broad inquiry into the economics of the relationship between television broadcasting and cable television" was premised on the concept that "[a] more complete understanding of the economics of the cable-broadcast interface [could] yield many benefits." The Commission predicted that "[i]t may be shown that certain of our rules are unnecessary; it is also possible that others should be adopted, or that familiar rules should be applied to different situations" (*Notice,* 1977, p. 14).

Notwithstanding its newly discovered interest in "the collection of economic data and analysis," the Commission did not await the outcome of its economic inquiry before modifying its distant signal rules. Rather, it placed the burden on broadcasters to prove that importation of a distant signal would have an adverse economic effect and adopted a general policy that presumed there would be little or no harmful impact (*Arlington Telecommunications Corp.,* 1977).

Two years later, the Commission released its Economic Inquiry Report, which concluded that distant signal carriage rules should be eliminated. The report, which spanned more than 350 pages in the FCC Reports, analyzed the supply and demand for cable television and attempted to assess the impact of distant signals on local broadcast audiences. The FCC's analysis unabashedly embraced economic analysis as the determinant of the public interest. Its principal criteria for defining the public interest in its cable regulatory policies included the economic concepts of consumer welfare, distributional equity, and external or spillover effects. Basing its conclusions on economic studies, the Commission stated its conclusions with a clarity and confidence "which is uncommon in matters of public policy" (*Inquiry*, 1979, p. 659).

On the strength of its conclusion that "few, if any, TV stations are likely to experience a reduction in real income" due to the growth of cable television, the Commission began to dismantle its web of regulations that previously protected broadcasters. In 1980, it eliminated its syndicated exclusivity and network nonduplication rules, which had protected local broadcasters from duplication of both network and syndicated programming via distant signals (*CATV*, 1980). These rules differed from the general limits on signal importation in that they prohibited only duplication of programming for which the local broadcaster had obtained exclusive rights. The Commission concluded that deletion of the rules would not lead to a reduction in the availability of programming or otherwise diminish service to the public.

The same consideration ultimately led to elimination of the FCC's "must-carry" rules. Like other measures designed to protect local broadcasters, the must-carry rules assumed that cable television could limit the ability of over-the-air television stations to serve their intended audience. These rules addressed that concern by requiring cable systems to carry a specified number of local television signals. Cable operators challenged the rules on constitutional grounds, arguing that the government lacked a sufficient interest to support restrictions on the operators' editorial autonomy. Citing the Economic Inquiry Report, the United States Court of Appeals for the District of Columbia Circuit found that if the Commission "has repudiated the economic assumptions that underlie the must-carry rules, the suggestion that they serve an important governmental interest (or any interest at all) would be wholly unconvincing" (*Quincy Cable TV Inc. v. FCC*, 1985). The court concluded that the findings of the report, combined with the FCC's inability after 20 years to demonstrate a tangible economic threat to broadcasters, made "the continued deference to the Commission's concededly unsupported determinations plainly inappropriate" (p. 714). Consequently, the court struck down the must carry rules.

Economic Adjustments and Reregulation

There is a fundamental difficulty with basing regulations on economic predictions—the predictions may be wrong. The 1979 Economic Inquiry Report, for example, was predicated on the FCC's "estimates of what will happen to cable and to broadcasting on the basis of the of the best economic information at our disposal" (*Inquiry*, 1979, p. 659). However, the "best economic information" in 1979 was not very impressive at the threshold of the 1990s. In 1979, the Commission found that "all of the available information suggests that under foreseeable circumstances cable penetration is unlikely to exceed about 48% of the nation's television households" (p. 713). But 10 years later, the FCC found that cable penetration had grown from 37.3% of all television households (32 million homes) in 1985 to 56.4% (50.9 million homes) by mid-November 1989. By 1995, cable penetration rose to 65.2% (61.7 million homes).

Growth of all segments of the cable television industry was phenomenal through the past decade. By 1990 there were approximately 9,010 cable systems in the United States—more than twice the number that existed in 1980. The average size of cable systems also increased. In 1984, 57.4% of all cable subscribers were served by systems with channel capacity exceeding 30 channels. By 1989, however, the number had increased to 86.8% and 96% in 1995. Cable systems with more than 53 channels accounted for the biggest growth during 1994, with a 9.9% increase in the number of such systems. Total cable revenues reached $9.94 billion (*Second Cable Report,* 1995)

Available programming also mushroomed. HBO became the first national cable network when, in 1975, it distributed uncut movies and sporting events to cable systems via satellite. By 1990, however, there were 104 cable-specific networks, including 39 regional networks and 65 national networks. By 1995, the number of national programming services increased to 129. Of these 129 services, 66 were vertically integrated, representing approximately 51% of all national services. Between 1984 and 1989, investment in cable programming doubled—going from $1 billion to $2 billion per year.

These vast changes led Congress and the Commission to reconsider the regulatory regime for cable television. The FCC in 1988 reimposed syndicated exclusivity and network nonduplication rules (*Amendment,* 1988). The resurrection of rules that were interred in 1980 was based on the conclusion that the economic situation had fundamentally changed. The Commission concluded that "time has proved these predictions [about the growth of cable television] inaccurate" (p. 5304). It found that cable had grown far faster than anticipated, thus presenting a serious competitive threat to over-the-air broadcasters. The FCC determined that "largely as a consequence of [measures deregulating the cable industry], the potential for duplicating broadcasters' programs, diverting broadcasters' audiences and advertising as a result of an unbalanced regulatory regime is far greater than we expected it to be when we rescinded our syndicated exclusivity rules" (p. 5305). Thus, it reimposed the rules in order to help shift the economic balance of power between the two industries, and to insure the economic value of programs for local TV stations.

In December 1989 the FCC initiated another far-reaching inquiry to determine whether cable television had abused its market power because the industry was substantially deregulated by the Cable Communications Policy Act of 1984 (*Competition,* 1989). It was prompted, in part, by increasing consumer complaints about high and rising basic cable rates, poor service quality, and the dropping or repositioning of broadcast signals. Additional motivation for the inquiry came from allegations that vertically integrated cable operators were denying other video service providers access to programming services such as HBO, ESPN, and other cable networks.

The common denominator of the complaints was that the cable industry was alleged to be excessively concentrated, allowing it to impede competition by alternative video services. Consequently, the FCC sought to gather "hard evidence and empirical analyses" to determine the validity of the charges. Given the nature of the allegations at issue, it was predictable that the proceeding would focus almost entirely on the economics of the cable television industry. The Notice of Inquiry asked, for example:

- What is the relevant product market in which the anticompetitive practices of the cable industry occur?
- How vigorous is the competition within the cable segment of that market?
- Who are the actual or potential noncable competitors in that market?
- What portion of that market is controlled by the cable industry?
- Does the cable industry's conduct reflect its abuse or accumulation of an undue degree of power in that market?

Given the economic focus of the questions, it is not surprising that the Commission's conclusions were cast in the same terms. The 1990 Cable Report concluded, for example, that "robust competition in the video marketplace has not yet fully evolved, but that the development of a fully competitive marketplace is possible" (*Competition*, 1990, p. 9). The Commission found that cable operators possessed varying degrees of market power over the local distribution of video programming, but did not recommend imposing a wide array of new regulations. Instead, the Report proposed reliance on market forces to curb abuses, interceding only when a lack of competition can be explained by naturally occurring market forces. Further, the Report proposed that the government should encourage a more competitive marketplace for cable and other video services. Thus, the Commission's policy recommendations were the direct product of economic analysis.

Shortly after the FCC released its general cable inquiry, it issued a Notice of Proposed Rulemaking to reexamine the standard for allowing rate regulation of cable television systems (*Competition*, 1990). In 1985, as part of its implementation of the Cable Act, the Commission adopted a "three-signal standard" for determining whether cable systems were subject to "effective competition" and thus exempt from regulation of basic subscriber rates. Under this standard, a cable system was not subject to rate regulation if the community in which the system was located received three over-the-air broadcast signals. As with other aspects of cable regulation, growth of the industry and evolution of the marketing aspects of the business led the FCC to reevaluate its initial standard.

The Commission eventually adopted a new standard for measuring "effective competition" in June 1991. Again, the policy choice was a function of economic analysis. The Commission noted that since the three-signal test was adopted, changes in the marketplace had rendered the standard obsolete. As the number of available cable channels increased, it took a great amount of over-the-air television signals to constitute a competitive alternative for viewers. Based on the comments filed by the various parties in the proceeding, the Commission found that six unduplicated over-the-air broadcast signals in a community would provide some type of market discipline for cable operators. Those communities with six broadcast channels are considered under the rules to be subject to "effective competition" and the cable operator exempt from rate regulation. Additionally, cable operators are exempt from rate controls in communities where there is a viable multichannel competitor to cable—such as in the form of a second cable system, direct broadcast satellite, microwave "wireless" cable system, or some other alternative (*Report and Order,* 1991).

Congress similarly took note of changes in the media marketplace, passing over President Bush's veto of the Cable Television Consumer and Competition Act of 1992. The new Act substantially reregulated cable television, imposing new standards for rate regulation, must-carry of broadcast signals, retransmission consent, cable programming access by competing technologies, customer service standards, and so on. Implementation of most provisions of the Act were vested with the FCC. Key economic concepts, such as when a cable system is subject to "effective competition" and what constitutes a "reasonable profit" were left to regulatory evaluation.

The 1996 Telecommunications Act, in turn, repeals many of the major provisions of the 1992 Cable Act. On rate regulation, current FCC rules capping cable service rates will be repealed by March 31, 1999, except the "basic tier" that includes over-the-air channels and public and educational channels. Price caps are repealed for "small" cable operators (less than $25 million in revenues) immediately or for any cable system once it faces "effective competition" from local telephone companies offering "comparable" video services over telephone facilities.

The Act also repeals the FCC's "telco-cable cross-ownership" restrictions. Telephone companies are authorized to offer video services either by distributing programming as a cable television system or by establishing an "open video system" for transport of video programming on a common carrier basis. State and local regulation of telecommunications services provided by cable systems is prohibited. As the marketplace changes, the Commission and Congress are forced to react and adapt to new conditions.

CONCLUSION

More than 60 years of experience with regulation of communications industries has proven, if nothing else, that the *public interest* is an elusive concept. Given the Communications Act's lack of specificity as to the meaning of this essential term, it has been up to the FCC, and the Federal Radio Commission before it, to come up with a definition that takes into account practical realities. The most significant reality confronting this quest is the fact that broadcasting is a business and it generally can provide greater service to the public when business is good. Thus, economic issues historically have been part of the Commission's allocation and licensing policies.

Because of its dependence on economic factors, the public interest also has been a moving target. The changing fortunes in the broadcasting industry have prompted the FCC to adopt, and later rescind, the *Carroll* doctrine. Likewise, marketplace changes led the Commission to adopt, then rescind, and finally consider reimposing AM/FM simulcast restrictions. A similar cyclical pattern of regulatory upheaval describes the FCC's experience with cable television.

The FCC's task of divining its regulatory mission through economic analysis has become more complex in an age of rapidly changing technology. As new methods of delivering video programming to the public are thrown into the marketplace mix, the effect of FCC action in one area may cause a chain reaction that spawns effects elsewhere. The question is not whether the cable industry will prosper at the expense of broadcasters or vice versa. Rather, the Commission must consider what effects its regulations may have on both existing and potential new market entrants. For example, regulation of the rate that a cable operator may charge its subscriber could have an inhibiting effect on the development of cable program networks by reducing the amount of money available to pay for programming. Dampening the growth of programming sources in turn might hinder the growth of alternative video delivery systems, which depend on such programming to create a competitive business. Multifaceted analyses of this type are now required for virtually any important regulatory decision the Commission must make, from the development of high-definition television to the deployment of direct broadcast satellites.

The increasing importance of media and the financial strength of media industries guarantees that economic analysis will continue to be a vital component of regulatory policy. However, the question still remains, as the number and complexity of necessary calculations increases, whether the tool will be sufficient to the task.

FURTHER READING

Brock, G., & Rosston, G. (Eds.). (1996). *The internet and telecommunications policy.* Mahwah, NJ: Lawrence Erlbaum Associates.

Carter, T., Franklin, M., & Wright, J. (1983). *The First Amendment and the fifth estate* (3rd ed.). Mineola, NY: Foundation Press.

Creech, K. (1996). *Electronic media law and regulation.* Newton, MA: Focal Press.

Pool, I. deS. (1983). *Technologies of freedom.* Cambridge, MA: Belknap.

REFERENCES

Amendment of Parts 73 and 76 of the Commission's Rules Relating to Program Exclusivity in the Cable and Broadcast Industries, 3 FCC Rcd. 5299 (1988), *aff'd sub nom. United Video Inc. v. FCC*, 890 F.2d 1173 (D.C. Cir. 1989).

Amendment of Section 73.242 of the Commission's Rules and Regulations in Regard to AM-FM Program Duplication, 59 Rad. Reg. (P&F) 2d 1611, 1613 (1986).

Arlington Telecommunications Corp., 65 F.C.C.2d 469 (1977), *recon.*, 69 F.C.C.2d 1923 (1978).

Carroll Broadcasting Co. v. FCC, 258 F.2d 440 (1958).

Carter Mountain Transmission Corp., 32 F.C.C. 459 (1962), *aff'd sub nom. Carter Mountain Transmission Corp. v. FCC*, 321 F.2d 359 (D.C. Cir.), *cert. denied*, 375 U.S. 951 (1963).

CATV Syndicated Program Exclusivity Rules, 79 F.C.C.2d 663 (1980).

Competition and Responsibility in Network Broadcasting, Docket No. 12782, 23 F.C.C.2d 382 (1970), *recon. denied*, 25 F.C.C.2d 318 (1970), *aff'd sub nom. Mt. Mansfield Television, Inc. v. FCC*, 442 F.2d 470 (2d Cir. 1971).

Competition, Rate Deregulation and the Commission's Policies Relating to the Provision of Cable Television Service (Notice of Inquiry), 5 FCC Rcd. 362 (1989).

Evaluation of the Syndication and Financial Interest Rules, 6 FCC Rcd. 3094 (1991), rev'd., *Schurz Communications v. FCC*, No. 91-2350 (7th Cir. Nov. 5, 1992).

FCC v. Pottsville Broadcasting Co., 309 U.S. 134 (1940); 309 U.S. 470 (1940).

FCC v. Sanders Brothers Radio Station, 309 U.S. 470, 60 S.Ct. 693, 84 L.Ed. 869 (1940).

First Report and Order, Docket Nos. 14895 and 15233, 38 FCC 683 (1965); *Second Report and Order in Docket Nos. 14895, 1523 and 15971*, 2 FCC 2d 725 (1966)

Inquiry Into the Economic Relationship Between Television Broadcasting and Cable Television, 71 FCC 2d 632 (1979).

National Association. of Regulatory Utility Commissioners v. FCC, 525 F.2d 630, 638 n.37 (D.C. Cir. 1976).

Notice of Inquiry, Docket No. 21284, 65 FCC 2d 9 (1977).

Office of Communication of the United Church of Christ v. FCC, No. 81-1032, slip op. at 27 (D.C. Cir., May 10, 1983).

Policies Regarding Detrimental Effects of Proposed New Broadcast Stations on Existing Stations, 3 FCC Rcd. 638 (1988), *aff'd. on reconsideration*, 4 FCC Rcd. 2276 (1989).

Quincy Cable TV, Inc. v. FCC, 768 F.2d 1434, 1455 (D.C. Cir. 1985), *cert. Denied, sub nom. National Ass'n. of Broadcasters v. Quincy Cable TV, Inc.*, 476 U.S. 1169 (1986).

Reno v. ACLU (1997).

Report and Order, Docket No. 15084, 45 FCC 1515 (1964).

Report and Order, Docket No. 20016, 59 FCC 2d 147 (1976).

Review of the Technical Assessment Criteria for AM Broadcast Service, MM Docket No. 87-267 (released Oct. 1991).

Sable Communications of California, Inc. v. FCC, 492 U.S. 115 (1989)

Second Annual Report to Congress on Cable Competition, Rep. No. DC 95-142 December 11, 1995

Washington Utilities and Transportation Commission v. FCC, 513 F.2d 1142 (9th Cir.), *cert. denied*, 423 U.S. 836 (1975)

4

Valuation of Media Properties

Benjamin J. Bates
University of Tennessee, Knoxville

One standard definition states that economics is concerned with the way in which resources are allocated among alternative uses in order to satisfy human wants. Such a definition provides an introduction to economics and a framework for analysis. It defines what economics does, what economics examines. It does not, however, really say much about what economics really is all about. What economics is all about is value: the creation of value, the exchange of things of value, the maximization of accumulated value (Ferguson, 1972). The concept of value, the idea that certain things are desired, is the foundation on which economics is built.

The economics of media reflect this concern. In fact, the evidence of the last few years would indicate that media properties are very highly valued. Broadcast stations, newspapers, and cable systems regularly are bought and sold for millions of dollars. *Broadcasting* magazine ("Station and Cable Trading," 1997) reported more than $25 billion in radio and television station sales, and more than $23 billion in cable system sales in 1996, while *Editor & Publisher* (Fitzgerald, 1995) noted more than $1.5 billion in daily newspaper sales. While the record sales in broadcasting and cable were fueled in part by the lifting of station ownership limits in the 1996 Telecommunications Act, the regular demand, not only for media but for access to the media, demonstrates that value is placed in media ownership. Although it is clear that media are valued, determining and measuring that value is much more problematic.

This chapter is devoted to exploring the factors that make media valuable and to considering the ways in which the value of media properties is measured. We explore the roots of the concept of value, and why value is often difficult to deal with in concrete terms. We also identify those factors influencing the valuation of media properties. Finally, we demonstrate some of the methods and procedures used to place a value on media properties.

VALUE AS A CONCEPT

> Economic value is not a material thing, any more than light and heat and sound are
> material things; and, like light and heat and sound, it cannot be represented or
> measured by a material thing. Economic value is sustenance, comfort, security, beauty
> and joy, whether contributed to by commodities, services, or order. The artist in us
> creates value; the technician in us amplifies values; and the critic in us determines
> value; for man, the maker, is also the measurer. (Atkins, 1925, p. 25)

In the purest sense, the value of any thing is whatever someone is willing to give,
or forego, in order to have it. It is a measure of desirability, of want. The problem
with this definition of value is that it is uncertain, and, in an absolute sense, it is
perhaps even unknowable. How can you determine what some individual, under
some circumstances, might be willing to exchange for an item? Is it even possible
for any *one* person to place a firm value on some good or service under all possible
conditions? Even if *you* can, then consider whether it is possible to determine a set
value out of every individual's set of values for that same good.

And even if we could, two other problems arise that make it difficult to ascertain
a precise, firm, value. First, situations change, and how much a person values
something can change with both their own situation and the general conditions
under which the valuation is being considered. Second, this conceptualization of
value is abstract; it considers what one *might* give for the item. It raises the problem
that although someone may value something highly, that person may not be in a
position to actually acquire the item. And does value, in a concrete sense, exist
when exchange is not possible?

These points illustrate the fact that, to the economists' chagrin, value is not some
fixed absolute measure, discoverable with relative ease by all who seek to determine
it. Value is variable, it differs from individual to individual, from situation to
situation. Value is influenced by an infinite range of conditions and factors. At the
very least, the concept of value is fraught with uncertainty.

Thus, value is not an easy concept for economists to deal with; it is not simple,
well-behaved, or certain. Most economic models presume that the participants
know everything, or at least almost everything, about the market and the goods in
that market. They also presume that things are relatively constant and fixed, at least
over the short term. Individual and market economic behavior is based on what is
known. So, if value is the basis for economics, and value is uncertain and perhaps
even unknowable, then the basic assumptions and laws of economics are broken
and the economists are out of business. How can you measure demand, or the effect
of market structure on demand, if you do not know how things are valued?

The situation for the economist, however, is not quite so grim, as they have
largely abandoned the pure, abstract, concept of value, and replaced it with more
concrete and measurable concepts. They have redefined value in ways that make it
at least theoretically knowable and certain. Thus, when looking at demand, value

has been replaced by the concept of utility, which is defined as a known set of preferences among a given set of goods and services. On the supply side, value is replaced by price, which in turn is determined in large part by costs; again, value is replaced by something a bit more certain, a bit more knowable. In both cases, the pure, simple, concept of value is replaced by measures that reflect more general, and more observable reflections of value. There are still some limits to these approaches, however, that sometimes creates problems in the application of economic theory to the real world.

The real world in which most of us operate, however, is in not quite so desperate a shape with regard to the question of value. For one thing, people tend to be able to tolerate a much higher level of uncertainty than the economists' models. Although the pure, true, exact and precise value of a thing may not be knowable, quite a lot can be determined about the level of value. That is, although one may not be able to nail down a precise, firm, value for any specific thing under all possible sets of conditions for all possible people, one can certainly get a fairly good idea of the general level of value under a general set of likely conditions. In fact, the business world has utilized such a notion for years, referring to it as *fair market value*, defined as the expected value under a set of normal or typical conditions. The notion of expected value is a statistical device that provides an averaging of individual values over a range of conditions or across a range of individuals, and thereby provides a means of generating a fixed value from a set of uncertain, but possible, values. The definition of fair market value as the expected value of a good under "normal" conditions restricts the consideration of certain extreme conditions, in a sense standardizing the process of valuation.

This section focuses on the concepts of value and fair market value as they are applied to media. In doing so, we consider first the nature of value and valuation, and the factors that affect the value of any given thing. Although we will deal primarily with a fair market value, it must be kept in mind that the standard conditions that such a valuation implies are almost never met in the real world, and thus the calculated fair market value may need to be adjusted for the peculiar situation and conditions of any media property and market.

Economic Theories of Value

How things are valued has been one of the central questions of economic theory. Early economic theories tended to fluctuate between three basic foundations for the determination of economic value: cost, exchange, and utility. The cost approach argued that the value of any one thing was the sum of the value of the inputs that went into its production. For many, that meant an emphasis on the amount of raw materials, including labor, that were involved in the production of the good or service. It was a nice, clean, definition of value in that costs were known and measurable, thus ensuring that value would itself be known and measurable.

A second approach emerged with the recognition that some things, like paper money, had value far in excess of the cost of their component parts. Their value lay, instead, in their ability to be exchanged or traded for other things that did have innate value. In 1776, Adam Smith (1937) argued for the valuation of products in terms of the labor that could be exchanged for the good. To Smith, only labor could create value where none existed before, and thus labor was the true source of value, whether it be through exchange or the creation of goods and services.

Although exchange value was a useful development and extension of the concept of value, it was limited in that it defined value as existing only in exchange. What about things that were not exchanged? Did they not have value? It was not long until some early economists argued that exchange value referred to the good's usefulness through exchange, and thus extended the concept of value in terms of usefulness, or utility. Etiennne de Condillac succinctly expressed the early utility perspective when he wrote in 1776, "Value is not an attribute of matter, but represents our sense of its usefulness, and this utility is relative to our need. It grows or diminishes according as our need expands or contracts" (cited in Rima, 1972, p. 60).

In contrast to cost-based theories, which put the determination of value in the hands of producers, the utility-based theories of value felt that it was the consumer who was important, and it was the consumer's concept and measure of value that was important. This is, because it was argued, no matter what the cost of a good, no exchange will occur unless the purchaser feels that the value of the good is at least as great as the cost. Utility-based theories also integrated exchange perspectives by recognizing that the utility of some items were based precisely on their usefulness as media of exchange. Pure utility theories are hampered by the fact that the true usefulness of any item can not be known until after it has been used. There are ways around this predicament, such as defining value as the expected utility of its future use. Nevertheless, this makes the utility approach to value somewhat speculative, and thus subject to the related problems of uncertainty.

From the modern perspective, all of these early theories are somewhat on the mark, and have contributed to the current conceptualization of value. Value, to an individual, is based on usefulness, whether that usefulness comes from the actual consumption of an item, its possession, or from its exchange for other valued things. However, the cost of a thing is a valid consideration in the determination of value, for cost is a constraint on availability and a thing cannot be valued if it does not exist or is not produced. Finally, but most importantly for our purposes, value can be objectively measured in terms of its exchange. When two parties exchange a good, they have reached an understanding about the value of that good, and have left a record of that negotiated value.

We need to remember, however, that this negotiated value, or exchange price, does not necessarily reflect the precise value placed on the exchange good by either of the parties involved. What an exchange price reflects is that sellers believe that their valuation of the good is no more than the exchange price. If the value to the seller was greater than the exchange price, the seller would not sell (unless forced to by other circumstances). Similarly, the exchange price reflects a minimum to the buyer; the buyer will not purchase the product unless she feels that its value is at least as large as the exchange price. Thus, what the exchange price actually measures is not true value, but some point in a range determined by the buyer's and seller's opinions about their own individual valuations of the good under the peculiar conditions of the exchange.

The Variability of Value

There are many factors that can influence value. Some are related to attributes of the item being valued. Some are related to the particular situation and needs of the potential purchaser. Some may be similarly related to the particular situation in which potential sellers find themselves. Yet others may be related to conditions of the exchange and the context in which it occurs.

In order to consider some of the sources of variability and their relation to value, look at water as an example. Water, unlike media properties, is a nice, simple product, one that is both familiar and used virtually every day. It is also one of the first, and most widely used, examples of products used in the study of value; Adam Smith (1937) had argued that although water was very useful, it had scarcely any value because water could not be exchanged for much (Smith, it should be remembered, lived in England where water was very plentiful). We know what water is, what its uses are. At first thought, we might also feel that we certainly know what the value of water is. But do we?

Although the concept of water might seem common and uniform enough that we do not often think of it in terms of having distinctive forms and qualities, certainly polluted water is distinctive from what comes out of your faucet at home (one would hope). Sea water is different from river water, which may be different from rain water or melted-snow water. Water may have different mineral contents, may or may not be fluoridated, may have different tastes and smells, indicating that there can be significant differences in the attributes, or properties, of the economic good water.

This also shows how we place different values on the different types of water. Polluted water is valued less than clean water, because its particular attributes are generally seen as being less useful and/or desirable. However, even clean water may not be enough; if it tastes bad or smells funny it may be fine for watering the lawn, but not preferred for drinking. So often we are willing to pay more for better water. Some people will even pay a premium for water that may not be chemically better or different, but has a prestigious label. Such "designer water" can be found today in most bars, restaurants, and grocery stores. In that case, the value is affected not only by the water itself, but by the manner in which it is packaged, which is, after all, an attribute of the product.

It is not only product characteristics that can influence value; so might various aspects of the situation under which the exchange takes place. Those aspects can include buyer characteristics, market (location) characteristics, and seller characteristics. One classic example of buyer characteristics involves water. It is based on the idea that a person dying of thirst might value a gallon of water differently from a person who is not only not thirsty, but has a reservoir tucked away in their backyard. Certainly, that additional gallon of water is needed and desired more by the thirsty person, and through the utility notion of value, that greater need and desire leads to a greater valuation of the water.

The example also extends to market/location characteristics, with the concept that water tends to have a greater value in the desert than in a region of lakes and rivers. The available supply and the ease of obtaining a product tends to influence its perceived value. Other specific market characteristics, like the degree of concentration among buyer and sellers or the amount of information available about the product and its availability, can also have an impact on the perceived value of the product. Monopolists are said to be able to manipulate price, if not necessarily value. Advertising is claimed to be able to increase the perceived desirability of a product, and hence its perceived value. On the other hand, the lack of information about a product, by increasing the uncertainty of its value, is said to lower perceived value. The value of water may also be affected by seller characteristics; they have acquired their supply of the good for some reason. Like the buyer, any number of things may affect that value. The amount of the product held, the perceived future needs for the product, and the perceived future supply (or availability) of the product may all easily influence the perceived value of the product to the supplier.

Thus, as the example of water amply illustrates, there are a number of aspects of economic goods, and the conditions of exchange that can influence the perception of value. Economists take into consideration some of these differences by specifying the market and the exchange conditions. Differences in buyer and seller characteristics are incorporated through the use of supply and demand curves, which reflect the fact that different people place different values on the same thing.

The Value of Businesses

An ongoing business operation is different from what is normally considered as economic goods. Businesses are not consumed, per se; nor are they typically held only for their exchange value. In that way, they are something like land. Land is not used up, and is not easily transportable, like most trade goods. However, land certainly has value. A question raised by many early economists was what was the *source* of that value.

English philosopher John Locke provided the central concept for the value of continuing goods such as land (or businesses) when he argued that the value of land depended on the income that could be derived from it (Rima, 1972). Sir William Pettey extended that notion when he suggested that the purchase price paid for land depends on the number of years a prospective purchaser is likely to enjoy its yield. In other words, the value of an continuing good was based on the expected yield of that good over a period of time. That is, the value of any business lies primarily in its ability to generate income over some period of time. There are three basic ways in which any business can generate a return to its owners, and thus create value.

First, all businesses have assets, the things that they own. Assets have value, both on their own and as part of an ongoing operation. One potential future for a business is to actually cease operations and to sell off their assets. This strategy has enjoyed some popularity among the so-called corporate raiders of the 1980s, who bought conglomerates, and were able to recoup their investments by selling off component parts. Firms may also have assets that are not necessary for their basic business operations, which could be sold without harming the ongoing main business operations. Thus, one possible determinant of the value of a business is its assets.

A second source of value for any business comes from its operation as a business, from its profits. An ongoing operation provides the owner with, hopefully, a flow of profits from its operation. These future profits certainly constitute a yield, and a value to ownership. That profit stream over time has a current value, which can be a possible determinant of the value of a business. Although profits may certainly continue well into the future, uncertainty and the normal risks of business suggest that one can accurately predict profits for only a short period of time. Thus, a business' value is usually based on a fairly limited period of profits.

The third source of value for a business is as an investment. Like any other non-consumed good, businesses may increase in value over time. If one expects the value of a thing to increase over time, one may purchase it in order to realize a future profit through resale, even if it provides no profit stream over that period. The investment potential of a property can also be a possible determinant of the value of a business.

The Value of Media as a Business.   Thus, there are three basic sources of value for businesses. However, as is pointed out in other chapters of this volume, the media are not typical. There are aspects of media, and media properties, which suggest that the primary source of the value of media properties lies in terms of their potential for generating profits over time. Ownership of media can also provide other sources of value that are not shared by other businesses.

Why the emphasis on future profits? For one thing, the physical assets of any media business tend to be only a fraction of that firm's value, and are not of significant value to any nonmedia operation. Those assets that may be of significant value to a nonmedia operation, such as a downtown office building, are usually not vital to the operation of the business, and thus may be sold off without ceasing operations. Furthermore, most media operations are self-contained, and the demand for used equipment is slight. This suggests that although certain valuable assets may affect the value of a particular property, this aspect of value is not central to the determination of the value of media properties as media.

Where media properties have been bought on the basis of their component values, it has been based more on the value of the component businesses rather than on the value of the physical assets. The purchase of media groups, or media conglomerates, has sometimes resulted in the subsequent sale of some of the media operations. Those operations, however, have usually been sold off as intact, although separate, businesses. Of course, separable physical assets can contribute to the value of the overall property.

In addition, considerations of value as an investment are at best speculative. They are based on the notion that the basic value of the investment will increase significantly over time, that someone at a future period will place a higher value on the media property. There are basically two reasons for this to happen. First, speculation that even higher demand for the good in the future might drive higher valuation for investment purposes. Second, the investor may feel that conditions affecting the future profit stream might change, leading to higher future profits, and thus higher value for the media property. There is a problem with the speculative nature of investment valuation. If it is based on reasonable expectations of even higher profit potential, then it is not so much based on investment as it is on future profit valuation basis. If not, then it is truly speculative, and has no reliable, rational basis. Rather, it is fueled by the expectation that other speculators will drive prices even higher. The problem with this is that eventually you run out of speculators, and have to value a property on its innate value, and the speculative basis collapses, much like many of the speculative development schemes that contributed to the recent savings and loan crisis in the late 1980s (where many S&Ls bought into the speculative fever, rather than basing loans on the asset or profit stream value of properties).

What this leaves, for media properties, is the general definition of value as being based on the expected future profits of the media property. Directly or indirectly, judgments are made about the expectations of future profits, and calculations are made as to the present value of those future profits. And that revenue stream is the primary basis for the fair market value of a media property. However, the presence of significant nonmedia assets can add to that basic valuation.

Other Sources of Media Value.   It should be noted that the utility theory of value suggests another source of potential value. Media properties can be useful in ways other than in their capacity to generate economic returns. Many media owners perceive a value in their properties related more to the prestige of being a publisher or broadcaster, in the potential to exert political or social influence through their media. This source of value, although certainly real to the owner and in some cases quite substantial, is not considered to be part of the conditions under which fair market value is determined. After all, potential buyers may not assign the same value to prestige or power. Therefore, we do not address this source of value beyond noting that sometimes premiums are paid above fair market value that represent such perceived value.

C0ALCULATING THE VALUE OF MEDIA PROPERTIES

So far, we have discussed where the value of media properties comes from, the factors that play a part in the determination of value. The important part, however, is the actual calculation of the fair market value of any specific media property. The discussion here suggests that the determination of fair market value should be based primarily on considerations of yield over time, defined in terms of future profits. The question then becomes how one determines the value of future profits.

Any value is uncertain, and to at least some extent speculative. Future values are even more speculative. There are, however, various guidelines that exist that can provide means of estimating future returns and the "fair market value" of a media property. There are simple procedures, sometimes using multiples of current returns, and there are the more complex and sophisticated analyses of the future profit stream. Generally, the more sophisticated and precise the procedure, the more accurate it should be, at least if it is done well. There are a number of firms that will be glad to value media properties for a price.

All of these guidelines and procedures are based on the general notion that the value of a media property is related to its future profit potential, the money it will generate over some future period. Where the approaches differ is in the means used to estimate that potential, and the assumptions made about the future profitability of the particular property. For greatest precision, it is best to perform an individual market/property analysis, with specific revenue growth projections and individualized profitability estimates that take into consideration the particular characteristics of the property being evaluated and the market in which it operates. Substituting certain simplifying assumptions and very general estimates of revenue growth and property profitability (usually industry averages) for more precise and individual consideration yields the multiples approach. This is where a very general range of values is generated by multiplying some figure by current revenues or profits. The use of "comparable sales," where one looks for sales of similar properties under similar conditions, offers a middle ground that gives some consideration to market and media characteristics without requiring a full individual treatment.

More Exact Calculations: Forecasting Revenues, Costs, and Profits

The previous discussion of business value argued that the value of media should be based primarily on future profitability. The difficulty comes in determining future states, in this case, future profits. Predictions can be made fairly simply, but they carry the potential for being quite inaccurate, if they fail to take into consideration the specifics of both present and future circumstances. The simpler the basis for the prediction, the less faith can generally be placed in the accuracy of that prediction.

More elaborate forecasts of market conditions and media profitability, although not necessarily any more accurate than simple predictions, are at least more precise in their statement and consideration of current and future conditions. And in making specific and explicit their assumptions about present and future conditions, forecasts provide the information necessary to judge their accuracy and validity. They can also often serve as goals for the media operator after the purchase. In this section, we consider what goes into forecasting future profit streams for the media, and how those forecasts are used to determine the value of media properties. There are several steps to this process.

Forecasting Revenues.   The first step involves the consideration and forecasting of revenues for the media property. This should involve more than just expecting current revenues to grow at a fixed rate. A media property's revenues are the product of two factors: market revenue levels and the media property's share of those revenues. Market revenue levels can be forecast on the basis of historical growth patterns, but should also take into consideration any unique characteristics of the market, anything that might enhance or diminish the market's revenue potential. Is the market booming or in recession? Are there major competitors for advertising revenues? Similar consideration should be given to the development of a station's share of the market. Can things be done to improve market share? Is better competition from existing competitors likely to decrease market share? What would be the impact of additional competition from new competitors, or from alternative media sources? Is new competition expected? All of these questions need to be considered when predicting market revenues, market share, and thus station revenues.

If data on current market revenues are available, they can be used to project a basic market trend for those revenues. If not, one can often find other economic data for the market. Many times, one can also find projections of this data. As research has indicated that media revenues tend to reflect current economic conditions in the market, these other indicators can be used to obtain an estimate of the probable growth of market revenues. Whether calculated directly or indirectly, this basic growth rate can be used to provide a foundation for forecasting future market revenues. Occasionally, other factors can create a shift in growth patterns. Industries may enter or leave a market. Shifts in policies may promote or hamper economic development. If there appear to be any such factors at work, or on the horizon, their potential impact should be considered and incorporated into the forecasts. It is often difficult, however, to determine precisely such effects. Thus, their impact is often included only as a minor increase (or decrease) in the projected market growth rate.

Once market revenues have been forecast, it is time to consider the particular media property's share of those revenues. As with market revenues, one can often base the estimate of market share on the property's historical share of the market. However, one also needs to consider whether it is likely that the share will increase or decrease. Most media buyers believe that they can increase market share, usually even beyond what would be considered to be normal or typical levels. Such normal shares are determined on the basis of the number and type of competitors rather than historical performance. Fair market value, based as it is on normal or typical behavior, requires that the projection of future market shares be at those normal levels. If current levels fall below normal shares, then one can presume that market share will increase over some period to those levels. Conversely, if the media property is currently performing above normal levels, market shares need to be reduced to those levels in the calculation of fair market value.

This does leave us, however, with the basic question of what is considered to be normal shares. This can be based on a combination of historical market patterns, industry averages, and a consideration of the competitive stature of the media property. Because those shares are forecast over time, consideration must also be given to potential changes in competition, whether it be from new properties entering the market, or from shifts in the relationship with alternative media. For example, future market shares of TV stations are influenced not only by the introduction of new broadcast television stations, but also by the rise of cable, satellites, and low-power TV stations, all of which can compete for audience and advertising.

Of course, one could bypass market revenues and shares forecasts and try to forecast the media property's revenues directly. However, this would tend to bypass consideration of shifting market patterns, and in a period when media competition is undergoing significant changes, to do so is to ignore important factors, and to most likely overestimate the value of the media property. Some critics have argued that such a process had indeed occurred in broadcasting, where the failure to consider the changing competitive environment led to unrealistically high prices being paid for stations in the late 1980s, and the consequent decline in prices when the new competitive situation was finally recognized.

There is one final note to be made on the consideration of revenues. Many media firms have additional revenue sources beyond their primary media business. Newspapers with their own presses often seek out additional commercial printing revenues. Broadcast media can earn additional revenues through the provision of production services to others. As these outside sources add to the revenue (and profit) stream, they should be considered in the forecasting of future profits. Today, with the convergence of media, and the rise of the Internet and the opportunities it presents to media outlets, this may be an increasingly valuable set of assets. However, as they are often emerging, secondary, and more competitive activities, they often can not be relied on as regular contributors to the revenue stream. As such, their contribution is normally discounted heavily.

Forecasting Costs. The second step involves the consideration of the media property's operations and costs. What costs are involved in the operation? What is the opportunity to reduce costs? What additional costs might have to be incurred in the future? All this points to the question of how much profit can be expected from a given level of revenues.

The best way to forecast profits is to obtain detailed information on the media property's current costs and operations. The consideration only of apparent profits can be quite misleading. For example, owners may choose to take profits in the form of higher salaries and benefits, inflating costs and reducing apparent profits. Conglomerates often use charges to shift profits among divisions. If details on the operation can be obtained, they can indicate opportunities for reducing costs, or areas where costs might be expected to rise, and those factors can be taken into consideration in the determination of future profit levels.

Another reason to try to obtain detailed information about the property's costs and operations is that there are actually several different measures of profitability, all of which provide useful information to a potential purchaser, and contribute to the calculation of media value. These measures differ largely in terms of what items of cost are included, or not included, in the calculation of profit. Having a detailed breakdown of costs permits the determination of all of these various measures.

Forecasting Profits.   The general definition of profits is whatever is left from revenues after all of the costs involved in doing business are subtracted (including taxes). As noted earlier, the differences in the accountant's definition of profits, the economist's definition of profits, operating profits, taxable profits, and cash flow all reflect differences in what are considered to be the applicable costs. To the economist, profits are the difference between revenues and the full opportunity costs of doing business, which include the owner's normal profits (their return for risk taking) and the return on capital. The accountant's version of profits does not consider either of these items to be costs; rather, they are considered to be an aspect of profits. Taxable profits are based on the accountant's definition of revenues less actual costs (before taxes), but include as costs depreciation, reinvestment, and certain other deductible payments. Operating profits remove reinvestment as a cost, and cash flow removes depreciation as a cost (in effect, adding those back into "profits"). What cash flow represents, generally, is the amount of internally generated funds that are available to the business, the actual cash yield of the firm. For the most part, it is cash flow that is considered to be the best indicator of the yield of the business, and is thus used to calculate the value of the firm.

Often, however, such detailed information is not available. In such cases, one can substitute other estimates of "normal" costs or profit margins, and apply those to the revenue estimates to obtain profit forecasts.

From Future Profits to Present Value.   A final step in this process involves the calculation of the present value of the future profit stream. The concept of present value reflects the fact that future profits occur in the *future*. They are not available at the present, and are thus not as valuable as they would be now. For example, inflation means that future dollars are worth less than today's dollar. In addition, you have to *wait* for the future dollars. Thus, future profits need to be discounted by a factor that takes into consideration the expected decline in value, and the opportunity costs lost from not having the profits immediately. This discount is often based on a combination of the expected level of inflation and the cost of money, that is, interest rates.

Finally, the process assembles these steps into a coherent statement of expected revenues, profits, and discounts that provides a prediction of the present value of future profits. The only thing left to be considered is how long a period is to be considered. For the most part, it seems that a period of 7 to 10 years tends to be used for calculations of value for media firms. There is a bit more than just normal judgment behind the specification of that period, however. For one thing, the reliability of revenue (and cost) projections decreases significantly the further one attempts to project. Second, present value discounts build up so that there is often little contribution to be made to present value from profits in the far future. Finally, the stability of markets and industries contributes to the determination of the period.

Although some very stable industries might utilize longer profits streams in their present value calculations, media operate in very volatile markets. New technologies bring new media competition. Shifts in regulations, such as the 1996 Telecommunications Act, can significantly affect media markets. Market demographics and economics can vary significantly over time. All of this reinforces the problem of predicting future media profits, and leads to the consideration of a fairly limited profit stream in value calculations.

A simplified example of this process is given in Table 4.1. The concept of the process is fairly simple. Getting good numbers that reflect specific market and media property characteristics and reflect future trends, is the difficult part.

Using Similar Properties

Often, a rough estimate of the value of a property can be calculated from the consideration of what prices have been paid for similar properties under similar conditions. This can be done by trying to match the prospective media property with others that have been recently sold, or it can involve the development of a statistical procedure that uses a wide range of sales to estimate the contributions made by various factors (including both market and media attributes) to the final price of the property. That formula is then applied to the prospective property in order to calculate its fair market value.

There are two potential hitches in the use of comparative sales in estimating the value of media. The first of these is the need to identify the price of other media sales. In broadcasting this is relatively easy, as the FCC requires such data as part of its license transferal process. That information is collected and published by several industry sources such as *Broadcasting* magazine. There is a certain lack of

TABLE 4.1
A Simple Model of Future Profits Valuation Calculation for a High-Power AM Station

					Year						
	Current	1	2	3	4	5	6	7	8	9	10
Market revenues[a] ($million)	22	23.54	25.19	26.9	28.8	30.8	33.0	35.3	37.8	40.4	43.2
AM share of market[b]	0.13636	0.136	0.136	0.136	0.136	0.140	0.140	0.140	0.140	0.140	0.140
AM revenues ($000)	3,000.	3,210.	3,434.	3,675.	3,932.	4,319.	4,622.	4,945.	5,292.	5,662.	6,059.
Station fair market share[c]	0.1327	0.15	0.19	0.23	0.27	0.30	0.30	0.30	0.30	0.30	0.30
Projected fair market station revenues ($)	39,823	48,150	65,259	84,528	106,174	129,595	138,667	148,374	158,760	169,873	181,764
Estimated operating expenses[d] ($)	35,049										
Operating profit ($)	4,773										
Operating profit margin[e]	0.1198	0.12	0.14	0.16	0.18	0.20	0.20	0.20	0.20	0.20	0.20
Estimated profits	5,778	9,136	13,524	19,111	25,919	277,335	296,748	317,525	339,747	36,353	

Using present value calculations of future profits to estimate value for station

	7 yrs	8 yrs	10 yrs
Present value of profit stream	$639,790.75	$733,366.82	$898,249.19
Present value rate	16.5%		

Thus, estimated value for this station would run from roughly $640,000 to $900,000.

[a] Start with current market revenues, then project growth slightly above projected national average (5% to 6%) at 7.5%.
[b] Based on existing share of audience, should grow somewhat as AM underachieving in market, and as new technology improves AM signal quality.
[c] Share of AM based on current audience share for station, projected to fair share based on comparable reach.
[d] Projected from NAB average for that type of station in that revenue range.
[e] Calculated from current estimate, to industry average of 20%.

detail to this information, however, and so the price given may not precisely reflect the actual price or value of the property. The price given, however, does reflect at least the level of value. The problem with knowing the price of media firms, however, lies more with print media. There is no regulatory agency requiring the collection of sales information for other media, and the final sales price is often not disclosed.

The second problem lies in the identification of "similar" properties. Media markets are notorious for their distinctiveness. There are considerable differences in levels of competition, in market/audiences served, and in the desirability of the market/audience to potential advertisers. Further, there is often great variation in the characteristics of media firms within markets. Differences in content and media characteristics can lead to variations in the values of firms. Although these distinctions do not preclude comparisons, they do force most comparisons to be with only roughly similar properties, and thus can provide only rough estimates of value.

The derivation of formulas from existing sales data avoids some of these potential problems. By basing the formula on a wide range of reported sales, this method avoids the problem of finding truly compatible stations. It also reduces the problem of missing data somewhat, by expanding the range of sales considered. The method is still hampered by measurement difficulties, however. Most formulae include only a few factors, and thus ignore station differences along other dimensions. Thus, this method also only provides a rough estimate of station value.

Some recent examples of price formulae for broadcast stations is given in Table 4.2. For example, the formula for television stations suggest that market size, bandwidth, and cable penetration all influence the price of stations.

Using Multiples

The concept of multiples is based on the idea that all well-run media properties are likely to be at least somewhat profitable, and that the future profit stream is more or less directly related to some set of current revenues or profits. The use of multiples assumes that profits are directly linked to revenue levels, and are likely to be consistent over time. Although that is not necessarily a bad assumption in that profits are usually positively correlated with revenues, the use of a single multiple also assumes that profit margins are constant for all levels of revenue, which is generally not true for media firms.

The thinking behind multiples goes something like this:

1. Assume that revenues will grow at roughly the same rate as the discount rate.
2. Assume a constant profit margin (e.g., 20%).
3. Assume a standard payback period of 7 to 10 years.
4. Then if growth and discount rates are roughly equal, then the expected value of future profits over the payback period is roughly profit margin times revenue times years. If the two rates are not equal, that could increase or decrease expected value somewhat.

TABLE 4.2

Broadcast Station Valuation Formulae

TV Stations [a]

---

ln(Price) = 0.926 + 0.675(ln(ADC)) + 0.398(ln(TVHH)) + 0.011(Cable%)

    − 0.726(if station is UHF band)

    + 0.970(if station is SIN affiliate)

    + 0.236(if buyer owns another TV)

Where ln = natural logarithm of value

        Price = station sales price, in thousands of dollars

        ADC = Average Daily Circulation for station, in thousands

        TVHH = television households in market, in thousands

        Cable% = basic cable penetration in market

Radio Stations [b]

AM stations

    ln(Price) = 26.261 + 0.349(ln(Income)) + 0.040(Station Power) − 0.001(Station Frequency)

        − 0.173(Year of Sale) − 0.249(if station held for less than 3 years)

        − 0.457(if station is daytime only)

FM Stations

    ln(Price) = 11.233 + 0.230(ln(Income)) + 0.014(Station Power) + 0.001(Antenna height)

    + 0.022(number of competing radio stations in market)

Where Price = station price, in dollars

        Income = total county income, in thousands of dollars

        Station Power = listed broadcasting power, in kw

        Station Frequency = AM frequency, in kHz

        Year of Sale = year in which station was sold, 19XX

---

[a] From Bates (1988). Reprinted with permission
[b] From Bates (1995). Reprinted with permission

5. This becomes revenues times multiple, or profits times multiple, or cash flow times multiple, where there are different multiples to use, depending on how much information you have about the media property.

With a presumed profit margin of 20%, the revenues multiple becomes 1.5 to 2, which falls within the current range for radio properties and weekly newspapers. Some examples of multiples are given in Table 4.3. As with the comparable sales figures, multiples are generally more widely reported for broadcast than for nonbroadcast firms.

TABLE 4.3

Some Recent Multiples

Newspapers	
Dailies	3–5 times revenues (Garneau, 1989)
	10–12 times cash flow (Garneau, 1989)
	22 times earnings (Fitzgerald, 1995)
Weeklies	1.1–1.5 times revenues (Fink, 1988)
	1–2.5 times revenues (Fitzgerald, 1990)
	6–8 times cash flow (Garneau, 1989)
Shoppers	1–1.5 times cash flow (Garneau, 1989)
Other Publishers	
Books	6 to 8 times profits (Shaw, 1987)
Magazines	6 to 10 times profits (Shaw, 1987)
	8 times cash flow (Kelly, 1995)
Radio	
Groups	3 times revenues (Condon, 1996)
	12 to 16 times cash flow (Station & Cable Trading, 1997)
AM only	5 to 7 times cash flow (Krasnow et al., 1991)
	1.5 to 2 times revenues
FM only	7 to 9 times cash flow (Krasnow et al., 1991)
	2 to 3 times revenues
AM/FM combinations	7 to 10 times cash flow
	1.5 to 2.5 times revenues
Television	
Network Affiliates	8 to 10 times cash flow (Krasnow et al., 1991)
	10 to 15 times cash flow (Station & Cable Trading, 1997)
Independent Stations	7 to 9 times cash flow ("Independent TV," 1990; Krasnow et al., 1991)
Cable	
	$2,000 to $2,500 per sub (Schneider & Peterson, 1990)
	$1,800 to $2,000 per sub (Station & cable trading, 1997)
	11 times cash flow (Moshavi, 1992)

The problem with multiples is that they make very broad assumptions about general values that may not be completely accurate. Thus, they provide only very rough indicators of value, and often incorporate a fairly wide range of values. Multiples are often expressed as a range, incorporating the uncertainties of the process, and integrating some leeway for the perceived risks of the deal. The more uncertain, or riskier, the market and assumptions, the lower the multiple tends to be. Uncertainty also tends to encourage the use of a wider range of multiples (i.e., 7 to 10 times profits rather than 8 to 9 times profits).

Media owners—broadcasters in particular—have been somewhat reticent about accepting the idea of constant profit margins. Years of FCC and NAB data show that profit margins tend to increase as revenues increase. There is too much range in the size of markets and levels of competition for a single estimate of profit margins to be accurate across all conditions. Thus a second form of multiples, based on operating profits or cash flow, has come into widespread use. Another variation on multiples has arisen in the cable industry, where some people use "per-subscriber" multiples, assuming that per-subscriber revenues and profits are fairly constant over time.

A problem has arisen in recent years with the assumption that profit margins should be stable over time. The rapid increase in broadcast revenues has slowed considerably in recent years, whereas costs have continued to escalate. The 1992 Cable Act forced revenue cuts and profit declines for most cable operators. Increased competition for audiences from new media look to continue to squeeze revenues and profit margins.

Special Concerns for Leveraged or Financed Sales

Very few media sales are made for cash up front. More often than not, the buyer finances much of the price through debt. This debt needs to be financed, and needs to be paid off from operating income, or through issuing more debt. The actual costs of this debt depend greatly on the prevailing interest rates. High interest rates increase the cost of debt and can influence the amount buyers are willing to finance, and thus the price they are willing to pay. The costs of debt thus become part of the value calculations for media properties. In addition, if a firm's cash flow is not sufficient to meet these payments, additional money must be borrowed, further increasing the true cost of purchase. Finally, media sales often include as part of the total cost (or value) of the sale consulting agreements, or agreements with the previous owners not to compete. Such agreements also must be paid out of cash flow, and can raise the total cost of the property.

Externalities and Expectations

As might be gathered from this chapter, determining the value of any good or service can be quite difficult, because many factors can influence that value, including the item being valued and the context of the exchange. Others may not be quite so directly related; such factors are called *externalities*. Externalities do influence value; they are not, however, normally considered as part of the typical valuation process, because they can influence values and prices, however, they should be considered in the valuation process, at least to the point of considering whether any externalities exist with a particular media property.

There often are externalities associated with media properties. Among them can be the prestige of certain media operations and the perceived ability to exert political, moral, or economic power through the media. *The Washington Times* was started at considerable expense and operated for years with significant losses, allegedly in part because its owner, the Reverend Moon, wanted access to the Washington media and the power it implied. Neuharth (1989) wrote of bidding high for some newspapers in the Gannett chain in order to help acquire a printing and distribution system for *USA Today*, or because they were prestigious properties.

Access to certain markets can also bring about higher than normal prices for media properties. Stories are told about Northern broadcasters paying a premium for stations in Hawaii and other vacation spots, so they can write off vacations as business trips. The Home Shopping Network grossly overpaid for a series of UHF stations, in part to guarantee their access to large markets and their cable systems. Fox paid a premium to acquire stations in the major markets, and with the recent spate of affiliation switches, other networks have also paid premiums to acquire stations in large television markets. Broadcast properties in the largest markets are generally thought to bring a premium (Levin, 1975).

Externalities can also arise when nonmedia property or operations are sold in conjunction with the media firm. General economic conditions can also influence the degree to which potential investors are interested in risk taking or speculative investing, which can drive up prices for goods with a limited supply, like media. Shifts in policy or technological developments can affect perceptions about long-term future viability.

There is one further issue to be considered. Values are based on perceptions and expectations: perceptions about sources of value and the factors affecting them, and expectations about the future of those sources and factors. Calculations of fair market value are particularly dependent on expectations, as fair market value is defined in terms of expected future profits. Media values, therefore, are heavily influenced by expectations about the future of the medium and the marketplace.

In stable times, this is not a big problem. Stability helps make people feel more certain, more comfortable with their expectations. Predictions seem more reliable. In periods of decline or when the future is more unpredictable, however, uncertainty about expectations increases and prices generally decline under uncertainty. Much of the decline in cable and broadcasting sales and prices in 1990–1991 was attributed to uncertainty about future competition and regulatory changes. In addition, we do seem to be entering a general period of media instability. The older media are still around, but new media and markets are emerging. Markets that were once considered stable are undergoing change as new forms of media compete for audiences and advertisers. The old boundaries between media are beginning to break down (Compaine, 1981). Cable has reshaped television markets (Bates, 1993), direct mail and shoppers have attracted advertising away from newspapers, videotape rentals have impacted on both theaters and pay cable, and DBS has started to make significant inroads into cable markets. The coming of what has been called the Information Age, or the Age of Convergence, threatens to transform most media and markets.

This raises certain questions about what can be expected in the future. Will market shares be cut as new competition emerges? Will new technology and new delivery systems change cost structures? Will world markets help control the costs of media product, or will the need to create for such markets increase production costs? Will Congress, or other regulatory agencies, impose new regulations and costs on media operations?

No one can predict the future with absolute certainty. Neither can we say that the future is absolutely unknown. Media expectations, at least for the purpose of valuation, are relatively short term; a matter of a few years. In the short term, things tend to be more stable, and thus more predictable. When valuing media properties, however, it does pay to consider whether expectations are realistic, just as it pays to consider the presence of any externalities.

CONCLUSIONS

Value, as long as it remains abstract, seems to be a nice, simple concept; it only becomes problematic when we attempt to precisely determine the value of any specific thing, when we try to make value something that it is not by inferring that value is an agreed-on constant. Too many factors influence value for it to be treated as a constant. Individual, market, and contextual factors, externalities, and expectations about the future can affect the value of media properties.

There are solutions to the issue of how do we value media properties. There is general agreement that the value of media is based primarily on its value as a continuing business, on its future profitability. Concepts such as fair market value can stabilize value by artificially fixing many of the variable factors, and by ignoring some potential influences. This consensual foundation can provide us with procedures for determining a basic value for media properties. Several of these procedures have been outlined in this chapter.

When media properties are valued, however, one must also be aware that these procedures will only provide a foundation. It must be remembered that there are many factors that can have an impact on value, particularly on the perceived value of any media property, and these factors do need to be considered when attempting to ascertain the precise value of any media outlet. Those who would value media need to be aware of these factors and how they can shape and determine value. Only then can one confidently assert the value of any particular media property.

FURTHER READING

Bates, B. J. (1988). The impact of deregulation on TV station prices. *Journal of Media Economics, 1*(1), 5–22.

Bates, B. J. (1995). What's a station worth? Models for determining radio station value. *Journal of Media Economics, 8*(1), 13–23.

Compaine, B. M. (1981). Shifting boundaries in the information marketplace. *Journal of Communication, 31*(1), 132–142.

Fink, C. C. (1988). *Strategic newspaper management.* Carbondale: Southern Illinois University Press.

Krasnow, E. G., Bentley, J. G., & Martin, R. B. (1991). *Buying or building a broadcast station in the 1990s* (3rd ed.). Washington, DC: National Association of Broadcasters.

McFadyen, S., Hoskins, C., & Gillen, D. (1980). *Canadian broadcasting: Market structure and economic performance.* Montreal: Institute for Research on Public Policy.

Miller, I. R. (1997). Models for determining the economic value of cable television systems. *Journal of Media Economics, 10*(2), 21–33.

Pringle, P. K., Starr, M. F., & McCavitt, W. E. (1995). *Electronic media management* (3rd ed.). Boston: Focal Press.

REFERENCES

Atkins, D. (1925) *The measurement of economic value.* San Francisco: Gelber, Lilienthal, Inc.

Bates, B. J. (1988). The impact of deregulation on TV station prices. *Journal of Media Economics, 1(1),* 5–22.

Bates, B. J. (1993). Concentration in local television markets. *Journal of Media Economics, 6(3),* 3–21.

Bates, B. J. (1995). What's a station worth? Models for determining radio station value. *Journal of Media Economics, 8*(1), 13–23.

Compaine, B. M. (1981). Shifting boundaries in the information marketplace. *Journal of Communication, 31*(1), 132–142.

Condon, B. (1996). Radio daze. *Forbes, 158(4),* 45.

Ferguson, C. E. (1972). *Microeconomic theory* (3rd ed.). Homewood IL: Irwin.

Fink, C. C. (1988). *Strategic newspaper management.* Carbondale: Southern Illinois University Press.

Fitzgerald, M. (1990, June 23). Evaluating an alternative paper. *Editor & Publisher,* pp. 24, 47.

Fitzgerald, M. (1995, January 7). All things to all people. *Editor & Publisher,* pp. 11–14.

Garneau, G. (1989, December 9). It's a seller's market. *Editor & Publisher,* pp. 11, 47.

Independent TV stations attractive to buyers. (1990, July 2). *Broadcasting,* pp. 45–46.

Kelly, K. J. (1995, March). Publisher profits driving up prices. *Advertising Age's Business Marketing,* p. 23.

Krasnow, E. G., Bentley, J. G., & Martin, R. B. (1991). *Buying or building a broadcast station in the 1990s* (3rd ed.). Washington, DC: National Association of Broadcasters.

Levin, H. J. (1975). Franchise values, merit programming, and policy options in television broadcasting. In R. E. Caves & M. J. Roberts (Eds.), *Regulating the product: Quality and variety* (pp. 221–247). Cambridge, MA: Ballinger.

Moshavi, S. D. (1992, February 10). Cable makes a comeback. *Broadcasting,* pp. 20–24.

Neuharth, A. (1989). *Confessions of an SOB.* New York: Doubleday.

Rima, I. H. (1972). *Development of economic analysis.* Homewood, IL: Irwin.

Schneider, A. J., & Peterson, M. O. (1990). Lending to the cable television industry. *Journal of Commercial Bank Lending, 72(6)*, 33–46.

Shaw, C. (1987, July/August). Aggressive foreign buyers bid up values for trade magazine and book publishers. *Buyouts and Acquisitions*, pp. 21–22.

Smith, A. (1937). *An inquiry into the nature and causes of the wealth of nations*. New York: Modern Library.

Station & cable trading. (1997, February 3). *Broadcasting*, pp. 18–48.

5

Mergers and Acquisitions: A Communications Industry Overview

Gary W. Ozanich
Access Media International (USA) Inc.

Michael O. Wirth
University of Denver

In recent years there has been substantial merger and acquisition activity in the communications industry. This activity has been based on the continued strong performance and perceived future prospects of this business sector, substantial barriers to entry, the continued trend toward technological convergence, a relaxation of regulatory policy, and the availability of capital to finance the transactions. These transactions are significant to considerations of firm conduct and performance on both an economic and First Amendment basis. This chapter provides an overview of this communications industry merger and acquisition activities and a discussion of their significance.

For the purposes of this analysis, the *communications industry* is defined as those companies that either directly or indirectly own and operate broadcast stations or broadcast networks, program production and distribution facilities, cable television systems, newspaper, magazine or book publishers, and telecommunications service providers. This broad definition is required due to the continued trend of technological convergence and associated competition, as well as increasing vertical and horizontal integration which has resulted from so-called "mega-mergers."

Mergers and acquisitions (M&A) are essentially a capital allocation decision where the purchasing company acquires operating assets for the purpose of growth. This decision is made within the context of overall corporate development and strategic planning. Similar to all capital budgeting decisions, the criteria applied to this process are return on invested capital analyses (Brearly & Myers, 1991). In a merger or acquisition, the purchaser is going outside the company for investment purposes. For example, Disney Company acquired Capital Cities/ABC instead of developing its own network from scratch.

Due to electromagnetic spectrum management and public utility regulation, communications companies have historically held a special place in public policy and have subsequently been subject to a unique degree of regulation. These policies have been critical in shaping M&A activities. Although these sets of policies largely define the structure of the marketplace, communication companies are not unique financial organizations. Thus, communication companies are well suited for examination via established theories and methodologies of finance.

OVERVIEW OF MERGERS AND ACQUISITIONS

In the broadest sense M&As involve the combining of all or part of two companies. The distinction between a merger and an acquisition is the means by which the transaction is accomplished (Abahoonie & Brenner, 1994). It is also worth noting that a joint venture represents another distinct form of deal structure that can allow a limited form of combination between two companies.

The technical distinction between a merger and an acquisition can be complex. In a merger transaction, two companies are combined into one company that assumes all assets and liabilities of both companies. In an acquisition, one company buys the common stock of another, thereby assuming ownership. In some cases, a company purchases all or a portion of a second company's operating assets instead of the common stock in a transaction referred to as an asset acquisition.

In the United States, the annual volume of M&A activity has varied greatly, although the activity can be described as having occurred in "waves" (Boisi & Essig, 1994). Macroeconomic factors have an obvious effect on M&A activity. Interest rates, inflation, and their volatility are the most important variables in valuation models. They affect the return on capital as well as the ability to secure financing. Business cycle factors must be considered in forecasts and are critical to valuation and deal structure.

These waves of activity are also tied to shifts in valuation methodologies. In the 1960s the focus was on income statements, resulting in M&As designed to bolster earnings per share. In the inflationary 1970s, the focus became balance sheets and the acquisition of assets at less than book value or replacement cost. In the 1980s and 1990s, the market discovered cash flow and mergers and acquisition were undertaken from valuations based on operating cash flow (earnings before interest, taxes, depreciation, and amortization—EBITDA; Boisi & Essig, 1 994). This last factor, an emphasis on cash flow, greatly changed the way in which communication companies were viewed and led to a substantial increase in transactions involving these companies.

Just as valuation methods evolved over time, so did investor sophistication and the associated ability to find new methods of finance. The M&A market changed dramatically in the 1980s with the advent of highly leveraged transactions (HLTs) financed through the use of high-yield or "junk" bonds and senior credit facilities provided by commercial banks.[1]

Table 5.1 provides a summary of aggregate domestic M&A activity in the United States during the period from 1980 to 1995 and a summary of M&A activity involving the communications industry during that same period.

The fundamental reason to undertake a merger or acquisition is economic gain. In other words, two firms combined are worth more than the sum of each individual firm, or the classic argument of synergy, $1 + 1 > 2$. In financial terms, the net present value of the gain associated with the combination must exceed the cost of the transaction to the acquiring company. Further, the price paid must be lower than the total resources necessary for the internal development of a comparable asset. For example, the discounted value of the future cash flow from the assets of ABC/Capital Cities when combined with Disney was viewed by Disney's board of

TABLE 5.1

1981–1995 Domestic Mergers and Acquisitions

Year	Total Domestic Valuation	Total Domestic Number of Deals	Communications Industry Valuation	Communications Industry Number of Deals
1981	59,272.3	816	1,946.3	30
1982	62,558.4	1,606	4,449.3	65
1983	77,168.9	2,669	2,988.9	125
1984	158,434.8	3,053	7,960.7	175
1985	148,754.2	1,979	10,193.0	114
1986	224,204.4	2,754	26,763.1	227
1987	196,459.2	2,869	19,659.5	206
1988	275,133.4	3,376	21,874.8	275
1989	298,716.1	4,338	31,860.6	341
1990	191,939.5	4,853	35,191.2	276
1991	133,620.1	4,201	23,640.0	253
1992	121,565.6	4,425	12,426.4	238
1993	175,765.5	4,805	20,406.0	298
1994	278,150.2	5,880	61,347.2	395
1995	254,949.1	4,705	59,044.6	373
	2,656,691.7	52,329	339,751.6	3,391

Note. Valuations = $Millions. From Securities Data Company. Reprinted with permission.

---

[1]High-yield or "junk bonds" are securities that are assigned a rating by a nationally recognized agency which is less than investment grade. This is a rating that is lower than Baa3 by Moody's and BBB- by Standard & Poors.

directors as being greater than the cost of the acquisition, and the cost of acquisition lower than developing a similar network internally.

The decision to undertake a merger or acquisition has become a function of the strategic planning and corporate development processes (Weston, 1994). Given the dynamic nature of business, the long-term survival of any corporation depends on its ability to develop strengths compared to its rivals. This often involves shifting corporate resources from maturing businesses into emerging opportunities. This is particularly true of the communications industry, which is subject to changing production and distribution technologies.

Mergers and acquisitions are often categorized as *horizontal, vertical* or *con-glomerate*. In a horizontal merger a company acquires a second company in the same or similar business. Examples of this are Telecommunications Inc. purchasing Viacom Cable, and the merger of the cellular telephone companies of NYNEX Bell Atlantic. The combined companies are expected to achieve economies of scale of operation resulting in greater efficiency or market power.

In a vertical merger, the company being acquired provides either input materials or it purchases output material from the acquiring company. This has been very common in the communications industry where there has been a perception of a software or programming shortage, or "bottleneck." Examples of vertical mergers are the Disney (software and programming) acquisition of Cap Cities/ABC (distri-bution company) and the Viacom (distribution) acquisition of Paramount Commu-nications (software and programming).

A conglomerate is a company that owns a portfolio of unrelated businesses. Thus, a conglomerate merger occurs when an acquiring company acquires another company in an unrelated business for the purpose of investment. Although not very common in the communications industry, examples of such transactions are the acquisition of CBS (program distribution) by Westinghouse (a conglomerate) and the acquisition of Madison Square Garden (software and programming) by ITT (a conglomerate). ITT has subsequently sold Madison Square Garden to Cablevision Systems Corporation.

Besides the horizontal and vertical economies, there are other economic reasons to undertake mergers and acquisitions. Tax issues are a consideration in every transaction. The economics of a merger can be partially premised on tax benefits such as sheltering earnings from taxation, the use of unused tax shields such as loss carry forwards, and the deferral of taxes through capital gains compared to ordinary income taxes. Other factors can include the acquisition of technology, and the general redeployment of surplus funds for the purpose of corporate development.

THE MERGERS AND ACQUISITION PROCESS

The actual process of undertaking and completing a merger or acquisition can be categorized into three distinct stages: the planning phase, the transaction phase, and the implementation phase (Weston, 1994). The time to successfully complete a transaction can vary greatly, but typically a merger or acquisition involving two publicly traded companies will take 6 to 9 months to close. The implementation phase, where the two companies are actually combined, can take a protracted period or occur relatively painlessly.

The internal analysis or planning phase generally begins within the context of corporate development and strategic planning. In general, this involves the question of positioning the company for long-term growth with the objective of long-term maximization of shareholder value. Once an objective is established, the question shifts to whether it should be accomplished through internal growth or though buying another company. If the determination is made to grow through acquisition, relevant acquisition criteria must be established, followed by a screening of candidates. Once a target company is identified, a price level must be established as well as a walk-away, or maximum price.

The difficult part of this internal phase is the valuation of the target company. There are three primary methods of valuation: discounted cash flow, comparable transactions, and replacement costs. In addition to valuing the target company as it currently exists, it is also necessary to forecast the performance of the combined companies once the merger occurs. Unwarranted optimism concerning future performance will mean that the acquiring company overpays for the target.

A second critical question concerns how the business transaction will be implemented. Among the issues are: Will it be a merger or acquisition? Will the target company be a subsidiary or will it be combined with other operations? Will the acquisition use pooling of assets or purchase accounting? These and other questions must be answered before a price can be placed on the bid.

The transactional phase begins when the acquiring company determines the structure of its bid for the target company. This includes whether the transaction is going to be presented as a friendly or hostile takeover as well as how it will be structured (i.e., all cash, all stock, or a combination). The terms of the offer must be communicated to the board of the target company and the shareholders of both companies. Other bidders may appear at this time.

For the target company, it is a fiduciary obligation of the board of directors to maximize shareholder value. Often the board will determine that a bid is not in the best interest of its shareholders and will turn it down. The board must consider all bonafide bids for the company. This can be a period of protracted negotiation and competing bids with complicated deal structures.

Once a tentative agreement is reached and approved by the boards of both the acquiring and target companies, an independent investment bank or accounting firm is typically contracted to provide a "fairness opinion" on the terms of the transaction. The acquiring company undertakes a "due diligence" investigation into the financial, legal and accounting activities of the target company. A tender offer is also launched to the shareholders of the target company soliciting their shares under agreed terms.

Mergers and acquisitions are subject to regulatory approval. A merger or acquisition can be blocked by the Department of Justice (DOJ) or the Federal Trade Commission (FTC) under antitrust law. As described in a later section, in some cases communication companies are subject to additional oversight from the Federal Communications Commission (FCC) and state utility commissions.

The final stage in the process is the implementation phase. The target company must be integrated with the acquiring company. This is where the theory of finance meets the reality of operations. Often the meshing of different operations and different corporate cultures produces diseconomies and unanticipated problems. However, if all goes according to plan, the combined companies become more valuable than the separate companies and the shareholders of the acquiring company are rewarded with a higher stock price. If the combination does not go according to plan, the shareholders of the acquiring company will likely face a lower stock price.

COMMUNICATIONS INDUSTRY M&A REGULATORY CONSIDERATIONS

Regulation plays a major role in determining the structure of the communications industry in the United States. It is necessary to understand the role of regulation before analyzing the specifics of M&A activity in the communications industry.

The communications industry is subject to unique regulation. This is due to four factors: (a) at the local exchange level, telecommunications service providers have historically been determined to have public utility economic cost structures; (b) mass media serve a special First Amendment role; (c) broadcasters and wireless communications companies are licensed to use a scarce resource, the electromagnetic spectrum; and (d) within at least some markets newspapers have cost structures that preclude economic competition (i.e., they are natural monopolies).

Historically, all U.S. telephone service (both local loop and long distance) was provided on a monopoly basis and regulated by state public utility commissions and the FCC. The primary reason for utilizing a public utility paradigm with respect to communication carriers was the notion that telephone service providers were natural monopolies (i.e., over the relevant range of operation, companies had a cost-based incentive to get larger such that the firm's average cost continued to decline as the firm's output increased. If true, this would make long run competition impossible). Secondary reasons for regulating via a public utility approach included (a) to guarantee universal telephone service on a national basis; (b) to insure that aggregate investment costs in a national telephone system would be minimized; and (c) to achieve a higher standard of telephone service quality. In short, telephone service was viewed as a necessity, and a competitive market approach was viewed as counter productive to achieving overall societal goals in this area.

With the passage of the 1996 Telecommunications Act, government regulators have moved away from the public utility regulatory paradigm toward a competitive model. An oligopolistic market structure (based on relatively free market competition) is already in place for long distance or interexchange carriers (IXCs). This move away from a monopolistic, public-utility approach has led Congress to pass legislation that allows for competitive entry in the provision of local-loop telephone services. As a result, a number of new competitors seem poised to challenge the current monopolies held by incumbent local exchange carriers (LECs). These include: cable companies, long-distance companies, competitive access providers, and even local power companies. Likewise, the Regional Bell Operating Companies (RBOC) are in the process of entering the long-distance business on a competitive basis. This movement toward a competitive market approach is having very significant short- and long-run impacts on merger and acquisition activity in this area. As the rules of the game are modified, entrepreneurs will move to strategically position themselves to survive given new competitive realities.

The special First Amendment role served by the media has proved to be a powerful tool with respect to preventing government regulation of the print industry. However, broadcast entrepreneurs continue to enjoy less than full First Amendment rights due to continued adherence to the theory that broadcasters are public trustees who are granted a limited privilege to use a scarce public resource (the electromagnetic spectrum). The U.S. Supreme Court has yet to determine the extent to which cable operators enjoy First Amendment rights. If it is determined that cable operators enjoy First Amendment rights similar to those possessed by the print media, regulation of cable would have to be significantly curtailed. If a broadcast regulatory model or some intermediate model is identified, much of the current approach to regulating cable will probably survive constitutional scrutiny. The recent U.S. Supreme Court decision upholding the must-carry rules (Turner Broadcasting vs. FCC, US, 1997) suggests that cable operators' First Amendment Rights will likely be governed by an intermediate First Amendment Model.

The criteria for gaining and keeping a broadcast license are of great significance to M&A activity in this area. As trustees of a scarce resource—the electromagnetic spectrum—broadcast station entrepreneurs are licensed to serve the public interest convenience, and necessity (47 U.S.C.A. Sec. 309(a)). As a result licensees are subject to periodic review (8 years for both television and radio licensees; 47 U.S.C.A. Sec. 307(d)), and any station transfer must be approved by the FCC (47 U.S.C.A. Sec. 310(d)). Most station transfers are approved without incident. However, all parties in a transfer must comply with the FCCs rules and procedures in this areas to avoid unnecessary and costly delay.

A third area of interest is cable regulation. Historically, most economists have believed that cable is a natural monopoly. As a result, very few of the nation's cable systems face direct competition from a multichannel wire line competitor. However, just as in the case of public utilities above, regulators are trying to create a more competitive local cable marketplace. Specifically, the 1996 Act allows LECs to enter the cable television business as either a traditional cable operator or as an open video system. Now that this approach has become law, cable companies are expected to lose their local monopoly positions in major markets and be forced to operate in competition with local telephone companies. Ameritech has been the most active RBOC to date with respect to launching local cable systems in competition with incumbent local cable operators. If these initial ventures are successful, direct, local wireline competition will exist in the future. Additionally, cable faces other forms of multichannel television competition from direct broadcast satellite (DBS) providers such as DirecTV, USSB (United States Satellite Broadcasting) PrimeStar and Sky, and from wireless cable operators. As with public utilities, movement away from a monopoly regulatory approach and toward a competitive approach can be expected to have a significant impact on cable merger and acquisition activity. Ultimately, increased competition increases entrepreneurial risk. Thus, cable companies can be expected to utilize varying merger and acquisition activities depending on their perception of the impact of competition on the longer term prospects for the cable marketplace.

In general, newspapers have not been subjected to extensive regulatory schemes established for broadcasting and cable. As a result, the primary regulation of newspaper M&A activity occurs through traditional antitrust oversight. The one exception is the Newspaper Preservation Act (1970), under which the U.S. Department of Justice may allow two directly competing same market daily newspapers to form a joint operating agreement (JOA) for the purpose of combining their business operations while preserving their editorial independence. Because the premise of the policy is the Failing Firm Doctrine, the Justice Department must determine that one of the two newspapers would exit the market in the absence of a JOA in order to approve the merger as a permissible exception to the antitrust laws.

In addition to the general regulatory considerations discussed here, a number of FCC ownership rules have had a significant impact on the structure of the marketplace under which media M&A activity has occurred. Of most immediate concern is the FCC's regulation of television and radio station ownership. Such regulation has taken three primary forms: limits on aggregate or national ownership (i.e., multiple ownership); limits in local markets (i.e., duopoly and cross-media ownership); and limits on network interest in program ownership and distribution. It is the relaxation of these rules during the past several years that has led to a substantial increase in merger and acquisition activity and increased industry consolidation. In particular, the rescinding of the FCC's financial interest and syndication rules paved the way for many large transactions by allowing for vertical integration between television networks and program production and distribution interests. Likewise, Congress' liberalization of the Radio Duopoloy Rules and its elimination of a cap on the number of radio stations an entrepreneur can own nationally has lead to an explosion of merger and acquisition activity in this segment.

Although the media (particularly broadcast and cable) are subject to national and local ownership constraints, limitations on cross media ownership and some limitations on vertical integration, the foci of these constraints are on who the purchaser is, not on the nature of the transaction. Thus, the transfer of media properties, whether through an acquisition or merger, is not subject to any additional special considerations. An example of this was a review by the FCC of a request by Storer Communications to intercede during a hostile tender offer to the company's shareholders by an outside company. Storer management requested intercession based on financial disruption and the Public Interest Standard. In this case, the FCC acted to prevent Storer from insulating itself from the challenge and remained neutral during the proxy challenge (Storer Communications Inc., 1985).

COMMUNICATIONS INDUSTRY M&As

The data concerning communications industry transactions are difficult to delineate. Many transactions may be between privately held companies where there is no requirement of public disclosure. In addition, if nonpublic securities (i.e., Rule 144A Private Placements) are used to finance the transactions, no public documents or details may be filed with the SEC. Finally, the definition of media or communications industry varies greatly by data collector.

According to Securities Data Corporation, (and as depicted in Table 5.1), the communications industry accounted for a significant portion of M&A activity during the period from 1981 to 1995. Using Census Bureau SIC Codes for the publishing (newspaper publishing, books and periodicals), telecommunications (cable, broadcast, telecommunication services) and motion pictures (motion picture production and distribution) industries as the identifying variables, the value of communications industry transactions accounted for 12.8% of merger and acquisition activity during the period.

As depicted in the table, the volume and number of transaction have varied over time. As described, major factors driving mergers and acquisitions in the communications industry are technology, availability of capital, and the relaxation of regulation. Perhaps most apparent in the data is the role regulatory liberalization has played. This is apparent from the pickup in the telecommunications sector (broadcast) following the relaxation of station ownership limits in 1992, and the substantial activity in 1995 following the abolishment of the financial interest and syndication rules.

The role that capital availability has played is also apparent in the data. The high-rolling days of junk-bond financing are apparent from the increase in transactions during the mid-to-late 1980s. The downturn during the early 1990s is correlated with an economic slowdown and tighter bank lending policies, followed by a pickup in the mid-1990s, a period of low interest rates and plentiful capital available from the banks and the capital markets.

Table 5.2 identifies merger and acquisition activity by industry groups. The substantial increase in telecommunications industry transactions during the mid-1980s was partially due to the consolidation of the cable television industry following its introduction and initial diffusion earlier in the decade. A similar pattern has occurred with the consolidation of the cellular telephone industry in the early 1990s following its startup phase. Such consolidation is a typical occurrence as companies in relatively new industries combine to capture economies of scale, as companies with superior management acquire less well run companies, and as entrepreneurs "cashout." Finally, technological convergence is probably the single greatest factor driving these activities during the last decade. Mergers and acquisi-

TABLE 5.2

1981–1995 Mergers and Acquisitions By Communications Industry Type*

Year	Publishing Industry Valuation	Publishing Industry Number of Deals	Telecom- munications Industry Valuation	Telecom- munications Industry Number of Deals	Motion Picture Industry Valuation	Motion Picture Industry Number of Deals
1981	254.8	7	1,311.5	22	380.0	1
1982	153.3	21	3,465.4	41	830.6	4
1983	625.2	27	1,847.0	94	516.7	4
1984	2,559.8	47	5,267.2	125	133.7	3
1985	2,471.3	36	7,183.7	72	538.0	6
1986	5,38.9	85	17,747.9	117	3,633.3	25
1987	3,544.0	74	10,706.1	113	5,409.4	19
1988	9,201.1	93	11,229.7	159	1,444.0	23
1989	7,134.2	111	17,510.2	200	7,216.2	30
1990	3,215.0	96	15,332.2	157	16,644.0	23
1991	3,045.0	85	12,256.3	137	8,338.7	31
1992	689.9	58	10,434.1	159	1,302.4	21
1993	4,439.5	75	12,279.3	186	3,687.2	37
1994	4,13.3	76	48,358.4	290	8,857.5	29
1995	1,449.8	79	51,650.2	218	5,944.6	23
Total	48,296.1	970	226,579.2	2,090	64,876.3	279

Note. Valuation = $Millions.
*Publishing consists of newspaper, periodicals, and books; telecommunications consists of telephone communications, two-radio telephone, radio, television, and cable television; motion pictures consists of motion picture production and distribution, and retail distribution.

tions are the logical manifestation of the redeployment of resources made by companies whose product and geographic markets are undergoing near constant redefinition.

During the past several years many communications industry transactions were "megadeals." These transactions were for companies carrying very high valuations. Table 5.3 provides a summary of the largest M&A transactions in the communications industry. These megadeals have attracted great attention from the press, public, and regulators. They have raised concerns about concentration of power and its implication for both economic and editorial power. This trend toward concentration of ownership into large media companies has been rationalized by the need for gigantic scope and size in order to compete in the currently unfolding global marketplace, and also to take advantage of economics of vertical integration (i.e., owning the distribution channel into the home as well as intellectual property or software).

Besides these megadeals there have been thousands of other communications industry mergers and acquisitions. There are a multitude of reasons for individual transactions. In many cases, the reasons for a merger or acquisition are firm or market specific. However, in a general sense, the factors driving the transactions are the same factors that drive any mergers and acquisitions in any other industry—namely, the purchase of or combination with the assets of another company for the purpose of growth.

TABLE 5.3

The Largest Communications Industry Mergers and Acquisition Transactions

Transaction	Valuation
Bell Atlantic/NYNEX	$23.0
Disney/Capital Cities–ABC	19.0
AT&T/McCaw/Cellular	18.9
SBC Communications/Pacific Telesis	16.7
U.S. West Cellular/Airtouch	13.5
NYNEX Cellular/Bell Atlantic Cellular	13.0
U.S. West/Continental Cablevision	11.8
Viacom/Paramount Communications	9.7
Viacom/Blockbuster	7.7
Time Warner/Turner Broadcasting	7.5
Matsushita/MCA	6.5
General Electric/RCA	6.2
CBS/Westinghouse	5.4

Note. Valuation = $ billions.

CONCLUSION

Although subject to unique regulatory constraints concerning aggregate ownership, cross ownership, and vertical integration, communication industry companies lend themselves to traditional financial analysis. Similar to any other company, merger and acquisition activity is a capital budgeting decision that is an alternative to internal investment.

In recent years, merger and acquisition activity in the communications industry has been driven by technological change, the liberalization of regulations governing ownership, and the ready availability of capital. Technology has played a role through the introduction of competition due to new distribution channels, a trend toward the convergence of technologies, and the rise of truly global companies. Regulatory liberalization has spurred transactions as broadcast ownership limits were relaxed and as the financial interest and syndication rules were rescinded by the FCC. Owing to its growth and cash flow characteristics, the communications industry has been an extremely attractive investment to bankers and investors. This has provided a ready source of capital to finance merger and acquisition activity.

The substantial increase in merger and acquisition activity, in and of itself, is of minimal policy concern. However, the resulting concentration of ownership, vertical integration, and rise of the megacompanies may have serious implications for both the advertising and information content markets. Existing antitrust policies provide an adequate framework for dealing with these considerations, but it is important to temper the expectation of the efficacy of these policies with the dynamic nature of technology and the inherently political nature of the communications industry.

FURTHER READING

Brearly, R. A., & Myers, S. C. (1991). *Principals of corporate finance* (4th ed.). New York: McGraw-Hill.

Fraser, L. M. (1995). *Understanding financial statements* (4th ed.). Englewood Cliffs: Prentice-Hall.

Investment Dealer's Digest (weekly publication). New York: IDD Information Services.

Rock, M. L., Rock, R. H., & Sikora, M. (1994). *Mergers & acquisition handbook* (2nd ed.). New York: McGraw-Hill.

Veronis, Suhler & Associates (annual publication). *Communications industry report*. New York: Author.

REFERENCES

Abahoonie, E. J., & Brenner, J. S. (1994). Tax planning for mergers and Acquisitions. In M. L. Rock, R. H. Rock, & M. Sikora (Eds.), *Mergers & acquisition handbook* (2nd ed., pp. 219–226). New York: McGraw-Hill.

Boisi, G.T., & Essig, E. M. (1994) Development of the M&A Market. In M. L. Rock, R. H. Rock, & M. Sikora (Eds.), pp. 15–26). *Mergers & acquisitions handbook* (2nd ed.), New York: McGraw-Hill.

Brearly, R. A., & Myers, S. C. (1991). *Principals of corporate finance* (4th ed.). New York: McGraw-Hill.

Cable Television Consumer Protection and Competition Act of 1992, Pub. L. No. 102-385, 106 Stat. 1460, 1465 (1992) (codified as amended at 47 U.S.C. pp. 521–555).

Newspaper Preservation Act. (1970). 15 U.S.C.A. Sec. 1801 et. seq.

Storer Communications Inc.(1985). *Shareholder's proxy statement.* Washington, DC: Securities and Exchange Commission.

Weston, J. F. (1994). The payoff in mergers and acquisitions. In M. L. Rock, R. H. Rock, & M. Sikora (Eds.), *Mergers & acquisition* (2nd ed., pp. 51–76) New York: McGraw-Hill.

Part II

Industries and Practices

6

The Economics of the Daily Newspaper Industry

Robert G. Picard
California State University, Fullerton

The newspaper industry is the second oldest mass-media industry in the United States, surpassed slightly by the book industry, and is now more than three centuries old. During its history, the newspaper industry has evolved to play important social and economic roles and now accounts for approximately $40 billion in advertising and circulation sales annually.

The mission of newspaper enterprises includes both commercial and social facets. Like most other media, newspapers play important roles as facilitators of commerce, promoting consumption by creating consumer wants for products through advertising, and serving the financial interests of newspaper owners as part of the competitive economic system. Newspapers, however, play a greater role as facilitators of social and political expression than other media. As a result, newspaper firms tend to emphasize conveyence of information and ideas about contemporary events and issues to a greater degree than other media that are more entertainment oriented. The mission of newspapers affects the structure of the industry and economic decisions made by managers.

The newspaper industry is the most profitable of all media industries and one of the most profitable of all manufacturing industries in the country. In order to produce its product, the newspaper industry combines technology (the capability for production), information gathering and packaging services, and financial support from advertisers and readers to produce a perishable product that is usable by literate audiences and whose usefulness to most consumers diminishes within a day. A variety of unique economic characteristics distinguish newspapers from other media. This chapter explores the industry and the impact of those characteristics on its operations and structure.

NEWSPAPER FIRMS AND MARKETS

The newspaper industry in the United States is characterized by monopoly and its attendant market power. Of the country's 1,538 daily newspapers in 1995, 96% existed as the only paper published in their markets. In addition, noncompeting local newspapers existed in 43 cities, with 26 cities served by joint monopolies in which a morning and evening paper were owned by the same company and 17 cities served by formerly competing newspapers in joint operating agreements (Busterna, 1988c; *Editor & Publisher International Yearbook*, 1995; *Facts About Newspapers '95*, 1995).

Only 38 newspapers existed in cities with competing locally produced newspapers. Where competition exists, it nearly always occurs between differentiated newspapers such as a broadsheet and a tabloid intended for different audiences or between papers that target substantially different geographic markets than their competitors.

The markets for most papers are the retail trading zones in which they exist. A national market is relevant for papers that circulate throughout the country and have the majority of their circulation outside the city of main publication. The national newspaper market in the United States includes papers such as *The Wall Street Journal, USA Today, Christian Science Monitor*, and *Journal of Commerce*. This national list is usually supplemented with *The New York Times*, which gains only about a quarter of its circulation in the national market, but is included because of its standing as the national newspaper of record (see Table 6.1). Because the national market includes a number of newspapers, publishers have differentiated their products to appeal to special segments of the audience so that there are greater differences between national newspapers than in those local markets in which more than one newspaper exists.

The nation's daily newspapers are primarily evening publications, with only one-third of the nation's papers publishing in the morning. Despite the higher number of evening papers, circulation nationally is split almost evenly between morning and evening papers because the majority of large circulation metropolitan papers publish in the morning.

TABLE 6.1
Daily Circulation of Nationally Circulated Newspapers

Rank	Newspaper	Circulation
1	Wall Street Journal	1,783,532
2	USA Today	1,675,091[a]
3	New York Times	1,071,120
4	Christian Science Monitor	97,170

Note. [a]From Monday through Thursday circulation.

A tidal wave of afternoon newspaper deaths taking place in the time between World War II and the 1980s, in which about 20% of all afternoon papers closed, led many observers to incorrectly assume that afternoon papers were becoming economically unviable and relics of the past. The deaths, however, were primarily among secondary newspapers and more attributable to advertisers' preferences for the largest paper in a town than the publication time (Benjaminson, 1984; Picard, Winter, McCombs, & Lacy, 1988).

In recent decades, advertisers have increasingly come to view newspapers as means of reaching mass audiences, rather than as means of reaching segmented audiences that were once available when multiple papers existed. Today, advertisers use other media—particularly radio, magazines, and cablecasts—to segment audiences and rely on newspapers, a print medium, for reaching mass audiences. In large local markets, some newspapers have begun to segment portions of their markets in geographic terms by providing cost-saving zoned editions that appeal most to local retail stores that serve customers only in a small portion of the entire newspaper's market and to classified advertisers only interested in reaching nearby readers.

The general reliance on newspapers as a mass medium by national and large advertisers has created a systemic economic problem that makes it nearly impossible for competing papers to survive. When more than one paper exists in a market, the secondary paper is disadvantaged because a disproportionate amount of advertising is given to the leading paper, regardless of how closely the second paper approximates its circulation (Picard, 1988b; Udell, 1978).

This "circulation elasticity of demand" (Corden, 1953, p. 182) creates an impetus toward failure known as the "circulation spiral." The paper with the largest circulation in a market has financial and economic advantages that enable it to increase advertising and circulation sales by attracting customers from the smaller paper. As the leading paper attracts more circulation, it attracts more advertising, which in turn attracts more circulation, trapping the secondary paper in a circulation spiral that ultimately leads to its demise (Engwall, 1981; Furhoff, 1973; Gustafsson, 1978).

Although several hundred daily newspapers died in the past four decades, an aggregate loss of only about 12% of the number of U.S. daily newspapers occurred because dying metropolitan papers were generally replaced with newspapers established in suburban communities that were created by migration out of major cities. Although it is popular to attribute the large number of closures to large metropolitan markets, the majority of newspaper deaths occurred because of the shakeout of secondary and joint monopoly papers in small and midsized markets.

In addition to daily publication, traditionally meaning Monday through Friday or Monday through Saturday publication, Sunday publication is important. Only about half of the newspapers in the country publish Sunday editions. Data on Sunday publication is reported separately in circulation reports because some advertisers and readers are interested only in Sunday sales.

The average newspaper's circulation is relatively small. In fact, about 85% of the nation's newspapers have circulations below 50,000 daily. Almost 70% of all newspapers have circulations below 25,000 daily, and only 1% of the papers have circulations exceeding 500,000 daily *(Editor & Publisher International Yearbook,* 1996).

The newspaper industry has experienced significantly increased economic concentration, and the amount of concentration found increases rapidly as the size of the market decreases. The term *concentration* refers to "the degree of market control enjoyed by the largest firms in an industry" (Heilbroner & Thurow, 1981, p. 646), and is measured by the total sales or assets of the top companies as a percentage of the total sales or assets of the industry as a whole. Definitions of the particular market under consideration are critical when considering concentration. The national market (that is, the market for nationally circulated newspapers) has been shown to be moderately concentrated and local markets are highly concentrated. Even in the largest markets, single-firm concentration surpasses 50% (Picard, 1988a).

When discussing the newspaper industry, the term *monopoly* is used to describe situations in which there is only one paper published in the market or in which joint monopolies exist. The term *competition* is often incorrectly applied to situations in which more than one paper exists, because situations in which two papers exist are *not* competitive in the economic sense but are more correctly labeled *duopolies.* In situations in which two or more papers exist, the papers often exhibit characteristics of *oligopoly* and *monopolistic competition* rather than competition in the economic sense (Litman, 1988). The nature of individual firms' responses to initiatives of competing firms is used in making such structural and behavioral distinctions.

The prospects for altering such concentration are poor, because barriers to entry in markets for existing papers are very high because of costs, advertiser preferences, and the unique properties of the local daily newspaper (Wirth, 1986). These monopoly situations can be expected to remain relatively intact absent unusually aggressive monopolistic behavior by the existing paper.

Financial Performance

The newspaper industry continues to be one of the most profitable industries in the nation, as well as one of the most profitable among communications industries. Throughout the 1980s, public newspaper firms averaged 17% pretax operating margins and asset growth of about 16% annually *(Communications Industry Report,* annual). Those numbers declined due to the recession in the early 1990s, but have been moving back toward the midteens since that time.

Increasing commercialization of the press after World War II, along with the growth of local newspaper monopolies, increased the profitability of the industry and led to the establishment of large newspaper groups and media conglomerates. These developments have led to extensive discussions of concentration of ownership, meaning the number of papers owned by the largest newspaper chains and media conglomerates and the amount of total daily circulation controlled by these major firms (Bagdikian, 1993; Compaine, Sterling, Guback, & Noble, Jr., 1982; Ghiglione, 1984).

The major newspaper companies are now among the largest corporations in the nation. The Gannett Co., for example, has assets totaling more than $6.4 billion, Tribune Co. has $3.7 billion, Times Mirror Co. has $3.5 billion and Knight-Ridder Inc. has assets of $2.9 billion (*Newspaper Stocks Report Annual Report Comparison, 1996*). Although not the size of firms such as General Motors, General Electric, IBM, and Exxon, the major newspaper companies rank 100 to 150 in terms of assets, in the range of companies such as Colgate-Palmolive, General Mills, Kimberly-Clark, Northrup, and Ralston-Purina.

Today, 105 U.S. dailies each are owned by Hollinger International, 92 by the Gannett Co., and 65 by Thompson Newspapers. Five other firms own 24 or more daily papers and 23 companies own more than 12 dailies (see Table 6.2 for the top 10 chains). Of the nation's newspapers, only one fourth are not owned by newspaper groups. For the most part, these are small newspapers whose profitability does not appeal to groups. Only a few iconoclastic publishers and newspaper families have managed to keep larger papers independent. Nearly 85% of the nation's daily newspaper circulation belongs to papers owned by newspaper groups. Table 6.3 reports the top newspaper firms by the amount of circulation each represents.

Newspaper groups enjoy the results of their profitable holdings. During the 1980s, companies such as Thomson and Dow Jones averaged about 30% pretax operating margins, Gannett Co. about 25%, Times Mirror about 16%, and Knight-

TABLE 6.2
10 Largest Newspaper Chains By Number of Papers Owned

Rank	Company	Number of Dailies
1	Hollinger International	105
2	Gannett	92
3	Thompson	65
4	Donrey	51
5	Morris Communications	32
6	Knight-Ridder	31
7	Freedom	26
8	Newhouse	25
9	MediaNews	25
10	Dow Jones	22

Note. From *Facts About Newspapers '95* (1995). ©1995 by Newspaper Association of America. Reprinted with permission.

TABLE 6.3

Daily Circulation of the Largest Newspaper Companies, 1996

Rank	Company	Circulation Total[a]	% of National Total
1	Gannett Co.	5,840,635	10.2
2	Knight-Ridder Nprs.	3,420,018	6.1
3	Newhouse Nprs.	2,811,832	4.9
4	Dow Jones & Co.	2,361,445	4.1
	Times Mirror Co.	2,314,303	4.1
6	New York Times Co.	2,278,094	4.0
7	Hearst Newspapers	1,743,510	3.1
8	Thompson Nprs.	1,338,567	2.4
9	Hollinger Internation	1,283,192	2.3
10	Tribune Co.	1,270,623	2.2

Note. Percentage calculated by author. From *Facts About Newspapers '97* (1997). ©1997 by Newspaper Association of America. Reprinted with permission.
[a]based on the average for 6 months ending September 30, 1996.

Ridder about 17%. To achieve such overall results, some of the most profitable companies expected their individual papers to achieve returns on sales of as much as 45% and 50%. By the mid-1990s, those margins and returns had declined about 17%, but the companies still produced margins and returns well above those for traditional manufacturing companies.

The high demand for newspapers by chains has pushed the values of papers consistently upward during the past two decades. A variety of methods for establishing the worth of a newspaper exist, but common formulas include circulation-based valuations based on $50 per subscriber and revenue or earnings-based valuations, such as 3.5 times gross revenue or 11 to 20 times earnings before interest and taxes. Purchase prices for larger papers often are much higher, depending on the willingness and ability of different newspaper companies to pay high prices in any given year. During the 1980s, purchase prices of $150 million to $300 million for large papers were not uncommon. Because of the recession and the unavailability of major papers, those numbers declined to the $100 million to $200 million range in the 1990s.

CONSUMERS OF NEWSPAPER PRODUCTS

Daily newspapers sell not one but two products (Corden, 1953; Reddaway, 1963), thus participating in what is called a *dual product market*, which includes sales of the newspaper to readers and sales of advertising (Picard, 1989). The tangible newspaper product is the information packaged and delivered in the form of the newspaper, information that includes news, features, and advertising. The second product sold is access to the newspaper purchasers, and advertisers purchase space as a means of conveying their information to the reader.

Circulation sales have an effect on advertising sales because the desirability of a paper to advertisers normally increases as circulation rises and decreases as circulation decreases. Readers find papers more desirable when they contain significant advertising because ads provides useful and wanted commercial information. Today, about two-thirds of the content of the average newspaper is advertising and a good portion of the nonnews editorial matter, such as articles in food and lifestyle sections, are devoted to promoting sales and use of products available from advertisers.

This interplay between the two newspaper product/service markets, the greater dependency on advertising than circulation sales, and differences in how fluctuations in the circulation submarkets affect advertising submarkets make the industry particularly complex.

Circulation

Although newspaper profits have risen in recent decades, consumer demand for newspaper circulation has been declining steadily. Newspaper sales grew from approximately 53 million copies daily in 1950 to 62.3 million in 1990, an 18.9% increase (*Facts About Newspapers '91, 1991*), but the nation's population increased by nearly 100 million persons during the same period (a 70% increase). As a result, penetration of newspapers declined from 37.9% to a worrisome 26.3% percent of the population during the same period. From 1990 to 1995, circulation declined 3.2 million (about 5%), primarily due to the loss of evening editions of morning papers (*Facts About Newspapers '95*, 1995).

About 20% of all newspapers charge $.25 for single daily copies today, and more than half charge $.35 for single copies. Prices charged for Sunday papers have increased rapidly in recent years. Nearly all the nation's largest papers charge $1.50, medium-sized papers charge $1, and smaller papers typically charge $.75. Studies in consumer behavior have shown that industrywide demand for newspaper circulation has been *inelastic* during the past three decades and is becoming more inelastic as local newspaper monopolies increase (Clark, 1976; Field, 1978; Grotta, 1977; Landau & Davenport, 1959). In other words, increasing prices for newspapers has not resulted in a decline in circulation as would be expected if elastic demand were present.

In large markets, where more than one daily may compete for the same newspaper audience, more elasticity can be expected to be found than in the overwhelming majority of one-newspaper markets. This occurs because the availability of a close substitute will result in consumers choosing that product at a lower price and thus creating elastic demand for the newspaper they have abandoned.

The ability of readers to find reasonable substitutes for a local daily newspapers is limited because newspapers are inherently local products, identified with a specific geographic market by the news and advertising conveyed about that market. Daily papers from outside the market can substitute in terms of state, national, and international information, but they do not provide substitutable local materials. Weekly and nondaily papers provide some local news, but not state, national, and international information. In addition, the range of news and advertising provided by weeklies is limited, so it is rare for consumers to substitute nondailies as information sources.

At times, readers may supplement the information and advertising in a local newspaper with a paper from outside the area. If a local paper provides only minimal national or international coverage or financial news, for instance, some of its readers may supplement the paper by also subscribing to *The New York Times* or *The Wall Street Journal*. Other readers may supplement their normal newspaper consumption by acquiring *USA Today* while traveling or to provide greater sports or entertainment coverage than they receive in their hometown paper.

Television, cable, and radio provide news and information, but the quantity and quality of their services differ and they do not serve as reasonable substitutes for newspapers for most newspaper readers. Magazines, especially weekly news magazines, provide more extensive information, but their frequency keeps newspaper readers from using them as substitutes.

Readers more than bear the cost of producing the editorial portions of newspapers. Only 16% of the cost of producing a paper is attributable to editorial or nonadvertising content, and circulation revenue accounts for 20% to 35% of newspapers' revenue (Busterna, 1988b).

Although newspapers have traditionally sought to achieve as high a circulation as possible, some newspapers in noncompetitive markets engage in profit engineering that maximizes their revenue by lowering circulation to achieve optimal output levels. This practice reduces costs and increases a newspaper's profit (Blankenburg, 1982). A newspaper selling 100,000 copies daily, with 10,000 in circulation areas far from its primary market, would achieve higher profits by selling only 90,000 copies daily if cost savings from ceasing service to customers in distant areas exceed revenues received by serving those areas. The decision to make such a change obviously would include consideration of whether it would adversely affect advertising sales. In situations in which such a change has not been expected to significantly harm advertising revenue, newspaper managers have chosen to voluntarily reduce circulation.

Advertising

Demand for newspaper advertising space has been more consistent than demand for advertising space and time in other media. Newspapers receive about 27% of all dollars spent for advertising (see Table 6.4), the largest amount devoted to any

TABLE 6.4
Newspaper Industry Shares of Total Advertising Expenditures

Year	Total Expenditures	Newspaper Expenditures	Newspaper Share
1981	$61,510,000,000	$17,420,000,000	28.3%
1982	$66,580,000,000	$17,694,000,000	26.6%
1983	$75,850,000,000	$20,582,000,000	27.1%
1984	$87,820,000,000	$23,522,000,000	26.8%
1985	$94,800,000,000	$25,482,000,000	26.6%
1986	$102,100,000,000	$26,990,000,000	26.4%
1987	$109,650,000,000	$29,412,000,000	26.8%
1988	$118,442,000,000	$31,197,000,000	26.3%
1989	$123,930,000,000	$32,368,000,000	26.1%
1990	$129,480,000,000	$32,280,000,000	24.9%
1991	$126,340,000,000	$30,349,000,000	24.0%
1992	$131,737,000,000	$30,639,000,000	23.3%
1993	$137,924,000,000	$31,869,000,000	23.1%
1994	$150,004,000,000	$34,109,000,000	22.8%
1995	$160,695,000,000	$36,092,000,000	22.5%
1996	$172,804,000,000[a]	$38,170,000,000[a]	22.1%[a]

Note. From *Facts About Newspaper '97* (1997). ©1997 by Newspaper Association of America. Reprinted with permission.
[a]Preliminary estimates.

one medium. Advertising expenditures in newspapers have grown from $1.16 billion in 1946 to $38 billion in 1996. When adjusted for inflation, the figures indicate that newspapers get five times more advertising revenue today than they did at the end of World War II.

Three major categories of advertising are published in newspapers: national advertising from large companies with business outlets or products distributed throughout the country; retail advertising (sometimes called display advertising) from local businesses making retail sales for goods and services; and classified advertising, small ads by businesses and individuals that are divided into categories by the type of goods or services offered or sought.

Nonprice issues significantly affect advertiser demand, which varies because of the day of the week, seasons, general business climate, and changes in the demographics of readers. Demand for space by retail advertisers is relatively inelastic with regard to price, except in larger markets in which substitute media are most prevalent. Demand is especially sensitive to price changes when there is another competing daily available and its audience demographics are similar and the disparity in circulation between the two papers is not great. There appears to be little cross-elasticity of demand in national advertising between newspapers and other media, because national advertisers make the majority of their placement decisions based on campaign needs rather than price (Busterna, 1987).

More substitutability is evident in the advertising than the information product market. This means that advertisers have a greater ability to use alternative media to reach similar audiences than readers have the ability to use alternative media to receive similar information. Large advertisers that prepare preprint and other insert advertising, for example, can choose to substitute nondaily and total market coverage newspapers, or mail delivery systems, for the daily newspaper if price becomes an issue. Nondaily newspapers and other types of media do not provide a close substitute for most daily newspaper advertisers, however, because their services are not similar and their formats and demographics vary substantially.

Individual newspapers receive between 20% and 35% of their revenue from circulation, with the remainder primarily coming from advertising sales (see Table 6.5). The resource dependency on advertising revenue affects newspaper content by making the average newspaper include advertising as about two-thirds of its content. Retail (local) advertising provides about 42% of total content, classified advertising about 10%, and national ads about 8%.

TABLE 6.5
Revenues and Expenses as Approximate Average Percentages of Operating Budgets

Operating revenues		
Advertising		65–80%
Local/retail	55–60%	
Classified	20–35%	
National	10–15%	
Circulation		20–35%
Operating expenses		
Editorial	7–10%	
Advertising	5–6%	
Circulation	9–10%	
Promotion	1–2%	
Mechanical	13–15%	
Newsprint	15–30%	
Administration	8–12%	
Building and land	1–3%	
Operating margin		
Before taxes and interest		15–20%

Because of the relationship between circulation levels and advertising, some observers argue that any decrease in circulation will result in less advertising demand and that papers will be forced to lower advertising prices and suffer advertising revenue loss. Although this concept applies in markets with direct competition, it does not apply in the 98% of all markets that have no local newspaper competitors. In these markets, newspapers tend to set their advertising rates annually, or less frequently, and rates are only infrequently adjusted for short-term fluctuations. In addition, research has shown that newspaper publishers most often set ad rates by implementing a target-return price strategy, in which business revenue and expenses are estimated, a rate of return (the target) is selected, and the advertising price is set accordingly, or by matching industry price averages (Picard, 1982a). Advertising rates are more dependent on industry norms for papers in certain circulation size categories, the local economy, and the type of advertising than specific circulation.

COST STRUCTURE OF NEWSPAPERS

Newspaper costs can be broadly distinguished by the costs of gathering and preparing the product and the costs of printing and disseminating the paper. Newspapers have relatively high "first-copy" costs—that is, the cost for procuring and packaging the information and preparing it for printing. In this view, only one copy of a newspaper is really produced and the costs are relatively high for that copy. In the second part of the process, newspapers face costs for reproducing the product (printing) and distribution. These costs decline as economies of scale develop when the number of copies produced increases (Rosse & Dertouzous, 1979).

When considering newspaper budgets, it becomes clear that the largest contributors to newspapers' expenses are production and reproduction costs associated with the printing aspects of the business (see Table 6.5). Even excluding overhead costs, expenses for "back-shop" activities account for 30% to 35% of a newspaper's operating expenses, and about half of that cost is attributable to newsprint costs alone. Administration (absorbing overhead costs), circulation, and editorial costs each contribute about 10% each to operating expenses.

Analyses of newspapers' cost structures and the impact of first copy and production expenses are given more specificity and strengthened if they are broken down into fixed and variable costs categories. *Fixed costs* are those for production that are not changed in the short run when the amount of product produced is increased or decreased (Litman, 1988). In the newspaper industry, fixed costs are generally accepted to be the nonprinting costs, such as the costs for facilities and equipment and the general costs of operating a newspaper (Corden, 1953).

Variable costs are those that change in direct relation to the amount of product, and such costs are well recognized in newspaper accounting (*Standard Chart of*

Accounts for Newspapers, 1979). The two most significant contributors to variable costs are ink and newsprint, and other important variable costs include plates and related production supplies and advertising commissions. If the number of pages changes or the amount of copies produced changes, these become important in calculating costs.

In considering short-run costs, one assumes that increasing the number of papers produced or the number of pages produced for an issue does not increase fixed costs by requiring facilities or press expansion; more administrative, advertising, or editorial personnel; more supplies or equipment; or any combination thereof.

Variable costs are affected if a change is made in the number of copies produced or the number of pages produced. If the number of copies changes, a newspaper experiences additional costs for newsprint, ink, and printing supplies, and it may incur larger costs for production and circulation labor and for circulation supplies.

Some observers have asserted that the weighting of costs toward the production side of the newspaper industry has been a primary impetus toward monopoly. It has been argued that *scale economies* are the single most important determinant of newspaper monopoly (Rosse, 1967). This view ultimately leads some to the conclusion that newspapers have the characteristics of *natural monopolies*. A natural monopoly is said to exist when ever-continuing economies of scale create conditions in which the growth of a firm makes it more efficient, lowers costs, results in competitors leaving the market and, inevitably, creates a perfect monopoly (Gill, 1975, p. 464). In such a situation, there is only one firm providing the newspaper in a market, and it controls the entire market for the good or service and can exercise great market power (Litman, 1988). The view that scale economies make newspapers natural monopolies, however, ignores the impact of large advertisers' normal practice of choosing to place ads in only one newspaper in a market, a policy that denies secondary newspapers revenues and promotes its circulation spiral and death.

Some observers have asserted that newspapers enjoy sharply falling average costs and relatively constant marginal costs of reproduction that result in nearly continuous economies of scale (Rosse, 1967; Rosse & Dertouzous, 1979). Because of high fixed and relatively low variable costs, a newspaper might be able to produce 10,000 copies of a newspaper at an average cost of $.19 each. If the fixed costs remained the same, the same paper might produce 20,000 copies at an average cost of $.14 each or 30,000 copies at $.09 each because the marginal cost (the cost of producing more papers) involves only the variable costs (ink, paper, etc.), which remain relatively constant and low on a per-copy basis.

This view of continuous economies of scale has been disputed by other researchers, who argue that this view considers costs in the short run rather than the long run, that it does not place sufficient weight on increased distribution costs, and that when average costs are considered in the long run, the constant decline is not evident because average costs for distribution rise much more quickly than evidenced in short-run analysis (Litman, 1988).

Technology

Significant changes in printing and production technology in the past three decades have altered the structure and functions of newspaper organizations. The developments of offset printing, phototypesetting, and prepress production by news and advertising personnel using computer-based equipment have altered the industry significantly.

The primary effect of new technology was a reduction in the number of personnel needed to produce a paper. Technology has allowed advertising and editorial departments to take the place of typesetters, has allowed national and international news and feature agencies to provide material in forms that no longer require typesetting, has reduced the activity necessary for laying out pages, and has simplified the printing process. These changes in technology have made it possible for contemporary newspapers to reduce personnel by one third to one half, depending on their sizes and the technology employed.

A second effect of the new technologies has been increased speed in preparing and printing the newspaper. This has been used by managers to make the content of the newspapers "fresher" because it has allowed them to shorten deadline time so that breaking news and information can be placed in a paper closer to the time the paper is distributed, thus increasing the paper's ability to compete with broadcast media in coverage of breaking news stories.

The impact of new technology on newspaper costs has been explored and indicates that economies of scale are not created equally across all sizes of newspapers (Dertouzous & Thorpe, 1982). The introduction of offset printing and phototypesetting equipment apparently reduces first-copy costs and minimum efficient scale, particularly for papers in the 10,000 to 100,000 circulation range, but the efficiencies are not equally enjoyed by papers below and above that size (Norton & Norton, 1986). The higher cost of the new technology makes some older technology more efficient for smaller papers. Larger papers often do not enjoy the same rate of cost savings because the newer technology must be specifically adapted for their requirements. Because there are fewer large papers that need the adaptations, the cost of the adapted versions are much higher.

Industry observers do not expect huge technological advances during the next decade, but look forward to the increasing development of new applications for electronic technology in composition and printing departments. Technological advances expected to be widely accepted include: conversion of plate departments (which photograph layouts onto metal plates for printing) to electronic darkrooms with computer-to-plate composition capabilities; acquisition of equipment for electronic integration and control of multiple press units and functions; computerized control of color printing; and automated folding, inserting, sorting, and labeling of newspaper bundles for carriers and mailed copies.

A result of the increasing reliance on advanced technology has been a rapid increase in equipment costs. Since the 1960s, the costs for composition and printing equipment have increased dramatically and today require extensive capital investments and financial planning. The types of equipment expected to enter newspaper plants in the 1990s are not expected to result in as significant labor costs as the introduction of offset printing and phototypesetting. Although some reduction in composition, printing, and mailing personnel will occur, a good portion of those salary savings will be redirected to technicians needed to operate and service the new machinery. In the long run, however, savings from reduced costs for employee benefits, reduced costs for supplies, reduced waste of newsprint, and increased desirability of newspaper advertising because of higher quality color printing are expected to result in favorable returns on the investments in the technology.

Labor

Despite the increasing reliance on mechanical and electronic equipment, labor is still a primary cost in the newspaper industry, requiring about 40% of operating revenue to pay for labor costs in newspapers. About half a million persons are employed in the newspaper industry nationwide and 44% of the employees are now women. About half of the employees are involved in prepress labor. Production and maintenance activities account for about 48% of the nation's newspaper workforce, editorial and administration (including executives) activities each account for about 15% of the total, circulation activities for about 12%, and advertising and promotion for about 10%.

In many large newspapers and geographical areas in which organized labor has historically been strong, newspapers and employees engage in collective bargaining. Primary labor unions involved in the newspaper industry include the Communication Workers of America (which includes the former International Typographical Union and the Newspaper Guild), the Graphic Communication Union, and the Brotherhood of Teamsters. In the smaller papers and in regions of the country in which right-to-work laws prevail or antiunion sentiments are strong—such as the southeastern states—unions represent employees in few newspapers. Unions representing composing and printing employees and vehicle drivers have had the most success in gaining members and agreements because of their specialized knowledge and historic strength nationwide. Nevertheless, unions play only a small role in the newspaper industry as a whole, but are an important economic factor in the largest newspapers.

Although unions have had a minor effect in the newspaper industry as a whole, the increasing power of large newspaper companies created by public ownership has led the unions to establish cooperative efforts to increase their representation of newspaper employees, particularly those working for newspaper groups, in the 1990s. As a result, large newspaper corporations are becoming more active in establishing and pursuing antiunion activities. These actions precipitated lengthy labor disputes at *The New York Daily News* in 1990 and 1991 and *The Detroit Free Press* and *Detroit News* from 1995 to 1997.

Distribution

The cost of getting printed copies of newspapers to readers now accounts for about 10% of most newspapers' expenses (Table 6.5). Although the costs of transportation and labor are high, newspapers rarely meet these costs directly but enter into subcontracts with distributors bearing the majority of the costs.

The most common delivery system is that of independent distributors, which is used by more than three-fourths of all daily newspapers (Picard, 1987b). Independent distributors purchase papers at wholesale prices and sell at retail prices. Their distribution territories are typically small, and the average newspaper has one carrier for each 100 subscribers (Thorn, 1987). Adult independent distributors typically serve routes ranging from 200 to 600 customers, and youth carriers usually have routes ranging from 20 to 100 customers. Because this type of distribution system uses independent business people who incur their own costs, newspapers typically need to provide only the administrative and supervisory mechanism for the delivery system.

Most newspapers consider these independent carriers to be the most cost-efficient distribution system because they can pass on a portion of the distribution costs, and because they are not subject to the higher costs of wage and hour laws, benefit payments, and transportation costs that increase costs if the work were done by employees.

About 15% of all papers use contract distributors—that is, agents paid a set fee for delivering papers, and 9% use employees who receive hourly wages or salaries (Picard, 1987b). In the latter system, newspapers' circulation costs increase markedly because of additional labor tax, benefit costs, and vehicle costs.

GOVERNMENT ECONOMIC POLITICS

No comprehensive economic policy toward the industry has ever been established in the United States, but a patchwork of policies apply, including a few policies established directly for newspapers. For the most part, government policies are oriented toward the maintenance of private enterprise and competition, but critics are increasingly charging that the policies have acted to prevent rather than encourage competition and that reconsideration of the policies is necessary (Owen, 1975; Picard 1982b).

Federal, state, and local governments have traditionally provided a variety of special economic supports to the industry, including exemptions from newspaper and advertising sales taxes and excise taxes on telecommunications equipment used for information gathering. In addition, a variety of fiscal advantages, including regulatory relief from wage and hour laws, have provided special support (Picard, 1982b).

The single most notable economic policies established by the federal government specifically for newspapers have been postal rate advantages and the antitrust exemptions for joint operating newspapers under the Newspaper Preservation Act (Busterna & Picard, 1993; Kielbowicz, 1989; Picard et al., 1988). Newspapers in York, Pennsylvania, Las Vegas, Nevada, and Detroit, Michigan, have been the most recent to use the provisions of the Newspaper Preservation Act to form joint operating agreements.

Newspapers enjoy the general tax exemptions and incentives available to other businesses and, with the exception of 34 papers operating with joint operating agreements, are subject to the same antitrust laws and enforcement as other industries. The result of application of general tax policies to newspapers has been an increase in chain ownership, because inheritors of independent papers have been forced to sell the papers to chains in order to pay estate taxes that are based on fair market prices. In addition, newspaper groups and conglomerates use pretax funds to acquire additional papers and the acquisitions can be depreciated over time, two factors that provide them significant tax advantages (Dertouzous & Thorpe, 1982). Antitrust laws are rarely invoked by government to halt concentration in the industry and are now primarily used by newspapers and other media against each other in disputes over marketing and pricing practices (Busterna, 1988a, 1989).

CONCLUSIONS

The future of the newspaper industry in the United States is unclear because of declining readership, growing illiteracy, and technological changes, but there is no reason to believe the functions of newspapers will no longer be required or that newspaper companies do not have the ability to adapt and survive. Newspaper companies are concerned because it appears that the decline in readership of newspapers among the population as a whole will continue. Many persons, especially young people, appear uninterested in the current content of newspapers and make greater use of other media. Persons of all ages who cannot read, or do not read well, can be expected to increasingly use broadcast and cable services for their news, information, and advertising needs.

Nevertheless, a great number of people can still be expected to want information of the type found in newspapers and there will continue to be a need for firms to gather and convey such information. Some futurists predict, however, that the newspaper itself will disappear because of changes in production and distribution. They argue that the printing aspects of the industry will disappear and the electronic product currently being produced by the news and advertising portions of newspaper companies will be transposed into an electronic newspaper delivered via cable or computer.

Traditionalists disagree, arguing that the portability of newspapers and the nonportability of video monitors will halt or delay such electronic distribution. To date, audience acceptance of electronic distribution of material traditionally found in newspapers has been low. Cable and other video-based experiments suggest a current unwillingness of newspaper consumers to give up newspapers for those services.

In the short term, the prospects for the newspaper industry remain good. Habitual use and steady demand for the information product, as well its continuing attractiveness to advertisers, indicate that it should remain a profitable industry well into the 21st century.

In the long term, the financial prospects of the newspaper industry are favorable even if technological and lifestyle changes lead consumers to accept electronic video-based distribution and the printing portion of the industry disappears. Under such a scenario, newspaper companies would replace their high-cost composition, printing, and distribution departments with a lower cost department that facilitates distribution or access through existing telecommunication or cable services, while continuing to use their prepress activities to provide the news and information for the new media product.

FURTHER READING

Bagdikian, B. (1983). *The media monopoly* (2nd ed.). Boston: Beacon Press

Dertouzous, J. N., & Thorpe, K. E. (1982). *Newspaper groups: Economics of scale, tax laws, and merger incentives.* Santa Monica, CA: Rand Corporation.

Owen, B. M. (1975). *Economics and the First Amendment: Media structure and the First Amendment.* Cambridge, MA: Ballinger.

Picard, R. G. (1989). *Media economics: Concepts and issues.* Newbury Park, CA: Sage.

Picard, R. G., Winter, J., McCombs, M., & Lacy, S. (Eds.). (1988). *Press concentration and monopoly: New perspectives on newspaper ownership and operation.* Norwood, NJ: Ablex.

Udell, J. G. (1978). *The economics of the American newspaper.* New York: Hastings House.

REFERENCES

Bagdikian, B. (1993). *The media monopoly* (4th ed.) Boston: Beacon Press.

Benjaminson, P. (1984). *Death in the afternoon: America's newspaper giants struggle for survival.* Kansas City: Andrews, McMeel & Parker.

Blankenburg, W. (1982). Newspaper ownership and control of circulation to increase profits. *Journalism Quarterly, 59*, 390–398.

Busterna, J. C. (1987). The cross-elasticity of demand for national newspaper advertising. *Journalism Quarterly, 64*, 346–351.

Busterna, J. C. (1988a). Antitrust in the 1980s: An analysis of 45 newspaper actions. *Newspaper Research Journal, 9*, 25–36.

Busterna, J. C. (1988b). Concentration and the industrial organization model. In R. G. Picard, J. P. Winter, M. McCombs, & S. Lacy (Eds.), *Press concentration and monopoly: New perspectives on newspaper ownership and operation* (pp. 35–53). Norwood, NJ: Ablex.

Busterna, J. C. (1988c). Trends in daily newspaper ownership. *Journalism Quarterly, 65*, 831–838.

Busterna, J. C. (1989, March). Daily newspaper chains and the antitrust laws. *Journalism Monographs,* No. 110.

Busterna, J. C., & Picard, R. G. (1993). *Joint operating agreements: The Newspaper Preservation Act and its application.* Norwood, NJ: Ablex.

Clark, J. (1976, February 4). Circulation increase despite higher subscription rates. *Editor & Publisher*, p. 32.

Communications industry report. (Annual). New York: Veronis, Suhler & Associates.

Compaine, B., Sterling, B. W., Guback, T. & Noble J. K., Jr., (1982). *Who owns the media? Concentration of ownership in the mass communication industry*. White Plains, NY: Knowledge Industry Publications.

Corden, W. M. (1953). The maximisation of profit by a newspaper. *Review of Economic Studies, 20*, 181–190.

Dertouzous, J. N., & Thorpe, K. E. (1982). *Newspaper groups: Economies of scale, tax laws, and merger incentives*. Santa Monica, CA.: Rand.

Editor & Publisher international yearbook. (1995). New York: Author.

Engwall, L. (1981). Newspaper competition: A case for theories of oligopoly. *Scandinavian Economic History Review, 29*, 145–154.

Facts about newspapers '91 (1991). Reston, VA: Newspaper Association of America.

Facts about newspapers '95. (1995). Reston, VA: Newspaper Association of America.

Field, R. (1978). *Circulation price inelasticity in the daily newspaper industry*. Unpublished doctoral thesis, University of Oklahoma.

Furhoff, L. (1973). Some reflections on newspaper concentration. *Scandinavian Economic History Review, 21*, 1–27.

Gill, R. (1975). *Economics: A text*. Pacific Palisades, CA: Goodyear.

Grotta, G. (1977). Daily newspaper price inelastic for 1970–1975. *Journalism Quarterly, 54*, 379–382.

Gustafsson, K. E. (1978). The circulation spiral and the principle of household coverage. *Scandinavian Economic History Review, 28*, 1–14.

Heilbroner, R. L., & Thurow, L. C. (1981). *The economic problem* (6th ed.). Englewood Cliffs, NJ: Prentice-Hall.

Kielbowicz, R. B. (1989). *News in the mail: The press, post office, and public information, 1700–1860s*. Westport, CT: Greenwood Press.

Landau, R., & Davenport, J. (1959). Price anomalies of the mass media. *Journalism Quarterly, 36*, 291–294.

Litman, B. (1988). Macroeconomic foundations. In R. G. Picard, J. P. Winter, M. McCombs, & S. Lacy (Eds), *Press concentration and monopoly: New perspectives on newspaper ownership and operation* (pp. 3–34). Norwood, NJ: Ablex.

Newspaper Stock Reports Annual Report Comparison. (1996). Riverside, CA: Carpelan.

Norton, S. W., & Norton, W. Jr., (1986). Economies of scale and new technology of daily newspapers: A survivor analysis. *Quarterly Review of Economics and Business, 26*, 66–83.

Owen, B. M. (1975). *Economics and the First Amendment: Media structure and the First Amendment*. Cambridge, MA: Ballinger.

Picard, R. G. (1982a). Rate setting and competition in newspaper advertising. *Newspaper Research Journal, 3*, 3–13.

Picard, R. G. (1982b). State intervention in U.S. press economics. *Gazette, 30*, 3–11.

Picard, R. G. (1987, September). Most papers use independent distributors. *ICMA* (International Circulation Managers Association) *Update*, pp. 6–9.

Picard, R. G. (1988a). Measures of concentration in the daily newspaper industry. *Journal of Media Economics, 1*, 61–74.

Picard, R. G. (1988b). Pricing behavior of newspapers. In R. G. Picard, J. P. Winter, M. McCombs, & S. Lacy (Eds), *Press concentration and monopoly: New perspectives on newspaper ownership and operation* (pp. 55–69). Norwood, NJ: Ablex.

Picard, R. G. (1989). *Media economics: Concepts and issues*. Newbury Park, CA: Sage.

Picard, R. G., Winter, J. P., McCombs, M., & Lacy, S. (Eds.). (1988). *Press concentration and monopoly: New perspectives on newspaper ownership and operation*. Norwood, NJ: Ablex.

Reddaway, W. B. (1963) The economics of newspapers. *The Economic Journal, 73*, 201–218.

Rosse, J. N. (1967) Daily newspaper monopoly, competition, and economies of scale. *American Economic Review, 57*, 522–533.

Rosse, J. N. & Dertouzous, J. N. (1979). The evolution of one newspaper cities. In Federal Trade Commission, *Proceedings of the symposium on media concentration* (Vol. 2, pp. 429–471). Washington, DC: U.S. Government Printing Office.

Standard chart of accounts for newspapers. (1979). Morristown, NJ: Institute of Newspaper Controllers and Finance Officers.

Thorn, W. J., with Pfeil, M. P. (1987). *Newspaper circulation: Marketing the news.* White Plains, NY: Longman.

Udell, J. G. (1978). *The economics of the American newspaper.* New York: Hastings House.

Wirth, M. (1986). Economic barriers to entering media industries in the United States. In M. McLaughlin (Ed.), *Communication yearbook 9* (pp. 423–442). Beverly Hills, CA: Sage.

7

The Economics of Television Networks: New Dimensions and New Alliances

Barry R. Litman
Michigan State University

After more than 50 years since its first inaugural season, the U.S. television broadcasting industry continues to survive and exercise leadership over the mass media landscape even in the midst of revolutionary changes in transmission of video programming to the household accompanying the cable, satellite, and VCR revolutions and the beginning of a new age of information. With the emergence in 1995 of two new "networks" and the fact that ABC has merged with Disney, CBS with Westinghouse, and NBC has been involved in several multibillion dollar takeover attempts by large media conglomerates, the broadcast industry continues to hold the spotlight of media attention. In this "era of the great networks," although their aura of dominance has eclipsed, it is instructive to focus on them as key players in the changing mass media mosaic, and observe how they have responded to the various internal and external shocks to the system surrounding them and propelling them to center stage status as the darling of the investment community.

The television networks have been the most powerful force in broadcasting over the last half century due to their position as the strategic bottleneck for the industry (Atkin & Litman, 1986; Litman, 1978). Occupying the key *distribution* stage of production, they reduce transaction costs by acting as the intermediary between producers who have programming to sell, broadcast stations who seek programming to fill air time, and advertisers who desire to expose their messages to the mass of interested viewers of these programs. Figuratively speaking, "they stand at the gateway of commerce and can extract a toll from all who wish to pass" (*Munn v. Illinois , 1877*).

Another source of power lies in the various efficiencies that arise from "networking"—that is, the brokering and transmission of high-cost/high-quality programming whose creative costs can be shared and spread across all participating affiliates and whose content can simultaneously be consumed by viewers across

131

the country without diminishing the utility for any person. The greater the penetration/reach of the network through its local market affiliates, and the more programs that can be packaged together in lineups throughout the broadcast day, the greater are the economies of scale that accompany national networking (see Thomas & Litman, 1991). Blessed with such cost-saving incentives to be large in size, the industry naturally gravitated toward the oligopoly market structure; yet, for such market power and excess profits to persist over a long time period, barriers to entry of one kind or another must be present.

BARRIERS TO ENTRY

Barriers to entry may take many forms in the mass media. As mentioned earlier, widespread economies of scale accompanying networking may act as one such barrier. If a firm must have access to 70% or more of the nation's households and broker entire dayparts of programming to reach the minimum efficient scale, then comparable unit costs can only be achieved by firms willing to invest on a similar scale. Of course, the ability to reach potential households is only the necessary—certainly not a sufficient—condition to having those households regularly view one's programs. Without significant viewership, new potential networks will not generate enough advertising dollars to cover the fixed costs of network overhead, programming, and satellite interconnection as well as the variable costs of affiliate compensation.

Because viewership is so fickle and slow to embrace new programming and ratings are heavily influenced by competing programming during the same time slots, it is very difficult for a newcomer to sustain enough popular programs while continuing to spend developmental money on new program concepts. This cash flow and program inventory problem becomes magnified if the new entrant wishes to compete on a full-fledged basis, through multiple dayparts *and* days of the week, with already entrenched firms (Thomas & Litman, 1991). This explains why new "weblets," as the trade press labels them, enter into competition on a gradual basis by "creamskimming" the most valuable nights and slowly expanding to other nights once their program lineup is solidified. When such structural problems as these are reinforced by network vertical integration into the production and exhibition stages, the barriers to entry become considerably higher.

GOVERNMENT BARRIERS

Perhaps the most difficult obstacles are those created by governments or governmental agencies that are often vested with full regulatory authority to unilaterally determine conditions of entry. If these agents deny the right to enter or establish extraordinary conditions, there is little appeal, and the courts generally do not second guess federal agencies on issues of judgment, only issues of due process.

Thus, when the FCC restricts the number of broadcasters by requiring a license to use the electromagnetic spectrum, this limits competition. It is tantamount to guaranteeing market protection from competition to the fortunate few.

In those hectic early days of the television industry, the FCC created a dual system of local TV frequencies, coexisting on the VHF and UHF bands. Given the superior reach and lower wattage of the smaller VHF band when compared to UHF, this created technical and economic handicaps for the use of these latter frequencies, especially as potential network affiliates. These factors thereby diminished the possibility for entry of new local stations and, paradoxically, frustrated the Commission's stated goal of encouraging the wider development of television (Long, 1974).

The paucity of high-quality local outlets was exacerbated by the FCC's concurrent localism policy that guaranteed originating stations to most reasonably sized cities throughout the country—a promise that could only be fulfilled by reallocating frequencies away from large metropolitan areas to smaller cities, thereby reinforcing the scarcity of such commercial stations within the most populous markets. Without comparable local stations as a base for affiliation, there would be no means of local access for new television networks. Hence, the number of viable networks was inextricably intertwined with the FCC's allocation and localism policies and the technological constraints of the new technology. When the DuMont network was unable to coexist with the other three networks due to an inferior affiliate lineup, it exited the industry in 1955, leaving the powerful network triopoly of CBS, NBC, and ABC virtually invincible for some 30 years (Long, 1974). Government policy (along with coercive network conduct) had reinforced the natural barriers to entry that existed from economic forces alone. Although there were many attempts to challenge the giant networks through creation of part-time networks, it was not until 1986, when technological alternatives had emerged to moderate the UHF handicaps and many new UHF stations had sprung up, that Fox Broadcasting could mount the most sustainable challenge from within the industry by combining superstation coverage on local cable systems with affiliation to the independent television sector. This is the same process being followed by the emerging Warner Brothers and United-Paramount networks as well.

VERTICAL INTEGRATION

Another important element of market structure that can be used to fortify market dominance is that of vertical integration—tying together of successive stages of production within an industry. In one form or another, all firms are vertically integrated as they internally produce what may have been purchased from outsiders at one point or another. In this sense vertical integration is a normal aspect of industry organization and should be considered as simply another means of achieving efficiencies. However, when industries have well-defined stages of production, vertical integration in combination with market power may be used to constrict the open portion of the market, create access problems, and thereby fortify existing positions of market power. New competitors may be compelled to enter at multiple stages to avoid dependence on rivals for supplies or access. Multiple-stage entry is always more costly, difficult, and riskier than single stage entry.

Network Vertical Integration

The television networks have always had some degree of vertical integration into the exhibition and production stages. In the exhibition area, each network has a base of owned and operated stations (O&Os) in the largest markets that collectively reach 19–23.5% of television households in 1995. This O&O base of affiliates provides virtually 100% clearance for all network programming and thus can be used to guarantee national advertisers coverage for their commercial advertisements. Being the most powerful group owners of broadcast stations also gives the networks considerable influence as buyers in the syndication industry, where they compete in local markets of the O&O stations for high quality programming for use during nonnetwork time periods (Litman, 1978).

The second form of vertical integration involves long-term affiliation contracts (with no upward bound anymore) with nonnetwork broadcast stations that are provided with an exclusive lineup of programs across the entire broadcast day that than may "clear" or reject for any reason. There are roughly 200 affiliates for each network, including their O&O stations. Although rejection rates vary across different networks and critically depend on the expected local rating for various programs, the average clearance rate for all network programs is roughly 90% (Litman, 1978). This indicates that networked programs generally deliver superior ratings, and that affiliates will only exercise their programming independence at the margins for fear of losing the valuable affiliation link to another local station. In sum, through direct ownership and long-term affiliation contracts, the historic networks have achieved virtually 100% access and self-sufficiency in the exhibition area. Yet, the historic stability of affiliation agreements has recently undergone turbulent changes due to raids by new networks (and even existing networks) seeking to achieve a better geographical affiliation lineup. Most recently, the complete shift of 10 New World broadcast stations to Fox caused havoc among the big three networks, forcing them to scramble to maintain representation in the affected markets.

In the production area, the networks have historically had less direct involvement. For many years, they produced roughly 10% to 15% of their prime-time programming in such areas as news, sports, features, and occasionally entertainment shows and made-for-TV movies while relying on the motion picture studios and truly independent producers for the vast amount of their fare. Their involvement in the other dayparts varied depending on the kind of programming involved. They produced some of their own soap operas and quiz shows during the daytime and some of their own late-night talk shows and all of their weekend sports programs.

This low degree of vertical integration into production is, of course, partially explainable by regulatory rules that for the last 20 years have limited network in-house production and prohibited coventuring with outside producers on an equity participation basis. However, the networks have also argued that even without the rules, the fundamental process of creativity would require many centers of development rather than the elitist attitude that only great program ideas can arise from network headquarters. Yet, the 1994 and 1995 seasons have witnessed a remarkable transformation of the network marketplace for prime-time programs. For the first time, the networks are the top suppliers of their own prime-time entertainment programs, due to relaxation of the Financial Interest and Syndication Rules and the greater security and potential profitability that comes from in-house production rather than outsourcing to the independent production sector.

According to Table 7.1, for the 1995–1996 fall season, 44 of the 76 hours (58%) of programming were produced in-house or in a reciprocal supply relationship for other networks. After the consummation of the merger between Disney and ABC in 1995, this trend became even more pronounced in 1997 with 48 of the 82 hours of prime-time programming produced in house. The distinction between network and supplier has continued to blur with Warner Brothers and Paramount continuing to fulfill both roles. This segment is clearly more vertically integrated and self-sufficient than anytime in its 50-year history.

Within the independent production sector, there are two kinds of production houses. The first group are the major motion picture studios (Universal, Columbia, and others) who abandoned their boycott of television in 1955 and began licensing theatrical movies and regular series to the networks. Their share of the prime-time program market has averaged in excess of 40% during the decade of the 1980s (Barrett, 1990) and early 1990s with the exception of the most recent seasons. The second group of program producers are large independent companies such as Spelling-Goldberg, MTM, Tandem, and Embassy and Lorimar (before their mergers with major studios). Often, these large independents had as large a market presence as some of the major studios. A subset of the third group are very small independent producers such as Dick Clark, Hanna Barbara, Michael Landon, or Marble Arch who were lucky with one or two shows for a period of time and then disappeared and were replaced by similar firms.

With the reappearance of deficit financing during the 1980s, producers needed to be of a particular size to survive; they needed a portfolio of programs of different vintages in their inventory. This meant they would have new scripts and pilots in development, new series, returning series, and series in syndication that would create a sufficient cash flow to cross-subsidize series operating under deficits. Alternatively, they may be a subsidiary of a large diversified parent corporation that itself has deep pockets. Many small- and medium-sized production houses that

TABLE 7.1
Network Supplier Market Shares of Prime-Time Hours: 1997 Fall Schedule

Supplier	Network Hours				Netlets Hours		Total
	ABC	CBS	NBC	FOX	WB	PARAMOUNT	
Major Networks[a]							
ABC/Disney-Touchstone	8.0				.5	.5	9.0
CBS		7.5		.5			
NBC			6.0				6.0
Fox	3.0	1.5		4.5			9.0
TOTAL	11.0	9.0	6.5	4.5	.5	.5	32.0
Netlets[b]							
Warner Brothers	2.0	1.5	3.0	1.5	3.0		11.0
Paramount	.5	.5	1.0		.5	2.5	5.0
TOTAL	2.5	2.0	4.0	1.5	3.5	2.5	16.0
Major Movie Co.[c]							
Universal	.5	2.0	1.5	1.0		1.0	6.0
Columbia		1.0	1.5				2.5
Tri-Star		.5	.5	1.0		.5	2.5
TOTAL	.5	2.5	3.0	3.5	.0	1.5	11.0
Independents							
Carsey-Werner	1.5	1.0	1.0				3.5
Brillstein-Grey		1.0			.5		1.5
Witt-Thomas	.5	.5	.5		.5		2.0
Spelling				2.0	2.0		4.0
New World	1.0						1.0
MTM			1.0			.5	1.5
Dreamworks SKG	1.5	.5					2.0
All Others	1.5	2.5	1.0	1.5		1.0	7.5
TOTAL	6.0	4.5	4.5	3.5	3.0	1.5	23.0
GRAND TOTAL	20.0	18.0	18.0	13.0	7.0	6.0	82.0

Note. Fox, Warner Brothers, and Paramount are all major movie company suppliers to other networks.
[a]Excludes movies that have various suppliers each week.
[b]Includes all co-productions with independent suppliers.
[c]Includes all co-productions with nonstudio suppliers.

lacked such financial capital were thrown into the arms of major studios through either mergers or coproduction deals. These companies could not approach the networks themselves because networks were forbidden from joint venturing programming with outside companies.

Although forbidden until recently from equity participation with outside suppliers, the networks have been able to exert their bargaining strength by successfully negotiating long-term option contracts with these suppliers, which has the effect of exclusively tying these programs to the networks for as long as they have a productive ratings life. Hence, although barred from owning these programs directly, they have extraordinary indirect control through exclusive use and monopsony buying power.

In essence what the networks did was establish themselves as the crucial bottleneck through which programming must flow and then reinforce this position by partial vertical integration through equity and long-term contracts. In this way, the vertical chain of power becomes an insurmountable barrier for potential entrants thinking of becoming full-fledged rivals.

THE IMPACT OF CABLE AND VCRS

Cable television has transformed the television industry from a medium of scarcity to one of abundance, and just as importantly, created direct consumer payments as the second source of revenues to cover the high costs of production, distribution, and exhibition of television programming. With 54 or more channels currently available and many more on the horizon, consumers now have the freedom and opportunity (aided by remote tuning devices) to choose a vast array of diverse programming from their TV set or video store as long as they have the discretionary leisure time and income available to consume it (Atkin & Litman, 1986).

In short, a new diverse program marketplace was created that featured significant consumer sovereignty, but no longer guaranteed favorable status to the historic networks. They would now be forced to compete with the vast array of alternative programs that individually posed only a mild threat (e.g., no basic cable network exceeding 2.4% of the prime-time audience) but that collectively eroded network market shares and profits. The once invincible giants would now have to redefine and rediscover their product niche if they wished to remain major players in the new television landscape. The alternative to innovation was to inevitably watch other program sources slowly nibble away and creamskim former positions of dominance in news, sports, theatrical movies, and even regular series. Such a process is similar to the fate of general-interest magazines, which eventually were replaced by the special-interest, narrowly defined and demographically targeted magazines that are so prevalent today.

NETWORK CONDUCT

Given the oligopoly structure described earlier, the next question is how the networks acted toward each other in the important areas of pricing, product differentiation and product development. This is known as their "conduct" and depending on several factors, it may range from the fiercest type of rivalry to coordination of practices in the form of a shared monopoly.

In an oligopolistic structure such as television networking, where there are few competitors and no new entries, one expects the network rivals to eventually come to an understanding that aggressive actions towards one's competitors in any dimension will be self-defeating. Such actions may merely provoke retaliation in kind, with no substantial reward of greater market shares (Litman, 1979a, 1979b). A far wiser strategy is a spirit of cooperation in which everyone understands the mutual benefits accruing from common standardized policies in as many areas of interaction as are feasible and workable. Such cooperation will maximize industry revenues, minimize expenses, and guarantee higher profits for the industry as a whole, and for each firm than if everyone took a more aggressive stance and tried to economically disadvantage its rivals.

Fortunately, there are many different points of stress in such cooperative strategies. Given the antitrust sanctions against direct consultation between rival firms, a signaling mechanism must somehow be fashioned to communicate how each firm should react under different economic stimuli. Often the dominant firm acts as a price or product leader by publicly announcing its forthcoming strategies to the print and electronic press who then relay the message to other competitors.

Although price/quality leadership are useful signaling devices, they are not infallible and the so-called "meeting of minds" in illegal conspiracy, which comes from knowledge about past industry responses to similar circumstances, may not be foolproof either. Similarly, when products have a high-quality differential or disparate cost structures, the common price or standardized practice may not be equally profitable for all competitors, thereby creating the incentive for one or more firms to cheat by offering what is best for itself rather than for the general benefit of all. Such forces inherently weaken and destabilize the cartel-like arrangement and trigger price or product differentiation wars for varying lengths of time until order is restored through effective sanctions or coercive conduct. The larger the number of significant firms in the industry, the greater the difficulty of reaching and maintaining a workable consensus, and the higher the likelihood of cheating.

Finally, it should be realized that the competitive instinct cannot totally be suppressed; often a pressure valve emerges to permit competition in one or more areas of contact. Nonprice competition in such areas as promotion, advertising, or other kinds of product differentiation are the usual areas in which rivalry is channeled and relative market shares are distributed in the industry.

The historic television networks have traditionally understood the financial logic of cooperative behavior and have been able to systematically standardize

many industry practices in such areas as advertising prices per thousand households, amount of commercialization per hour (across different dayparts), number
and timing of reruns, affiliation compensation for comparably sized markets, and
payments to program producers (packagers). The one area in which cooperation is
impossible lies in program quality and the associated ratings game. It is impossible
to predict audience tastes, much less standardize program quality (Litman, 1979a;
Owen, Beebe, & Manning, 1974). Hence, this has been the one escape valve by
which rivalry surfaced in this industry, and market shares accrued to whichever
programming team could most accurately gauge and respond to audience tastes. As
indicated earlier, the ratings game has become even more hectic and more volatile
with the emergence of new competitive over-the-air networks like Fox and strong
cable alternatives like HBO and the most popular group of basic cable networks.

THE STEP PROCESS OF PROGRAM ACQUISITION

Perhaps the most interesting area of cooperation has been that of payments to
program producers. Because this area accounts for nearly two thirds of all costs, it
is imperative that the networks restrain program inflation. However, because this
is an integral part of ratings rivalry, it is potentially the most explosive area for
competition.

In the early era of networking, the big three networks would act as common
carriers by selling time and access to the associated audience to interested national
advertisers who in turn would arrange for programming to be produced by an
independent production house and commercial spots to be interspersed within the
program content. The risk of ratings failure lay solely with the national advertiser
who would reap a bonanza (e.g., low cost per thousands) with hit programs and
suffer losses with flops. This "sole sponsorship" form of program financing soon
gave way to alternate sponsorship as time charges increased and became unaf-
fordable to all except the largest national advertisers. By the late 1950s, with
charges of negligence from the quiz scandals still fresh in their minds, the networks
changed the form of sponsorship to the participation model, in which the networks
would take full responsibility for all program scheduling and sell spots in network
programs to advertisers interested in collectively sponsoring a program. They
would thus share in the risks as well as the rewards from successful programming
(Litman, 1979a).

Advertisers could now diversify their own risks by purchasing time in a portfolio
of program investments, each with different levels of ratings risk. Most importantly,
this narrowed the points of access available from 50 to 100 national advertising
agencies to only the three networks. In their role as both powerful buyers and sellers
of programming, the networks could make their products irresistible if they could
cooperate in these and other important cost areas.

What emerged was a step process of program acquisition that followed a
long-term option contract from the idea, treatment, script, and pilot stage up through

the first 5 to 7 years the program remained on the network. This contract gave the network the option to cancel at any discrete point, yet bound the program producer for the entire contract length at fixed prices for each successive year of programming, regardless of ratings success. Often, the networks paid license fees that did not fully cover all the production costs, forcing the producers to deficit finance. It was also alleged that a positive network decision often was tied to use of network facilities at high overhead charges, surrender of valuable syndication rights or profit shares, or both (Litman, 1979a).

Why did the networks engage in such standardized programming practices? And more importantly, why did the packagers accept such one-sided deals? The networks wanted to prevent the kind of bidding wars that accompany payments for hit shows by tying up the shows with long-term contract proposals before ratings information became available. If the networks had to renegotiate after a successful season, then prices for hit shows would escalate because their true market value would be known.

The producers had to accept such offers if they wished to get on the airwaves because there were only three sources of access (all of whom followed identical policies). Furthermore, the programs were so risky that developmental investments were only forthcoming from the networks, the only entities who could average out the successful and unsuccessful programs, and the program supply industry was monopolistically competitive and therefore could not countervail the monopsony bargaining strength of the consolidated networks. Although the motion picture companies could easily coventure with the smallest independents, they too were completely dependent on networks for program access, survival, and program payments. Furthermore, there was always the hope that the program would be so long-lasting and successful during the initial network contract that its true value would be established and rewarded during subsequent network contracts and, of course, through multiple runs in the syndication industry. Thus, the networks became financially successful because they were able to control both sources of potential profits—profits from uncertainty of program quality and profits from interindustry coordination (Litman, 1979a). It should be noted that some economists believe that monoposony power never really existed; rather, the networks simply shared and shifted risks from themselves to suppliers because of distorted incentives accompanying the Financial Interest Rules (see Owen & Wildman, 1992, chap. 2).

Although the focus here has been on network program acquisition, this is not to imply that the other areas of interaction should be totally neglected. Forming a spirit of cooperation in areas dealing with setting of advertising prices, amount of commercialization and reruns, as well as affiliation payments is crucial to the consensus. Fissures in the foundation may spread to the entire superstructure, that is, instability in any one area may cause a ripple effect across all areas. To a certain extent, all these areas involve very public actions by the networks that are reported to the nth degree by the trade press. Given such visibility, cheating on agreed-on standards is easily detected and retaliation in kind can be swift, especially when prices or payments are involved, thus punishing the maverick firm by removing its advantage. The futility of such cheating should remove the incentive to engage in such activity, thereby strengthening the consensus (Owen et al., 1974). The fact that network profits have stabilized in recent years indicates that they have been only partially successful in maintaining their industry consensus in the wave of new competitive thrests from within and outside their industry (see Table 7.1).

REGULATION OF NETWORKS

There has always been widespread public interest in the degree of market control possessed by the traditional networks. This has prompted regulatory oversight by the FCC and Congress seeking to limit this power, modify its use or introduce new competitive elements. Public policy has been most successful when it was targeted at the structural aspects that compel good conduct rather than its manifestations.

Going back to the earliest years of radio, there has been a continual fear of private monopolization of the airwaves because of their centrality to the free marketplace of discourse. During the early 1940s, this concern led the FCC to enact the *Chain Broadcasting Rules* (FCC, 1941), which limited the number of networks that a single organization could own and the corresponding *Multiple Ownership Rules* (FCC, 1953), which limited the number of broadcast stations of different kinds that any single organization could own both within a market and across the nation. The Multiple Ownership Rules initially limited group ownership to 7 TV stations but were changed in 1985 to a maximum of 12, provided they did not exceed 25% of all TV households in the country. There were also a series of *Cross Ownership Rules* that forbade joint ownership within a single market of competing mass media such as daily newspapers and broadcast stations, TV stations and cable systems, and cable systems and telephone systems (FCC, 1975). The implications for such restrictions are quite intriguing. By limiting the number of owned and operated stations, the networks cannot be totally self-sufficient across the exhibition stage by equity means alone; they must rely on nonowned stations to achieve sufficient program clearance. What was surprising was the degree of vertical integration permitted, given the *Paramount* case precedent in 1948–1949 that required the motion picture producer/distributors to vertically disintegrate, that is, to divest all their motion picture theaters (Litman, 1978).

With the fundamental alteration of the mass media landscape, all of these ownership rules have come under very severe scrutiny during the 1990s, and the tide of regulatory change indicates either liberalization or elimination in the near future. For example, The Telecommunications Act of 1996 increases the ownership caps to 35% reach and facilitates telephone entry into the fiberoptic home market.

Prime-Time Access Rules

In the mid-1960s, the FCC also noticed an unhealthy condition in the syndication market. It had hoped that the abolishment of option time would give first-run syndication program producers the boost they desired, and they could then effectively compete against networks in prime time. However, the evidence indicated a decline in first-run syndicated fare and an upsurge in network reruns. To restore the health of independent producers, an affirmative action program guaranteeing their access during prime time needed to be instituted. The adopted rule (FCC, 1970b) limited network service to an affiliate to three prime-time hours between 7 p.m. and 11 p.m. in the top 50 markets in the country, and these affiliates were not allowed to substitute network reruns for the lost network service. In keeping with the new momentum toward network deregulation, the FCC has recently decided to sunset these rules in 1996 and open up this market to the forces of competition.

Financial Interest and Syndication Rules

During this same time frame, the networks were accused of demanding syndication rights and profit shares in subsidiary markets as a quid pro quo for access to the airwaves and as a means of increasing their share of the syndication market. The FCC became concerned with the potential leverage and conflict of interest that this power created and enacted the *Financial Interest and Syndication Rules* (FCC, 1970a) to force the networks out of the syndication business. Furthermore, they were forbidden from obtaining profit shares (e.g., joint venturing) in programs they obtained for network showing from outside producers. Once again, as the program marketplace has become more fractionalized and network control has diminished, the rationale for retaining these rules has similarly waned and they are scheduled to be phased out in November of 1995. This is expected to open up new investment and partnership incentives for networks and program producers alike and appears to be one of the driving forces behind the recent acquisitions of CBS and ABC and the aborted takeover attempts of NBC by TBS in 1995. It also may explain why this was the optimal time for two of the strongest network program suppliers, Warner Brothers and Paramount, to establish their own competing networks. If the foreign ownership restrictions were to be lifted, additional interest would be expected by those media conglomerates seeking to build global empires.

The Consent Decrees

When CBS and ABC attempted to produce theatrical motion pictures in the late 1960s, they were sued by the major movie studios for antitrust violations under the *Paramount* case precedent that no mass media should be vertically integrated across the production, distribution, and exhibition areas. The studios feared that network production of theatrical movies would deny their movies access to the lucrative network window. Eventually the private antitrust case was superseded by the

Justice Department case that broadened the case against vertical integration to include network production of all program forms and sought judicial approval for the same prohibitions contained in the *Financial Interest and Syndication Rules.* This case was eventually settled through separate consent decrees with each network that ratified the FCC rules and severely curtailed the permissible amount of the networks' in-house production of programming. The Consent Decrees expired in November 1990, thereby providing further incentive for rethinking network strategy in balancing in-house versus outsourcing of their program needs.

INTERNAL DECAY OF THE CARTEL

To understand the decline of network control and the prospects for the future, it is important to distinguish three periods during the last 30 years: the era of network stability (1960–1975), the era of internal strife (1976–1981) and the era of competing technologies (1981–present). Each of these periods is now being examined in turn.

During the 15-year period ending in the mid-1970s, television grew to become the dominant mass medium in the United States, occupying an ever-increasing amount of discretionary leisure time and advertising dollars. The chief beneficiaries of this growing status were the television networks, who through their program supply of nearly two thirds of the broadcast day and their ownership of many of the largest VHF stations in the country, were the kingpins of this industry and the central focus of both wonderment and criticism. It was also during this era that the networks matured and came to understand the financial logic of forming a spirit of cooperation and standardization in many areas of interaction rather than taking an independent, self-defeating, aggressive stance toward each other. At the zenith of their power, only the ratings popularity game remained competitive and determined relative market shares (Litman, 1983; Owen et al., 1974).

The result of this cooperation/competition posture meant record profits for the networks and what has been described (and criticized) as a degree of sameness, homogenization, or lack of diversity in terms of programming. It was hypothesized that commercial support of television broadcasting, with its emphasis on mass appeal, created a corresponding incentive for networks and local stations to cater to the mass taste or least common denominator of program taste rather than supply distinctive high-quality programs of cultural or uplifting educational value (Owen et al., 1974). Network programming risks could be minimized by imitating what current or past program concepts pleased the audience rather than experimenting with new ideas or untested talent. When such financial incentives to copy were coupled with the oligopolistic structure of the industry and the desire to standardize practices in most areas of contact, the end result was even less of a desire to innovate or experiment with new program forms, lest the delicate industry consensus be overturned.

INTRAINDUSTRY WARFARE

The fragile network consensus began to disintegrate during the 1975–1976 season when ABC, the perennial third-place finisher and most flamboyant programmer, suddenly jumped to the number one position because its mixture of nostalgia, sexual appeal, and double entendre comedy struck a resonant chord with the audience. CBS and NBC were so shocked by this reversal of fortune that they went on a crash competitive course toward regaining their ratings dominance. They began spending enormous sums of money on program development, substituted more expensive original programming in place of reruns, took programming risks, and made cancellation decisions at a much faster rate (Litman, 1979b).

Most importantly, the step process of program acquisition was relaxed as the networks sought to gain a competitive advantage vis-à-vis each other by courting the favor of the program production community. In real terms, this meant that the length of the option contracts was reduced to 4 years, the production deficit was considerably narrowed or eliminated, and the networks began to renegotiate payments upward for successful series during the life of the contract. All of these actions collectively translated into greater program diversity for the American public.

Surprisingly, during the first few years that this intraindustry warfare persisted, network profits did not seriously decline because rivalry seemed limited to the programming sphere; the other areas of network interaction were largely unaffected, because of the continuing bull market for network advertising. However, by 1980, network profits began to decline as the advertising revenues could no longer sustain the double-digit annual increases in program prices and expenditures (Litman, 1983).

THE EXTERNAL THREAT AND FOX

With restoration of CBS and then NBC to the top of the ratings roost in the early 1980s, the timing seemed right for reestablishment of the spirit of cooperation since the fundamental raison d'être for its appearance had not altered. However, other industry atmospherics had indeed changed with the arrival and spectacular development of cable and pay-cable television, followed shortly by the home VCR revolution. These new technologies and services represented an exogenous shock to the system and posed a new life-threatening dimension to the carefully planned spirit of cooperation (Atkin & Litman, 1986; Litman, 1983). The market power of the historic networks was further eroded from within by the growing strength of the independent television sector, initially buoyed by the success of first-run syndicated programming and then through their affiliate relationship with the Fox Broadcasting Company toward the end of the decade. The combination of the external and internal threats has seen the aggregate network share of the prime-time audience fall more than 25% during the 1980s to slightly above 60% and below that in the 1990s, so that the networks can no longer be properly called a shared monopoly.

Industry critics and financial analysts blamed the networks' problems on excessive costs, poor management, and a failure to be innovative with new programming. Beginning in the mid-1980s, as the networks began to institute various cost controls, they simultaneously were put into play because it was widely believed that their stock prices were undervalued relative to their earning potential. Shortly thereafter, each of them was acquired or reorganized in highly publicized multibillion-dollar deals (NBC by General Electric, ABC by Capital Cities, and CBS by Lawrence Tisch) and new corporate managements installed. Each became a subsidiary of a giant American media conglomerate, rationalized as a defense against unfriendly takeovers by foreign corporations—a strategy that turned out to be clairvoyant when Sony and Mashushita acquired major motion picture studios at the end of the decade and Rupert Murdoch first purchased Twentieth Century Fox and then the Metromedia Broadcast Group to act as a foundation for his proposed fourth television network.

Murdoch believed that a new network that was both innovative in its programming and cost conscious could selectively compete for viewership against the bigger networks. Even in the face of new competition from cable and other services, Fox believed that the timing was right to establish a fourth network because the technological and regulatory handicaps that made network entry so risky before seemed to be lower due to the entrance of many new independent stations in the top 100 markets as potential affiliates. Recognizing the hazards of full-scale entry, they sought to first establish their presence in the weekend prime-time hours. Furthermore, Fox believed that viewers were ready for a more exciting kind of network programming that contrasted with the staleness and predictability of the traditional broadcast networks and was targeted to youth and young adults. The economics of networking seemed irresistible to both Fox and the independent stations; they could both improve their economic position through forming a network partnership.

During its first several years, the audience for Fox programming continued to grow and the network's survival was assured. By 1995, it had developed a consistent lineup of successful programs across seven nights of the week and established a very successful children's network as well. Fox still has not achieved ratings parity with the Big 3, leaving open the question of why Warner Brothers and Paramount would now enter into this crowded, fiercely competitive marketplace.

Understanding the harsh realities of establishing new networks, after 6-month planning horizons, both Warner Brothers Television Network and United-Paramount (UPN) debuted in mid-January, 1995. Warner Brothers began with a single night of prime-time programming while Paramount had two nights. As expected, neither network had comparable affiliate clearance to the established networks. By September 1995, UPN had access to 88% of the nation's television households whereas Warner Brothers had only 81%. Warner achieved this clearance only after utilizing superstation WGN to enter some broadcast markets where no affiliates were available while Paramount was forced to accept secondary affiliation status in many markets, covering some 15% of the country, which means that the stations could position the programs in different slots than originally broadcast.

The Paramount network was based around the *Star Trek* franchise program and consisted of hour-long dramatic fare targeted to males while Warner Brothers utilized half-hour situation comedies to attract a predominantly "yuppie" demographic target. With the exception of *Star Trek*, none of the programs showed acceptable ratings during the abbreviated first season, most earning ratings in the 1% to 3% range, which is comparable to that of a basic cable network or an access hour syndicated show. Paramount replaced all its shows save *Star Trek*, whereas Warner Brothers retained its shows, added a second night, and began planning for expansion into the children's market. Unless their programming achieves acceptable ratings next year, the planned expansion of Paramount to a third night in 1996 will be torpedoed and fate of these new netlets may be sealed.

COMPETITION

Given that the role of the traditional networks has now diminished, it is interesting to see how they have responded to the internal and external shocks and to try to predict their role in the new telecommunication mosaic. With the days of double-digit advertising price increases long past and the added demand from the new programming services raising programming costs, the networks' profit margins appear to be squeezed from above and below (Atkin & Litman, 1986). They are clearly disadvantaged vis-à-vis their new rivals by their sole reliance on advertising as a single source of revenue. Furthermore, the network window for some high-profile and popular programming such as theatrical movies has been pushed further back behind pay cable, pay-per-view and VCRs. Their sports franchise has proven to be more of a loss leader than cash cow and is now parceled off to other cable players as well. It goes without saying that following the mergers and corporate reorganizations, the networks have slimmed down their overhead in every operating division, most notably in news, and have sought greater economies in transmission of programming via satellites, in affiliation compensation, and even in the explosive programming area. Unfortunately, their attempts to enter the cable programming area directly or through joint ventures with existing services have largely met with failure (e.g., CBS Cable, CNBC, Arts and Entertainment) except in the sports arena with ESPN.

Yet what still rings true even with the fractionalization of the programming marketplace is that the networks remain the industry leaders; only HBO when it has a premiere movie can equal the attraction of the TV networks. Also, although some national advertisers have left network television to more closely target their audience on cable, there is still a large residual advertiser demand for the kind of broad appeal programming that only the networks can efficiently deliver. This is also what makes them especially attractive takeover targets.

THE FUTURE OF NETWORKS

From the programming perspective, the networks must clearly find their market niche rather than do every conceivable type of programming. They should concentrate on the program forms where they have a comparative advantage such as soap operas, quiz programs, regular series, made-for-TV movies, news, information, reality programs, and live programs while deemphasizing theatrical movies (which are readily available in VCR stores), high-profile sports, and special events that seem better suited to cable and pay cable, which have a second revenue source.

The real-world evidence seems to confirm these expectations. The networks have greatly expanded their use of made-for-TV movies at the expense of theatricals, have shifted away from hour-long dramas toward more situation comedies and reality-type programs, have increased their use of news and information type programs, and have grudgingly relinquished their monopoly control on major-league sports and special sporting events. Most importantly, they have achieved greater self-reliance in the process—no longer as dependent on others for their programs. With the exception of the sports programming whose license fees have greatly escalated in recent years, all of these moves also introduce greater efficiencies because the programs are typically shot on videotape, are live, and require less editing than hour-long dramas. The networks have also sought to exploit current and controversial topics through their information and feature type programming and made-for-TV movies. In short, the new competition coming from Fox and others with its heavy emphasis on youth, and the new cable program services with their siphoning of traditional network fare and diverse demographically targeted programming have forced the networks to search for those unique series and other program forms that are their trademarks and comparative advantage (Thomas & Litman, 1991). This has meant greater attention to program development and more program experimentation with such series as *Twin Peaks* and *Cop Rock*, and most recently *ER*.

The networks must also position themselves to be major players in the coming information age, thanks to the information superhighway. In addition to the infusion of new revenues from new corporate giants like Westinghouse and Disney, and possibly TBS in the near future, they appear to be forming strategic alliances with telephone and computer companies as evidenced by NBC's joint venture with Microsoft and Fox's link to MCI. What will be critical to them is being at the forefront of the new digital broadcast technologies in addition to high-definition and interactive television and new animation techniques. Far from being pessimistic, the fact that they are being pursued and acquired by large media conglomerates suggests great confidence and security in their future. Like Odysseus, they must chart a steady strategic course amidst all the potential obstacles that lie in their path.

REFERENCES

Atkin, D., & Litman, B. (1986). Network TV programming: economics, audiences, and the ratings game, 1971–1986. *Journal of Communication, 36*(3), 32–50.

Barrett, M. (1990, May–June). Financial interest and syndication rules: An examination. *Broadcast Financial Journal,* 41–49.

Federal Communications Commission. (1941). *Report on chain broadcasting* (Docket 5060).

Federal Communications Commission. (1953). Multiple ownership report and order. *Federal Communications Commission Reports, 18,* 288.

Federal Communications Commission. (1970a). Financial interest and syndication report. *Federal Communications Commission Reports, 23,* 382.

Federal Communications Commission. (1970b). Prime time access report and order. *Federal Communications Commission Reports, 23*(2), 387.

Federal Communications Commission. (1975). Cross ownership report and order. *Federal Communications Commission Reports, 50* (2), 1046.

Litman, B. (1978). Is network ownership in the public interest? *Journal of Communication, 28*(2), 51–59.

Litman, B. (1979a). The economics of the television market for theatrical movies. *Journal of Communication, 29*(4), 20–33.

Litman, B. (1979b). The television networks, competition and program diversity. *Journal of Broadcasting, 23*(4), 393–410.

Litman, B. (1983). U.S. TV networks' response to new technology. *Telecommunications Policy, 7*(2), 163–177.

Long, S. (1974). *The development of the television network oligopoly.* Unpublished doctoral dissertation, University of Illinois, Urbana–Champaign.

Munn v. Illinios, 94 U.S. 113 (1877).

Owen, B., Beebe, J., & Manning, W. (1974). *Television economics.* Lexington, MA: Heath.

Owen, B., & Wildman, S. (1992). *Video economics.* Cambrdige, MA: Harvard University Press.

Thomas, L., & Litman, B. (1991). Fox Broadcasting Company, why now? An economic study of the rise of the fourth broadcast network. *Journal of Broadcasting and Electronic Media, 35*(2), 139–157.

GLOSSARY

Cartel—a formal or informal arrangement of companies that attempt to eliminate competition between themselves by agreeing to common prices, quality standards, advertising, and the like.

Consent Decree—a negotiated settlement of an antitrust case before a judgment is rendered. No admission of guilt is implied by such a settlement nor may it be the foundation for assessing damages to injured parties.

Concentration of Market Power—a situation where the top firms in an industry collectively control the vast majority of industry sales or assets. It is measured by the cumulative market shares of the four or eight largest firms.

Creamskimming—to take the most desirable and valuable part of a business, akin to skimming cream off the top of milk bottles prior to pasteurization.

Deficit Financing—a situation where the costs of production (including normal profits) are not fully covered by payments, forcing producers to either sacrifice normal profits or cross-subsidize operations from revenues derived in other areas.

Economies of Scale—declining levels of average cost accompanying greater expansion of product output and optimal use of plant and equipment.

Equity—ownership of a company arising from purchasing shares or stock or building the enterprise from scratch.

Excess Profits—profits over and above normal profits.

Monopsony—a monopoly from the buyer's (rather than the seller's) perspective.

Network—the simultaneous transmission of a program by two or more stations or systems, interconnected by wire or satellites; it also refers to organizations that provide a continuous flow of such programs to a prearranged groups of stations or systems that are affiliates.

Normal Profits—the rate of return on invested capital for entrepreneurs that provides adequate compensation to them to invest their scarce time and funds in the enterprise rather than switch to another one; also referred to as the opportunity cost of entrepreneurship.

Oligopoly—a market structure composed of a few very large and powerful firms than control an industry. The higher the market concentration, the stronger/tighter the oligopoly.

Opportunity Cost—the economic value of the next best alternative to what one is currently doing.

Self-Sufficiency—the condition in which a firm is totally reliant on itself for its supply of inputs into the production or distribution process. Widespread self-sufficiency indicates significant vertical integration.

Shared Monopoly—when a cartel arrangement is so stable and successful that the several firms operate in unison as if a single monopolist controlled the industry.

Stages of Production—product is said to flow through several stages from its earliest origins as raw material through various manufacturing, distribution, and wholesaling levels until its final appearance as a retail consumer product. Each successive stage adds complexity and value to the product.

Vertical Integration—the situation where a company occupies adjacent stages of production in an industry, thereby removing this stage either partially or wholly from access by outside companies (depending on the level of self-sufficiency).

8

The Economics of the Cable Industry

Sidney L. Carroll
Herbert H. Howard
University of Tennessee

Cable television began around 1949 as a grass-roots endeavor to bring television signals to areas of difficult reception. Throughout the 1950s and 1960s, it expanded rapidly, mainly in small cities and towns across the country, usually providing subscribers with retransmission of one or more affiliates of each TV network, educational television, and, in some cases, one or more independent stations depending on the availability of off-air or microwave signals. In contrast, cable at the end of the 20th century is a major telecommunications industry. Of the 97 million households in the country, cable is available to an estimated 97%, and subscribed to by about 67%, or 64.3 million households (A. C. Nielsen Company, personal communication, April 10, 1997, phone call with H. Howard). For comparison, only 94% of households have telephones.

In 1996, the cable industry's revenue was an estimated $26.6 billion (*Cable TV Facts*, 1997). Annual spending on basic cable in 1995 was $15.59 billion, on pay cable $5.26 billion, on pay-per-view movies $708 million, and on interactive television $6.1 billion. Direct broadcast satellite (DBS) brought in an additional estimated $420 million. This exceeded the amount spent on recorded music ($12.068 billion), newspapers ($9.5 billion), consumer books ($15.23 billion), consumer magazines ($6.6 billion), home video rentals and sales ($14.029 billion), theatrical movies ($5.396 billion), CD-ROMs ($910 million), or online services ($708 million; Gregor, 1995). The Cable Television Advertising Bureau (CAB) predicts that by the year 2002, the American public will devote 42% of its entertainment dollar to subscription cable (*Cable TV Facts*, 1995).

Although broadcast programming is still an integral part of its service, cable television has become a significant electronic delivery system for a myriad of broadcast and cable originated services. Nearly all subscribers (95%) are served by systems with 30 or more channels, and nearly one half (47%) have service from 54 or more channels. Many of today's modern cable systems have capacities of 100 or more channels, and systems of 500 channels have been predicted for the next century. A typical system in the mid-1990s provides programming from local network affiliates and independent stations, a few distant "superstations," a vast array of satellite delivered cable networks, pay television (movie) channels, pay-per-view programming, and audio services.

VIEWING OF CABLE TELEVISION

Over the past decade, viewing patterns have shifted noticeably as viewers have increasingly tuned to cable networks and premium channels, while watching broadcast television less than before. Two factors are largely responsible for these trends: (a) expanded availability of cable service, resulting in more subscribers and greater audience potential; and (b) cable network programming has grown in diversity and popularity. In general, families that subscribe to basic cable tend to watch more television than noncable families, and households that subscribe to pay cable services view more television than those that subscribe only to basic service.

The share of viewing of basic cable networks in all U.S. television households (all-day average) rose from 7.2% in 1982 to 31% in 1996 (Coleman, 1996). Viewing to network affiliated broadcast TV stations, including Fox affiliates, declined from 69.3% in 1984 to 58.9% in 1994, and viewing to all broadcast TV stations dropped from 86.3% in 1984 to 69.9% in 1994 (Veronis, Suhler & Associates, 1995).

In cabled households, viewing of cable network programming has become significantly greater. For the first time ever, the combined prime-time ratings of the basic cable networks surpassed the three major broadcast networks in the cable only universe during the third quarter of 1995 ("Cable Beats," 1995). The basic cable networks received a combined 39.0 share versus 36.9 for the three major broadcast networks (excluding Fox) combined within the cable universe (*Cable TV Facts*, 1997). Although a few of the leading cable networks attract average audiences ranging from 1 to 2 prime-time rating points, most networks reach fragmentary audiences of less than 1. However, some individual programs have won substantial ratings in the 5 to 10 point range. For the 1995–1996 season, within the cable universe, all cable networks combined attracted about 51% (43% for basic and 8% for pay TV) of 24-hour-day viewing, compared with 40% for the broadcast networks, 17% for independents and an estimated 3% for public stations (*Cable TV Facts*, 1997). Totals exceed 100% due to multiset usage.

ECONOMICS OF CABLE DISTRIBUTION AND NETWORKS

Two elements comprise the modern cable industry: local systems, mostly owned by multiple system operators (MSOs), and cable network companies, many of which provide several satellite distributed networks or program services. There are more than 11,000 local systems in the United States, ranging in size from less than 25 to more than 1 million subscribers. Ownership of individual systems ranges from small proprietorships to major multinational firms. Table 8.1 shows the 15 largest multiple systems operators as of April 1, 1997.

Cable Distribution Revenues

Once in operation, cable systems tend to generate substantial amounts of cash. Revenues come from four sources: basic and pay-TV subscription fees, pay-per-view fees, advertising, and extra customer charges for multiple TV hookups or remote control boxes. The bulk of a local cable system's revenues (85%) come from basic and pay-TV subscriber fees. In 1995 subscriptions per household averaged about $22 per month for basic service and $0.74 for pay services. (Veronis, Suhler & Associates, 1995). Average revenue per subscriber has varied from $32.18 in 1993, down to $30.35 in 1994 in response to Congressional action to control rates, then rising to $32.26 in 1995—a 4.1% increase in subscriber rates when the Consumer Price Index rose only 2.5% (Fox, 1995). Price hikes averaged 10% in 1997 as cable companies struggled under enormous debt loads. The number of

TABLE 8.1

15 Largest Multiple System Operators as of April 1, 1997

Rank	MSO	Basic Subs	TVHH	Cable HH
1	Tele-Communications, Inc.	14,742,086	15.4	22.9
2	Time Warner Cable	7,321,000	7.6	11.2
3	US West Media Group	4,716,948	4.9	7.3
4	Time Warner Entertainment-Advance/Newhouse	4,479,000	4.7	6.9
5	Comcast	3,923,536	4.1	6.1
6	Cox Communications	3,923,536	4.1	6.1
7	Cablevision System	2,807,575	2.9	4.4
8	Adelphia Communications	1,800,850	1.9	2.8
9	Jones Intercabel	1,524,500	1.6	2.4
10	Marcus Cable	1,271,140	1.3	2.0
11	Century Communications	1,250,600	1.3	1.9
12	Falcon Cable	1,167,850	1.2	1.8
13	Lenfest Group	1,141,519	1.2	1.8
14	Charter Communications	1,139,354	1.2	1.8
15	InterMedia Partners	937,399	1.0	1.5

TV HH Universe = 96 million (A. C. Nielson, 1996–1997). Cable vision = 64,320,000 (A. C. Nielson, 1996–1997) [67% penetration].
Note. From *Cable Vision* magazine. [On-line, April 1997]. Used with permission.

subscribers, rising at a 4.26% pace for the year ended July, 1995, slowed to 1.1% in the first six months of 1996 under intense pressure from DBS (Lesly, Grover, & Gross, 1996).

Revenues for cable companies from pay-TV are twofold: (a) monthly charges to subscribers of about $2.75 a month for an "addressable box" and (b) the sale of "tiers" of pay programming where the content can be movies, sports, cartoons, operas, or other topics too numerous to list. These channels can be sold separately or in packages for monthly rates ranging from $1 per month per channel to $20 for combinations of channels in packages and pay-per-view. These charges are in addition to the basic cable charges.

Cable advertising revenues have surged, accompanying cable's audience growth. Spending for cable advertising, including cable networks and local systems, reached the $2.5 billion level in 1990, increasing to $6 billion in 1996 (*Cable TV Facts*, 1997). In addition to national advertisements carried by cable networks, cable systems have attracted significant and steadily increasing amounts of local revenue from advertising inserted on various cable networks. Advertising agencies have become aware of cable's numerous benefits, such as more targeted programming audiences, lower costs-per-thousand for audiences reached, better opportunities for program sponsorship, greater flexibility in message lengths and formats, and lower overall costs. Advertising sales on local cable systems are expected to increase dramatically during the next few years, from $634 million in 1990 to an estimated $1.9 billion in 1997.

Although premium pay-TV services have leveled off at about 44 million household subscriptions, pay-per-view is just beginning to fulfill its promise. In 1995 pay-per-view revenue, usually from movies or sporting events, amounted to only $583 million, barely 2% of the cable industry's $23 billion total. However, pay-per-view revenue is expected to increase at a moderate rate for the next few years.

Systems with 150 or more channels based on fiber-optic and satellite technology are beginning to be offered by cable, phone, and satellite companies. New revenue strategies are producing results: DirectTV, a direct satellite broadcaster, by devoting 50 or so of its 150 channels to movies at any one time, offers up to 40 movies that start at frequent intervals. The strategy has produced a monthly "buy rate" of 1.5 to 2 movies per subscriber per month, about five times greater than the typical pay-per-view subscription rate (Robichaux, 1995b). In October 1996, for the first time, a movie debut on HBO outdrew all four networks ("Debut," 1996).

Sporting events are another engine of revenue. The Tyson versus McNeeley fight on August 21, 1995 (which lasted 89 seconds) was sold for $49 to 1.4 million subscribers (2.2% of cable subscribers) and brought in an estimated $63 million (Robichaux, 1995b). Fierce bidding wars are breaking out for the rights to sporting events: NBC paid $1.25 billion for the rights to the 2000 Summer and 2002 Winter Olympic Games for a combination of broadcast and cable network distribution

(Nidex, 1995). The price may have been justified: NBC's rating for the 1996 Olympics were well more than double their previous summertime ratings (Carter, 1996). Cable networks are joining bidding coalitions for major sporting events and are offering many college games or professional sports not being broadcast by television networks as pay-per-view events.

Cable Distribution Expenses

Revenues from a cable business must cover all essential costs of doing business. These costs fall into two categories: capital and operating. Essential fixed capital costs for a cable franchisee are for signal reception and transmission facilities. Operating costs include both the variable transmission costs and the variable costs of operation.

Reception costs usually do not vary much after initial construction (or purchase) of the system. Included are the headend, which consists of the receiving antennas and electronics necessary for access to satellite and broadcast signals and the building to house this equipment. Engineering and other costs for the building vary with options chosen.

Transmission capital costs cover purchasing and installing cable and amplification equipment to carry the signals from the headend to the customers and the equipment the customer must have to receive the various levels of service offered. These costs typically vary with the number of subscribers, the terrain, and density of population in the community among other factors.

The variable costs of operating a cable company are twofold: transmission and operating costs. Variable transmission costs are those associated with the number and turnover of customers (replacement of decoder boxes) and continuing expenses for ongoing customers (depreciation of decoder boxes in use by customers).

Cable owners face an array of variable operating expenses including:

1. A required franchise fee, typically about 3% of gross subscriber revenues payable to the local franchising government.
2. Technical costs, including installation of cable, maintenance of the cable plant, including the headend and the distribution system, as well as the tuner boxes rented to subscribers.
3. Program expenses, including payment for network services (ranging from $0.05 to $1 per subscriber per month per network), copyright fees for distant TV stations carried (approximately 3.75% of gross revenues per station), and costs of any local program origination.
4. Marketing/promotion costs involved in soliciting subscribers.
5. Customer servicing costs, including service calls, billing, and collecting monthly fees.
6. Advertising sales and service costs involved in soliciting and servicing advertising clients on various local and network channels.

7. General and administrative expenses incurred in operating the system's business offices.

   In addition to operating expenses, most cable companies have debt obligations incurred in building or acquiring their systems. Such reduction obligations generally are scheduled in installments and must be met on a regular basis in addition to monthly operating expenses. Property and equipment depreciation also are included as costs, as well as in cash flow figures. Because of heavy depreciation, the cable industry's financial performance is usually evaluated on a cash flow basis.

   One recent source of debt for the industry has been the widespread replacement of older cables with fiber-optic cable. Although fiber-optic cable is hugely capital intensive, it is a true technological breakthrough. Capable of transmitting a vast number of two-way audio and video signals simultaneously, this technology greatly expands the range of services technically available through a television set. In addition, cable operators face the expense of converting to a digital system with the approaching debut of high-definition TV (HDTV) broadcasting.

Cable Network Revenues and Expenses

Cable networks provide the programming shown on cable television. Although there were about 200 satellite-delivered cable networks in 1997, 12 firms own most of these programming services. Much of the media frenzy today is focused on determining who controls the resources necessary to provide programming—film libraries and movie studios—and the distribution facilities for exhibiting the programming.

   Table 8.2 shows cable network owners and subscribers to basic cable networks. Conceptually, the revenues and expenses related to cable networks are straightforward. Producing and purchasing programming for cable or broadcast networks—whether sitcoms, movies, game shows, or sports—requires the commitment of resources. The sale of these products to cable systems, usually at a set amount per subscriber, or to television broadcasters raises the revenues to cover these expenses. In the past, the functions of cable distributors and cable programming producers were required by law to be carried out by independent companies. In 1992, the FCC began relaxing this ruling, putting in motion the consolidation of the cable television functions.

A CHANGING INDUSTRY STRUCTURE

The world in which cable television operates today is radically different than the one which existed less than 5 years ago. It is changing so rapidly that no one can predict whether in 5 years there will even *be* a cable television industry or whether it will have become an indistinguishable part of the telecommunications industry that provides households with an array of services. Theoretically, a householder

TABLE 8.2

Major Cable Network Owners as of April 1, 1997

Cable Network Owner	Basic Cable Networks	Networks Owned or Partially Owned
Time Warner (Turner)	11	CNN, Headline News, CNNFN, CNNSI, TBS, TNT, Turner Movie Classics, Cartoon Network, HBO, COURT TV, Comedy Central (50%), BET (17%)
Viacom, Inc. (Paramount)	7	MTV, VH-1, Nickelodeon/Nick at Night, Nick at Nite TV Land, Lifetime (33%), Comedy Central (50%), USA Network (50%), Showtime, The Movie Channel
Disney/ABC	6	ESPN (80%), ESPN2 (20%), ESPNews (80%), Lifetime (33%), A&E(33%), History (33%)
Hearst Publishing	6	ESPN (20%), ESPN2 (20%), ESPNews (20%), Lifetime (33%), A&E(33%), History (33)
Liberty Media (TCI)	5	Home Shopping Network (42%), The Family Channel (28%), Court (33%), BET (17%), FiTV (18%)
NBC (General Electric)	4	CNBC, MSNBC (50%), A&E (33%), History (33%)
CBS (Westinghouse)	3	The Nashville Network (TNN), Music Television, Eye on People
Discovery Communication	3	Discovery, The Learning Channel, Animal Planet
News Corporation	3	Fox, fX, Fox News
Cablevision Systems	3	American Movie Classics, Bravo, Sports Central
Landmark Communications	2	The Weather Channel, The Travel Channel
International Family Entertainment	2	The Family Channel, Game Show Network
Black Entertainment Television	1	BET
Scripps Howard	2	Home and Garden TV, The Food Channel
MCA, Inc. (Universal)	1	USA Network (50%)
Comcast	1	QVC

could mix and match both the company (or companies) and the services they offer. Over fiber-optic cable or with an 18-inch direct broadcast television receiver or wireless technologies one could receive all currently available television, local and long-distance telephone, connection to the Internet and the World Wide Web, home banking, and home buying services among other products limited only by imagination. The communications media are currently undergoing extensive changes, manifested in technological and ownership convergence. There are at least seven reasons:

1. In 1992 the Federal Communications Commission (FCC) began dismantling the barriers separating the producers and distributors of cable television.
2. The FCC began to lift rules that had prevented phone companies and cable companies from competing. Several federal courts in different sections of the country ruled that phone companies could buy cable companies if the same company did not offer both services to the same market.
3. Congress, responding to changes occurring elsewhere, passed the 1996 Telecommunications Act specifying how competition between local and long-distance phone companies and between cable companies and the various phone companies would work.
4. Technological breakthroughs occurred. Fiber-optic cable that can carry enormous numbers of two-way signals at the speed of light became technically feasible and both phone and cable companies began installing it at a furious pace. Direct broadcast systems that can deliver digital phone and television signals to a householder's 18-inch dish were perfected. Effective wireless systems that can compete with other technology became feasible.
5. Both governments and companies began realizing what can be done with these new technologies that create incredible new capacity for phones and for television. Signals can be delivered by land (fiber-optic) or by air (satellite or wireless). Although all technologies are enormously expensive, costs can be spread among the world population.
6. Phone and cable services in much of the world are nonexistent at worst and barely developed at best, offering enormous potential financial rewards to those capable of offering them these services.
7. Phone, television, and Internet services can be offered as one system for the first time.

In the mid-1990s merger mania accelerated. In the nation's second biggest merger ever, Walt Disney bought Capital Cities/ABC for $19 billion. Moreover, Time Warner purchased Turner Communications for $7.5 billion, and Westinghouse bought CBS for $5.4 billion. Cable television distributors also consolidated. U.S. West's 1996 acquisition of third-ranked Continental Cablevision rocked the industry. Telecommunications, Inc. (TCI) bought Viacom's 1.2 million subscribers. Cox Cable, Comcast, and other cable operators also made major acquisitions.

Motives driving these mergers are strategic, not financial. They include at least:

1. Gaining position and expertise in the imminent national and international race to provide households and businesses with all phone, television, and computer services.

2. Reaping economies of scope—where one company can provide multiple communications services more cheaply than separate companies can supply each. Duplicative expenses in equipment, lines, billing, and management can be eliminated.
3. Vertical integration of production and distribution. Disney has enormous programming capabilities and by owning ABC it can control all facets of distribution—to whom the programming is sold, for how much, and when. It can cut costs on the boundaries of production and distribution—it no longer, for example, has to exert effort to sell its programs to another company. Moreover, it controls all rights to coordinate and promote its products from toy ducks to theme parks over its media properties worldwide.
4. Increasing market power over markets.

These changes have affected the current value and ownership structure of cable properties.

Value of Cable Systems

The market for cable systems has been active, but per subscriber rates have become less variable than in the past. Major 1989 sales/mergers ranged in value from about $1,850 to $2,850 per subscriber ("Brokers," 1990). In 1995 Comcast paid $2,000 per subscriber for Scripps Howard's 800,000 subscribers (Robichaux, 1995a), and TCI bought Viacom's 1.2 million subscribers for $2.25 billion or a per subscriber rate of $1,875 (Landler, 1995).

Another standard measure of the value of a company is the ratio of the value of the outstanding stock to annual cash flow. At $8 billion, the Time Warner/Turner merger was priced at 17 times cash flow; Disney paid 12 times cash flow for Capital Cities/ABC (Grover & DeGeorge, 1995) and Comcast between 10 and 11 times cash flow for Scripps/Howard (Robichaux, 1995a).

Ownership

Concentration of cable distributors is increasing. The percentage of households served by the 10 largest cable owners grew from 56% in 1994 to 73.6% in 1997, and the percentage served by the 50 largest MSOs leapt from 87% in 1994 to 96.6% in 1997(see Table 8.1). Spatial concentration is also a factor as MSO firms strive to develop clusters of systems that, in close proximity to each other, allow for greater management efficiency. Interlocking ownership is a further complication. The largest three cable distributors and Turner, one of the largest programmers, each has ownership stakes in the others. In 1997 local cable television markets still tend to be monopolies, but that could change in the ongoing telecom convergence.

In recent years, another type of affiliation among cable owners has emerged in most large markets. Under arrangements known as "interconnects," all of the cable systems in a metropolitan area, regardless of ownership, join together to sell and disseminate advertising messages on a market wide basis. The New York Interconnect is the largest with 4,336,000 aggregate subscribers (*Cable TV Facts*, 1997). Through such joint activities, cable owners can compete with radio, broadcast television, and newspapers for marketwide advertising budgets.

Companies are picking elements from many entertainment fields to form multifaceted organizations that combine such formerly separate operations as cable system ownership, cable networks, telephone service, film/video studios, broadcast networks, and video rental and sales outlets. Focus is shifting from the U.S. market to international arenas. Disney, for example, expects international revenue to increase significantly as the company begins to take advantage of synergies and cross promotions, particularly in television programming and distribution of networks such as ESPN and the Disney Channel (Trachtenberg, 1995). Both Disney and ABC/Capital Cities already have a significant presence overseas. Revenues could expand and turn into a mix similar to that at Time Warner, where overseas revenue from music and film production is larger than domestic revenue (Bannon, 1995).

Ownership concentration of various national industries, including the communications media, has long been a matter of public policy concern with respect to potential anticompetitive practices. A second traditional policy concern relates to the vertical integration of the production and distribution of products, a practice outlawed in the film industry in the Paramount case of 1948 (*U.S. v. Paramount Pictures, Inc.*). A third national issue is the need to assure an adequate diversity of media voices in the film and electronic media industries.

Concentration in ownership on all levels is worrying some. FCC Commissioner Andrew Barrett, a Republican, noted that "by the year 2000 we'll probably see 10 to 12 companies controlling everything we see, hear and convey in voice and data" (Pearl, 1995b). For those who believe that there should be many voices, predictions for specific media groups are dire: within a few years, 75% of the national radio audience may be served by four major groups; a similar shakeout is expected among TV affiliates. Analysts and executives expect the major networks to keep on buying, along with newspaper giants such as the Tribune, Hearst, and Gannett Companies.

What do these consolidations portend for the future? Concentrated ownership creates power. The clout of multiple-station ownership is already clear in radio in such markets as Cincinnati, Denver, and Rochester, where a single company has captured 40% to 50% of the local advertising market by segmenting the audience over four to eight radio stations either owned by the company or operated through sales agreements with other operators. This strategy already has begun to emerge among TV broadcasters in some markets.

Ownership structure also can affect effective management. Culture clashes between individuals, firms, or both are common as mergers occur. Rupert Murdoch of the News Corporation and Sumner Redstone of Viacom have succeeded in expansion by maintaining a single controlling shareholder. Such an arrangement gives the CEO the ability to plan and enforce a coordinated strategy and to weather tough times without worrying about losing his job. Time Warner's Levin does not have such leeway in his firm's merger with Turner (Fabrikant, 1995).

Motives for Mergers

In the current wave of mergers several strategic themes have emerged as companies assess value in choosing partners. Factors that appear to have influenced Disney's decision to acquire Capital Cities/ABC are: (a) ABC's extensive expansion overseas and in cable made it a more interesting property than CBS (Ramstad, 1995), (b) Disney views the key to future growth as greater control of both creation and distribution of telecommunication products, and (c) the uncertainty of predicting how digital entertainment will eventually be delivered to households—telephone lines, cable television, wireless or satellite broadcasts—makes outright control of distribution channels preferable to the current system of fuzzy alliances with independent entities. Alliances, by their nature, are slow and hard to control. By acquiring more segments of the media-communications field, Disney upped its odds of putting together the right combination (Wysocki, 1995).

Economic forces are also at work. Buying existing properties is cheaper than building new ones. Westinghouse recognized in buying out CBS that it is not possible to build a comparable media company from scratch—at least not at reasonable cost (Narasetti, 1995). Economies of scope enabled Turner Broadcasting to launch an all business channel for about $10 million, approximately one-tenth the startup cost of most new cable-TV channels.

THE MECHANISMS FOR CHANGE

Federal laws and regulations as determined by Congress, the Federal Court System, the Federal Communication Commission, the Justice Department and the Federal Trade Commission, all are moving in the direction of changing the rules for competition in the telecommunications industry. However, the Federal government is aiming at a moving target as many changes are being put into action by companies and by states responding to market opportunities. Eighty percent of phone revenues are regulated by state public utility commissions, and commissions all over the country are opening up competitive trials. Before the enactment of the Telecommunications Act of 1996, some observers feared that the resulting myriad of independent actions could create a "regulatory crazy quilt" (Arnst, 1994). The future economic course of the cable industry now depends on the competitive forces that were released by the passage of the Act of 1996.

Governmental Bodies

Congress: The Telecommunications Act.   Before the passage of the Telecommunications Act of 1996, Congress had been moving toward massive telecommunications restructuring for several years. For example, bills were passed by both
the House and Senate that would permit direct competition between phone and
cable companies and between long-distance and local phone companies. Media
competitors began making strategic moves in anticipation of passage of some form
of new legislation for the telecommunications industries. Finally, after several years
of consideration, the new and far-ranging Telecommunications Act was passed in
February 1996. This Act, passed on a nonpartisan basis, was intended to spur
competition in radio and TV broadcasting, cable and telephony, as well as to
"benefit the public through lower prices, new jobs and innovative services" (Stern,
1996, p. 9). Many unresolved questions that had plagued the media and telecommunications industries for years were resolved. Others were passed on to the
Federal Communications Commission for further consideration. The following are
among the important questions that were decided in the Act.

Can telephone companies enter the cable field?   Under previous regulations, a
phone company could acquire or begin a cable system, but only in markets outside
its franchised telephone service area. Such acquisitions continue to be allowed.
However, the Act also repealed the statutory ban against phone operators providing
video programming in their own service areas.
Can cable companies enter the telephone business?   The Act, which supersedes
state and local regulations, allows cable operators to provide local telephone
services. The law requires local phone operators to negotiate with new telephone
providers for interconnection, number portability, dialing parity, access to rights-
of-way and reciprocal compensation.
How may telephone companies participate in the cable business?   In addition
to acquiring cable systems outside their operating telephone service areas, telephone companies may establish new cable or video services within their service
areas to compete with cable systems. Telephone companies may not acquire cable
systems within their service territories except under limited conditions in non-urban
areas with fewer than 35,000 population. However, ownership of up to 10% of a
cable system by the local telephone company is allowed. Thus, cable and phone
companies without major ownership stakes in each other are allowed to compete.
What rules govern the operation of telco-owned cable services?   The telephone
operators were required to choose from among three forms of regulation for their
new services: cable system, common carrier, or a new designation of "open video
system." Open video systems must adhere to the same rules on network nonduplication, syndicated exclusivity, must-carry and retransmission consent that cable
systems are required to follow. However, they are not subject to other federal cable
rules and are not required to obtain a local franchise.

What happens to cable rate regulation? In anticipation of heightened competition for cable service from telephone companies in the near future, the Act lifted the regulation of rates cable systems may charge subscribers for extended basic service within 3 years. It deregulated the rates of small systems with fewer than 50,000 subscribers that are owned by small companies immediately upon the Act's passage. Furthermore, the Act deregulated the rates of any system that receives "effective competition" from a telephone company providing comparable video service by any means other than direct broadcast satellite.

What limits would TV broadcasters face? The Telecommunications Act eliminated the numerical limit of 12 stations previously imposed on broadcast TV owners, while also raising the coverage limit from 25% of the nation's television households to 35%.

Could a cable company buy a broadcast network or TV station? The 1996 law permits common ownership of broadcast networks and cable systems. Previously, a cable company that covered more than 10% of cable-ready homes could not own a national broadcast network. Several cable networks already were owned by cable-system operators. The Act also repealed the previous law that barred common ownership of TV stations and cable systems within a market, but it did not overturn the FCC's rule barring such combinations.

What ownership limits would cable multiple-system operators face? Multiple ownership of cable systems resembles group ownership of broadcast stations and chain ownership in the newspaper and magazine publishing industries. Unlike radio and TV ownership, however, no limits had been imposed previously on cable MSO ownership, although a 25% cable household limit had been mentioned at one time by the FCC. The Telecommunications Act of 1996 maintained the status quo. No ownership limits were imposed on the number of cable systems any single organization may own.

What about the must-carry requirement? The Act provided for a continuation of must carry protection for local television stations within their Designated Market Areas. Subsequently, the cable industry sought court relief from the must carry requirement on First Amendment grounds. However, in March 1997, the U.S. Supreme Court upheld this requirement because of the importance of preserving local television service.

Federal Communications Commission (FCC). The FCC is the federal government agency that has primary responsibility to maintain a strong, diverse communications industry. FCC rules govern how the media mergers of today are being structured.

In 1992, 2 years before the Telecommunications Act was passed, the FCC changed two major rules affecting cable: It removed the barriers that formerly prohibited telephone companies from cable ownership, permitting them to own systems outside their operating telephone territory (FCC: Telephone Company-Cable Television Cross-Ownership Rules, 1992b); and it relaxed its rules to permit limited ownership of cable systems by the broadcast networks (FCC: Network-Cable Cross Ownership Rule, 1992a). Those changes, now codified into law, resulted in much of the acquisition activity in the telecommunications industry in the mid-1990s.

The FCC has the power to shape the telecommunications industry, and it uses it. Among its decisions, the FCC, in recent years, released AT&T from rate caps, required News Corporation to reduce control of some Fox-TV stations, barred a phone company from choosing what programs may be carried on its network, and required an auction for a hotly contested satellite-TV license.

With respect to cable, more recently the FCC has dealt with specific cases of rate deregulation based on a determination of when a cable system experiences "effective competition," as well as developing rules for spectrum auctions for multipoint distribution services or wireless cable, setting national standards for prices telephone companies may charge cable firms that hook up with the local phone network, and promoting universal availability of telecommunications services.

Courts.   The courts interpret the laws and FCC and FTC actions. A series of court decisions have changed the fundamental relationship between cable companies and the communities they serve. Not surprisingly, some decisions have helped, others have hurt the cable industry. In one of its most important decisions for the communications field, the Supreme Court, in 1997, upheld the must-carry rule that requires cable systems to carry the signals of local television stations in their designated market areas. While cable interests held that their First Amendment rights were violated by the must carry rule, the Court held that the need for citizen access to local stations broadcasting local information was of greater importance as a public issue.

Other cable issues for Court action include access to cable private property when property owners prefer to operate satellite master antenna television (SMATV) systems; taxation of cable service by states; retention of franchises from communities that may become dissatisfied with cable owners' service; the legality of the traditional franchise fee levied by local governments; and the provision of the 1996 Act that requires cable operators to scramble any program a subscriber deems unsuitable for children. In a deregulated environment, the question of competition among local companies raises such interesting questions as: Who has access to poles and whether just anyone can string a cable? Do cities retain control of the installation of fiber optics beneath their streets?

The Justice Department and the Federal Trade Commission (FTC).
The antitrust division of the Justice Department and the Federal Trade Commission (FTC) are the guardians of competition for the government and are responsible for

scrutinizing mergers for anticompetitive impact. Since the passage of the Telecommunications Act allowing common ownership of as many as eight radio stations in most large markets, the Justice Department has stepped in to limit some radio mergers when those combinations would result in control of more than 40% to 45% of the local radio advertising expenditures.

Other issues taken under consideration by the Justice Department include whether merged companies will create market power in content or distribution, whether competing content providers will have enough outlets remaining, and whether other distributors will have sufficient access to content (Pearl, 1995b). The FTC is studying whether control over enormous amounts of programming could be used to stymie new rivals, what the impact would be, for example, of giving TCI cable systems the right to receive Turner programming at discounted prices for 20 years, and how the concentration arising from the new company's control of approximately 35% of the U.S. cable market would affect competitiveness in the industry (Gruley, 1995).

Regulatory Issues. Although the Telecommunications Act determined public policy on cable service in many respects, a number of issues remain to be decided by the FCC and the courts. Issues include alleged abuse of power by cable owners who dictate what cable networks and stations are available to viewers (in an environment of ever-increasing sources of cable network programming), the public's access to popular sports broadcasts, and issues regarding exemption of systems from rate control based on significant competition. Cable companies have flagrantly dropped or refused to carry some local TV stations before the Supreme Court upheld the must-carry rule. They also have shifted some stations and cable networks to undesirable channel positions while giving more favored channels to program services in which the MSO had a financial interest. TV stations also are concerned that major sports events may be siphoned away to pay-TV. Still another issue relates to control of cable programming by MSO companies that also have ownership interests in cable networks. At issue are the rights of SMATV and wireless cable to carry such programming in competition with traditional cable systems.

Other unresolved issues at the time of this writing include proposed changes in the copyright payment schedule for cable operators, and the question of granting more than one cable franchise in a given community. How these issues are ultimately decided clearly will affect the profitability of individual systems and, therefore, their value as media properties.

Market Forces

Domestic Markets. How serious are the competitive challenges facing large cable operators? The stock market provides a comprehensive assessment of the future profitability of each industry. That competition is serious for the industry is reflected by the fact that a 3-year index of the stock of large cable operators trails the Standard & Poor's 500-stock index by 60% (Lesly, Grover, & Gross, 1996). The cable industry ranked at or near the very bottom of the Standard & Poor industry rankings in early 1997. A danger of such poor stock price performance is the threat of unfriendly takeover bids. At this point the market seems quite wary about cable's future.

Cable operators, however, believe they have the most enticing new business opportunity in years. Cable as it now exists can offer ultra-high-speed access to the global computing web, a feature neither telephone nor satellite services can yet match (Landler, 1996a).

International Markets.   Driving the consolidation in the U.S. telecommunications industry is the burgeoning global market and the need for expertise in designing and running diverse telecommunications empires as worldwide markets explode. Germany is drawing particular interest with an audience of 80 million, advertising revenues of almost $4 billion, and advertising growth rates among the highest of any media market in Europe, a relatively high percentage of cable subscribers, and a tradition of poor local programming (Nash, 1995). The ultimate prize, however, is the Asian market, home to roughly two thirds of the world's population. A number of U.S. companies, including Time Warner and Turner Broadcasting, have been stepping up their operations in Asia to compete with Murdoch's Star TV. Satellites are already major transmission channels for cable systems. Driving further development of such wireless technologies is the lure of a billion Chinese customers to whom both phone and television could be offered. In that situation, fiber-optic cable is too slow and too expensive to install.

How these new markets may work can be seen in Great Britain, which opened its doors in 1991 as a laboratory for telecommunications deregulation. By 1995, 146 organizations had been licensed to supply every form of telecommunication service. The most important of these were television and telephone over the same lines and competition in local phoning. Competitors are being drawn from all over the world and from many different industries, all spending big money to learn how to compete in this environment. NYNEX, Britain's Number 2 cable operator, has invested $540 million and plans to spend up to $3 billion by 1998. Companies such as Energis, owned by 12 regional British electric companies, are in the fray along with U.S. media and phone companies (Flynn, 1994). Telephone rates have come down: In 1993 British Telecommunications (BT) cut its long distance rates by as much as 60% on weekends and nights. At that time New York-based NYNEX, which was providing phone service over its British cable television network, had been undercutting BT's long distance rates by 13% (Hudson, 1993). In business markets Mercury has skimmed top corporate accounts, helping pare BT's share from 94% to 88% in 3 years. Some 26,000 residential customers a month are switching to the cable operators and analysts predict that the upstarts could win up to 35% of the market by 2000. BT held 100% of the market in 1991, and still had 90% as late as 1993 (Hudson, 1993).

How cable operators fare in their new world created by a new regulatory and technological scene in the domestic markets and an explosion of opportunity in the international markets remains to be seen. The cable industry is spending billions to upgrade its systems, while continuing to consolidate into a small number of large and super-large MSOs.

COMPETITORS OF CABLE DISTRIBUTORS AND NETWORKS

Distributors

Phone Companies. As part of their aggressive new stance, almost every important telephone company has merged with, acquired an interest in, developed an alliance with one or more cable organizations, or done any combination thereof, since the FCC allowed the telcos to enter the cable field in 1992. With the enactment of the Telecommunications Act of 1996, telephone companies have gained permission to enter into the cable (video transmission) business as well as to transmit information services. One transaction that had great impact on the telecommunications landscape was the 1996 merger of Continental Cablevision into US West, a $11.3 billion deal. Various telcos reportedly have been developing their own "one line" systems for providing cable, telephone, and Internet service. Ameritech, for one, has launched new cable service in communities located in four midwestern states in competition with franchised cable systems.

In a strange turnaround, some cable companies have bought interests in cellular telephone companies and data transmitting centers and have gained authority to provide telephone services on their own systems. Limited trials of telephony service have been undertaken by some of the larger cable operators. Many cable executives believe their industry will have a bright future in the delivery of 500 video channels, high-speed Internet access, and telephony.

The long-distance companies are seeking ways to get around dealing with local phone companies. AT&T, frustrated by the slow pace of talks with the regional Bells, is negotiating to lease local phone networks from alternative carriers and is in talks with Winstar to provide voice and data service in 150 markets nationwide in 1997 or 1998 (Rosenbush, 1997).

Phone and cable companies have plotted for years to invade each other's territories. In the turmoil following the passage of the Telecommunications Act of 1996, some in each camp who had been actively pursuing invasion plans have dropped them, while others have seen this as the time for entry. Long-distance and local phone companies have refocused their attention on their core businesses while cable companies are fending off the satellite companies. Liberty Cable, for example, plans to combine residential cable and telephone service in New York City with rates 15% lower than those now being offered by NYNEX and Time Warner (Landler, 1996c). TCI, on the other hand, is concentrating on upgrading its service with digital cable boxes that match satellites' ability to deliver up to 150 channels with high-quality digital signals, dropping efforts to provide telephone service (Robichaux, 1997). At the same time Ameritech—owned by four phone companies and the Walt Disney Company—will begin offering television programming to a potential audience of 200,000 telephone customers early in 1997 (Landler, 1996b). All the new technologies are capable of handling phone, video, and computer needs, and so the long-term prospects are for a renewal of widespread turf invasion.

Direct Satellites. Following the 1994 launch of digital television from direct broadcast satellites, more than 1 million digital satellite receivers were sold during the first year of DBS service. This public reception of DBS receiving dishes made them the hottest new product in the history of the consumer electronics industry. Subscribers praised the crisp picture quality and the availability of up to 150 channels from DBS (Trachtenberg, 1995).

At present, three major and two smaller companies are offering DBS to the public on a subscriber basis, much like cable service. The combined customer base of the five entities totaled about 4 million subscribers in November 1996 (Robichaux, 1996).

Both United States Satellite Broadcasting (USSB) and DirecTV (Hughes Electronics) offer an array of programming that includes most of the most popular cable networks, but local programming is not available. Primestar, a third service owned by TCI Satellite Entertainment and four other MSO partners, offers 94 channels of video. At the beginning of 1997, DirecTV led with about 2 million subscribers, followed by Primestar with 1.5 million and USSB with 950,000. The two smaller DBS players, EchoStar and Alphastar, had 400,000 and 8,500, respectively. Some overlap exists between the DirecTV and USSB subscriber base (Robichaux, 1996). An even more intriguing entry into DBS was announced by Rupert Murdoch's News Corp. in 1997. The Murdoch plan calls for News Corp. to pay $1 billion for a 50% interest in EchoStar Communications. The converted EchoStar service, known as "Sky," will include spot-beam transmission of local TV stations, as well as an array of traditional cable channels (Hall & Schneider, 1997). Projections are for 75% of the United States to have local service by the end of 1998. The possibility of DBS offering local TV stations for the first time has resulted in great competitive concern by the cable industry.

Although the principal target of DBS at present is rural noncabled areas, subscribers may be found in many cities as well. Including local broadcast TV would overcome one of the biggest obstacles to the growth of DBS, making the Sky service fully competitive on a technical basis with wired cable. The potential of these DBS systems in both urban and rural areas is enormous.

Other ancillary means of distribution of DBS services have been proposed, including one by Southwestern Bell (SBC) to sell and rent DirecTV satellite to home television systems in two test markets. Further, airlines are moving toward offering DirecTV on flights of over 2 hours for a charge of $5 to $10 per flight. This would provide to the flying public a quick sample of the power and range of DirecTV services (Cole, 1995b).

By 2002, more than a dozen entrants—including General Motors's Hughes Electronics, AT&T, and General Electric—plan combined investments of about $23 billion to launch satellite systems (Cole, 1995a). AT&T, for instance, is proposing a network of 12 satellites, which would rely on spacecraft positioned at fixed spots around the earth at a distance of more than 22,000 miles. Such a system, which would cost several billion dollars, could handle 10 million customers worldwide and each system would have data-carrying capacity of 1 billion bits of information per second (Markoff, 1995). The technology of DBS dishes has spurred the interest of Microsoft's Bill Gates and cellular pioneer Craig McCaw who announced a plan to put a whopping 840 satellites into orbit and create a "global Internet" that would allow voice and data communications between handheld devices. GM's Hughes Aircraft has plans for a similar system (Pearl, 1995a). The skies will be crowded.

Wireless.   The FCC auctioned segments of the radio broadcast spectrum that have become the new wireless technology fueling the explosion of portable phones. AT&T is claiming new technology that will vault this transmission method to compete with fiber-optic cable and satellites in capacity, quality and error-free data transmission. AT&T's intention is to use the new technology to bypass the Bells' in providing local telephone service (Kerber, 1997). However, the potential exists for this new technology to become a major new challenge for cable operators.

Microwave wireless cable is already a competitor of traditional cable in numerous markets, and new technology is enhancing its power. Digitized programming is transmitted by fiber-optic cable to mountaintops where it is broadcast to rooftop antennas via microwave in a 10- to 30-mile radius. Using this method, PacTel is offering up to 5 million Southern California households the option to get up to 135 channels plus pay-per-view for $2 less than the local cable competition. At stake is between 15% and 20% of that cable market (Gross & Grover, 1996).

Private Cable.   Two other less-regulated and lower cost competitors also may be found in many large cities: SMATV and multichannel multipoint distribution services (MMDS). Both of these types, however, have inherent limitations that prevent them from engaging in full-blown competition with franchised cable. SMATV, commonly known as "private cable," is an unfranchised and unregulated cable system that is restricted to operation on properties such as apartment complexes, mobile home parks, and hotels. MMDS, also known as "wireless cable," is unfranchised but FCC licensed and transmits programming via microwave signals. Now permitted to feed multiple channels, MMDS can provide an array of cable networks to subscribers in apartment complexes and individual houses in competition with franchised cable. Also, SMATV operators are taking advantage of new FCC spectrum rulings intended to make private cable more competitive.

Utilities. The 1996 Telecommunications Act lifted the New Deal era ban that prohibited utilities from entering the telecommunications industry. Utilities—also in the throes of deregulation—are eyeing telecommunications as a logical extension of their services. With long-established rights-of-way, billing systems, experience in customer relations clearly the equal of telephone companies and superior to many newcomers to subscription services, the utilities have many economies of scope. Boston Edison is a case in point. Massachusetts regulators are urging electric utilities to chose either transmission or generation. Boston Edison with a 200-mile ring of fiber-optic cable already installed and paid for by ratepayers, much of that cable running past valuable downtown properties, is choosing transmission. It still plans to deliver electricity, but it also will develop telephone, video and data services for apartments and offices in the Boston area (Kerber, 1997).

Networks

Broadcasters and HDTV. The broadcast TV networks also have become increasingly active as cable network operators. Under a FCC ruling in 1992, the networks were allowed to acquire and operate local cable systems on a limited basis. Thus far, the networks have refrained from any large-scale system operation. However, they have expanded their cable network activities greatly.

The initial foray into cable network operation was ABC's purchase of 80% of ESPN. ABC, now a unit of Disney, holds a similar interest in ESPN-2 and ESPNews, plus the Disney Channel, and a 33% interest in Arts & Entertainment and 33% in the Lifetime Channel. NBC launched its financial service, Consumer News and Business Channel (CNBC) in 1990 and acquired the Financial News Network (FNN) in 1991. NBC and Microsoft embarked on an ambitious joint venture with the 1996 debut of MSNBC Cable, a 24-hour news and information network. NBC also owns 33% of Arts & Entertainment and 50% of Bravo. In 1996, Westinghouse–CBS took a major step into cable networking with the purchase of The Nashville Network (TNN) and Country Music Television (CMT) from Gaylord Entertainment. CBS also started Eye on People Channel in 1997. The Fox network also operates the Fox Network, fX, and Fox News, launched in 1997. Such cable services offer the broadcast networks a ready-made outlet for programming, with economies of scale, at a time when network viewing is slipping.

HDTV offers another avenue of competition for broadcasters with cable. This digital technology can be used in one of two ways. HDTV broadcasters can send much clearer pictures, but the same broadcast space also can be used as standard definition TV (SDTV) to pack four or five channels of ordinary quality into the one digital channel, competing with cable (Andrews, 1995). The FCC intends to provide one new digital channel to each broadcaster for a transitional period, such as 9 years, during which time television in both the analog and digital formats would be broadcast. By the end of that time, unless it was extended, all TV sets in the country would have to be replaced to receive over-the-air TV or a conversion box purchased at about $200 for cable use. The supposition is that the analog channels, once they have been abandoned by broadcasters, will be auctioned off for other telecommunications purposes to raise money for the U.S. Treasury.

Direct broadcast satellites and the new digital TV converter boxes already are digital and thus ready for HDTV transmission. Even with current technology they provide TV pictures with higher quality and sound than conventional over-the-air or cable-TV. The HDTV signal can also be used for the Internet (Rose, 1996).

VCR. The VCR rental industry is still another important competitor of cable, particularly for pay television services, because hundreds of movie titles can be obtained at modest rental cost. In 1995, 25 million subscribers had "addressable boxes," whereas 80 million homes had VCRs, making home video sales and rentals a powerful competitor (Robichaux, 1995b). VCR sales and rentals generated over $14 billion in revenues in 1995, while basic cable generated $15.59 billion and pay-TV raised $5.26 billion (Gregor, 1995).

Web-TV. For much of its history, cable-TV has flirted with interactive schemes, but until the Internet burst on the scene, none was compelling enough to endow a large segment of the population with a desire to pay for televised interactivity. The massive publicity given to cyberspace by the media and the availability of high speed two-way communications has finally bridged that gap. In 1996, Web-TV made its debut connecting televisions directly to the Internet. Microsoft's Bill Gates purchased the service in 1997 setting aim on the 98% of homes with television sets. Although Microsoft currently provides the software that controls 80% of the world's computers, only 40% of homes have personal computers. Web-TV gives Microsoft direct access to the remaining TV homes (Hof & McWilliams, 1997).

New Programming Products. Bell Atlantic Video Services, a joint venture of "Baby Bells" Bell Atlantic, NYNEX, and Pacific Telesis, has been given $300 million and one mission: to steal customers from cable systems and direct-broadcast companies. The venture promises a new dimension of entertainment and programming by allowing subscribers to customize programming to individual needs. Viewers will be offered the networks, MTV, CNN, and the laundry list of other channels, as well as films from Hollywood, just as cable systems do. The distinguishing factor will be interactive services: online banking, games, shopping, and video-on-demand.

Another similar joint venture costing an estimated $500 million would deliver interactive services and video programming over telephone lines. Partners in the venture, announced in 1995, are Disney, Ameritech, SBC Communications, Bell-South, GTE, and Americast (The Walt Disney Co. Annual Report, 1995).

Interactions Between Cable and Its Competitors

Turning all of these new technologies and theories into working systems never proceeds smoothly. Pacific Telesis had planned to offer multimedia services to more than 1.5 million homes by the end of 1996. In trying to deliver 21st-century technology, it compiled a list of 30,000 milestones that must be addressed before the plan could become reality (Cauley, 1995a).

Because Congress provided for competition in telephony in the Telecommunications Act of 1996, the Bells, instead of dabbling in cable-TV, may need to concentrate on their local telephony markets, which still provide 90% of their profits. Cable operators face increasing competition for subscribers from DBS, requiring management concentration on the basic cable business.

More than 90% of the Bells' 2.7 million miles of telephone lines is antiquated copper wiring that cannot transmit large volumes of video signals (Cauley, 1995a). Although fiber-optic lines can easily do that, they are expensive to install and require costly transmission equipment. Rewiring all of the United States with such fiber-optic lines could cost more than $120 billion—plus the cost of billing systems, computers, boxes atop TV sets, and the like (Cauley, 1995b). In the early and mid-1990s, phone and cable companies raced to install fiber-optic cable, and a glut of capacity developed causing rates for leased lines to drop 80% between 1989 and 1994 in some cities. In today's telecom market, demand for fiber-optic cable is far outstripping supply (Schiesel, 1996).

Phone companies are inflicting what pain they can as cable companies try to enter local phone markets. Tactics include refusals to allow seamless switching of calls generated in the cable systems, cuts in service to cable clients, and requiring cable companies to have a Bell escort to inspect their own equipment once it is installed (Cauley, 1995b).

Cable Industry Trade Groups

As the cable industry has matured and its competition has increased, it has relied on the National Cable Television Association (NCTA) to defend itself against incursions by over-the-air broadcasters, telephone companies, various competitors, regulators, local officials, and any others who would infringe on its domain. The industry also has formed the Cabletelevision Advertising Bureau, Inc. (CAB) to promote advertising on cable and to assist local systems and interconnects in securing advertising clients. Both the NCTA and the CAB give the industry the ability to disseminate favorable information and to rebut negative materials.

CONCLUSION

Traditional cable may be an interim technology in the classic sense of technological determinism. Although the precise shape of the cable industry in particular and the telecommunications industry in general in another 5 years cannot be predicted, it is clear that it will be nothing like what exists today. The fireworks will continue to be spectacular as the competing interests of consumers, cable-TV distributors and network owners, broadcasters, phone companies, and regulators continue to clash.

FURTHER READINGS

Cable TV Facts. (Annual). New York: Cabletelevision Advertising Bureau
Kagan, Paul & Associates. (Annual). *Cable TV buyer broker.* Carmel, CA Author.
Report on Television/Nielson. (Annual). New York: A.C. Nielson.

REFERENCES

Andrews, E. L. (1995, July 10). Quest for sharper TV is likely to produce more TV instead. *The New York Times,* pp. C1, D8.
Arnst, C. (1994, October 17). Telecom reform is becoming a local call. *Business Week*, pp. 178–182.
Bannon, L. (1995, August 2). Expanded Disney to look overseas for fastest growth. *The Wall Street Journal*, p. A3.
Brokers see slow but steady cable sales for 1990. (1990, February 5). *Broadcasting*, pp. 44–45.
Cable beats b'cast in 3rd qtr prime. (1995, October 9). *MultiChannel News*, p. 3.
Cable TV Facts. (1995). New York: Cabletelevision Advertising Bureau.
Cable TV Facts. (1997). New York: Cabletelevision Advertising Bureau.
Carter, B. (1996, July 29). Ratings vault above promises made by NBC. *The New York Times*, p. B1.
Cauley, L. (1995a, July 24). Phone giants discover the interactive path is full of obstacles. *The Wall Street Journal*, p. A1.
Cauley, L. (1995b, October 2). Rivals are hung up on Baby Bells' control over local markets. *The Wall Street Journal*, p. A1.
Cole, J. (1995a, October 10). In new space race, companies are seeking dollars from heaven. *The Wall Street Journal*, p. A8.
Cole, J. (1995b, October 5), Travelers may get a chance to channel surf while flying. *The Wall Street Journal*, p. B1.
Coleman, P. (1996, December 9). Nowhere to go but up. *Broadcasting & Cable*, pp. 64–78.
Debut of HBO movie draws more viewers than network. (1996, October 18). The *Knoxville News Sentinel Detours*, p. 7.
Fabrikant, G. (1995, September 18). Time Warner deal to acquire Turner overcomes hurdles. *The New York Times*, p. C8.
Federal Communications Commission: Network-Cable Cross Ownership Rule, 57 F.R. 35468, (1992a).
Federal Communications Commission: Telephone Company-Cable Television Cross-Ownership Rules, 57 F.R. 41106, (1992b).
Flynn, J. (1994, September 26). The sparring match being fought in Britain. *Business Week*, p. 124.
Fox, L. (1995, October 16). Cable operators view robust quarter as the number of subscribers increases. *The New York Times*, p. B8.
Gregor, A. (1995, September 15). Entertainment & technology: Decisions, decisions. *The Wall Street Journal*, p. R21.

Grover, R., & DeGeorge, G. (1995, September 11). Time Warner Turner: Nice script, but. *Business Week*, pp. 40–41.

Grover, R., & Gross, N. (1996, October 14). A wireless weapon in the cable wars. *Business Week*, p. 105.

Gruley, B. (1995, November 8). Phone companies find an ear at FTC. *The Wall Street Journal*, p. B13.

Hall, L., & Schneider, M. (1997, March 3). Sky vows air war on cable. *Electronic Media, 1*, 38.

Hof, R. D., & McWilliams, G. (1997, April 21). Digital TV: What will it be? *Business Week*, pp. 35–37.

Hudson, R. L. (1993, November 2). BT cuts rates on phone calls as much as 60%. *The Wall Street Journal*, p. A19.

Kerber, R. (1997, January 27). Utilities reach out to add phone, cable service. *The Wall Street Journal*, B1.

Landler, M. (1995, July 26). Viacom and Tele-Communications revive a cable deal. *The New York Times*, p. C1.

Landler, M. (1996a, January 31). Where on line is on cable. *The New York Times*, C1.

Landler, M. (1996b, June 19). Partner joins Disney-backed phone group in TV venture. *The New York Times*, pp. B1, C9.

Landler, M. (1996c, July 16). Cable concern plans to offer phone service in Nynex home. *The New York Times*, p. C1.)

Lesly, E., Grover, R., & Gross, N. (1996, October 14). Cable TV: A crisis looms. *Business Week*, pp. 101–106.

Markoff, J. (1995, October 4). AT&T plan links Internet and satellites. *The New York Times*, p. C1.

Narisetti, R. (1995, July 21). A Westinghouse bid for CBS could set buyer on a new course. *The Wall Street Journal*, p. A1.

Nash, N. C. (1995, August 28). A dominant force in European TV. *The New York Times*, p. C1.

Nidex, S. (1995, August 8). Olympic TV double costs NBC $1.25 billion. *Chicago Tribune*, p. C1.

Pearl, D. (1995a, July 14). FCC resolves radio-spectrum dispute, giving big boost to wireless cable TV. *The Wall Street Journal*, p. B8.

Pearl, D. (1995b, August 1). Regulators see results of their work in mergers between networks, producers. *The Wall Street Journal*, p. B8.

Ramstad, E. (1995, August 1). Disney to buy Capital Cities/ABC: Merger will form world's largest entertainment firm. *The Knoxville News Sentinel*, p. C2.

Robichaux, M. (1995a, October 30). Comcast to buy E. W. Scripps cable systems. *The Wall Street Journal*, p. A3.

Robichaux, M. (1995b, September 15). Ready for prime time? The pay-per-view era has arrived. Again. *The Wall Street Journal*, p. R17.

Robichaux, M. (1996, November 7). Once a laughingstock, direct-broadcast TV gives cable a scare. *The Wall Street Journal*, pp. A1, A10.

Robichaux, M. (1997, January 2). Malone says TCI push into phones, Internet isn't working for now. *The Wall Street Journal*, pp. A1, A3.

Rose, F. (1996, December 23), The end of TV as we know it. *Fortune*, pp. 58–66.

Rosenbush, S. (1997, January 17). AT&T maps shortcut to providing local service. *USA Today*, p. B1.

Schiesel, S. (1996, November 4). Fiber optic cable demand outstrips supply. *The New York Times*, p. B.

Stern, C. (1996, February 5). New law of the land. *Broadcasting & Cable*, pp. 8–12.

The Walt Disney Company. (Annual) *1995 Annual Report*.

Trachtenberg, J. (1995, September 7). Sony says it's stopping selling satellite dishes. *The Wall Street Journal*, B1.

Veronis, Suhler & Associates (1995). *The Veronis, Suhler & Associates Communications Industry Forecast*. New York: Author.

Wysocki, B. Jr. (1995, August 29). Improved distribution, not better production, is key goal in mergers. *The Wall Street Journal*, p. A1.

9

The Economics of Hollywood: Money and Media

Douglas Gomery
University of Maryland

The 1990s have been an exciting time for the titans of Hollywood. The decade began with the $15 billion consolidation of Time and Warner, bringing Hollywood's Warner Bros. studio into the largest media company in the world. Halfway through the decade, Disney spent $19 billion to purchase of Capital Cities/ABC. In between, Matsushita took over—and then sold—MCA's Universal Studios, Viacom acquired the Paramount studios, Rupert Murdoch's Twentieth Century Fox studio expanded, and Sony's Columbia Pictures reorganized. In summary, these six Hollywood operations—defining the world's dominant makers and distributors of movies and television—have never done better. Although many fans look back to the 1930s and 1940s as the Golden Age of the movie business, in fact the end of the 20th century stands as the era when Hollywood—as a diversified set of corporations—achieved its greatest power and profitability.

Remarkably, the handful of companies that presently define Hollywood have been with us since the Great Depression. They have weathered wars, recessions, the introduction of wide-screen and color technologies, the coming of over-the-air and cable television, and the diffusion of home video. These factors, plus a host of other technological, social, and economic changes in life in the United States, from suburbanization to changing roles of men and women, have not shaken Hollywood's hold. Indeed the Hollywood studios have gotten ever more powerful.

As the 20th century ends, a listing of the major Hollywood corporations looks remarkably similar to an inventory of the business institutions that dominated the film industry 60 years ago. In 1928 the Radio Corporation of America and the Keith-Albee-Orpheum theater chain merged to create Radio Keith Orpheum. RKO survived on the margin through the 1930s and 1940s, but was taken out of the movie making business during the mid-1950s by eccentric billionaire Howard Hughes. In recent years there have been other dropouts. Former powers United Artists and

175

MGM have faired badly and presently function as marginal operations. The most significant change has been the rise of the Disney company. Until 1984 Disney represented a minor Hollywood operation, making most of its profits from theme parks. However, with an injection of new management, led by Michael Eisner, the Disney Corporation has arisen to become Hollywood's leading corporation (Gomery, 1985; Grover, 1991; West, 1995).

Six vertically integrated operations represent today's Hollywood: Time Warner's Warner Bros. studio, Disney, Murdoch's News Corp.'s Twentieth Century Fox studio, Sony's Columbia, Viacom's Paramount studio, and Seagram's MCA's Universal studios. (This is a rank order based on *Variety's* estimate of revenues in 1995; rankings change.) Only these six studio corporations can fully exploit film and television market products around the world, to the full complement of mass-media outlets. The six "majors" function as parts of a set of vast billion-dollar media conglomerates, possessing deep financial pockets and diversified in a varied line of mass media (West, 1995).

Not only has Hollywood's basic structure remained remarkably constant, so has its fundamental operating tenets. Principles developed in the 1920s continue to be exploited. Through skillful use of cross-subsidization, reciprocity, horizontal and vertical integration, and price discrimination, the Hollywood majors have maintained and, indeed, increased their considerable economic power. Hollywood corporations are able to retain and even expand their control while keeping all possible competitors at bay (Gomery, 1989).

What has changed in recent years has been Hollywood's expanding participation into nearly all phases of the mass-media production, distribution, and presentation. For example, although we associate Hollywood companies with film and television, the leading book publisher in the world is Simon & Schuster, owned by Viacom's Paramount division. Disney's Capital Cities/ABC division not only represents the world's leading broadcast TV network, but also functions as a major publisher of magazines and newspapers. And Rupert Murdoch, owner of the Twentieth Century Fox studio, stands as the leading exponent of diversification into all media marketplaces on all continents throughout the world.

THE SIX MAJORS

• Time Warner, parent owner of Warner Bros., stands as the quintessential media conglomerate and by certain measures the largest media company in the world. This corporate empire grew out of a 1969 merger between Kinney National Services, Inc. (which dealt in parking lots, construction, car rental, and funeral homes) and the then-struggling Warner Bros. Pictures, Inc., a maker of both movies and television programs. Warner Communications' empire expanded to include popular music, publishing, and cable-TV interests as well as the core Hollywood movie making and movie distribution operations. Time added publishing and cable-TV properties. As of the mid-1990s, Time Warner was the number one music distributor, the second largest collection of cable systems in the United States, the most profitable pay-cable network in HBO, and a host of mass-media outlets from Turner Broadcasting to Comedy Central, from magazines (including *Time* and *Sports Illustrated*) to the WB television network. Its Warner Bros. studio continues to be a significant producer of television series (*Murphy Brown*), a leading distributor of syndicated fare (*Night Court, Dallas*, to name but two examples), and has counted a number of the top-grossing films, most notably its *Batman* series, "properties" that began in Warner's DC Comics unit (Bruck, 1994; West, 1995).

• Disney challenges Time Warner for the mantle of the world's largest media corporation. Led by Michael Eisner, Disney has taken bold steps to become a full-service media conglomeration. Its heralded 1995 takeover of ABC/Capital Cities climaxed a decade of expansion. Disney began making R-rated films for adults through new releasing subsidiaries Touchstone and Hollywood Pictures as well as acquiring distributor Miramax. The company also opened new theme parks in Japan and France. The Disney cable channel consistently made money, targeting its youthful audiences and their parents. Disney makes TV's *Home Improvement* and *Ellen*, and syndicates *Siskel & Ebert* to television stations around the country. During the latter years of the 20th century and into the early years of the next millennium, Michael Eisner will try to lead Disney to ever greater profits and power (Grover, 1991; West, 1995).

• Twentieth Century Fox's owner and CEO, Rupert Murdoch, has taken billions from his worldwide News Corporation conglomerate and transformed it into a media empire with formidable film and television operations. The Twentieth Century Fox studio continues to turn out hit movies as well as serving as the basis for Fox's television network. Its production of television programs includes not only traditional fare, but also NFC football from Hollywood, programming cable's FX channel, and syndicated "evergreens" such as *M*A*S*H*. Fox's *Cops* represents an innovation in programming in that it costs so little to provide and has achieved relatively high ratings. However, the Fox studio will most efficiently serve to supply the ever-expanding global distribution outlets that Rupert Murdoch will develop (Block, 1990; Shawcross, 1992; West, 1995).

• Sony, the giant electronics manufacturer from Japan, paid more than $3 billion for Columbia Pictures Entertainment, as well as assuming more than $1 billion of Columbia's debt. Sony acquired not only an ongoing movie and television studio, but an extensive library of nearly 3,000 movies and 23,000 television episodes. Through the bulk of the 1990s, however, Sony has been unable to turn this Hollywood studio colossus into a money-making operation. Sony also owns a major music label that does earn profits. The challenge for Sony as the 20th century draws to an end is to restructure its Hollywood operations or sell it to a colossus like NBC, which could use Columbia to supply its NBC television network. Sony's experiment to use Columbia movies to help sell Sony VCRs never worked out (Dick, 1992; West, 1995).

• Paramount was acquired by Viacom and now encompasses not only television and film units, but also an active TV syndication operation, a home video division, a group of television stations, and the largest book publisher in the world, Simon & Schuster. Viacom also added its TV production, MTV, Nickelodeon, and Showtime cable TV channels, and chain of movie theaters to the mix, making the new Viacom/Paramount one of the multi-billion-dollar powers in the mass-media business. Together they have created the UPN television network, acquired Blockbuster video stores, and seek to market MTV and Nickelodeon into every media market in the world (O'Donnell & McDougal, 1992; West, 1995).

• Seagram, the giant liquor manufacturer based in Canada, acquired MCA and its Universal studios in 1995. In 1990 Japanese electrical manufacturing giant Matsushita had taken over MCA, but then failed to exploit its movie-making, theme parks, music, cable networks, chain of movie theaters, and other mass-media operations. Thus as the 20th century draws to a close, Universal seeks to rejoin Time Warner, Disney, Fox, Sony, and Viacom in forming Hollywood's oligopoly of dominant studios (West, 1995).

THE CAUSES AND CONSEQUENCES
OF THE HOLLYWOOD OLIGOPOLY

Hollywood is defined by six companies, a classic oligopoly. The successes and riches associated with the economic power of these major operations provide incentives so that every few years bold pretenders will come along and try to create a new major Hollywood studio. During the 1980s, the most serious challengers came from Cannon, New Line, New World Entertainment, Orion, and Vestron. For brief moments each captured headlines in the business press; none survived save as an absorbed division of one of the six majors (Yule, 1987).

The six Hollywood media conglomerates possess a host of advantages that enable them to maintain their considerable economic power and keep out the competition: Cross-subsidization enables a Hollywood media conglomerate with interests in a number of media markets to take profits from a thriving area to prop up another less financially successful area. Single-line corporations do not have this luxury and as a result aspiring Hollywood operations fail. Reciprocity enables Hollywood media conglomerates to choose to whom they will sell and then only deal with those companies that cooperate with other units of the media conglomerate. For example, Viacom's Paramount studio might not sell movies to Time Warner's HBO unless Time Warner's cable franchises offer Paramount's Sci-Fi cable channel.

In the end this leads media conglomerates that own the Hollywood studios to integrate horizontally and vertically. All generate considerable profits from a wide spectrum of mass media enterprises, including theme parks (Seagram's MCA and Disney), recorded music (Seagram's MCA, Sony's CBS Records, and Time

Warner), publishing (Paramount, News Corp., Time Warner, and Disney), and television production (all). And make no mistake about it—the major Hollywood companies will continue to be the big winners with this horizontal diversification. Consider that Paramount, Warner, Universal, and Twentieth Century Fox all "instantly" became the defining producers in home video at the end of the 20th century; they had the films people wanted to rent or buy (Gomery, 1992).

However, the significant change in the 1980s came as the Hollywood majors built up considerable vertical power by spending millions to acquire interests in movie theaters, cable television operations, over-the-air television stations, and even networks. All felt that controlling the markets "downstream" (here distribution and exhibition) was vital for the long-term survival and prosperity of any Hollywood-based operation, be it found in a movie theater, a television station, or a rented videotape. Two economic motivations lead the CEOs of the major Hollywood companies to spend millions to secure vertical control.

First, vertical integration enables a company to take full advantage of reductions in costs associated with only having to "sell" to another part of the same company. Time Warner can, thus, take a Warner movie or book it into a Warner-owned theater, present it on HBO, show it to the millions of households that subscribe to a Time Warner cable system, and then tender sales through Warner's video arm. This can be coordinated without a fleet of salespeople to drum up business.

More important, however, is the issue of market control. A vertically integrated company need not worry about being shut out of one of those key ancillary markets. Indeed, one of the majors would rather work with a known "rival" than see a new competitor arise. So, despite all their alleged struggle in the merger talks of 1989, Paramount and Time Warner continued to always jointly own and operate vast theater circuits that gave both a strong, dependable position in key cities (principally Los Angeles), guaranteeing that their movies would receive the best possible opening in their jointly owned chain. Indeed today's "theatrical window," despite all the talk of the impact of cable television and home video, remains the most important venue to create the blockbusters that can be exploited in other media (Gomery, 1992).

However, the vertical stream extends far past traditional theaters and video outlets. In 1995 Disney stunned the world by purchasing ABC/Capital Cities. There were many reasons for this acquisition, but the most significant was that Disney gained control over access to a major over-the-air TV network as well as to cable TV outlets. Vertical integration has extended to all forms of media.

For Hollywood studios most notable product, feature films, the process begin in theaters, and then goes downstream to revenue streams in the ancillary markets of pay-cable, home video, foreign distribution, and over-the-air television only if they do well at the theatrical box-office. There are rare exceptions. A handful of films that fail in theaters do garner significant box-office returns overseas. Fewer still provided sizable sales and rentals in home video. However, these cases are the exceptions. In the vast majority of cases, the theater remains the voting booth where the return on the $25 million investment for the average theatrical feature is determined. A theatrical blockbuster guarantees millions of additional dollars from the home video and pay television arenas. That is why the major Hollywood companies work so hard to craft a hit in the theaters, for once they have a proven commodity there, the rest of the way is usually smooth sailing.

Interestingly the continuing importance of theaters has only become obvious in the last few years. Consider that at the beginning of the 1980s, a number of serious pundits, including Arthur D. Little, Inc., the multinational consulting firm, studied the film industry, and predicted that there probably would no need for movie theaters by 1990. Everybody could (and would) stay home, and view Hollywood's best through the new television technologies. Instead, going out to the movies has remained a viable leisure time activity. The movie theater is still where the blockbuster is determined.

Few predicted that during the 1980s hundreds of new movie theater complexes would be built, creating nearly 24,000 available theatrical screens in the United States, virtually all in multiscreen complexes. This is a greater number than any other time in film history. Theatrical release requires more and more theater screens so Hollywood can take full advantage of the economies of scale from television advertising. Because the cost of marketing, a film can often exceed $10 million, if it is spread over lots of theaters, marketing costs per theater per film can remain relatively low. The economies of scale of television advertising of theatrical features provides the foundation of the multiplex and the creation of the blockbuster that then leads to millions in the ancillary markets.

Crucially, it should not be forgotten that the market for Hollywood's films spreads far beyond the 24,000 screens in the United States. Hollywood films play all over the world, whether the profits eventually made their way to the ledgers of corporations headquartered in New York City or Tokyo. Indeed, since the 1920s, the Hollywood majors have held dominion in distribution throughout the world. Hollywood's trade association, the Motion Picture Association of America, expends a great deal of time and energy making sure that the economic power of the major studios is not threatened. Through the 1980s and into the 1990s, the movie business functioned as one of the few positive signs for international trade by corporations based in the United States.

Year in, and year out, the Hollywood majors control markets from Sweden to Australia, from West Germany to nearly all the nations of Africa. Hollywood derives roughly one third to two fifths of its theatrical box-office revenues from overseas (in excess of $3 billion annually by 1991 and climbing). Only in the rare nation does Hollywood not capture more than half the business. At considerable expense, the Hollywood majors maintain offices in more than a dozen cities in North America (and up to 50 overseas), where their representatives are in constant contact with the heads of the dominant theater chains. Hollywood's regular production of hit films provides a strong incentive force for foreigners to consistently deal with the six majors rather than take a flyer with an independent.

This has led, in recent years, to joint deals with foreign companies to build theaters in Britain, Australia, Germany, Spain, and France, to run cable-TV networks all over the world. As cable television spreads across Europe, Hollywood stands at the core of programming strategies. Indeed various proposals for uniting the economics of European nations will grapple with attempting to limit Hollywood's access.

Finally, skill at price discrimination stands at the core of Hollywood's enormous power. During the 1930s and 1940s, the Hollywood majors, through their ownership and control of production, distribution, and exhibition set the prices for the movies shown and, through careful use of runs, zones, and clearances, were able to maximize revenues from box-office take. One paid more to see a film in its first-run and then less down the line. If a viewer waited for a 12th run in Chicago, for example, then the price in the 1940s would have been as low as $.10 or $.20 (Gomery, 1985).

In other words, the major studios worked together to enforce a system of classic price discrimination. A generation ago the process was simple. Features opened with big premieres and publicity. Then they played off from first-run to second-run to third-run, so on down the line. The coming of television simply added two runs at the end. A film earned the bulk of its money from play in theaters; television, even with a sale for showing on one of the three major television networks, accounted for less than one tenth of total revenues (Gomery, 1993; Philips, 1983; Vogel, 1995).

Feature films, for example, still begin their marketing life in theaters. If one can fashion a theatrical blockbuster during the crucial first weekend of release, then it should be possible to reap added millions from the home video and pay television arenas. Even as recently as 10 years ago, movie theaters supplied more than three fourths of the revenue for an average Hollywood feature film. Today, theaters provide about one fourth because of the extraordinary cable-TV and home video markets. In 1980, the Hollywood majors collected about $20 million from worldwide sales of video cassettes. In 1995 the figure stood at well in excess of $16 billion. Ten years ago an average film expected to take in precious little from home video; today that ancillary revenue contribution usually amounts to the leading contribution to the revenue stream (Lardner, 1987; Miller, 1990).

Yet home video hardly stands alone in Hollywood's ancillary markets. HBO and its cousins continue to rake in millions in the mature pay-cable market, both for feature films and made-for-cable TV movies. The final runs for feature films and Hollywood-made TV shows comes with presentation on basic cable and reruns by an over-the-air television channel. It usually takes a couple of years for important feature films to make their way to independent television (less for box-office failures), but once released into syndication, the feature films are repeated to faithful audiences. Reruns of hit TV series come to syndication after about 100 episodes have been made and then seemingly run forever (Gomery, 1992).

Through TNT, the Family Channel, Arts and Entertainment, and American Movie Classics, among others, cable reruns the best and worst of Hollywood's products, providing vast and reliable revenue streams based on these "libraries." Whatever additional new television technologies appear in the future, the business of the Hollywood major studios will continue to be to seek additional ways to maximum revenue. Starting with a theatrical showing, then home video, pay-cable, cable television, network television, local over-the-air television, and any other possible venues that come along in the forthcoming years, the object of this price discrimination will continue to be to get as much revenue from a product as the various markets will permit (Gomery, 1993).

THE FUTURE

In summary, through cross-subsidization, reciprocity, horizontal and vertical integration, and skillful price discrimination, the Hollywood majors have maintained and, indeed, increased their considerable economic power. To this observer nothing seems on the horizon that might change that vice like grip. Indeed, the takeovers of Columbia by Sony, MCA by Seagram, and Paramount by Viacom only point out that it is far easier to buy into the Hollywood oligopoly than to form a new company.

Is there anything on the horizon that might change the domination of the major Hollywood companies? Many who find fault with Hollywood's excess power look to the coming of some new technology to alter Hollywood's long-held economic power. One new technology that many argue will make us stay home and never venture out the movies again is high definition television (HDTV). Presumably its superior, wide-screen video image will finally allow new entrants into the oligopoly.

Media economics suggests that HDTV will not reconstitute the current Hollywood oligopoly. First, HDTV is not a perfect substitute. The quality of the motion picture image, for example, has not "stood still." Chemical celluloid images provided more information per square inch than the best HDTV can offer. More importantly, during the 1980s we learned that image quality does not matter so much. If it did, why did the technically superior Beta format for home video fail so badly in market competition with the inferior images of VHS? Fans seek out their favorites for many reasons, not simply to experience the most technologically advanced image reproduction.

As we end the 20th century, nothing looms on the horizon that will threaten the oligopolistic power of the major studios. The major Hollywood studios will continue to enjoy the fruits of their formidable economic power. Their influence will keep reaching throughout the world, more powerfully than any other mass medium. The Hollywood oligopoly has learned to thrive in the age of advanced technologies, based on skilled use of media economics.

FURTHER READING

Block, A. B. (1990). *Outfoxed*. New York: St. Martin's Press.

Dick, B. F. (Ed.). (1992). *Columbia Pictures: Portrait of a studio*. Lexington: University of Kentucky Press.

Gomery, D. (1992). *Shared pleasures*. Madison: University of Wisconsin Press.

Vogel, H. L. (1995). *Entertainment industry analysis: A guide for financial analysis* (3rd ed.). New York: Cambridge University Press.

REFERENCES

Block, A. B. (1990). *Outfoxed*. New York: St. Martin's Press.

Bruck, C. (1994). *Master of the game: Steve Ross and the creation of Time Warner*. New York: Simon & Schuster.

Dick, B. F. (Ed.). (1992). *Columbia Pictures: Portrait of a studio*. Lexington: University of Kentucky Press.

Gomery, D. (1985). *The Hollywood studio system*. New York: St. Martin's Press.

Gomery, D. (1989). Media economics: Terms of analysis. *Critical studies in mass communication, 6*(1), 43–60.

Gomery, D. (1992). *Shared pleasures*. Madison: University of Wisconsin Press.

Gomery, D. (1993). The centrality of media economics. *Journal of Communication, 43*(3), 190–198.

Grover, R. (1991). *The Disney touch: How a daring management team revived an entertainment empire*. Homewood, IL: Business One Irwin.

Lardner, J. (1987). *Fast forward: Hollywood, the Japanese, and the VCR wars*. New York: Norton.

Miller, M. C. (Ed.). (1990). *Seeing through movies*. New York: Pantheon.

O'Donnell, P., & McDougal, D. (1992). *Fatal subtraction: How Hollywood really does business*. New York: Doubleday.

Philips, L. (1983). *The economics of price discrimination*. New York: Cambridge University Press.

Shawcross, W. (1992). *Murdoch*. New York: Simon & Schuster.

Vogel, H. L. (1995). *Entertainment industry analysis: A guide for financial analysis* (3rd ed.). New York: Cambridge University Press.

West, S. (1995, September 3). The global 50. *Variety*, 27–38.

Yule, A. (1987). *Hollywood a go-go: An account of the Cannon phenomenon*. London: Shere Books.

10

The Economics of Contemporary Radio

Jonathan David Tankel
Indiana University-Purdue University Fort Wayne

Wenmouth Williams, Jr.
Ithaca College

"The report of my death was an exaggeration" wrote Mark Twain in 1897 to the London correspondent of *The New York Journal* (Bartlett & Kaplan, 1992). This oft-quoted quip describes accurately the current state of the radio industry in the United States. For many, radio is seen as an industry dying at the feet of the MTV generation. Although industry experts were wondering how radio would rebound from economic recession and media competition (Simon, 1992), aggregate radio revenue continues to expand at acceptable rates to date. As of July 1995, radio revenue increased for the 35th-consecutive month according to the Radio Advertising Bureau (1995). With an average of 5.6 radios in 99 out of 100 households and a typical listener who tunes in for 3 hours and 20 minutes each week, radio maintains its niche in the evolving and competitive media marketplace (Standard & Poors, 1995).

Radio's unique characteristic—communicating by sound via the electromagnetic spectrum—has continued to prove valuable to audiences, broadcasters, and advertisers. Radio has withstood the many challenges presented over the years by the vagaries of the national economy, newer technologies, changing patterns of media consumption, developments in popular culture, and confused regulatory oversight. Facing these constant challenges has forced innovators in the radio industry to rethink radio as an economic entity in order to remain viable for more than 70 years. This chapter, therefore, describes the historical development of the radio industry, its current status, and some perspectives on its future.

RADIO AS NATIONAL MEDIUM, 1920–1950

Radio as an industry in the United States emerged from a confluence of technological innovations, industrial interests, and governmental imperatives in the aftermath of World War I (see Douglas, 1987, for an excellent description of the process). Because of the limitations of broadcast technology, radio was first conceptualized as a local economic entity. Revenue was generated through the sale of radios by manufacturers (such as Westinghouse and General Electric) and through the public recognition of local merchants through their identification as radio broadcasters (such as the Joseph Horne department store in Pittsburgh, Pennsylvania). The entry of AT&T into the radio business in 1922 pushed the developing economic structure from radio broadcasting as an *indirect* generator of revenue toward the *direct* generation of revenue through the sale of air time (see McChesney, 1994).

Simultaneous with the conversion to an advertising-based economic structure, the local nature of radio broadcasting was effaced by the development of radio networks. The ability to broadcast to audiences in more than one location was made possible by wire connections between stations. Program production costs (underwritten primarily by advertisers during the era of network radio dominance from 1927 to 1950) were rationalized by spreading those costs across multiple audiences. In this way, the increase in cost of program production due to networking was marginal compared to the increased advertising revenue derived from the enlarged audience. This parsimony was, and remains, the organizing principle for radio, and later television, networks (see Head, Sterling, & Schofield, 1994, for a more detailed description).

The Federal Radio Commission, later the Federal Communications Commission (FCC), conceptualized radio as a local medium based on the technical limitations of broadcasting. In economic terms, radio was considered a national programming medium by 1927 with the formal organization of the National Broadcasting Company's Red and Blue networks. The economic structure of radio at that time was based on this seeming contradiction. A limited number of radio stations in each market were supplied programming by networks in exchange for "compensation," a fee for using the local station's air time. Network affiliates were most often the dominant stations in the market based on broadcast coverage and dial position. In most markets, therefore, network-affiliated stations were supported indirectly by national and directly by premium local advertising revenue, while weaker stations provided locally produced programming of varying quality supported by local advertisers. Radio in the 1930s and 1940s was a national medium in the minds and pocketbooks of most listeners by bringing the nation a common set of entertainment (and later information) programs and product advertisements (see Barnouw, 1978).

Radio dramatically changed as an industry in the post-war period: a demonstration of the capacity of an advertising-supported medium to adapt its economic structure. These changes originated at the national level in the wake of earlier actions on the part of the radio networks and the FCC. On one hand, the radio networks shifted financial resources from the mature radio networks to the development of television. On the other hand, the FCC placed restrictions on the radio networks, in particular reasserting the localness of radio (*National Broadcasting Company, Inc. et al v. United States et al.,* 1943). The Big 3 networks controlled radio by broadcasting from the most powerful stations that dominated evening, and therefore effective, broadcast hours. NBC was forced to relinquish one of its networks, and, more important for network affiliates, CBS and NBC were forced to liberalize their restrictive affiliate contracts. The network settlement and the limitation of one outlet per medium per market formed the ownership structure of radio for the next 40 years.

RADIO AS LOCAL MEDIUM, 1950–1990

After World War II, the networks and advertisers proceeded to abandon radio as a national medium. Television proved quickly to be more attractive to national advertisers and to be less suspect as a restrictive economic practice than radio (see Litman, 1993, for an explication of television networks). Faced with economic dislocation in the 1950s, radio became increasingly local. Three developments intertwined to restructure the industry: (a) the switch to primarily local advertising, (b) the switch to primarily format programming, and (c) the shift in audience from the AM band to the FM band (see Fornatale & Mills, 1980). These three developments together transformed radio from a national medium for *mass* advertising to a local medium capable of targeting specific demographics for large and small advertisers alike.

The switch to local advertising was inevitable, although national advertising did not disappear. By the early 1960s, network radio service was reduced to hourly news services and live sports, so national advertisers seeking radio audiences utilized local spot sales. The bulk of radio revenue, however, was generated from local advertisers. From 1960 to 1980, local spot sales constituted more than 85% of a typical station's revenue (Sterling, 1984). With the reemergence of network radio in the 1980s, the ratio has declined somewhat, but local sales still average around 75% of total advertising revenue (Standard & Poors, 1996).

Radio stations today are positioned as the quintessential local advertising medium when compared to its competitors. Costs for radio spot production and transmission are low when compared with local broadcast television. Radio's programming practices target specific demographics unlike newspapers. Radio's most serious competitor in the local advertising marketplace, local cable television services, can match price point, but have a limited audience compared to radio (Petrozzello, 1995a). It is clear that the broadcaster's conceptualization of radio as a national medium from the 1920s to 1950 was maintained artificially. As a local medium, "[t]he radio industry is probably in the best position it's been in for decades and will be the best positioned medium for at least the next five years" according to Fritz Beesemyer, Oppenheim & Company (quoted in Petrozzello, 1995a, p. 45). Radio's capacity to localize its advertising derives from the programming strategies that replaced those employed by network radio. From the early 1950s to today, radio broadcasters refined the practice of using programming that appeals to limited and well-defined demographic groups. In this way, format radio refers both the content and presentation of on-air materials and the intended target demographic to be sold to advertisers, both local and national (Hesbacher, Clasby, Anderson, & Berger, 1976; Rothenbuhler & McCourt, 1992). The early development of format radio proceeded only slightly the serendipitous emergence of the teen as commodity and *rock and roll* as the music of that teen culture (Denisoff, 1975; Fornatale & Mills, 1980). The need on the part of the popular music industry for an inexpensive vehicle for advertising and promotion and the need of the developing local radio industry for inexpensive and simple programming were mutually satisfied in format music radio. The synergy of these two industries was most notable in the unintended shift of audience from AM to FM, the most notable development in the radio industry in the 1970s (see Tankel & Williams, 1993, for a detailed description).

By the mid-1980s, the major transformation of the radio industry complete. The bulk of the radio audience listened to music format radio, primarily broadcast in stereo in the FM band (see Braun, 1994, for a discussion of the ill-fated attempt to establish AM stereo broadcasting). AM broadcasters were turning to formats shunned by the increasingly profitable FM band, such as talk radio, ethnic, and religious broadcasting. In general, local radio broadcasters generated most of their revenue from local advertising based on target demographics defined by the format. This economic structure was supported by deregulation at the federal level, in which programming restrictions and administrative burdens were removed from radio broadcasters. In particular, the FCC repealed the requirement for radio stations to report ascertainment surveys. These detailed public documents were the means by which the station was judged to have fulfilled the public interest standard of the Communications Act of 1934. Also, the lapsing of the Fairness Doctrine in the late 1980s was welcomed widely by the radio industry.

RADIO ECONOMICS IN THE 1990s

Contemporary radio economics involve activities at the level of the specific station and of the industry as a whole. The remainder of this chapter examines radio economics at these micro and macro levels.

Radio Economics: In The Station

At the station level, radio in the 1990s has continued to refine format programming practices. These trends are made possible primarily because the growth of the radio audience has matched the growth in the U.S. population, creating room for new formats (Piirto, 1994). In turn, the "demographic profiles of listeners to different radio formats are highly consistent" (p. 43), making radio a predictable purchase for advertisers. Format innovation also seems to be motivated by the changes in ownership rules and the reemergence of network product (Wilke, 1994).

Format renovation tends to occur in two ways: (a) creation of new formats for underserved audiences, and (b) increasingly narrow definitions of already popular formats. For example, African-American-oriented radio programmers tend to seek particular demographics through increased segmentation (Brandes, 1994). Rock programmers continue to look for underserved audiences with new formats such as New Rock (formerly the noncommercial college radio artists), the Adult Album Alternative (a revival of aspects of the underground FM format of the 1960s), and All-70s (Goldman, 1994; Wilke, 1994). Country music formats seem less likely to either segment or increase since the traditional formats reach more listeners than any other format in the AM and FM bands combined (Heuton, 1994). New/Talk has increased market share in the Top 25 markets and now accounts for almost 15% of the radio audience in those markets ("N/T Big," 1994).

Accompanying this proliferation of formats was a major change in the way local stations broadcast their programming. ABC, CBS, Westwood One, and many other proliferating smaller networks now supply formats to local stations that cannot afford local in-studio talent. In 1994, radio networks experienced a 1.7% increase in listenership (Heuton, 1995). Packaged programming supplied by satellite and/or run by computer programs are replacing local instation personality-driven music and talk formats that dominated local radio from 1950 to the early 1990s. The change in ownership rules have led to situations where three or more stations in one market are being programmed by one staff. Satellite and computer-driven programming marginally increase programming costs while overhead costs remain fairly constant, thus increasing profitability foi the radio operation as a whole.

During the bleak days of recession in the early 1990s, radio station management also began to rethink how to sell radio. While ad rates were relatively cost-effective, radio sales personnel became more active in soliciting business for their stations and for the industry as a whole. The trade journals were filled with various suggestions on how to market radio as a local advertising medium that created intense listener loyalties with clear demographics that go beyond pure cost-per-point tactics (see, e.g., Guild, 1992; Kim, 1992; Yorke, 1992). Changes in these attitudes on the part of broadcasters and advertisers contributed to radio's rebound in the mid-1990s (Standard & Poors, 1995).

One area of station operation that should attract more attention in the near future is the use of FM subcarriers, which are a byproduct of the stereo transmission technology. The technology of FM broadcasting uses limited bandwidth within the channels assigned by the FCC. A licensee can therefore offer this bandwidth to operations that can use these frequencies for limited transmission purposes, such as background music services and date transmission (see Inglis, 1990). FM subscriber leasing, therefore, allows FM broadcasters to take advantage of the demand for high speed data-transfer channels. Radio Broadcast Data Systems was introduced in 1993, which permits data transfer transmitted on subcarriers at speeds of 9,600 bps and higher. While the radio industry awaits the introduction of the most obvious manifestation of new technology in the form of digital audio broadcasting, local FM broadcasters already have the technology to become part of the new information infrastructure. The NAB reported in 1994, however, that only a small proportion of station operators were actively marketing their subcarrier capacity (Springer & Fratrik, 1994).

Radio Economics: In the Corporate Office

The most significant "macro" economic development in the radio industry in the 1990s derives from the change in ownership rules. The relative success of the radio industry reflected in the continued increase in aggregate revenue belies the fact that specific stations in specific markets were not profitable. According to a study conducted by the Mass Media Bureau, more than half of the radio stations licensed in 1990 lost money (FCC,1992a, p. 2776), despite the fact that actual advertising dollars have steadily increased since 1975 (Veronus, Suhler, & Associates, 1995). In order to rectify this situation, changes in ownership rules in form of the local marketing agreement (LMA) and the loosening of the duopoly rules have been instituted. These changes seem to have had the effect of eroding the diversity of radio stations in individual and overlapping markets while strengthening the remaining stations. A closer examination of these changes is therefore in order.

The economic recession of the early 1990s had a devastating effect on the radio business. Smith, Meeske, and Wright (1995) reported that 100 stations declared bankruptcy and several others were suffering from the downturn in the economy. A partial solution to this problem was the LMA. These agreements allowed a successful station to share programming and the cost of selling time and personnel with a not so successful station. Both stations would then share the advertising revenue. The FCC counted LMAs against the station ownership limits. LMAs are affected by attributable ownership (at least 5% of the stock in a given radio station) unless one person or group owns more than 50% of the stock. The application of this concept is discussed later.

The duopoly rules (as well as many others such as ascertainment and the Prime Time Access Rules) were intended to ensure diversity of viewpoints and economic competition in every market. The first ownership rules, passed in 1953, dealt specifically with multiple ownership. Under the Carter Administration, the Commission began the investigation of these and other rules that seemed burdensome to the business of radio (Williams, 1993). This deregulatory emphasis continued during the 1980s and led in part to changes in the ownership limits from 7 stations per service to 12 of each.

The ownership rules were designed initially to enhance competition. The impetus for their abolishment was indicative of a movement away from the limited resource model responsible for those ownership rules in the first place. Former commissioner Mark Fowler, a proponent of "unregulation" of the communication industries, thought that the marketplace should determine what forms radio and other information and entertainment services should take (Williams, 1993). The major deregulatory decisions in the 1980s that directly affected the economics of radio included increasing limits on the number of radio stations owned by one person or group and the relaxing the anti-trafficking (sale of radio stations) rules (Smith et al., 1995).

In 1987, the FCC issued a *Notice of Proposed Rulemaking* for the purpose of relaxing certain duopoly and one-to-a-market rules. The resulting rules allowed common ownership of stations with overlapping contours that may be licensed to the same market. However, common ownership of two or more AM or FM stations in the same community (different from markets in many places) was still prohibited. Cross ownership of television and radio stations (one-to-a-market) was also considered, on a waiver basis only, under certain station contour criteria. These waivers were most likely in Top-25 markets that had at least 30 separately owned and controlled licenses or "voices" (*First report and order*, 1989). One test of the waiver procedure was *In re Application of Alta Gulf FM, Inc. and Citicasters*. Citicasters argued that the Tampa/St. Petersburg market was a Top-25 market (actually number 16) and by allowing joint operation of WTBT-FM, WTSP-TV and WXTB-FM, the licensee would save in excess of $600,000 annually. Further, the public interest would be served because WTBT would be able to use more news personnel from the other stations and to provide their hurricane warning information to more listeners.

In 1991, the FCC issued a *Notice of Proposed Rulemaking* with the intention of further relaxing the local and national ownership rules and time brokerage rules (LMAs). The rationale for this consideration was the dramatic change in radio economics since the ownership rules were first issued. As a result of this increased competition for advertising dollars and the concomitant decrease in revenue for radio stations, the FCC pursued further relaxation of the ownership rules. The FCC stated that the national radio market was "extremely fragmented" with no dominant owner or power (FCC, 1992a, 2757). The number of 24-hour cable music services increased from 6 in 1984 to 15 in 1992. Further complicating radio's ability to compete in the economic marketplace was a significant decrease in revenue growth and share of the local advertising market because of increased dollars spent on cable television. The economic fragility of individual radio stations was most pronounced in smaller markets, because approximately 50 stations in the larger markets accounted for half of radio's profit. According to the FCC, more than 300 stations were "silent" in the 12 months preceding the 1991 order (FCC, 1992a).

The FCC argued that if the economic viability of radio is in jeopardy, then it can not fulfill its public interest requirements. In fact, many stations in smaller markets had significantly decreased their staffs, with news being reduced the most. The FCC was convinced that this economic trend would continue with little relief in sight. This opinion was substantiated by problems with bank loans for existing stations that were "highly leveraged." With revenues decreasing, station owners who borrowed heavily dependent on predicted economic growth in the industry were faced with the prospect of selling their stations at a loss because they could not meet their loans (Radio, 1990).

A 1990 Mass Media Bureau study found 246 AM, 17 FM, and 20 UHF television stations not operating. About 5% of the authorized AM stations were not on the air. The solution, according to the FCC, was to allow radio stations to combine operations to reduce costs. If these savings were put back into programming, the FCC felt that diversity in the local market would increase. The national radio rule changes were as follows:

1. Increase the Rule of 12s to 30 AM stations and 30 FM stations, nationwide.
2. Except in the smaller markets, limit local ownership to any combination that does not exceed 25% of the local market.
3. Limit simulcasting is limited to 25% of the broadcast day.
4. Make all time-brokerage agreements part of the public file (*In re revision*, 1992).

The intent of the local radio rules was to encourage and maintain economic competition and the diversity of ideas. However, increased competition within and outside of the radio industry in local markets at least partially assured the diversity of ideas. Therefore, some relaxation of local rules were thought to be in order, especially given the cost savings possible for individual stations. These changes were:

1. A single licensee could own up to 3 stations (no more than 2 in one service) in markets with fewer than 15 stations as long as the audience does not exceed 50% of the market.
2. A single licensee can own no more than 2 AM and 2 FM stations in markets between 15 and 29 stations, with a market share of less than 25% allowed.
3. In markets with 30 to 39 stations, the ownership limit is 3 AM and 2 FM stations with the 25% audience share cap.
4. In markets with more than 40 stations, the ownership limit is three AM and 3 FM stations with the 25% share cap.

The FCC argued that these rule relaxations would not lead to market monopolies because there were so many radio stations operating today. For example, a study concluded that over 96% of the markets would have at least four different licensees.

The tiered approach to these rules would add other economic safeguards for the local markets (FCC, 1992a).

Shortly after releasing the 1992 *Report and Order* modifying the local and national radio station ownership rules, the FCC announced its first reconsideration later that same year. The new rules changed the rule of 30s to the rule of 20s: each licensee could own up to 20 AM and 20 FM stations. To enhance minority ownership, three additional stations could be brokered (LMA) if they were owned by minority licensee or small business (FCC, 1992b).

A second reconsideration of the ownership rules in 1994 changed the national cap for minority owners to 25 AM and 25 FM licenses. The cap was raised for nonminority brokered stations to five stations. The four tiers of the 1992 rules were reduced to two. In markets of 15 or more stations, one licensee could own only 2 AM and 2 FM stations as long as the audience share did not exceed 25 %. In markets of fewer than 15 stations one licensee could own up to 3 stations and no more than 2 per service with a 25% share cap (Second Memorandum, 1994).

The analysis accompanying this *Opinion and Order* defined the public interest as a combination of competition and diversity and "preventing undue concentration of power" (*Second Memorandum*, 1994, p. 7184). Based on this assumption, the FCC believed that economic competition was best achieved by market forces and not government regulation. The rules as published prevent undue monopolization of the radio spectrum, yet provide sufficient latitude for economic forces to regulate the market.

The economic analysis explained by the Commission in the *Opinion and Order* divided radio into a *programming production market* and a *programming distribution market*. In the first market, licensees can produce programming locally or purchase it from national sources. The distribution market consists of buyers (advertisers and listeners) and sellers (radio stations). The ownership rules dealt with the horizontal concentration of station licenses at the national level and prohibit monopolies. The most stations a licensee can own is 46, which is a small percentage of the 9,995 commercial stations on the air in 1994.

The local ownership rules also prohibit monopolies in markets of more than 15 stations. In small markets, those with fewer than 15 stations, 3 licensees could own all the available radio stations. Although this would be a monopoly situation as defined by the Justice Department, it would only affect 25% of the available radio audience. These new entities were dubbed "*megacombos*" and have brought some economic stability to those small market broadcasts able to afford the upfront cost of purchase (Gallagher, 1993; Viles & Foisie, 1992).

The philosophy undergirding these changes in ownership rules was codified in the Telecommunications Act of 1996. Going even further than the *Opinion and Order*, the Act first required the FCC to eliminate all caps on ownership nationally. Under the heading "Local Radio Diversity," the Act set the following local ownership caps:

1. In a market with 45 or more commercial stations, a party may "own, operate, or control" 8 stations, with a limit of 5 in a given service (AM or FM).
2. In a market with 30 to 44 stations, a party may be involved with 7 stations, with a limit of 4 in a given service.
3. In a market with 15 to 29 stations, a party may involved with 6 stations, with a limit of 4 in a given service. However, a party may not be involved with more than 50% of the stations in the market (Telecommunications Act of 1996).

These ownerships rules reflected the trends set by the FCC as far back as the late 1980s. Megacombos as an economic formation were now approved by agency action and legislation. With the uncertainty removed from ownership caps, many local radio markets have witnessed consolidation of radio holdings placing ownership, operation and control in stronger, but fewer, hands.

A prime example of the viability of radio in general in the late 1990s in the formation of the largest radio network and syndicator by Westinghouse with its 1995 purchase of CBS and its 1996 purchase of Infinity, which had earlier gained control of the Westwood One network. Another example of the new radio macroeconomics at the national level is the proposed formation of a new radio group, Triathlon Broadcasting Co., which purchased duopolies in several medium-sized and small markets through the acquisition of Pourtales Radio (Petrozzello, 1995b). In 1994, duopoly operations and LMAs made up 23% of radio stations according to *Radio Business Report* (as reported in Standard & Poors, 1995). These national and local trends are reflections of the economic stability where marginal costs involved in multiple station operations are more than offset by lower cost for consolidated advertising sales.

THE FUTURE OF RADIO

Radio continues its gains from the most recent low points in the early 1990s. Advertising gains are expected to come at the expense of local newspapers because of radio's cost and targetability. Radio's portability and flexibility still gives it an advantage over television for advertisers who want to attract mobile consumers and who want to quickly adapt to cultural trends. As Standard & Poors noted in its 1996 survey, radio is not an advertising afterthought and will remain viable as a mature medium that exudes stability in an ever-changing media environment. As James Marsh of Prudential Securities told *Fortune* magazine, "You're not going to see any technology that's going to put radio out of business tomorrow. It's got staying power, and it's very profitable when it's done right" (quoted in Gunther, 1997, pp. 112–113).

There is one irony, however, in radio's seemingly enviable position in the marketplace. The post-World War II transformation from a national to a local medium is undergoing a reversal. Programming is being packaged nationally and regionally, although the advertising revenue base remains primarily local. The product being delivered to the home, therefore, is more homogenous. The unique local twist on program format and content, which was a major attraction at first for local advertisers, is being eroded. The basic principles of parsimonious programming strategies are still viable: Radio stations seem to be using programming with quality that is underwritten by a large audience base. In this way, their distinct identities as local service providers is becoming illusory. The consolidation of radio services resulting from the change in ownership rules and the LMA is having the intended effect of removing underfinanced stations from the market. The net effect may be more services, but fewer owners. Local radio broadcasters may be unintentionally building the foundation of a smooth transition to national and regional digital audio broadcasting services. In other words, the irony is that the current success of local radio broadcasting maybe the harbinger of its inevitable demise.

FURTHER READING

Barnouw, E. (1978). *The sponsor: Notes on a modern potentate*. New York: Oxford University Press.

Braun, M. (1994). *AM stereo and the FCC: Case study of a marketplace shibboleth*. Norwood, NJ: Ablex.

Fornatale, P., & Mills, J. (1980). *Radio in the television age*. Woodstock, NY: Overlook Press.

Greve, H. (1996). Patterns of competition: The diffusion of a market position in radio broadcasting. *Administrative Science Quarterly, 41*(1), 20–61.

McChesney, R. (1994). *Telecommunications, mass media, and democracy: The battle for control of U.S. broadcasting, 1928–1935*. New York: Oxford University Press.

Tankel, J. D., & Williams, W. (1993). Resource dependence: Radio economics and the shift from AM to FM. In A. Alexander, J. Owers, & R. Carveth (Eds.), *Media economics: Theory and practice* (pp. 157–158). Hillsdale, NJ: Lawrence Erlbaum Associates.

REFERENCES

Bartlett, J.,& Kaplan, J. (General Editor). (1992). *Bartlett's familiar quotations* (16th ed.). Boston: Little Brown.

Barnouw, E. (1978). *The sponsor: Notes on a modern potentate*. New York: Oxford University Press.

Brandes, W. (1994, September). Black-oriented radio is more segmented. *The Wall Street Journal*, p. B5.

Braun, M. (1994). *AM stereo and the FCC: Case study of a marketplace shibboleth*. Norwood, NJ: Ablex.

Denisoff, S. (1975). *Solid gold: The popular music industry*. New Brunswick, NJ: Transaction Books.

Douglas, S. (1987). *Inventing American broadcasting, 1899–1922*. Baltimore: The Johns Hopkins University Press.

First reconsideration order, 7 FCC Rcd 6387 (1992).

First Report and Order, 4 FCC Rcd 1729 (1989).

Fornatale, P., & Mills, J. (1980). *Radio in the television age*. Woodstock, NY: Overlook Press.

Gallagher, J. (1993, February 8). Duopoly rules spur radio activity. *Broadcasting*, pp. 38–43.

Goldman, K. (1994, September 7). "Triple A" format attracts sponsors. *The Wall Street Journal*, p. B8.

Guild, R. (1992, April 27). Monday memo: Differentiation begins with a well-planned marketing program. *Broadcasting*, p. 71.

Head, S., Sterling, C., & Schofield, L. (1994). *Broadcasting in America* (7th ed.). New York: Houghton Mifflin.

Hesbacher, P., Clasby, N., Anderson, B., & Berger, D. (1976). Radio format strategies. *Journal of Communication, 26* (1), 110–119.

Heuton, C. (1994, December 12). Country fills the airwaves. *Mediaweek*, p. 12.

Heuton, C. (1995, March 13). More ears for networks. *Mediaweek* p. 8.

In *re application of Alta Gulf, FM, Inc. and Citicasters*. 10 FCC Rcd 7750 (1995).

In *re revision of radio rules and policies*, 7 FCC Rcd 2755 (1992).

Inglis, A. (1990). *Behind the tube: A history of broadcasting technology and business*. Boston: Focal Press.

Kim, J. B. (1992, September 14). Cost per point still rules: Sale execs. *Advertising Age*, pp. 41–42.

Litman, B. (1993). The changing role of television networks. In A. Alexander, J. Owers, & R. Carveth (Eds.), *Media economics: Theory and practice* (pp. 225–244). Hillsdale, NJ: Lawrence Erlbaum Associates.

McChesney, R. (1994). *Telecommunications, mass media, and democracy: The battle for control of U.S. broadcasting, 1928–1935*. New York: Oxford University Press.

National Broadcasting Company, et al. v. Unites States, et al. 319 U.S. 190 (1943).

N/T big in top 25. (1994, February). *Billboard 106*(8), 97.

Petrozzello, D. (1995a, March 20). Advertisers expected to favor radio in '95. *Broadcasting and Cable*, p. 45.

Petrozzello, D. (1995b, April 24). Ownership clock ticking for Evergreen. *Broadcasting and Cable*, p. 35.

Piirto, R. (1994, May). Why radio thrives? *American Demographics 16* (5) 40–46.

Radio (1990, October 15). *Broadcasting*, pp. 65–67.

Radio Advertising Bureau. (1995, August 30). *Radio advertising revenues increase 7% in July to maintain solid growth rate in 1995*. [press release].

Rothenbuhler, E., & McCourt, T. (1992). Commercial radio and popular music: Processes of selection and factors of influence. In J. Lull (Ed.), *Popular music and communication* (2nd ed., pp. 101–115). Newbury Park, CA: Sage.

Second memorandum opinion and order, 9 FCC Rcd 7183 (1994).

Simon, C. C. (1992, September 14). Rethinking the business in tough times. *Mediaweek*, p. 64.

Smith, F. L., Meeske, M., & Wright, J. W. (1995). *Electronic media and government*. New York: Longman.

Springer, K., & Fratrik, M. (1994). *1994 FM Subcarrier Market Report*. Washington, DC: National Association of Broadcasters.

Standard & Poors (1995, July 20). *Industry surveys: Media: Radio and tv broadcasting*.

Sterling, C. (1984). *Electronic media: A guide to trends in broadcasting and newer technologies 1920–1983*. New York: Praeger.

Tankel, J. D., & Williams, W. (1993). Resource dependence: Radio economics and the shift from AM to FM. In A. Alexander, J. Owers, & R. Carveth, (Eds.), *Media economics: Theory and practice* (pp. 157–158). Hillsdale, NJ: Lawrence Erlbaum Associates.

Telecommunications Act of 1996. [Online]. Available: http://www.callthemonit.com/legislation/tele-com_act.

Veronus, Suhler, & Associates (1995). *Communications industry forecast*. New York: Author.

Viles, P., & Foisie, G. (1992, September 7). Radio's new age: The dawn of the mega-combos. *Broadcasting*, pp. 4–12.

Wilke, M. (1994, November 21). Radio tunes in fresh ideas. *Advertising Age*, p. 23.

Williams, W. (1993). Impact of commissioner background on FCC decisions: 1975–1990. In R. J. Spitzes (Ed.), *Media and public policy* (pp. 43–60). Westport, CT: Praeger.

Yorke, R. (1992, November 23). Monday memo: Many stations seem to utilize a retail and wholesale strategy. *Broadcasting*, p. 20.

11

The Economics of the Music Industry

Eric W. Rothenbuhler
John M. Streck
University of Iowa

In this chapter we provide an overview of the structure and performance of the recorded music industry. After an initial discussion of industry size, providing historical notes where appropriate, we define the industry in terms of its core technologies, key contingencies, and capitalization strategies. A second section discusses key issues in industry structure: oligopolization, conglomeration, economies of scale, and barriers to entry. A third section discusses key issues in industry decision making and the strategies used to manage the high levels of uncertainty characteristic of the business.

OVERVIEW OF THE INDUSTRY

Making music is big business. According to the Recording Industry Association of America (RIAA), sales of recorded music in 1994 reached approximately $35.5 billion worldwide. With its large and relatively wealthy population, the United States was responsible for approximately one third of these sales. In 1996, consumers in the United States spent just over $12.5 billion on 1.1 billion records, cassettes, compact discs (CDs), and music videos (Recording Industry Association of America, 1997). This performance, moreover, represents a continuation of the recording industry's 15-year trend of increasing sales (Fig. 11.1). Prior to this, the years between 1978 and 1982 had plunged the recording industry into a major recession; and in constant dollars it was not until 1992 that the industry was able to return to sales levels set in 1978. Hence, much of the record industry's apparent growth in the mid-1980s and early 1990s was actually due to inflation.

The record industry, however, has long been characterized by cycles of rapid growth and relative decline. A boom of record production and sales in the first half

199

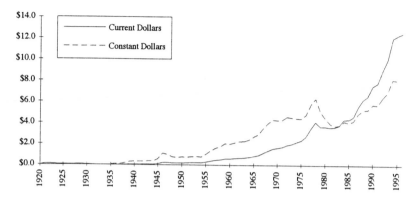

FIG. 11.1. Value of domestic music industry shipments by year, in billions. Adapted from Recording Industry Association of America (1982, 1997).

of the 1920s was followed by decline, and the depression of the 1930s nearly eliminated the record industry (Ennis, 1992; Sanjek, 1988; Sanjek & Sanjek, 1991). The 1940s were a period of steady growth, but in the early 1950s record sales in constant dollars leveled and declined. The year 1955 brought rock and roll, and with it a rapid increase in record sales with the growth lasting through 1969 (e.g., Sanjek, 1988).

Moving beyond dollars, Fig. 11.2 displays the number of units (i.e., cassettes, singles, LPs, etc.) sold each year since 1973 when the RIAA first began to monitor sales in units. Looking at units rather than dollar figures eliminates the influence of price increases as well as inflation. This graph shows the 1978 peak to be less precipitous than the dollar figure—it was produced in part by an increase in prices—but the same broad slough in sales following 1978 remains. Nevertheless, the ups and downs in recorded music sales rest on a foundation of steadily increasing levels.

It is also worth noting the performance of the recording industry in comparison to other media industries. Table 11.1, for example, shows consumer expenditures in dollars and hours for seven major media. The time devoted to recorded music exceeds that for every medium but television and, with home video and books, is one of the few media attracting increasing amounts of time over these years. The money spent on recorded music, moreover, is just under half that spent on television and exceeds that spent on film (and in more recent years, magazines). Although no doubt in part a function of the associated price structures (i.e., the average list price of a book versus the average list price of a CD, cassette, or LP versus the average cable bill), Americans spend more hours per dollar on recorded music—over 5 hours per dollar in 1993—than on any other medium except television. By contrast, in 1993 Americans spent less than half an hour per dollar on film.

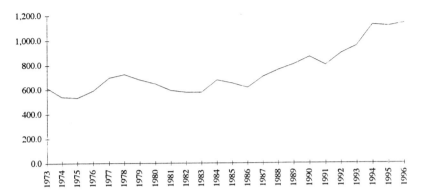

FIG. 11.2. Domestic music industry unit shipments by year, in millions. Adapted from Recording Industry Association of America (1982, 1997).

Core Technologies

From the beginning, the core technologies of the recorded music industry have been, and remain, the manufacture and distribution of recorded music products such as records, tapes, and CDs. The infrastructure surrounding these core technologies includes manufacturing plants, warehouses, trucking contracts, wholesale distributors, retail chains, independent stores, and the contract system, conventions and work habits that hold it all together. To that end, every major record company—currently WEA, Sony, BMG, Polygram, Thorn/EMI, and MCA—owns its own manufacturing facilities and operates a wholesale distribution system. Neither the most glamorous part of the record business, nor the part that attracts public attention, this manufacturing and distribution is the essential foundation of the industry.

Mass manufacturing imposes certain requirements on the recording medium. In the early days of recording one of the most important advantages of Berliner's disk recording method over Edison's cylinder recorders was that the disks were easier to reproduce, handle, and store. Thus, although cylinder recording produced a superior recording in terms of fidelity, the disk soon emerged as the industry standard because manufacturing advantages mattered most for business success. In more recent decades the different manufacturing requirements of records, tapes, and CDs have also impacted the conventions and standards of the music industry. Records, for example, are pressed, whereas tapes must be copied from beginning to end. Modern tape-duplicating machinery runs at very high speeds, which makes such duplication economically viable but reduces the sound quality of the recording. Speed and ease of production, however, are not the only issues. When only one or two CD manufacturing plants existed, manufacturing costs were high. Today, however, with the duplicating machinery being standard and several manufacturing plants in place around the world, the cost of CD manufacturing has fallen below

TABLE 11.1

U.S. Consumer Media Expenditures

	1985	1986	1987	1988	1989	1990	1991	1992	1993
Hours Per Person									
Television	1530	1522	1485	1490	1485	1470	1513	1550	1529
Recorded music	185	173	200	215	220	235	219	233	248
Daily newspapers	185	184	180	178	175	175	169	172	170
Magazines	110	103	110	110	90	90	88	85	85
Books	80	88	88	90	96	95	98	100	99
Home video	15	22	29	35	39	42	43	46	49
Film	12	10	11	11	12	12	11	11	12
Dollars Per Person									
Television (i.e., cable)	45.43	49.71	56.66	66.89	75.58	85.31	92.36	96.71	101.06
Recorded music	22.39	23.52	27.92	31.01	32.25	36.64	37.73	43.05	47.42
Daily newspapers	41.84	43.28	44.76	46.15	47.48	49.35	48.38	50.31	52.02
Magazines	25.62	26.89	29.31	29.88	31.49	33.14	33.45	34.26	35.27
Books	43.39	44.81	49.72	54.29	61.24	63.9	68.18	71.37	74.9
Home video	20.43	28.45	35.58	44.04	50.84	56.48	58.88	63.41	69.42
Film	19.13	19.11	21.33	22.1	24.67	24.4	23.13	23.24	24.33

Note. From U. S. Bureau of the Census (1995). ©1994 by Veronis, Suhier and Associates Communications Industry Forecast, New York, NY, TCI: (212) 935-4990. Reprinted with permission.

that for vinyl records—which have become the more exotic technology. Furthermore, CDs have additional advantages for manufacturing and distribution as well. Most importantly, the manufacturing process is more reliable than that for pressing records, and thus there is a smaller defect rate. Pressing vinyl records also requires more human handling than manufacturing CDs, which raises labor costs, and the compact discs themselves are smaller and lighter, considerations important for shipping costs.

Although the manufacture and distribution of recorded music remains the music industry's raison d'être, recently there have been plans and experiments with alternative systems for delivering recorded music products. One idea considered has been to use satellite networks to deliver digital data from central databanks to in-store CD printing devices. Consumers could browse computer listings of available CD titles, order a CD, and have it printed in-store from the satellite-delivered data. Such a system would save the record company distribution costs and save the retail store inventory costs, but on the other hand the system would involve complex data processing and communication problems. Even if such problems could be overcome, success would ultimately depend on the quality of the in-store print, and on overcoming existing consumer habits. The record-buying public is used to browsing in bins of product, often using album cover graphics to inform their decisions. Consequently, the idea to date remains just that: only an idea. There is no central database, no satellite network, no in-store CD printing device.

There have also been recent experiments with delivering samples of music over computer networks, making them available to anyone who chooses to download them. So far this has mostly been used as a promotional device and record company willingness to distribute the data for free most likely results from the fact that few consumers have the facilities to transfer it to a tape or CD for later use. Such experiments have also been limited by the logistics of processing the quantity of data required for quality musical sound. Thus, given the diverse range of technical problems that have yet to be overcome, as well as the force of the established conventions which define record retailing, such experiments and any future developments are for now dwarfed into insignificance in comparison with the existing infrastructure for the manufacture and distribution of records, tapes, and CDs.

Key Contingencies

In addition to the central requirements for the manufacture and distribution of recorded music products, the industry is structured in response to a number of other key contingencies. These can be addressed under three main headings: there must be music to record; it must be recorded; and there must be consumers of recorded music products.

Obviously the point of manufacturing and distributing records is the music that is recorded on them. Record companies, however, are neither musicians nor songwriters; they must contract with other parties to provide those services. There must, then, be an incentive system to induce musicians and songwriters to offer their services. Record companies use a variety of contracts for those purposes. Studio musicians may perform under a work-for-hire contract. This means they are employees of the record company and anything they produce in that capacity belongs to the record company; such artists are paid for their services and relinquish all rights to the products and profits of those services. A lump sum fee for a featured artist usually works the same way, and so, for instance, when early blues musicians signed contracts to record a certain number of songs for a certain fee they also relinquished control over, and profits from, those recordings. Although now controversial, this was standard practice for several decades and allowed the profits from successes to cover losses incurred on records (the majority of releases) that did not generate profitable returns (e.g., Sanjek, 1988).

In contrast to that system, a normal recording contract today offers the featured musicians royalties on future sales—a common range is 7% to 15%, depending on the musician's status (Weissman, 1990). However, the costs of recording, equipment purchases, and various other costs are advanced to the musicians and charged against royalty earnings. In other words, until enough copies of an album have been sold to pay the costs incurred in producing the record the artist will not earn royalties on that album. The recording contract becomes, in essence, a loan from the record label to the artist, with the loan to be repaid out of the artist's royalties. Moreover, in those cases where an album fails to recoup its initial investment, that album's "debt" will be applied to any follow-up album the artist records.

Although the royalties paid to musicians are stipulated in a recording contract as a percentage of the income from sales of the record itself, songwriters can earn additional income from publishing royalties. Publishing royalties are income generated by fees charged for the right to use and reproduce a published item, in this case a song. Record companies pay these fees, based on the number of copies of a song they reproduce whether they sell those copies or not. Radio stations, jukebox operators, night clubs, television stations and networks, movies, advertising, and any other business user of copyrighted music also pay into the system. Publishing royalties are established by copyright law and handled for songwriters by ASCAP, BMI, and other rights fees organizations. Although this system is distinct from the recording business proper, the entire industry obviously depends on it. Without a source of income from the sale of recordings of their work, songwriters would have little incentive to allow the use of their material by recording companies (as was the case prior to the 1909 copyright law). Indeed, enough money is made from copyright fees that songwriting and publishing have been at the center of the more enduring forms of music industry subterfuge since the 1920s. Whoever claims to have written a song, registers its copyright or both becomes the legal collector of the fees. Over the decades many a producer, executive and prominent disc jockey have taken songwriting credits in return for helping to make a hit (e.g., Eliot, 1993).

In addition to the straightforward necessity for business arrangements assuring a supply of music to record companies, the industry is also dependent on a dynamic musical culture it does not control. In the early days of the industry this required recruiting established musical performers from opera, vaudeville, and theater. Then, in the growing competition of the 1920s, record companies had to find new sources of music. The result was the first recording of southern, rural, and African-American musics. In the 1950s, recording entrepreneurs followed musical changes as much as they produced them. At first the major companies ignored rock and roll, but then learned that their success was to be dependent on that new force in musical style and culture whether or not they chose to produce and promote it (e.g., Ennis, 1992; Gillett, 1983).

Just as the record industry must have music to record, it must also have facilities for recording and technicians to do the work. Prior to the development of tape recording technology after World War II, music was recorded by disc-cutting machines. These cutters were neither cheap nor easy to use. The norm was for record companies to build and equip their own studios and hire their own recording engineers. Tape recording technology quickly became smaller, cheaper, and easier to use than disc cutting recorders, allowing a boom in recording activity. Kealy (1979) estimated that the number of record companies in the United States increased from 11 to nearly 200 within the first 5 years of tape recording. Access to recording facilities had been a dear resource; suddenly it became common. This trend, moreover, has continued in recent years with the increasing proliferation, growing ease of use, and falling prices of recording and musical technologies, including the most recent digital devices (Jones, 1992). Whereas early musicians depended on record companies and recording engineers for access to studios and equipment, more musicians now own portable or in-home recording equipment. Recording experience is becoming common, with attendant changes in recording and musical practices. The so-called "rave" movement, for example, was rooted in amateur musicians creating music on their home computers; and as exemplified in Beck's Grammy Award-winning *Odelay* and U2's *Pop*, the techniques perfected there have become mainstream.

The final major category of contingencies for the recorded music business is the consumers themselves. Here we mention three key issues, moving from the most concrete to the most ephemeral. Although it is often overlooked, the record industry is crucially dependent on an infrastructure of in-home equipment. These days the consumer electronics industry is huge and we take for granted the presence of TVs, VCRs, radios, and stereos in the home. However, when the format of the recorded music product changes, the industry is reminded of their vulnerable dependence on the consumer's choice vis-à-vis another (although in terms of corporate ownership, not always separate) industry's products. Whatever the format of the recorded music, be it cylinders, acetate discs, vinyl discs, reel-to-reel tapes, cassettes, 8-tracks, CDs, digital audiotape (DAT), minidiscs, or CD-ROMs, sales of that music are dependent on the music buyer's ownership of the necessary playback equipment. By example, then, the success of the CD, which brought record companies higher profit rates, lower shipping and handling costs, and a new opportunity to capitalize on back catalogs, depended on consumers buying CD players. Moreover, although the CD eventually emerged as one of the music and home electronic industries' more stunning successes, at the time of the CD's introduction success was by no means a foregone conclusion. Indeed, while the CD represents the current standard for the music industry, its most direct predecessor, the video laser disc, has become more or less a specialty item. The "war of the speeds" in the late 1940s between RCA's 45 and Columbia's LP was another contest over hardware compatibility, although in this case each was able to carve itself a niche in the home electronics market. Tied to the market for home electronics, then, new formats may, like the CD, become industry standards, effectively eliminating competing formats; they may, like the video disc or quadraphonic sound, fail to capture the interest of electronics manufacturers, record labels or consumers as competing standards leave investors wondering which system to choose; or they may, like the LP and 45, develop distinct niches in the market for recorded music and, by extension, home electronics. Regardless of the particular technology, however, one thing that can be said of them all is this: All will eventually be replaced by something new. The duration may change—the analog disc has lasted for more than a century, the 8-track tape for 20 years, and quadraphonic sound barely left the labs—but occasional claims for "perfect sound forever" and problems for retailers notwithstanding, recording formats are now largely intended to become obsolete. The home electronics industry wants to sell new machines, and the recording industry wants new profits from old (i.e., proven) recordings rereleased on new formats.

Whatever their relationships to one another, however, each of the technologies of music recording and playback is both dependent on and constructive of a culture of music listening for entertainment in the home. Again, we largely take this for granted but the culture of listening was historically constructed and without it the record industry as we know it would not exist. Prior to the boom of the record industry in the 1920s, the music business depended on ticket sales for live performance and on sales of musical instruments and sheet music. The production and sale of pianos in America grew increasingly from 1870 on, peaking in 1909 when 364,545 pianos were built (Roell, 1989). Musical instruments, music lessons, sheet music, and the idea of music in the home were promoted as morally uplifting from the mid-1800s on. These ideas were continued by the early phonograph industry and the early players as well as the phonographs were sold as educational, musically accurate, "good for the children," and so on (see magazine advertisements from the era; Thompson, 1995). The difference between playing music and listening to music had to be elided. This was usually accomplished through claims of bringing the worlds greatest musicians, composers, and performances "into the home" (e.g.,

Thompson, 1995; Welch & Burt, 1994). The later development of the radio industry helped cement habits of listening for entertainment in the home.

Finally, the most commonly noted area of dependence on consumers is the industry's vulnerability to shifts in taste. No other media audience has such a range of available choice, nor so regularly displays such massive shifts in taste as the audience of the record industry. By comparison, newspaper audiences have hardly changed in decades while magazine audiences are easier to predict, film and television audiences easier to manipulate. No element of commercial culture and communication changes as much and as constantly as popular music. Furthermore, most of this change is in restless pursuit of an audience that cannot say what it wants until it hears it.

Capitalizing on the Structure

Once an industrial apparatus has been built that is responsive to the contingencies for the manufacture and distribution of recorded music products, it is logical for recording companies to attempt to reap the most from their investments. Any additional investments or activities that serve to increase the financial return on initial investments are deemed necessary; hence the promotion of the recorded music product is a standard industry activity. Indeed, promoting hit songs has for so long been a major activity in the music business that we can think of that type of success as one of the industry's products. From this perspective, record labels manufacture hits, positions on music charts, and popularity as much as they do records; hype is as important in the industry as music (Harron, 1988).

Music promotion goes back to the "song pluggers" of the publishing industry in the 1800s. These promoters were employees of music publishing companies who worked to get songs played by vaudeville, theater, and touring orchestras. The public would hear the songs and be disposed to buy the sheet music. As early as the 1890s there were already complaints that the "necessary" expense of promotion was cutting into profits (Sanjek & Sanjek, 1991). Yet promotion so greatly increased the profits from the most successful songs that the investment was deemed worthwhile, no matter how expensive. Radio, moreover, accelerated the process of making a hit by allowing a few name orchestras who played in prominent time slots on network shows to have nationwide effect (e.g., see Ennis, 1992; MacDougald, 1941). Naturally, then, promoting songs to those orchestras became much more important for the publishers—and that much more difficult as they competed for the same few orchestras. Promotion became a bigger, and more necessary, part of the music industry.

Eventually, of course, the record industry would replace sheet music as the core of the music business. However, the importance of promotion and the power of radio for that purpose remained. Since the mid-1960s, promotion has been the single largest expense in the music industry, and crucial to the success of a recording (Hirsch, 1972; see also Dannen, 1990; Haring, 1996). The importance of promotion, moreover, has at times led to an obvious extreme: promoters paying radio industry gatekeepers (i.e., DJs and programming directors) to play their songs—that is, bribery, or, in the terms of the record industry, "payola." Far from rare, although Congressional hearings in the late 1950s attempted to both position payola as the product of rock and roll and to suggest that it had been effectively eliminated, neither is the case. Payola emerged with the sheet music industry in the 1880s and continues to this day (see: Dannen, 1990; Ennis, 1992; Segrave, 1994).

CHARACTERISTICS OF INDUSTRY STRUCTURE

Oligopoly

Through most of its history the record industry has been dominated by a small number of major firms. At the same time, however, the character of this domination has changed from year to year, and there have been periods in which the majors lost control of key aspects of the industry. The most famous of these was the explosion of rock and roll in 1955. The majors lost touch with the sources of hit popular songs, and in the ensuing years an unusual diversity of labels, artists, and musical styles prevailed. Eventually a new group of labels rose into prominence. Both before and after that period of time, however, nearly all of the top-of-the-chart popular hits were controlled by a few, large firms: a clear case of oligopoly. Nevertheless, behind any generalizations about oligopoly in the popular music business lie a number of complications. In the early 1950s for example, while the eight largest record companies controlled 95% to 100% of the weekly top-10 hits and the pop music charts were relatively stable and homogeneous (Peterson & Berger, 1975), the rhythm and blues charts were bubbling with activity and new artists (see, e.g., Gillett, 1983; Shaw, 1974). Moreover, new record companies like Atlantic, Chess, Modern, Specialty, and Sun—to name only a few of the most famous—were springing up throughout the United States. In the 1980s and 1990s, to consider another example, although six major record companies control the distribution of nearly all of the most successful popular music, their control is obtained via a multilayered system of ownership or interest in a diversity of subsidiary labels and distribution, promotion, and artist development contracts with smaller labels. This era of oligopolization would appear to be very different from the oligopolization of the early 1950s (Burnett, 1992; Lopes, 1992). Nevertheless, with appropriate qualification, some generalizations can be made.

Most of the money in the record business is made from music at the top of the popular music charts. The largest expense and most important logistical factors in making that money are national distribution and promotion. If we examine the companies that control distribution and promotion for the music that reaches the top of the popularity charts we can establish a reasonably clear record of oligopo-listic control over that portion of the music business. Figure 11.3 reproduces data

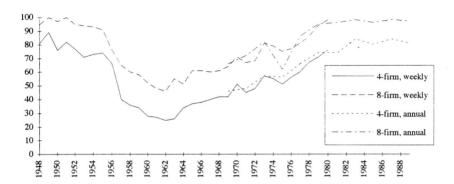

FIG. 11.3. Percentage of the weekly and annual "Hot 100" charts controlled by the top four and top eight firms by year. Adapted from Peterson and Berger (1975), Rothenbuhler and Dimmick (1982), and Lopes (1992).

from studies by Peterson and Berger (1975), Rothenbuhler and Dimmick (1982), and Lopes (1992). It is clear that except for the 14-year period from 1956 to 1970 this portion of the record industry has been controlled by very few corporations. Both the Peterson and Berger study and the Rothenbuhler and Dimmick study showed clear negative correlation between concentration of control in the industry and the diversity of music on the charts. In the years covered by these studies, periods with a high degree of concentration were characterized by fewer successful songs per year, fewer artists, and more established stars. When control of the industry was less concentrated among the few largest firms popular music was characterized by greater variety of songs and faster turnover on the charts. The period was characterized by more styles, more artists, and more new stars. Although the correlation is not consistent over all years, there also appears to be an association between these indicators of diversity and total annual sales in the industry. Years of greater diversity tend to be associated with greater sales levels.

Lopes (1992) and Burnett (1992) both argued that a different pattern emerged beginning in the late 1980s. The industry has returned to, or even exceeded, historically high levels of concentration of control. Some evidence indicates that musical diversity has *not* fallen however. Our own opinion is that there has been more diverse and better music available in the pop market in recent years that in the late 1970s to late 1980s. Certainly annual recorded music sales have continued to grow, which Lopes and Burnett argued calls into question the usual assumption of association among these factors. The explanation offered is that the industry is now structured differently than before and follows commensurate changes in operating procedure. The idea is that the majors have become a loosely coupled system in which financial control is centralized while musical decision making is decentralized. The majors allow their many subsidiary and contracted labels to operate relatively autonomously in making musical decisions, thus maintaining the musical diversity of product while keeping centralized corporate control of finances.

This may be a tale of successful conglomeration, or it may be a bubble of success produced by circumstances beyond the record industry's control. The 1980s and 1990s have also witnessed a growth of television and radio outlets for popular music and a growing diversity of radio formats. The CD has also allowed record companies to capitalize on back catalog, the box set allowing them to do so multiple times. And as never before in the history of the record business, people have continued buying records as they age into their 30s and 40s. All of these trends represent growing markets and thus new economic opportunities. Most of them also present pressure for diversification.

Vertical Integration

Vertical integration is the term used to describe the coordination under a single corporate ownership of the elements of different businesses or industries necessary to the production and provision of a finished good or service. The businesses are "vertically" linked as in the flow from raw materials to manufactured goods to retail sales. For example, if a paper goods manufacturer also owns forest land, sawmills, wholesale distributors, and office supply stores then they are vertically integrated, using their ownership umbrella to coordinate the provision of raw materials, manufacturing, wholesale distribution, and retailing.

The major record companies have always been vertically integrated to one degree or another. At most points in the history of the business the majors have included publishing arms, recording facilities, manufacturing plants, distribution, and promotion businesses; in recent decades most of the majors have had record clubs for mail-order retailing, and some of them have been invested in record store chains. Occasionally record companies have invested in, or have been owned by corporations invested in, the manufacture of musical instruments and recording equipment (e.g., CBS records' ownership of Fender for several years, or the more recent purchase of CBS records by Sony). Over the years important record companies have been owned by film studios (e.g., MGM, Warner Brothers) or developed corporate ties to the production of films—this bringing a major method of cross-media promotion under the umbrella. It has not been unusual for record companies to be financially associated with talent and entertainment booking agencies, aiding in the control and supply of musical talent.

Vertical integration has been one of the key forces in the major record companies' ability to maintain their oligopoly (Peterson & Berger, 1975). By controlling each step in the link between the musician and the audience vertically integrated companies achieve four distinct advantages over smaller, less integrated competitors. First, they increase the number of potential revenue sources. A record label that also owns a publishing company can place the rights to the songs it records with that company and transform copyright fees from a cost to a source of income.

Second, the vertically integrated company is able to economize its use of the various resources by essentially selling to itself as well as centralizing administrative functions such as management and accounting. Third, these companies are able to coordinate and control their use of resources, manipulating schedules in order to maximize the performance of the companies' offerings as a whole rather than individual records. Finally, through their control over the complete chain of the production process, vertically integrated companies can inhibit competitors' access to these goods and services, profit from it, or both. So, for example, as the largest of the record distributors WEA profits not only from the music of its own subsidiary labels, but also from any label that contracts with WEA for distribution—while also denying access to their distribution and promotion machinery to anyone from whom they cannot profit.

Interestingly, vertical integration has occasionally been used to maintain the power and independence of smaller companies. Motown is the best example. The artists that recorded for Motown performed songs written by Motown staff writers and published by Motown's publishing company. Their performances were backed by Motown staff musicians and recorded in Motown's studios by staff engineers. They were signed to Motown's artist management staff and worked through Motown's booking agency. So long as Motown could keep producing hit songs this system worked spectacularly well. However, when the hits became fewer and farther between, the company became financially vulnerable and was bought out.

Conglomeration

Conglomeration is an extension of vertical integration; the businesses under a conglomerate umbrella may be more horizontally than vertically related (e.g., film and records vs. record production and record distribution) and they may even be largely unrelated. The conglomerate can be more efficient in the use of basic administrative resources such as accounting and legal departments, while taking profits in whatever industries they own parts of, and trying to benefit from synergies across industries (e.g., Turow, 1992).

Ties between the film and recording industries go back to the beginning of sound film. However, recent years have seen the increasing incorporation of record labels into the multinational corporations that do business not only across the media, but, in some cases, outside the media as well. So Warner Records, for example, is not only a part of the recorded music industry but through its connections to parent company Time Warner can be linked to cable television, the film industry, book and magazine publishing, and other media-oriented endeavors. Parent companies like Sony, Philips, and Matsushita, moreover, not only link record labels to other media but to the professional and home electronics markets as well.

Although conglomeration principally enables the major record labels to vertically integrate within the confines of the recorded music industry, it can also allow recorded music to be incorporated into the revenue streams of the parent companies.

Although revenue streaming is generally discussed within the context of the motion picture industry, where feature films move from domestic theaters to foreign theaters, pay television, network television, syndication and so forth, recorded music rights—specifically in the form of soundtracks—can be an important market as well. Thus, in some cases (e.g., *Reality Bites*) decisions regarding the soundtrack of a film have been made not with specific regard to the demands of the narrative or the desires of the filmmaker, but rather for the sake of the soundtrack in and of itself. Songs, in other words, will often be included in a film only to make the associated cassette or CD more appealing.

The next extension of such thinking is more aggressive use of cross-media corporate ties to exploit the profit potential of the company's properties and contractees. By placing a mix of established stars and new artists from the company's roster on the soundtrack of a film, having the stars from the film appear in the music video for the soundtrack, having film and recording stars appear on television talk shows and in interview magazines (all owned by the corporate parent), and selling licensed t-shirts and souvenirs in the lobbies of both movie theaters and concert venues—and when the song is old enough, selling the right to use it to an advertiser and putting out a box-set on the artist—the parent corporation gets maximum exposure for their artists and song properties at minimum cost, squeezing profit from every possible use of them. As Frith (1988) said:

> In the music industry itself, a song—the basic musical property—represents "a bundle of rights"; income from the song comes from the exploitation of those rights, and what happened in the 1980's was that some of these (the "secondary rights" [i.e., licensing and copyright fees from other users]) became more profitable, others (the "primary rights" [i.e., selling your own records]) less so. (p. 105)

Conglomeration can also lead to an exploitable linkage between home electronics and recorded music—almost a replay of the early decades when the manufacturers of phonograph machines had to also record and distribute phonograph records so that their customers would have something to play (e.g., Kennedy, 1994; Welch & Burt, 1994). This becomes particularly important as corporations making consumer electronics search for new recording formats, as access to the libraries and artists of a record label can, or at least so some think, potentially give a new format an advantage over competitors. Under situations of conglomeration, the recorded music and home electronics industries can become not only interdependent, but strategically linked. For example, the importation of the DAT recorder was blocked for nearly a decade by the lobbying of American record companies who argued to Congress that DAT would allow consumers to easily and cheaply make perfect copies of CDs to an extent that would damage their legitimate rights to the sales of those CDs. Despite the Congressional Office of Technology Assessment's study demonstrating the fallacious and self-serving nature of the record companies' arguments, their lobbying was successful—probably because the record companies were American and the importers of DAT were Japanese at a time of great economic nationalism.

Finally, then, there is one more advantage conglomeration offers to corporations: Risk and loss can be spread from one division or area to another. The fortunes of a record label that is only a record label will, for the most part, rise and fall with the performance of the music industry as a whole. However, a record label tied to other industries—be it publishing, home electronics, television, film, or what have you—can both support and be supported by those industries as their various economies rise and fall.

Economies of Scale

Although the advantages of conglomeration to a large extent depend on the particular configuration of a given corporate entity—that is, a company cannot take advantage of, say, linking recorded music to the motion picture industry if it does not own both film production company and record label—conglomeration and oligopoly both lead the major record companies to a more universal advantage: the exploitation of economies of scale. Economies of scale are not unique to the music industry; they do, however, define it. From recording to manufacturing to promotion, as the business of creating and selling recorded music currently operates, there are clear advantages to those who operate at high volume.

Although such issues as how much to spend on artist royalties, recording, and promotion are "fixed" arbitrarily (that is to say, either the product of a particular negotiation or company policy), once these are decided the bulk of the costs of selling a given CD are fixed costs. Because these fixed, "first copy costs" are incurred regardless of whether a given album sells one copy or one million, they must be spread across each of the individual units sold. As a result, the more copies are sold, the lower the percentage of the fixed costs which each must account for and, assuming the price to the consumer stays the same, the higher the profit margin for each disc or tape. Put simply, in an economy of scale the more copies that are sold the more that is made on each copy.

Although economies of scale exist wherever there are fixed costs of doing business, they become most important in situations, such as the manufacture of recorded music, where fixed costs account for the bulk of the cost of doing business. Consider, for example, the difference between producing music and producing athletic shoes. In both cases there are first copy costs: the aforementioned royalty rates, and recording and promotion budgets in the case of recorded music; research and development, design, production plants, and so forth for athletic shoes. Additionally, there are, in both cases, marginal costs: blank media and packaging for recorded music; leather, rubber, thread, and so forth for athletic shoes. However, although both forms of manufacturing involve fixed costs and marginal costs, the ratio of fixed costs to marginal costs is far higher in the case of recorded music. According to Vogel's (1994) estimate, the marginal costs for manufacturing a single

CD are roughly $.60 per disc. Assuming the wholesale rate of $8, this means roughly 93% of the record label's revenue from the sale of a disc is directed at covering the first copy costs. The consequences of this are twofold: first, the high rate will lead to a quick payoff of those fixed costs; and second, once enough copies of the disc have been sold to cover the fixed costs, 93% of the company's revenue from each subsequent disc sold will be profit. Hence, at the breakeven point, known only to company policymakers, the marginal rate of return (i.e., profit per unit) goes up in a single huge step, whereas the overall rate of profit goes up exponentially. Nike should be so fortunate.

Barriers to Entry

Barriers to entry are any conditions that inhibit the success of new businesses in a market or industry. If the capital, technology, skilled labor, or other such necessities are not available, then new businesses cannot be started; such conditions would be considered a barrier to entry. All new businesses face difficulties, failing at a much higher rate than do established businesses. However, if new businesses in a particular market or industry face unusually large difficulties in access to suppliers or customers, ability to compete on price, and so on, then these too would be considered barriers to entry.

In principle there are few or no barriers to entry in the recorded music industry. There is an oversupply of underemployed musicians and songwriters. Recording technology has never been cheaper, more readily available, or easier to use. The price of printing CDs has now dropped below that of pressing records, so the total financial investment could be small and access to the skilled labor and facilities easily arranged. Indeed, although unassailable evidence would be impossible to compile, there are some indications that in recent years more musicians and small studios may be producing more recordings for local and regional distribution than ever before (e.g., Robinson, Buck, & Cuthbert, 1991). In classical, jazz, and audiophile music markets, small, specialty labels are not at all unusual. Many of these specialty labels market their music through magazines and mail-order catalogs.

The big money (and the big celebrity) in the music business, of course, is not in local and regional markets, but in national and international popular-music markets. Access to these markets, and a chance to sell copies of an album in the multiple millions, depends on both huge amounts of capital and controlling a large and complex system for distribution and promotion. This is indeed a huge barrier to entry. Control of distribution is so important that the traditional distinction between "majors" and "independents" is based on whether a company owns its own distribution system. The majors can control their own distribution; independents have to contract with other companies—these days usually the majors themselves—for that service. This requires them to share the profits as well as put their own products in part at the mercy of another corporation's business plans.

Both the importance of the national market and the difficulty of entering it successfully were exacerbated by the steadily increasing nationalization of popular musical culture since the 1950s. In the 1950s and 1960s, radio formats and record sales varied from city to city and region to region, and it was not unusual for records to become national hits by first gathering industry attention as city or regional hits (Marsh, 1993, provided a case study). Of course, that was an era in which the majors did not control the market to the extent they did before 1955 and have since. In the later 1970s radio formats became more nationally standardized, today being nearly identical from one city to another (Barnes, 1988; Fornatale & Mills, 1980; Rothenbuhler, 1985; Rothenbuhler & McCourt, 1992), and nationwide cable services such as MTV and VH-1 are now essential in making a hit. At the same time, national record store chains, with nationally coordinated inventory, have come to dominate recorded music retailing. Partly in response to these other trends and partly as a producer of them in their own business interest, the major record companies have coordinated their own distribution and promotion efforts to work the whole nation as a single market.

The combination, therefore, of vertical integration, economies of scale, the nationalization of popular-music culture and its business, and the sheer size of the distribution and promotion activities commensurate with a hit record creates insurmountable barriers to entry in the national or international recorded popular-music market. The result is the oligopolistic control of that market by six major corporate conglomerates.

UNCERTAINTY AND DECISION MAKING

Based on the previous discussion of economies of scale, it should be intuitively clear that within the recorded music industry once the break-even point has been reached—that is, once enough units have been sold to pay for the first copy costs of recording, promotion, and so forth—profits accumulate at a stunning pace. This leads to an important consideration for understanding the performance of the music industry. Because not every recording will pass the break-even point and yet sales of those that do become almost pure profit, it is a common characteristic of the music industry that the burden of the financially unsuccessful albums is carried by the few that are successful. One *Thriller* (91 weeks on the chart, 37 weeks at #1, 24 million copies sold as of 1994) can carry a vast quantity of unsuccessful experiments. The problem is recognizing the difference between the next *Thriller* and the next failure.

Like all manufacturers of cultural products, the record industry is faced with unusually high levels of uncertainty (cf. DiMaggio & Hirsch, 1976; Hirsch, 1972;). Many products today have cultural features; cars and clothes, for example, are characterized by style as well as functionality. Consumer decisions will be based in part on these cultural features, and hence on taste. However, the appeal of style to consumer taste is less predictable than the functionality of features that can be decided by engineering criteria. Clothes of essentially identical functionality and durability may be received as being of very different value in a market characterized by decisions made according to taste.

Some products, such as recorded music, are all but entirely cultural and hence their market is essentially entirely dominated by decisions of taste. The buyer of a CD, for example, is probably not motivated by a need for a plastic-coated aluminum disc, but by a desire for music. Therefore the best value in the store will not necessarily be the cheapest plastic-coated aluminum disc, but the one that contains the most desirable music. Predicting what will be considered the most desirable music by millions of strangers is a most uncertain business.

Yet all businesses, and the recorded music industry is no exception, require certainty for routine prediction, planning, and control. They must make payroll, make regular payments on borrowed capital, pay taxes, make leases, depreciate, maintain, and replace equipment, and so on. These needs are of course much exacerbated by the size of a mass manufacturing and distribution business.

The structure of the industry, reviewed in the previous section, can be seen to be characterized by attempts to isolate and control sources of uncertainty. For example those parts of the business that deal with creative activities or the public are set up as separate offices and kept organizationally isolated from those parts of the business that allow and require predictability and control (Peterson & Berger, 1971). In the remainder of this section we review characteristics of organizational decision making that are designed to cope with the characteristic uncertainty of the recorded music business.

Contracts and Independent Producers, Studios, Engineers, and Promoters

One uncertainty management strategy is the use of the structured contract. Rather than supporting a staff to engage in highly uncertain activities, such as recording hit records, companies can contract with people who present themselves as professionals in these uncertain activities. The contracts can be structured such that the work of the outside professional is evaluated routinely, rewards tied to specific performance criteria (e.g., X% when the record is done, Y% if it goes gold), and the company given the option of renewal or cancellation of the contract (see Peterson & Berger, 1971). This is exactly how artist contracts have been written since the rock and roll era began. In the more stable business environment of pre-1955 pop music, 5-year contracts for singers and musicians were normal among the major labels (Gillett, 1983). Since then a series of five renewable 1-year contracts has become the norm (Weissman, 1990)—of course, the record company, not the artist, holds the renewal option.

In the mid-1960s, such contracts for independent producers, studios, and engineers rose in prominence—sometimes only because record companies were responding to star-artist demands to hire their own producers. However, they have become the norm in the industry. No major record company now maintains a staff of company producers and engineers (other than for classical music), though some still have company studio facilities. On the other hand, independent record companies more often have their own studios and staff, and often the independent company is built on the sound of their producer, staff, and studio.

In the 1980s even independent promoters became fairly common, although no major company gave up its own promotion staff, that being too big an investment of too much importance. According to more than one exposé, it would appear that the primary purpose of the independent promoter system was to obtain services that were too shady, or even outright criminal, for a major corporation to ask of its own staff (Dannen, 1990; Knoedelseder, 1994).

Track Records and Star Systems

Another response to uncertainty in the music industry is to rely on track records and reputations. The star system, for example, promotes celebrity because it is typically a safer investment than is music. Bruce Springsteen, for example, remains a good commodity even as the sales potential of his changing musical style varies. Moreover, although the most obvious manifestation of track records is the music industry star system, musical performers are not the only ones who, at times, will be judged by their past performance and established reputation rather than their current work. From the executives who decide which artists will be signed, to the producers who shape and control the recording and the engineers who record, those who have a reputation for producing hits, selecting hits, or both, will inevitably be called on for their expertise—at least until their first failure. As a decision-making short-cut, decisions are quite often based on the track records of the people involved more than the merits of the project, which are far more difficult to evaluate.

Preselection Systems and Surrogate Consumers

Successful products in the record industry must pass through a series of decisions: Songs must be published and recorded; recorded songs must be selected for an album and released; the number of albums to be manufactured and distributed must be decided; a promotional budget and strategy for its deployment must be developed; record stores must stock and promote the records; radio stations must pick songs to play. All of this occurs before the first buyer makes his or her choice. This whole sequence works as a preselection system in that the items ultimately made available to consumers are those selected as the most likely to succeed at each preceding stage of the process (Hirsch, 1969; cf. Ryan & Peterson, 1982).

The preselection system of the record industry is a staged filtering of overabundant product, in anticipation of uncertain demand. At each stage decisions are made by comparing the product in question with successful products in the recent past.

However, each stage of the decision making is also carried out by players in different positions in the industry who have different interests and use somewhat different criteria. For example, songwriters want to be published, musicians want to be recorded, producers want their contracts renewed, executives want work on time and under budget (and they want a hit), promoters want to spend their time where it will pay off, radio programmers want songs that fit their formats, and record store owners want the hits as well as a diverse back catalog. However, making a hit requires the active participation of all of these players and at each point in the decision chain there are more products being considered than can possibly be used. The few products that emerge with large promotional budgets, prevalent radio play, music videos, in-store displays, concert tours, and talk-show appearances are those that gave no decision maker along the way a reason to worry. The preselection system of the recorded music industry is, therefore, conservative.

Overproduction and Differential Promotion

Overproduction and differential promotion is a business strategy by which more products are produced than can possibly be successful, whereas promotional efforts are differentially assigned to minimize risk (Hirsch, 1972). This is made possible by the fact that the biggest investments are in promotion and distribution, which fall late in the decision-making chain (star musicians may get huge recording budgets, but ordinarily they then command even larger promotion budgets). Until it is time to make the big decision about investment in promotion, it is safe to continue making small developmental investments in a large number of products. In this way the system always has a large number of products in the works at any one time. Then the largest proportion of promotion budgets can be spent on the products that appear to be the safest bets to become hits while the rest of the records are released with little or no promotion. Because promotion budgets are the best predictors of hits (either because budgets make hits, because budgets are assigned to things that are accurately predicted to be hits, or both—likely both to some degree), this is a safe way to invest the largest single piece of the total investment made in a product. Only a fixed number of records can be successful at a time; however, the record companies are constantly turning out more records than that. This apparently nonsensical business practice does have the advantage of allowing record companies to cover their bets, which is important because the next big hit might emerge unexpectedly. At the same time labels can assign the biggest promotion budgets to those records most easily predicted to be successful or reassign bigger promotion budgets to records that begin to show promise on their own. In the latter case, promotion is not used to make a hit so much as to increase the rate of return on a hit by increasing the total sales.

SUMMARY AND CONCLUSION

The recorded music industry is a producer of cultural goods, working in what may be the most uncertain, most volatile of the media businesses. Consumer taste in recorded music is more ephemeral than consumer taste in newspapers, magazines, popular novels, TV shows, or movies, and they also have more options for expressing that taste than in most of those other categories. Yet the industry has succeeded, attracting consumer dollars and time at equivalent levels.

The core technology of the industry remains the manufacturing and selling of copies of recorded musical performances. Income from associated activities such as song publishing has always been important and, due to the prevalence of corporate conglomerate structures, is probably more important today than ever before. Capitalizing on the core technology requires meeting contingencies in three major categories: assuring a supply of music, songwriters, musicians, and performances; achieving the recording itself; and assuring the interest of an audience. Having built a system to meet these contingencies and capitalize on the core technology, the industry invests in promotion to increase the rate of return on their business activities.

The industry structure is characterized by vertical integration and conglomeration, capitalizing on economies of scale, and the promotion of the nationalization and internationalization of the music market, all of which create barriers to entry that aid the maintenance of the oligopolistic control of the industry by a few major corporations.

The characteristic uncertainty of the business is managed by strategic decision making. Among the techniques are the prevalent use of external parties working under short-term, renewable contracts; the use of track records as a decision-making shortcut and the promotion of star celebrities as more predictable investments than their music; the elaboration of a preselection system in which industry players operate as each other's surrogate consumers; and overproduction and differential promotion, in which the biggest investments are made in the safest products while many smaller investments are spread over more diverse musical products.

As would any business of the size of the major companies in popular-music recording, the overall system is as conservative as it can afford to be. However, below the top of the business, beneath the level of the most popular, most money-making albums and artists controlled by those few international, conglomerate corporations, bubble the activities of a diversity of specialty labels, regional labels, independent musicians, home tapers, night clubs, and bars. As 1955 stands to remind us, a breakout of new music that upsets the controlling structure of the majors can happen.

FURTHER READING

Chapple, S., & Garofalo, R. (1977). *Rock'n'roll is here to pay: The history and politics of the music industry.* Chicago: Nelson-Hall.

Frith, S. (Ed.). (1988). *Facing the music.* New York: Pantheon.

Gillett, C. (1983). *The sound of the city: The rise of rock and roll* (rev. ed.). New York: Pantheon.

Gray, H. (1988). *Producing jazz.* Philadelphia: Temple University Press.

Jones, S. (1992). *Rock formation: Music, technology, and mass communication.* Newbury Park, CA: Sage.

Stokes, G. (1977). *Starmaking machinery: Inside the business of rock and roll.* New York: Vintage Books.

REFERENCES

Barnes, K. (1988). Top 40 radio: A fragment of the imagination. In S. Frith (Ed.), *Facing the music* (pp. 8–50). New York: Pantheon.

Burnett, R. (1992). The implications of ownership changes on concentration and diversity in the phonogram industry. *Communication Research, 19,* 749–769.

Dannen, F. (1990). *Hit men: Power brokers and fast money inside the music business.* New York: Vintage.

DiMaggio, P., & Hirsch, P. M. (1976). Production organizations in the arts. *American Behavioral Scientist, 19,* 735–752.

Eliot, M. (1993). *Rockonomics: The money behind the music* (rev. ed.). New York: Citadel.

Ennis, P. H. (1992). *The seventh stream: The emergence of rocknroll in American popular music.* Hanover, NH: Wesleyan University Press.

Fornatale, P., & Mills, J. E. (1980) *Radio in the television age.* Woodstock, NY: Overlook.

Frith, S. (1988). Video pop: Picking up the pieces. In S. Frith (Ed.), *Facing the music* (pp. 88–130). New York: Pantheon.

Gillett, C. (1983). *The sound of the city: The rise of rock and roll* (rev. ed.). New York: Pantheon.

Haring, B. (1996). *Off the charts: Ruthless days and reckless nights inside the music industry.* New York: Carol Publishing Group.

Harron, M. (1988). McRock: Pop as commodity. In S. Frith (Ed.), *Facing the music* (pp. 173–220). New York: Pantheon.

Hirsch, P. M. (1969). *The structure of the popular music industry.* Ann Arbor, MI: Institute for Social Research.

Hirsch, P. M. (1972). Processing fads and fashions: An organization-set analysis of cultural industry systems. *American Journal of Sociology, 77,* 639–659.

Jones, S. (1992). *Rock formation: Music, technology, and mass communication.* Newbury Park, CA: Sage.

Kealy, E. R. (1979). From craft to art: The case of sound mixers and popular music. *Sociology of Work and Occupations, 6,* 3–29.

Kennedy, R. (1994). *Jelly Roll, Bix, and Hoagy: Gennett studios and the birth of recorded jazz.* Bloomington: Indiana University Press.

Knoedelseder, W. (1994). *Stiffed: A true story of MCA, the music business, and the mafia.* New York: Harper Perennial.

Lopes, P. D. (1992). Innovation and diversity in the popular music industry, 1969 to 1990. *American Sociological Review, 57,* 56–71.

MacDougald, D., Jr. (1941). The popular music industry. In P. F. Lazarsfeld & F. N. Stanton (Eds.), *Radio research 1941* (pp. 65–109). New York: Duell, Sloan, and Pearce.

Marsh, D. (1993). *Louie Louie.* New York: Hyperion.

Peterson, R. A., & Berger, D. (1971). Entrepreneurship in organizations: Evidence from the popular music industry. *Administrative Science Quarterly, 16,* 97–107.

Peterson, R. A., & Berger, D. (1975). Cycles in symbol production: The case of popular music. *American Sociological Review, 40,* 158–173.

Recording Industry Association of America. (1982, April 5). *News from RIAA.* New York: Recording Industry Association of America.

Recording Industry Association of America. (1997). *The top ten fact book.* Washington, DC: Recording Industry Association of America.

Robinson, D. C., Buck, E. B., & Cuthbert, M. (1991). *Music at the margins: Popular music and global cultural diversity.* Newbury Park, CA: Sage.

Roell, C. H. (1989). *The piano in America, 1890–1940.* Chapel Hill: University of North Carolina Press.

Rothenbuhler, E. W. (1985). Programming decision making in popular music radio. *Communication Research, 12,* 209–232.

Rothenbuhler, E. W., & Dimmick, J. (1982). Popular music: Concentration and diversity in the industry, 1974–1980. *Journal of Communication, 32*(1), 143–149.

Rothenbuhler, E. W., & McCourt, T. (1992). Commercial radio and popular music: Processes of selection and factors of influence. In J. Lull (Ed.), *Popular music and communication* (2nd ed., pp. 101–115). Newbury Park, CA: Sage.

Ryan, J., & Peterson, R. A. (1982). The product image: The fate of country music songwriting. In J. Ettema & D. C. Whitney (Eds.), *Creativity and constraint: Individuals in mass media organizations* (pp. 11–32). Beverly Hills, CA: Sage.

Sanjek, R. (1988). *American popular music and its business, Vol. 3: From 1900 to 1984.* New York: Oxford University Press.

Sanjek, R., & Sanjek, D. (1991). *American popular music business in the 20th century.* New York: Oxford University Press.

Segrave, K. (1994). *Payola in the music industry: A history, 1880–1991.* Jefferson, NC: McFarland & Company.

Shaw, A. (1974). *The rockin' 50's: The decade that transformed the pop music scene.* New York: Da Capo.

Thompson, E. (1995). Machines, music, and the quest for fidelity: Marketing the Edison phonograph in America, 1877–1925. *The Musical Quarterly, 79,* 131–171.

Turow, J. (1992). *Media systems in society: Understanding industries, strategies, and power.* New York: Longman.

U.S. Bureau of Census. (1995). *Statistical abstract of the United States* (115th ed.). Washington, DC: U.S. Bureau of the Census.

Vogel, H. (1994). *Entertainment industry economics* (3rd ed.). Cambridge, England: Cambridge University Press.

Weissman, D. (1990). *The music business: Career opportunities and self-defense* (rev. ed.). New York: Crown.

Welch, W. L., & Burt, L. B. S. (1994). *From tinfoil to stereo: The acoustic years of the recording industry, 1877–1929.* Gainsville: University Press of Florida.

12

The Economics of International Media

Rod Carveth
University of Bridgeport

James Owers
Georgia State University

Alison Alexander
James Fletcher
University of Georgia

As the U.S. media industry positions itself for the 21st century, it faces major macroeconomic forces that are reshaping its business and marketing strategies: the regional integration of national economies, such as the European Community and NAFTA; advances in technology; the emergence of an economic world based more on pragmatism than ideology; and a borderless economy resulting from global competition. These forces will dramatically alter the structure, function, and strategy of the U.S. media industry in the decade ahead (Carveth, 1992; Carveth, Owers, & Alexander, 1993).

Many countries of what Ohmae (1990) termed the "Triad"—the United States, the European Union and the Pacific Rim nations (especially Japan)—are looking to new markets for their products and services, such as China and post-Communist central and eastern Europe. Ohmae suggested that many previous variable-cost items, such as technology and promotion, are now really fixed costs for business. If Ohmae is right, contemporary businesses will be hard-pressed to reduce fixed costs, and thus will need to seek new markets, acquire competitors to reduce their fixed costs through economies of scale, or both. Adopting a global strategy allows companies to achieve these goals.

This chapter reviews the factors within the domestic and international marketplace that are important to the economic future of U.S. media companies. Our method draws from macroeconomic theory, specifically Porter's "diamond" model (cf. Carveth,

223

1992), to explain the changes occurring in one segment of the media industry. The chapter first reviews the basic elements of TV and film syndication. It then uses Porter's model to analyze the role of the United States in the international film and television marketplace, particularly the factors that contributed to the erosion of the competitive advantage of the United States in the international syndication marketplace. Although the focus of this chapter is on the U.S. television industry, due to the increasing integration of both the media industries and the media marketplaces, the principles reviewed here are generalizable to media business overall.

INTERNATIONAL FILM AND TV SYNDICATION

Before discussing the international syndication business, we present some basics of the syndication process.

Syndication

The *syndication marketplace* is the place where the rights to presentation of films, audio programs and video programs are sold to media outlets such as TV and radio stations, cable program networks, and pay-per-view services. The marketplace is driven by two principles. First, syndicators—those who deal in program rights—will seek to sell these rights as often as the relevant regulations and their agreements will allow. Second, each buyer will be charged as much as the marketplace will bear.

Unlike manufactured products, the value of film and television entertainment is intangible, referred to as "frame of mind" (Fletcher, 1993). Frame of mind can refer to positive critical reviews, industry awards, box office receipts, viewer ratings, positive critical reviews, industry awards, and other measures of familiarity and popularity. However, previous box office performance or audience ratings is considered to be the most important reflection of a favorable frame of mind among the public.

In the syndication marketplace, those who make rights available for sale deal with stations or networks who hope to take advantage of economic opportunities by buying these rights. For example, a syndicator's package of reruns (off-network series) represents the opportunity for a station to run a weekday strip (Monday through Friday) of programs. Similarly, first-run syndicated programs (such as *Star Trek: Deep Space Nine*) represent an opportunity for an independent station to air an alternative to network prime-time programming.

The Syndicator

The economics of syndication mean that the syndicator *earns* when rights move from supplier to customer. As a result, maintenance of a desirable volume of transactions is characteristic of the successful syndicator. Because they are often not involved in production, syndicators do not have to be expert writers or producers (although some are). They make their business successful by commanding an inventory of program sources (producers and studios) and a separate inventory of program buyers. Matching the two produces syndication revenue.

There are a number of products available for syndication.

Motion Picture Packages. Motion pictures made available for presentation on cable and over-the-air television come from recent theatrical productions, from archives, and from foreign-produced imports. In recent years, theatrical production has run in the vicinity of 500 titles per year. Relatively few are the well-promoted blockbusters that drive patrons to the theaters. An additional smaller number are made-for-TV movies produced for the networks for presentation in prime time.

Motion picture archives include large numbers of titles, many out of distribution long enough that large audiences are unfamiliar with them. However, major stars connected with these titles can create a positive frame of mind in an audience large enough to increase a film's commercial potential. The largest of these archives is undoubtedly that of Turner Broadcasting based on the acquisition of the MGM film archive.[1]

Every package for syndication must be organized to fit the programming and marketing opportunities valued by local stations, networks, and cable programmers. This may include playing in prime time (the time of peak viewing, 7 p.m. until 11 p.m. local time), and "stripping" (offering the films at the same time on consecutive days of the week).

In negotiating prices for film packages, the syndicator is concerned with the number of stations or networks interested in the package. A package sold to many customers will produce more revenue while permitting price incentives to customers. The result will be a greater difference between revenue and cost. When the number of customers for a package is low, the syndicator has less latitude in

---

[1]A certain number of foreign films have found significant audiences in theaters and on television in this country. While estimates vary widely, the figure most often cited in the film industry is that roughly 500 foreign titles suitable for release in the United States complete production each year. "Suitable for release" is a judgment made either on the basis of language (English and Spanish are both languages appropriate for release in the United States), suitability to dubbing or subtitles, theme, pace of action, and quality of sound and picture in the available prints. The best known productions from abroad are those from the United Kingdom and presented by such prestigious programmers as public television or the Arts & Entertainment cable service. Spanish-language programmers in the United States (the third largest nation in terms of Spanish speakers) have made use of the large number of programmers abroad who produce in Spanish.

On the whole, however, importation of theatrical titles represents an area with great potential for development in the future. With a shortage of theatrical product given the increased demand generated by cable and videocassette growth, more entrepreneurs will be able to acquire film and video entertainment abroad for dubbing and release in the United States. The market for additional imports appears to be present if an organization has the means to make more of the available titles "suitable" for presentation in the United States by editing, dubbing, preparing new release prints and video masters, and so forth.

negotiating a package price agreeable to both parties. Deals typically include multirun, multiyear financial commitments which are among the largest a station or service undertakes. As a result, establishing the value of the film package is critical to a buyer's financial success.

Off-Network Reruns.   The principal frame of mind value for off-network series is the popularity of the series during its network run, and the popularity (or "drawing power") of performers appearing in the series. Ratings, particularly across demographic groups, are the most important evidence carefully analyzed by customers in the market for such series.

The most attractive off-network series is one with a record of beating competition, a history of drawing large and broad audiences, and a sufficient inventory of episodes. For a station to strip a program for 13 weeks requires about 65 episodes. A full season of the typical prime-time network series is about 22 original episodes per year, with the remaining weeks of the year being filled by reruns of those 22. This means that a series needs to air on a network for a minimum of 3 years.

The number of prime-time series annually available on the four largest television networks is somewhere between 60 and 70. However, the number of successful programs entering off-network syndication from this number of series is perhaps 2 or 3. Consequently, successful new off-network series are in great demand by local stations and cable programmers, and demand drives prices upward. A solicitation for bids for these very popular off-network series goes to stations, and rights to these programs are optioned off. Often, series are sold in syndication 12 to 18 months before the first episode of the series is broadcast by the station or cable programmer who wins the auction. The practice of auctions for off-network series increases the pressure on syndication customers to manage their program acquisition activities prudently.[2]

First-Run Syndication.   First-run or original syndication consists of programs and series produced specifically for the syndication market. Evidence of favorable audience frame of mind for these series consists of previous program performance in markets where they have been syndicated or their performance in test markets and in other program research. The first-run syndication market is identified by a large number of half-hour series that are programmed by affiliates

---

[2]The rules of an auction are dictated by the owner or syndicator. Rights to off-network runs of the series may be exclusive or nonexclusive (most rights to series are exclusive). Under exclusive arrangements only one station per market may be granted rights to the series. Terms of payment vary; the buyer may be required to make a significant payment at the time of sale, or payments may be scheduled over some period of time. The sale may involve promotional materials or personal appearances on the part of performers. The conditions of the auction are dictated by the owner/syndicator's desire to maximize revenues from the property. Terms of sale are typically arranged to control the revenue stream from the sale to accommodate the seller's financial plan. In some cases, the seller may not wish to receive large cash payments at the beginning of the contract period because of an already strong cash position.

early in the evening. These include game shows (such as *Wheel of Fortune*) and so-called "reality-based" programs (such as *Hard Copy*).[3]

In addition, the first-run syndication market includes talk shows for daytime and late-night scheduling and "prime-time alternative" programming. Prime-time alternatives are purchased by independent television stations hoping to steal audience from affiliates during prime time and by cable channels with the same intent. Prime-time alternatives are usually offered on the basis of one episode per week or as limited series. Examples include *Highlander* and *Xena: Warrior Princess*.

In understanding the first-run syndication market it may be helpful to review the lifecycle of these programs. Planning for such a series typically begins in late summer or early fall when producers have already put their present series into production (network and syndicated series production typically begins in July). The producer of a proposed first-run syndication series examines the concept (or main idea) of a proposed series in the market to be sure that the market can accommodate additional programs of the kind envisioned. Investigation into the availability of stars, hosts, writers, and production facilities may also be involved.

To elicit station interest in a proposed series, producers commonly make a rough of the proposed program with lesser known performers and relatively simple settings. The rough allows the producer to discuss the proposed program with potential advertisers and customers of the series. The aim of these early discussions is typically to solicit upfront money. Upfront money represents bargain prices for the advertiser or syndication customer. For the producer it reduces the amount of loans needed for production of the series. In addition, securing upfront investors amounts to a strong endorsement of the proposed program, which may sway syndication customers later on.

Barter Syndication. This has become a major factor in encouraging additional first-run syndication. In barter syndication an advertiser purchases some or all of the advertising opportunities in a program prior to its being offered in the syndication market. The syndication customer pays less for barter programs because there are fewer advertising opportunities to be sold by the station. The advertiser is offered—in addition to time for commercials—an identity with the program and an assured environment for commercials.

For the most part, stations and cable programmers make their program decisions for the fall season in the first quarter of the year. There are no assurances that

---

[3]There is little doubt that the *prime time access rule* (PTAR) has been one of the most important stimuli to the production of first-run syndication programs. The PTAR was adopted by the FCC in 1971 and provides that the commercial television networks may not program more than three of the weeknight block of four prime-time hours. In addition, in the top 50 television markets, local stations may not schedule off-network programming in the hour of prime time that they schedule. An exception is made in the case of news: Network news may be used during the prime-time access hour of the local television station. Many affiliates do use a half hour of network news in access time leaving a half hour to be filled with programming from first-run syndication.

first-run series under consideration for purchase will play well in the marketplace. Sometimes the program will be broadcast in a test market or submitted to other forms of program research to examine the appeal of the program and its parts or to details of predicting the ratings of the program when it is broadcast in various program slots.

Suppliers and Syndicators

A supplier is a production firm that provides programs either to a network or to syndication. The largest suppliers of entertainment are the studios and independent producers in Hollywood, such as Warner Brothers and Carsey-Werner Productions. The supplier may or may not syndicate its own productions. A case in point is MGM. MGM Television is a producer of television series and of made-for-television movies. Its series *thirtysomething* was syndicated by MGM/United Artists. By contrast, many older theatrical films produced at MGM, such as *Gone with the Wind*, are now owned by others, such as the Turner Entertainment division of Time Warner.

An independent producer often is associated with a studio. The studio may provide office space and other resources to the producer and may be a regular partner in production deals for television put together by the independent producer. Many but not all independent producers will rely on a separate syndicator to sell their programs in the syndication marketplace.

The largest of the syndicators, Viacom, was established to isolate the syndication rights held by the networks at the time that the Financial Interest in Syndication ("finsyn") rules came into being. The finsyn rules permitted the networks merely to lease the shows they aired and left to others the lucrative business of selling the rights for reruns of popular network programming. Viacom produces some programming, but the syndication of such programs as *The Honeymooners, I Love Lucy*, and *The Cosby Show* is the principal business of the company.

Overall the syndication marketplace experiences gross sales to syndication in excess of $6 billion with about 10% growth per annum since 1985. Although syndication performance will experience ups and downs, this rate of growth is likely to continue for some time.

It is likely that the total inventory of syndicated programs available for purchase will increase steadily in the foreseeable future. There will be large increases in the number of film packages available, as archives are uncovered and made suitable for presentation on television. Foreign production is underutilitized by U.S. television. As foreign producers and distributors make more material available, they are likely to do so with production costs lower than those of U.S. producers. As a result they will find opportunities in late-night and daytime time slots in broadcasting and cable. Off-network syndication will continue to represent an important staple in syndication, even though national network shares during prime time are not likely to increase.

Even more growth is likely to occur in first-run syndication. As cable program-mers become more influential, the impact of broadcast network concentration will have less influence on public frame of mind value. The economics of first-run syndication encourage participation in production by a large number of individuals and organizations. As a result this part of the syndication market is most responsive to increasing demand for programs.

The potential for imported programming has not been realized and represents an important opportunity. Syndication opportunities with narrow-interest viewers have been developed to some extent in the cases of sports programming and programs related to business and finance, but the potential of specialized program-ming for specialized audiences is likely to continue to be a trend in the next several decades, and the syndication marketplace will benefit.

Factors Affecting the Domestic Marketplace

Porter (1990) developed what is known as the "diamond model" of industrial competitive advantage. He observed that four environmental attributes of a nation help determine whether its firms will achieve international success. These attributes are: (a) factor conditions; (b) related and supporting industries; (c) firm strategy, structure, and rivalry; and (d) demand conditions. Factor conditions include a country's human, natural, and capital resources. A domestic industry is more likely to be internationally competitive if its related and supporting industries are inter-nationally competitive. Domestic rivalry helps keep firms innovative and striving for improvement. Finally, demand conditions refer to the composition, size, and pattern of growth of demand for the product/service in the domestic economy, as well as how transferrable the nation's domestic preferences and products are to foreign markets. In addition to the aforementioned four environmental attributes, Porter observed that firms are also affected by government policy and chance events.

For years, the U.S. television syndication industry was strong in all four of the attributes identified by Porter. U.S. television companies possessed superior factor conditions for producing content. A 250-million-person marketplace provided plenty of demand for broadcast programs. Supporting industries, especially the electronics industry, were internationally competitive. The nature of domestic rivalry was different. Television broadcasting was dominated by three major networks (ABC, CBS, and NBC), who competed only among themselves and commanded the attention of 90% of the prime-time broadcasting audience. How-ever, during the last 10 years, the industry has become much more competitive, as the audience share for the three major networks has dropped under 50%.

The strength of U.S. television across these four attributes allowed them to attain competitive advantage in the global media marketplace. Each year, U.S. media companies earn considerably more from the export of media products than is paid for media imports. Thus, the media industries in the United States are net exporters.

The television programming industry alone has a net trade surplus of more than $2 billion per year (Carveth, Alexander, & Owers, 1994).

Traditionally, U.S. television companies have considered foreign countries as ancillary (or secondary) markets for the exporting of programs. The revenue stream provided by sales of programs to other countries paled in comparison to domestic sales. Nevertheless, U.S. television programs have long enjoyed wide international popularity, with many U.S.-made programs ranking in the top 10 in countries ranging from France to Australia. The international popularity of U.S. television programs (such as *Baywatch*), combined with the economies of scale accruing from a large domestic market for such product, gave the industry international competitive advantage.

During the last few years, however, it has become evident that the United States has lost some of its competitive advantage in certain sectors of the international television marketplace, specifically western Europe. To stem the erosion of its competitive advantage, U.S. television companies are attempting to enter the nascent markets of the central and eastern European countries, while concomitantly making adjustments in the way to conduct business in western European markets. The next section illustrates the erosion of the competitive advantage held by the U.S. in the international television marketplace utilizing Porter's diamond model of competitive advantage.

Factor Conditions

The U.S. television industry has long enjoyed the benefits of several different factor conditions (i.e., human, natural, and capital resources). Over the last 45 years, viewing television delivered by the major networks became a habit. The size of this viewing population meant that the industry could produce high-quality programming at a relatively inexpensive price. In addition, the prices charged to advertisers could be expected to rise at least 10% per year.

As reviewed elsewhere (Carveth, Owers, & Alexander, 1993), during the late 1980s, the U.S. television industry suffered from many of the same conditions that plagued the U.S. economy as a whole: the loss of the preeminent position in human resources; the sale of technologies to international competitors; and a lessening of the money available for research and development. Additionally, as Auletta (1992) has observed, the networks were extremely slow in responding to the threat of cable television. The conflicts between the networks and the program suppliers over the financial interest and syndication rules meant that foreign investors could obtain positions in the lucrative syndication marketplace.

The television industry was also hurt by its inability to keep down costs. The oligopolistic structure of the television industry (which reduces price competition), combined with the high cost of technology and labor, make the creation of TV programs costly ($1.3 million per hour in production costs), and strain the economic support system (advertising).

Efforts have been made to hold down costs. Seeing outsourcing as an effective cost-reduction strategy for the auto and computer industries, TV producers outsourced cartoon animation to Taiwan. Live-action TV productions have been moved to less costly, nonunion states (such as Georgia) or to other countries (such as Canada). Joint venture arrangements are another method to hold down production costs.

Another area of cost containment has been the move to produce less costly content: infotainment programming such as talk shows and "reality programs." Talk shows cost roughly $250,000 per week to produce, although the figure rises for major talk show hosts such as Oprah Winfrey. Despite a generally crowded market for talk shows, more than 20 will appear during the 1997–1998 television season. Reality programs (such as *Real TV* and *America's Most Wanted*) cost approximately $500,000 per hour to produce, less than one third of the $1.3 million per hour average of dramatic programs.

It is likely that broadcast companies will be looking for more innovative ways to hold down costs. One such way may be a shift in accounting practices to activity-based costing (see chapter 1, this volume). To date, no major television company has adopted activity-based costing. However, General Electric, which owns NBC, has had success with activity-based costing at its medical systems division, and may be the most likely to adopt such a practice. One of the problems facing entertainment companies, however, is that success in the programming marketplace tends to fluctuate more wildly than for other industries. For example, after a decade when situation comedies did well in the syndication marketplace, programmers discovered that public tastes shifted to more expensive, hour-long adventure shows, such as *Highlander* and *Hercules*. Such a shift is not only one of cost, but a complete production changeover (situation comedies are generally videotaped using interior sets; dramatic shows are filmed using more exterior shots). Although holding down costs is one area for improvement within the U.S. television industry, we argue that the single biggest factor condition change was that of the restriction of available capital for investment.

The Role of Investment

A number of factors changed the nature of investment in the broadcast industry. From 1970 to the mid-1980s, interest rates were generally high and consumer savings were low. The federal deficits were the largest in history, absorbing much of the investment monies available, and contributing to inflated interest rates. Banks that made substantial loans to developing countries in the 1960s and 1970s found there was little prospect of such loans being repaid. Thus, the supply of funds for domestic investment was substantially reduced (Porter, 1990; Toffler, 1990; Zengage & Ratcliffe, 1988).

There was a dramatic upturn in the number of institutional investors who had short-term appreciation of assets as a goal, and whose only real influence comes from voting in merger and acquisition activity, which brings immediate capital gains advantages. Consequently, the 1980s saw a record number of mergers and acquisitions take place, including those involving all three television networks and many major station groups. The debt taken on in much of this restructuring did not go to reinvestment, but to paying off shareholders. Many businesses had highly leveraged themselves through acquisitions (more debt) or stock buybacks (exchanging debt for equity), thereby increasing the vulnerability of the domestic economy. This was particularly true in the media industries. Following the October 1987 stock market crash, traditional bank lenders became more conservative. The government issued rules limiting the amount banks can lend to highly leveraged transactions.

At first, to secure financing for their debt loads and facing increased domestic competition, U.S. media companies increasingly turned to the international marketplace for revenues. At the same time, the economies of scale that made the United States best able to create slickly produced media content also made these U.S. companies attractive investment and acquisition targets for international firms. Until the 1980s, international media firms did little investing in U.S. media firms. Rather, the relationship between the United States and other countries could be characterized by two trends: (a) the United States competed with other countries in the communications hardware market, such as consumer electronics, and (b) the United States exported their software (i.e., programming) to very receptive international markets. As the 1980s began, the United States lost international market share in developing communications hardware, especially to Japan. Japan's consumer electronics industry benefitted from high productivity rates resulting from such factors as a well-educated workforce and lower labor costs. In 1981, Japan's consumer electronics output was valued at approximately $16.8 billion, whereas the U.S. share was approximately $11.7 billion. By 1986, Japan's share grew to slightly over $26 billion, while the U.S. share dropped to $6.5 billion (Zengage & Ratcliffe, 1988). By 1990, the Japanese held dominant positions in most of the consumer electronics industry, including VCRs, computers, and facsimile machines. The United States was able to maintain a national competitive advantage in the communications "software" industry (i.e., films, TV programs, recording).

Hence, the mergers between Sony and Columbia, Matsushita and MCA, or Philips and A&M Records merely reflect a combining of two firms from different countries holding international competitive advantages in their respective industries. Sony, Matsushita, and Philips are the largest producers of home entertainment and consumer electronics in the world (Levine, 1991; Zengage & Ratcliffe, 1988). These companies sought U.S. media firms who could provide software, such as films and music, to go along with their communication hardware. Such mergers allowed the companies to combine strengths, and to potentially achieve savings in production, distribution, and exhibition of media product.

Eventually, both Japan and the European Union suffered from the recession of the early 1990s, and foreign investment slowed significantly. U.S. broadcasters had to turn to more "creative" ways of financing expansion and acquisition (Noglows, 1990).[4] Several companies, such as Time Warner and News Corp., became active in the public debt market in order to restructure their balance sheets and take advantage of lower interest rates (Noglows & Rothman, 1993). Generally speaking, however, capital has became far more difficult to obtain than in the mid-1980s.

Broadcasting was one industry that was essentially bypassed in terms of direct foreign investment. Historically, the industry was relatively immune to the trend toward major foreign investment in U. S. corporate assets, because of regulations preventing foreign ownership. For example, in 1985, Australian and British media baron Rupert Murdoch (News Corporation) acquired the Metromedia broadcast station group, and the Fox production and syndication divisions. Those acquisitions positioned Murdoch to be able to launch the Fox Broadcasting Network as a challenger to ABC, CBS, and NBC. In terms of foreign companies acquiring broadcast companies, however, Murdoch is the exception rather than the rule. In

---

[4]Some of the strategies are outlined as:

1. Liquid yield option notes (LYONS). These are 15-year zero coupon notes on which interest is never paid if the note is converted into common stock. That conversion price increases every year, so that the company seeking financing gets to sell its stock at a premium price. Turner Broadcasting raised $200 million in late 1989 through LYONS.

2 Private market guarantees/assets as acquisition currency. During the McCaw Cellular Communications/Bell South pursuit of Lin Broadcasting, McCaw offered to buy 50% of the company at a bid price, and then would purchase the other 50% in 5 years. If McCaw failed to buy the other half of the property in 5 years, LIN properties would all be put up for sale, auctioned off to the highest bidder. Bell South proposed merging its cellular phone interests with that of LIN's and then spin-off the broadcast properties. They then offered to make a "back-end" guarantee for the half of LIN it will not own after the proposed merger which consisted of agreeing to pay, for any shares that they might acquire in the future, a price equivalent to what an outsider would pay. Bell South did not oblige themselves to purchase shares in the future.

3 Pay-in kind securities (PIKS). Also known pejoratively as "cram-downs," these are preferred stock that pay-out interest. In the Time Warner deal, preferred stock was issued to Warner stockholders that can be convertible into Time Warner stock at a premium above the market value. The stock's dividends accrue at an 11% rate, and the stock can be paid out in cash after 3 years. What was unusual about this PIK was that it was that it had an equity conversion feature (buying common stock) that many do not. Although some analysts believe that PIKS are essential to some media deals, others object because shareholders of a takeover target often are obliged to take these securities.

4 Commercial banks. Commercials banks have remained a player in the financing of broadcasting, but are more selective in what they finance. For example, commercial banks provided the major portion of the capital for the 1989 $1.5 billion Viacom refinancing deal (which, ironically, helped Viacom replace its high-yield debt with commercial bank debt). Commercial banks are becoming more creative in their financing, and, by doing so, are helping to stabilize the media finance market (Noglows, 1990).

In addition, a number of U.S. banks (such as Bank of Boston and Manufacturers Hanover Trust) are seeking more business in Europe. U.S. banks are investing in a wide range of European media properties, such as Echo, a French sell-through video firm; a British company that is converting single screens into multiplexes, and U.K. cable. U.S. banks were also poised for the possibility of takeover of the ITVA stations when bids were tendered in 1992, but were unsuccessful in obtaining a franchise.

order to qualify as an owner of a broadcast group, Murdoch was forced to become an American citizen.

As a consequence of the explosion of merger and acquisition activity during the 1980s, many companies were forced to hold the line on costs, particularly in the area of program development. Seeking partners to spread the risk is one of the current methods of containing program-related expenses.

Related and Supporting Industries

As noted, until the 1970s the United States not only held a dominant position international media content production, but in consumer electronics as well. This related industry was critically important to the U.S. broadcast industry because consumer electronics represents a major portion of the exhibition arm of the media industry (i.e., TVs, VCRs, radios). Slowly, however, the U.S. began to face competition from both Europe and Japan in the consumer electronics industry. By the late 1980s, most major U.S. consumer electronics manufacturers had abandoned the industry. Consequently, domestic media companies and consumer electronics companies missed an opportunity to take advantage of possible synergistic economic relationships.

However, there have been two areas that affect broadcasters in which the United States has made a major investment: fiber optics and high-definition television (HDTV). Investment in fiber optics is critical for the burgeoning information industry, and will potentially allow the telephone companies to deliver cable television into the home (thereby increasing the coverage of cable television, and, of course, broadcasters). The promise of HDTV is its ability to deliver twice the picture resolution of NTSC (currently 525 lines) standards; its digital stereo sound and a 16:9 aspect ratio (similar to 70mm film). Before HDTV becomes a reality, the FCC first has to approve a domestic standard among several technological options. Because so many of the other related and supporting industries have merged with media companies, further issues are addressed in the next section, as well as in chapter 13.

Corporate Strategy, Structure, and Rivalry

Porter (1990) observed that firms that achieve an international competitive advantage most often have strong competitors within their own industry. In terms of television, there was very little intraindustry competition, as the industry was dominated by the three major networks, and television production was controlled by a handful of major producers. Thus, the television industry became competitively complacent. However, two major events took place that forever changed the nature of the domestic rivalry.

The first of these events was an acceleration in the process of corporate restructuring, particularly a sharp upturn in merger and acquisition activity (cf.

Carveth, 1992). Restructuring activity usually takes place when the previous organizational form is perceived to be nonoptimal. For example, if a conglomerate is too unwieldy as a result of bureaucratic considerations, a breakup of the firm into smaller units may be efficient. However, the media merger activity that took place in the 1980s was largely the result of a unique combination of factors, such as more liberal regulations, lessened governmental oversight of business, and a rapidly growing economy that poured capital into the acquisition marketplace. Thus, multibillion-dollar media merger deals became commonplace, and even local TV stations were bought at between 12 and 20 times cash flow. For example, the $2 billion that Rupert Murdoch spent for the Metromedia stations represented 13 times cash flow.

The stock market crash of October 1987 slowed down the frenzy surrounding media restructuring, but it did not stop it. As was observed during the stock market crash in 1929, media restructuring, once it begins, appears to be somewhat immune to conditions of severe market swings. Whether this is a general business truism, or one that applies only to media industries is uncertain. Nevertheless, the efficiencies caused by both economies of scale and by cost-trimming left the media in a position to withstand the October 1987 shockwave. In fact, in the months after the October 1987 crash, media stocks not only survived, but, as a class, outperformed the Dow Jones index (Owers & Carveth, 1988).

For broadcast companies, most of the restructuring occurred during the spate of mergers and acquisitions occurring from 1984 to 1986. Restructuring activity slowed down due to a reevaluation of broadcast companies' value. After the crash, the investment community began looking not at earnings, but at assets. Thus, the major changes in the broadcast industry over the most recent years have less to do with corporate ownership restructuring but business practice restructuring. Deals that were consummated had to make economic sense.

The second major event that occurred was the 1987–1992 recession, which resulted in a substantial downturn in the advertising marketplace. Much of the restructuring activity during the 1980s assumed ever-increasing levels of revenue generation, an assumption that turned out to be overly optimistic. For most of the decade, revenues did increase. For example, in 1987, advertising accounted for 2.43% of GDP, up from 1.87% in the 1970s. As the decade ended, however, sources of media revenues flattened or declined. No longer could advertiser-supported media depend on annual advertising price increases of 12% to 15%. With the increasing competitiveness of the cable television and home video industries, fewer advertising dollars were being split up in more ways. Consequently, many major broadcast companies faced slow or zero growth as the 1990s approached. Companies that based their financial decisions on multiples of 12 to 15 times earnings found that they had overpaid for their media properties. Media companies, especially those with a substantial debt, were forced to adopt one or more of the following business practices: (a) laying-off personnel, (b) reducing production costs, (c) pursuing additional revenue streams, especially the international market-place, or (d) any combination thereof.

The downturn was especially painful for companies that were leveraged "to the tilt," financed their deals with "junk bonds," or both. Not only did they find that the earnings potential of their media properties was no longer strong, but Congress, as part of the savings and loan (S&L) bailout, forced the S&Ls to divest themselves of junk-bond portfolios. Some companies, such as Grant Broadcasting, folded; some, such as CBS, had to realign themselves by selling off assets to lessen their debt burden (a problem made more acute because banks became increasingly reluctant to lend money to finance acquisitions); some, such as Turner Broadcasting, undertook further restructuring to finance earlier deals; finally, some companies, such as Cap Cities/ABC and GE/NBC, tried to reduce costs through layoffs (Noglows, 1990).

It appeared unlikely that we would soon see a period with the type of restructuring activity the U.S. media experienced during the 1980s. Not only did many media firms struggle with high debt loads, but the government issued new rules regulating the financing of highly leveraged transactions. However, there are too many benefits to the strategy of restructuring for it to disappear. In fact, a considerable amount of restructuring activity began in 1995, largely in anticipation of the Telecommunication Act of 1996, which substantially loosened media ownership limits. In economic terms, long-term equilibrium is a condition of ongoing change and evolution.

Demand Conditions

The most important factor accounting for the decline of the competitive advantage of the U.S. broadcasting industry in the global media marketplace is the change in demand conditions. Porter (1990) proposed that in order to be competitive, firms must choose a position within the industry. For example, a firm can choose to market a serviceable product that is affordable to the broadest possible consumer market (such as fast food), or it can market a product for an elite market (a fancy restaurant). Positioning stems from two factors—*competitive advantage* and *competitive scope*. Competitive advantage can be achieved through either lower costs or by differentiation—offering unique products or ones with superior values. Competitive scope is either *broad* (going after the widest possible audience) or *narrow* (focusing on consumers who want very specific product attributes).

The competitive strategy that a firm might employ depends on the combination of competitive advantage and competitive scope. If the competitive advantage is product differentiation and the market is a broad one, then the strategy becomes *differentiation*. The U.S. television networks reach more than 50% of the available television audience through its variety of slickly produced television programming. If the competitive advantage is differentiation and the scope of the market is narrow, then the strategy is called *focus differentiation*. Cable television services such as

Cable News Network (CNN) and Entertainment and Sports Programming Network (ESPN) employ focus differentiation by providing specific programming to narrow audiences.

In the domestic media marketplace, the competitive strategy has largely shifted from *differentiation* to *focus differentiation*. More and more the broadcast media's corporate strategy dictates that companies target narrower audiences to differentiate themselves from the competition. Rather than striving to attract the largest audiences possible, broadcasters are focusing on specific demographic and psychographic groups. The success of the Fox Television Network can be attributed to its strategy of focus differentiation, targeting the younger demographic market with such shows as *Beverly Hills 90210* and *The Simpsons*, and culturally diverse markets, with shows such as *In Living Color*.

One of the most important factors affecting consumption is demography. Statistics show that the fastest growing age group in the United States are the elderly. Between 1990 and 2020, the number of people over the age of 50 will increase by 74%, whereas the number of those under 50 will grow by 1%. This shift will be meaningful in terms of media content and marketing, especially as older people tend to read more, and to consume television more than other age groups.

Demand conditions are not only changing domestically, but internationally as well. Porter (1990) noted that if the competitive advantage an industry enjoys is due to lower cost, and the competitive scope is broad, then the competitive strategy will be one of *cost leadership*. Game shows, talk shows and "infotainment" programs (such as *Jeopardy, Oprah* and *Inside Edition*) are sold in the syndication marketplace to TV stations as low-cost alternatives to off-network reruns. Internationally, the U.S. has maintained a cost leadership position in media exports. U.S. television companies, because of economies of scale caused by a 250-million-person domestic marketplace, have generally been content to rely on a media product export business.

It became apparent during the 1980s, however, that the United States would no longer have the same freedom to operate in the international marketplace. Many countries—including such close neighbors as Canada—began to impose restrictions on U.S. media exports. These countries began to step up their own domestic media production, thereby creating more programming supply to compete with U.S. media product. In addition, content preferences began to change.

Changes in World Demand

Some businesses adopt a concentration strategy in conducting international business. All production activities take place in their domestic environment, and these same products are exported to other countries. Aircraft, machinery, and agriculture are typical industries that have a concentration strategy. Other businesses *disperse* their activities, locating production and distribution activities among a variety of nations to take advantage of the different competitive features (such as lower labor costs) or characteristics (cultural differences) that affect the potential success of their products. An emerging dictum in conducting international business—"Think Globally, Act Locally"—reflects this dispersing strategy (Porter, 1990).

Until the 1990s, the United States was able to adopt a concentration strategy in exporting media content. However, the changes in the structure and function of both U.S. and international media institutions forced U.S. firms to adopt a dispersing strategy. Such a strategy allows the United States to overcome host-country language, cultural, and institutional barriers by tailoring media product to suit local needs.

For example, in addition to the proposed import restrictions, the United States is also facing changes in European content preferences. Where once the U.S. companies dealt with friendly state broadcast systems, and an audience hungry for its films and TV programming, now they are finding a more uncertain marketplace, with many more outlets and European audiences who demand more domestic product. Although American television still does well in the international market-place, it is not as dominant as it once was. As the U.S. marketplace has begun to produce less standardized programming fare (*Picket Fences, Northern Exposure*), it has found that those shows do not travel overseas as well as programming such as *Baywatch*. In addition, while some domestic situation comedies (such as *The Cosby Show*) do well, others do not translate. *Roseanne*, with its abrasive humor, failed to gain an audience in Greece and Australia, and achieved only a cult following in Great Britain.

To compete successfully in the "new Europe," U.S. broadcast companies will have to reexamine their notions about the European market. The United States has generally conceived of the European market as an international market. However, as Carlo Freccero of LaCinq (France's first commercial TV network) has observed, there are now two markets—an international market and a national market. The international market is a young market, "extremely open to the American style, which is more popular, less literary and closer to a comic strip or cartoon style" ("La Cinq," 1990, p. 18). By contrast, the national market is one where program-ming (largely family-oriented) is tied to each country's national experience. A dramatic sign of the changing marketplace occurred at the 1992 MIP-TV conven-tion. There, Italian media mogul Silvio Berlusconi announced that his networks would only buy U.S. shows in which his companies are involved in at the development stage. Other programmers, such as Helmut Thomas of RTL-Plus (Germany) declared "We have no word for 'sitcom' in German, but we are utilizing the expertise of Columbia and the producers of 'Married ... with Children' to localize the show for our viewers. Our advertisers love this kind of show" (cited in Guider, 1992).

The Role of Government

The political philosophy governing regulatory policy is a critical issue in assessing the role of government. The shift from the Carter administration to the Reagan and

Bush administrations was more than just a matter of Republicans replacing Democrats in the Oval Office. The ideology of the Reagan and Bush administrations rested on the assumption that Americans were tired of "big" government, and wanted government to be less intrusive in matters of the business. Thus, the Reagan–Bush years resulted in fewer restrictions for media industries. The Republican Party's regain of Congress in 1994 helped accelerate the deregulatory process with the passage of the 1996 Telecommunications Act.

For example, the concept of what constituted antitrust was shifted from a within-industry perspective to an interindustry perspective. In broadcasting, practices such as audience ascertainment, programming logs, commercial time restrictions, and even the Fairness Doctrine were eliminated. In addition, the number of broadcast stations an individual or company could own increased from 7 per class (AM, FM, or TV) to 12, and the 3-year mandatory period for owning a station was eliminated. With Federal Communications Commission (FCC) Chairman Mark Fowler leading the way during the 1980s, the marketplace rather than regulation became the operating principle for media operations.

The 1995 abolition of the finsyn rules allowed the networks to participate in the distribution revenues from the sales of programs to other countries, thereby sharing in the "back-end" profits from the sale of TV programs. The FCC decision could eventually result in less competition in the TV production industry, with a few major companies dominating in that area. On the other hand, those new combinations will be better positioned to compete on an international basis.

The elimination of the finsyn rules represents an opportunity for the TV industry to redefine business arrangements. By taking equity positions in new programs, the networks can generate a new revenue stream while lessening the risk to smaller program suppliers (which, in turn, exerts more cost controls on suppliers in a more competitive TV production marketplace).

The recent events in international media economics reflects a shift away from historical patterns of global media ownership. Media systems can be classified as *laissez-faire, permissive, paternalistic, state-controlled* or *mixed* (cf. Head, 1985; Merrill, 1984). Laissez-faire systems are characterized by private ownership of the media industry and government guarantees of freedom of the press. The U.S. newspaper industry is a prime example of this type of media system. Permissive systems allow private ownership of media firms, although the government does have limited regulation in place designed to promote media operations in the public interest. This system is typified by the U.S. broadcasting system. Paternalistic systems own the media, but they are run by quasi-government agencies who are shielded by law from interference from either the government or the public. Their operating charters require these agencies to run the media system with an eye on the public interest. A classic example of such a system is the British Broadcasting Corporation. State-controlled systems are owned by the state, and operate under strict governmental operation. The Soviet print and broadcasting systems are examples of state-controlled media systems. Mixed systems use some variation of the previous four classifications. One example would be Sveriges Radio AB (Swedish Broadcasting Company). The Swedish government owns and controls the transmission facilities of broadcasting, but leaves programming and production to a private, nonprofit corporation—the SBC. The SBC issues stock that is distributed among key "national groups" (publishing, electronic, and social groups). Sweden refers to this arrangement as a "partnership in the public interest" (Head, 1985). Another example of a mixed system would be that of Australia, where the public broadcasting company, Australian Broadcasting Company, competes with privately owned broadcasting networks. A similar pattern is emerging in New Zealand.

Historically, with the exception of the United States and Latin America, almost all countries began with a public broadcasting system (usually paternalistic or state-controlled), and then slowly began to allow some form of private competition. In Latin America, broadcasting began with private (laissez-faire) ownership, but political upheavals left most media systems under the control of the government. Only in the United States was private, commercial broadcasting in place before the legislation designed to control it.

During the 1980s, many Western European countries either initiated the privatization of media systems (especially television) or increased the rate at which previous privatization trends were taking place. This move came about for several reasons. The swing to political conservatism, and, in particular, the free-market capitalist foundation on which it is based began to sweep across Europe. Technology, especially the dramatic increase in the use of satellite technology (such as direct broadcast satellite—or DBS—systems), reduced the scope of governmental control over the media within their respective national borders. Finally, the movement toward the formation of the European Union (EU) dictated a more complete opening of trade markets. Hence, privatization is philosophically in line with the new relationships of the Western European countries.

One of the countries to benefit most from the new financial liberation has been Spain. Until 1990, the Spanish television market was controlled by state-run RTVE. Market deregulation led to the debut of three private television networks—Telecinco (25% owned by Italian media mogul Silvio Berlusconi), Antena 3-TV (17% owned by foreign banks), and Canal Plus (25% owned by France's Canal Plus). Private TV's share of the audience grew from 1.3% to 12.3% from January 1990 to June 1990. During the same period, the government's two TV network shares dropped from 82.6% to 72.8% (Besas, 1991).

Many of the popular shows airing on the Spanish networks are Latin American soap operas ("telenovellas") and Spanish versions of American game shows. The popularity of such shows has forced state-run Spanish Television (RTVE) to revamp some of its programming to reflect popular tastes. Although it once considered them to be unsuitable, RTVE has found that Latin soap operas, such as the Venezuelan-produced series *Crystal,* have become major hits, drawing about 25% of the Spanish TV audience. RTVE has since partnered with Brazil's TV Globo to produce similar series.

The loosening up of restrictions in Europe has not, however, made it a totally free marketplace. The French government tends to protect TF-1, prohibits commercial breaks, and has stringent programming import restrictions. La Cinq, one of France's new private TV networks, found it could not survive financially in competition with TF-1, and was taken over by media giant Hachette during November 1990. Similarly, broadcasting is dominated in Italy by the public broadcaster RAI, which has little broadcast, and no cable or satellite competition.

Sometimes, the protectionist media practices, the monopolistic media practices, or both have worked to the advantage of European countries. In Germany, Leo Kirch (owner of the Kirch Group which runs Beta Film and Sat 1) has traditionally dominated the German media market, especially film and television. In the 1960s, the Kirch Group became the principal distributor of films and TV programs to the two major German public broadcasters, ZDF and ARD, and, by locking up the rights to Hollywood, had virtual monopoly control over such programming. When German TV introduced private TV channels in 1984, these competing services were forced to look elsewhere for programming. As a result, competitors, such as traditionally conservative RTL-Plus, have had to go to other types of programming, which has indirectly led to their success. The importation of somewhat more erotic French and Italian programming has meant that more Germans are now watching or talking about RTL-Plus. With Kirch losing some control over the media market, Hollywood has now begun to bypass Kirch, and are negotiating directly with ARD and ZDF (Ilott, 1991).

Despite some obstacles, media companies have far greater room to maneuver than they ever had. One result of increasing private ownership is that there now exist Pan-European media companies (such as Hachette and Pathe) with sufficient size to compete in the global media marketplace.

The Role of Chance Events

Porter (1990) noted that so-called "chance events" play a role in determining the national competitive advantage of an industry. These also have a major impact on the management of individual media firms. Among the chance events that apply to the U.S. electronic media industry are acts of pure invention, such as the development of HDTV and the struggle to adopt a global standard. War is another chance event that has played a role. The 1991 Persian Gulf War and the more recent O.J. Simpson murder trial signaled a major shift in news viewing from the major broadcast networks to CNN. Not only did these events help CNN significantly increase its share of the viewing audience, but Times-Mirror polls have revealed that it is the news network with the most credibility. The major chance events that have affected the U.S. television industry, however, are political decisions by foreign governments.

Political Decisions by Foreign Governments

One result of increasing private ownership was the creation of Pan-European media companies (such as Berlusconi Communications, Hachette, and Pathe) with sufficient size to compete in the global media marketplace.

The increasing privatization of Europe normally would result in more economic opportunities for U.S. media companies. However, the formation of the European Union, and the changing content preferences of European audiences have resulted in a tougher time for U.S. media exporters. Consequently, the United States will see its role as worldwide media industry leader challenged. The formation of the European Union in 1992 has resulted in tougher import restrictions for U.S. media product. Some of the restrictions debated include prohibiting alcohol and tobacco advertising as well as regulating comparative advertising (Giges, 1990).

Perhaps an even more discomforting aspect of the EU is the Council Directive on the Coordination of Certain Provisions Laid Down by Law, Regulation or Administrative Action in Member States Concerning the Pursuit of Television Broadcasting Activities, which was passed by the European Council on October 3, 1989. The directive specified a plan, entitled "Television Without Frontiers," which imposes quotas on each country in terms of their importation of foreign content. The United States will be most directly affected by such quotas. At the end of 1993, the United States attempted to have those quotas eliminated as part of the General Agreement on Tariffs and Trade (GATT) treaty, but, as a compromise, the issue of TV programming and film trade was taken out of the treaty.

Fortunately for the United States, foreign broadcast media were organized on a national framework with public monopolies and local regulations of production and broadcasting of local productions. All of these monopolies were financed through licensing fees, which were sufficient for local productions. However, they were not sufficient to finance the thousands of hours of programming needed. It is estimated that EU countries will need up to 440,000 hours of programming (Moebes, 1991). Although media firms of the EC are becoming bigger, they still lack sufficient resources to provide that much media product. Hence, many European companies are trying to form alliances with U.S. media companies to provide such a product. Television companies may also have to develop creative financial strategies in their syndication arrangements, such as countertrade (Dupagne, 1992) or through coproduction and coinvestment arrangements.

The change in the financial interest and syndication rules have allowed U.S. broadcast networks to have a financial interest in coproductions with international media companies. Three of the networks have made moves into this area: ABC and the ZDF (West German) TV network, NBC and London-based Yorkshire Television, and CBS and Italy's Reteitalia Productions (Young, 1992). An advantage of coproductions is that they guarantee ongoing access to the European marketplace. U.S. broadcast companies still possess the greatest expertise in providing entertainment content to large markets. What these companies lack is an understanding of how to accommodate the changes currently taking place in the international media marketplace. It would appear that alliances that combine U.S. broadcast production expertise with knowledge of and access to international markets would help reverse the erosion of U.S. competitive advantage in the international media marketplace.

Coproduction arrangements also provide more content for a U.S. domestic marketplace that lacks sufficient program supply. Several syndicated broadcast and cable series airing in the United States (*La Femme Nikita, Silk Stalkings*) are globally produced.[5] Another form of partnership involves licensing agreements. Domestic U.S. programs such as *Wheel of Fortune* have been licensed to a number of European countries who produce their own local versions.

The shakiness of the European media market may portend problems for the EU/U.S. media alliances. Companies usually enter alliances to achieve economies of scale, obtain access to local markets, spread out the risk element, or offset competitive disadvantages. However, international alliances are tricky to maintain, requiring skills at coordinating industrial activities across countries. In addition, alliances are generally formed as a transitional combination to combat market uncertainty. Most fail, with the result either being competition or merger (Porter, 1990). The instability created by a shaky European media market may just create enough uncertainty for these alliances to fail. A potential problem for the importation of U.S. TV programs into central and eastern Europe is whether those countries eventually become accepted into the European Union, and thus have to adhere to their program import rules.

---

[5]In addition to coproduction ventures, some EC countries are passing legislation designed to spur U.S. investment. Such legislation tries to keep a delicate balance between encouraging investment on the one hand and preventing control on the other. In October 1990, Rupert Murdoch's Sky Television merged with British Satellite Broadcasting. In its wake, the United Kingdom's Office of Telecommunications (OFTEL) proposed to end the telecommunications duopoly of British Telecom and Mercury. As a result, a number of North American companies indicated interest in providing capital investments ("Cignarelli," 1990).

The U.K.'s Independent Television Commission (ITC) announced in November 1990 that it would allow non-European countries to own up to 29.9% of commercial TV and radio franchises. The ITC considers 30% of the voting stock to be a controlling interest, and non-European countries are forbidden by law to control a British broadcasting company. However, given that British law says that any group with more than 25% of voting shares in a company can call a shareholders' meeting, such a stake would give U.S. media companies a large say in how a British broadcasting company is run.

CONCLUSION

U.S. television companies continually will have to monitor and adjust their notions about global marketplaces. Even wide-open opportunities for investment by U.S. media firms are not without their risks. First, the rising nationalistic movements in the "new" Europe, as exemplified by the ethnic turmoil in Central and Eastern Europe (especially in the former nation of Yugoslavia) creates political and economic instability in the region. Beyond that, companies seeking to set up media ventures in the former command economies of Eastern and Central Europe will not only have to overcome a myriad of regulatory obstacles, but ideological ones as well (Winter, Carveth, & Parrish-Sprowl, 1994). On the other side of the globe, the vast market of China poses great opportunities and tough potential obstacles. It is unclear whether the annexation of Hong Kong by China in 1997 will result in more open media markets in China, or more closed ones.

No matter what happens, the U.S. TV industry is learning to play by new rules. These new rules have forced the industry out of its competitive complacency, compelling it to be more creative in maintaining its position in the domestic and international marketplace.

ACKNOWLEDGMENT

We acknowledge the assistance of Professor James Fletcher. Substantial portions of this chapter discussion of syndication were based on his chapter on syndication in the first edition of this text.

FURTHER READING

Hilliard, R., & Head, S. (1996). *Global broadcasting systems.* Newton, MA: Focal Press.
Ohmae, K. (1990). *The borderless world.* New York: HarperCollins.
Porter, M. (1990). *The competitive advantage of nations.* New York: The Free Press.
Toffler, A. (1990). *Powershift.* New York: Bantam.

REFERENCES

Auletta, K. (1992). *Three Blind Mice.*
Besas, P. (1971, April 15). The TV boom in Spain creates a new source of partnerships. *Variety,* p. 179.
Carveth, R. (1992). The reconstruction of the global media marketplace. *Communication Research, 19*(6), 705–723.
Carveth, R., Owers, J., & Alexander, A. (1993). The global integration of the media industries. In A. Alexander, J. Owers, & R. Carveth (Eds.), *Media economics: Theory and practice.* Hillsdale, NJ: Lawrence Erlbaum Associates.
Carveth, R., Alexander, A., & Owers, J. (1994). Paper presented at the annual convention of the Association for Education in Journalism and Mass Communication.
Cignarelli is out, MGM/UA syndication future is in doubt. (1990, November 19). *Broadcasting,* pp. 27–28.

Dupagne, M. (1992). Factors influencing the international syndication marketplace in the 1990s. *Journal of Media Economics, 5*(3), 3–29.

Giges, N. (1990, June 18). Int'l split on fighting ad rules. *Advertising Age*, pp. 1, 84.

Guider, E. (1992, October 19). Europe's TV tactics outflank the Yanks. *Variety*, pp. 1, 182.

Head, S. (1985) *World broadcasting systems*. Belmont, CA: Wadsworth.

Ilott, T. (1991, April 15). Germany's media giant keeps competitive edge. *Variety*, p. 190.

La Cinq programmer sees dual market. (1990, October 22). *Electronic Media*, pp. 18, 47.

Levine, J. (1991, August 5). Philips' big gamble. *Business Week*, pp. 34–36.

Merrill, J. (1983) *Global journalism*. New York: Longman.

Moebes, A. (1991). Structuring media joint ventures in the European Community. *Hastings Communication and Entertainment Law Journal, 14*(1), 2–34.

Noglows, P. (1990a, February). After junk: Street-wise financing. *Channels*, pp. 58–63.

Noglows, P. (1990b, December 17). Banks say: Bah, humbug. *Variety*, pp. 1, 78.

Noglows, P., & Rothman, M. (1993, June 28). Showbiz floats on debt flood. *Variety*, p. 35.

Ohmae, K. (1990) *The borderless world*. New York: HarperCollins.

Owers, J., & Carveth, R. (1988, November). *The party's over: Media acquisition activity after the "crash."* Paper presented at the Speech Communication Association Conference, New Orleans, LA.

Porter, M. (1990) *The competitive advantage of nations*. New York: Free Press.

Toffler, A. (1990). *Powershift*. New York: Bantam.

Winter, M., Carveth, R., & Parrish-Sprowl, J. (1994). Communicating capitalism: The challenge of Eastern Europe. *Arizona Communication Association Journal*.

Young, D. (1992, October 12). Reteitalia sets sights on U.S. *Variety*, pp. 42, 207.

Zengage, T., & Ratcliffe, C. (1988). *The Japanese century*. Hong Kong: Longman.

13

The Economics of Online Media

Rod Carveth
University of Bridgeport

James Owers
Georgia State University

Alison Alexander
University of Georgia

INTRODUCTION

A phrase heard frequently in the news media during the 1990s is "the Information Superhighway." News reports illustrate how quickly and how extensively the "information highway system" is being built, connecting the home to an infinite array of information and entertainment services. In actuality, discussion should really focus on the information superhighways—the cable industry version, the telephone company version, even the electrical power company version.

One such information superhighway exists already; it is called the Internet. Every day, millions of messages travel along the hundreds of computer networks that make up the Internet. There is "gold" on the information superhighway, as a number of online services, including America Online, Compuserve, and Prodigy have discovered. Each of these firms has millions of subscribers to their information services, access gateways to the Internet, and sites on the World Wide Web (WWW or the Web). These big three are joined by smaller national and regional online services vying for potentially billions of dollars in the information business.

In addition, many companies are poised to pour hundreds of thousands and even millions of dollars into new media advertising budgets. For example, in 1996 Proctor & Gamble allocated an estimated $8 million to promote Web sites for several of its brands, Visa poured $6 million into the "Sony Station" site jointly

247

developed with Sony, and General Motors spent as much as $3 million for each of its divisions to construct an umbrella site for the whole company.

In fact, most companies banking on selling their content online will not see a profit until the year 2000. For example, Forrester Research predicts the typical Web site, such as an electronic newsletter or magazine, will lose $3.9 million beyond the initial investment before it starts making money ("Web Profits," 1996).

To date, three basic revenue streams for online media have been identified: subscription fees, advertising, and online sales. To date, no one is quite sure which of the revenue streams can be counted on to bring in the profits many predict will soon be coming their way.

This chapter reviews the economics of the current online media. The first section reviews the growth of online subscription services such as America Online (AOL) and Compuserve. The second section explores online advertising, especially as it applies to the WWW. The third section examines financial security issues related to the Internet, a major obstacle to online sales. The chapter concludes with a discussion of the future of the economics of online media.

THE DEVELOPMENT OF ONLINE SERVICES

The rapid evolution of the Internet has been matched by a torrent of news and predictions about it, making it difficult to keep the medium in perspective. One way to envision the Internet, and to speculate on its future development, is to think of it as part of a continuing history of online services rather than as a sudden and singular phenomenon. Here, the term *online* refers generally to services that are delivered over a narrowband connection. There are three intervals of narrowband services, called (a) videotex, (b) online services, and (c) the Internet.

As argued elsewhere (Carveth & Metz, 1996), the growth of the Internet occurred in three stages. The first of these stages was initiated by the "pioneers"—mostly scientists and engineers who were concerned with the need for national security. The original network proposed and accepted was designed by individuals who had a notion of linking together computers for the sole purpose of communication. These scientists and programmers initially worked through the funding of the federal government (commissioned by the Advanced Research Projects Agency—ARPA) to explore the possibilities of branching out a new form of technology that would enable people to work together despite great distances.

The second stage began with the arrival of the "settlers"—academics and scientists who were using the machines sharing resources and communicating with one another. Those who continually used the system began establishing comfortable communities in which interests were shared. This group of people believed that the realm of computer networking was limitless, and that there seemed to be enough room for all types of people to coexist peacefully. The primary goal for the settlers was to communicate with similar "cybernauts"—explorers who tended to be interested in technology that the mainstream population eschewed. The Internet was seen by these initial settlers as a public good, an expansive cyberfrontier that could be shared by all.

The third online era came with the arrival of the "people of capital." It had an aborted beginning in the early 1980s, but returned in the 1990s. The people of capital tried take advantage of a new world of information, available by turning on a computer hooked up to what is called *videotex*—text transmitted online (e.g., over the telephone) to be displayed on a video screen (Major, 1990). Although it is not absolutely necessary to own a computer (e.g., public terminals were made available in areas such as Santa Barbara, California [Hanson, 1992]), the services provided and information available is easier to access and store with a home personal computer (PC). Despite a plethora of opportunities available, it was not until 1994 that a critical mass of consumers in the United States began to take advantage of videotex opportunities.

The U.S. Videotex Experience

In the 1980s, marketing experts predicted that videotex would revolutionize the marketing, advertising, and broadcasting industries, and become a $5-billion-a-year industry (Major, 1990). Videotex enabled customers to use a keypad to call up screens of content from a centralized database for display on a home viewing screen. It was seen as a natural result of combining the television, the telephone, and the computer.

This hybrid technology frequently evoked notions of social and technological revolution. Videotex promised to change shopping, banking, news delivery, travel, and messaging. Many of the more optimistic predictions came from vendors offering such services.

Market researchers projected billions of dollars of revenue from equipment sales and service usage. As a result, $2.5 billion was invested in videotex. However, the videotex industry in the first half of the 1980s generated only $400 million annually in revenues from 1.5 to 2 million customers. By March 1986, three U.S. videotex providers had ceased operation after consumer disinterest led to combined losses of over $100 million (Major, 1990).

The original failure of the videotex revolution could have been that early marketers of videotex were promoting a system that did not exist: Consumers lacked low-cost, user-friendly PCs and applications. Consumers preferred to get news from traditional media, PCs were not widely distributed, pricing was based on the minute rather than the month, and videotex offerings were limited. As a result, videotex producers abandoned their original target of replacing traditional media and repositioned themselves as a supplemental information service provider (Major, 1990).

Another possible explanation could be that the market for videotex services was narrower than companies originally anticipated (Truet & Hermann, 1989). In this area, it is difficult to analyze the market without first understanding France Telecom's Teletel service, dubbed "Minitel." France had long been the world leader in videotex activity, with 5 million active users of more than 15,000 different services by 1990.[1]

Maital (1991) traced Minitel's success to three major factors. First, France Telecom invested substantial time and money designing Teletel, concentrating on long-term evolutionary planning. Second, they spent millions on a technologically advanced switching system known as Transpac, providing a more efficient cost structure of the service overall. This switching system enables data bits to be grouped and then transferred as a "bundle" through the system, cutting the cost of sending messages and making "the cost independent of the geographical distance between the consumer and the seller" (p. 8). Third, France Telecom's monopolistic position made it possible to launch a mass-market product for which market demand did not yet exist. As Maital observed, "Who would invest massively in such terminals without first being assured of the demand for their services? The answer: A government with deep pockets, a clear purpose, and a national technology strategy" (p. 8).

By contrast, the United States government historically had none of those three requisite criteria, despite some attempts by a handful of governmental officials recommending immediate execution of a nationwide construction of electronic superhighways (Gore, 1991). Market observers attribute Teletel's success to France Telecom's farsighted planning, cost-effective service rates, and monopoly position in telecommunications. America's initial inability to compete globally in the information services arena may be traced to the fragmentation of American telecommunications after the breakup of the American Telephone and Telegraph Co. (AT&T) monopoly (Maital, 1991). During the period from 1984 to 1990, France Telecom installed 6 million Minitel terminals in France—1 for every 10 people. Comparatively, in 1990 there were only 1.5 million subscribers to online videotex services in the United States, or 1 for every 165 people (Hawkins, 1991).

Yet another problem was the overall poor performance of videotex systems. These problems included overall economic viability of videotex, involving costs of specialized equipment and costs of communications; benefits not seen as sufficient to justify costs; a lack of industry standards with a consequent incompatibility among systems; and human–social factors involving new and different ways to do things (Grover & Sabherwal, 1989). Obviously, a change in strategic orientation would be needed to repair all of these problems.

Although the launch of Prodigy in 1988 led to another round of optimistic predictions, the modest overall performance of online services dampened talk about their social impact. By 1993, three national online services, Prodigy, AOL, and Compuserve, claimed about 3 million subscribers, although Prodigy had already suffered cumulative losses of more than $1 billion.

---

[1]The authors want to thank Dr. J. Michael Metz for his observations about U.S. videotex development.

The videotex industry began to rebound in 1990 when car manufacturers became some of the first major advertisers to tap into the videotex market (Fahey, 1990). To accommodate these new clients, Prodigy began taking steps toward making the service a mainstream advertising medium (Fahey, 1989a). Prodigy began by charging advertisers by "measured response pricing," where viewers could see teaser ads across the bottom of a screen and could access the full ad for more information (Fahey, 1989b). While the average length of most ads was 30 screens, if a viewer viewed only 5 screens, the marketer was charged for only those 5 screens. This new method of advertising was hailed as "a no-risk medium," because it charged on the basis of actual advertising exposure (Fahey, 1989b)

However, Prodigy began running into trouble. General Motors' Buick division re-evaluated the videotex systems, and decided to pull its advertisements from Prodigy, although maintaining the advertising campaign on Compuserve (Fahey, 1990). Audi renewed its contract only after serious deliberation, saying that they may have obtained a large number of leads, but the concern was whether or not they were qualified leads. Audi wanted to make sure that the Prodigy subscribers were good targets for Audi automobiles.

Such criticism evoked a strong response from Prodigy, which complained that it was "unfair for advertisers to expect videotex to provide information they don't request from other media" (Fahey, 1990, p. 54), claiming that no magazine client requires that medium to prove that it delivered enough sales to justify the ad dollars. Unfortunately, although this may have been a valid argument, the fact remains that videotex advertising in 1990 was still an experiment.

By 1994, there were between 1.5 and 2 million loyal users who used the various networks religiously. Nevertheless, the event that propelled explosive growth in videotex services occurred in the spring of 1994 when AOL finished its gateway onto the Internet. Since that time, growth in online services has wildly exceeded expectations. AOL now serves more than 10 million customers. With the creation of the Microsoft Network (MSN) in August 1995, the number of commercial online service users will exceed 18 million by the end of 1997.

The development of narrowband services demonstrates a pattern of progressive decentralization of the technology and content components. Videotex was a top-down model of centralized providers furnishing centralized services through a specialized terminal. The design reflected the technology of the time, but it also then emphasized centralized (i.e., transaction- and information-oriented) interactive services. These services were assumed to be desirable, but consumers were not interested; prognosticators (and suppliers) confused technological capability with market demand.

Prodigy was a centralized provider offering mostly centralized interactive services. However, a key component changed with the use of consumers' own standards-based computers. The change in delivery device from a passive terminal to a multipurpose machine changed the assumed model for services, although

Prodigy's marketers did not seem to take this fully into account. Consumers followed the pattern of text-based online services such as Compuserve and showed greater interest in electronic mail and bulletin boards—something for which Prodigy was architecturally and strategically unprepared.

Today, the Internet operates on a completely different model than that of the first videotex experiments. The network features decentralized content that can be created by anyone and accessed on a standardized technological platform. If the original assumption was that consumers would access online services in their homes to save time, current research suggests that consumers are more interested in using online services to produce or peruse content (Web pages, e-mail, news-groups) as a new, enjoyable way to spend time. Thus, online services have found their success through decentralization: content is now more in the hands of users than providers, and services to communicate with others, such as e-mail and chat rooms, are highly popular.

THE ECONOMICS OF ONLINE SERVICES

In understanding the economic underpinnings of online media we need to clarify several concepts. The first of these is the *unit of production*. The unit of production is a *packet* of information (bits). Messages are often made up of a number of these packets. Service is measured by the number of received bits per second. The average bit rate the Internet delivers is about 200 to 400 bits per second. Consumers want to send items of different sizes on the Internet, from a few characters to many bytes for images. Thus, there are two factors affecting consumer response to information transfer: how big the transfer is, and how long we can wait for it to be delivered.

There are two major consumer cost factors. First, a consumer pays in dollars for access and amount of service. A second cost to the consumer is time— the time it takes for the receipt of information and the time it takes to transmit information. Most research suggests that consumers will pay for quality service.

DETERMINANTS OF ONLINE SERVICE FIRM VIABILITY

The most basic determinants of an online service firm's viability are the initial subscriber base, and the continuous growth in the subscriber base. An important factor influencing the size of the subscribership base is the relationship between hardware and software. Look, for example, at the diffusion of the personal computer. The initial costs of PC hardware for the consumer were a disincentive in other areas—with limited hardware sales, no incentives existed to produce a variety of software. Thus, with a limited choice of software, consumers hesitated before investing in expensive PC hardware; with limited hardware sales, PC prices remained high; with high PC prices, we go back to the beginning. This pattern remained cyclical over several years until a critical mass of PC owners spurred growth in PC software availability and subsequent PC hardware sales.

Following this reasoning, the most basic unit of viability is the subscribing household. Potential households can be categorized into initial subscriber households and intraindustry competitive households.

Initial Subscriber Households

Initial subscriber households are those households who do not currently subscribe to an online service. They may be able to afford the costs associated with an online service, or they may not be. An understanding of the factors involved, both in facilitating and impeding the diffusion of any new communication medium, however, can be furthered from an examination of diffusion and marketing research literature on high technology consumer product. The four variables to be considered are (a) compatibility of the product with existing products, (b) trialability and observability of features of the new product, (c) characteristics of potential adopters of the product, and (d) pricing.

Compatibility and Complexity

Rogers (1985) defined compatibility as the degree to which an innovation is perceived as consistent with existing values, past experiences, and needs of the potential adopters. An idea that is more compatible is less uncertain to the potential adopter. An innovation can be compatible or incompatible with adopters' values and beliefs, adopters' needs for innovation, and ideas introduced previously. Complexity is the degree to which innovations are perceived as relatively difficult to understand and use. Any new idea may be classified on the complexity–simplicity continuum. The complexity of an innovation, as perceived by the members of the social system, is negatively related to its rate of adoption.

For example, in early 1996, AOL entered into two major agreements designed to simplify the use of their service and make it more compatible with major software systems. Although AOL has benefitted a great deal from the popularity of the Web, many users are not impressed with its browsers that were slow during peak hours. In February 1996, AOL and Netscape announced a marketing and technology alliance. AOL agreed to license the Netscape browser for all of it services. Initially, the browser would be integrated with AOL's GNN Internet service. AOL would get some exposure on Netscape's home page, one of the most popular pages on the Web. Putting Netscape's browser in the hands of 8 million AOL subscribers would better position both Netscape and AOL in their respective battles versus Microsoft's Internet Explorer and MSN.

The day after announcing the Netscape deal, AOL and Microsoft announced their own technology and marketing agreement. Microsoft's Internet Explorer would be seamlessly integrated into America Online's client software later by the end of 1996. In return, America Online would be preinstalled with future versions of the Windows operating system in a folder on the desktop called "Online Services." This move was designed to significantly reduce AOL's customer acquisition costs.

As part of the cross-licensing agreement, Microsoft would license the ART compression technologies of Johnson-Grace, a fully owned subsidiary of AOL. Instead of dealing with different compression formats for photos, graphics, streaming audio and MIDI, developers could use the ART format to produce highly compressed files that will function on AOL and Internet Web sites at very low bandwidth.

Trialability and Observability

Trialability is the degree to which a new product or service may be experimented with on a limited basis. New concepts or products that can be adopted on a temporary or trial basis represents allows the consumer to reduce uncertainty associated with the new product and to "learn by doing." The trialability of a new product or service is positively related to its rate of adoption. *Observability* is the degree to which the results of an innovation are visible to others and details positive consequences. AOL, as well as other online services, help promote both trialability and observability by sending disks along with computer magazines so that readers can try the service.

Characteristics of Product Adopters

The number of households with at least one computer has more than doubled since 1984, from 16% to 36%. However, online service penetration remains low; only 12% of American households subscribe to one or more online services (Vonder Haar, 1995). The PC market is "young," as 58% of PC owners have had their PCs for less than 2 years (Zeigler, 1995). Major studies of computer and other high-technology consumer products compare the demographic and psychographic characteristics of those who adopt with those who do not (Perse & Dunn, 1995).

Most studies that have focused on adopters of personal computers have supported propositions of diffusion of innovations research (Rogers, 1983). For example, socioeconomic status (SES) and educational level have been the two most consistent predictors of home computer ownership (Dutton, Rogers, & Jun, 1987). Home computer owners are "techno-savvy," and generally have more disposable income to spend on technology products such as video games and CD-ROMs (Ogilvy & Mather Direct, 1994). Home computer ownership is more common among those employed in technical and higher-status occupations where computers are part of work and there is likely to be experience with technology (Vitalari, Venkatesh, & Gronhaug, 1985). However, gender and race do not seem to be stronger predictors of ownership.

Modems, or electronic devices that allow computers to connect to telephone lines, are in more homes than ever before, in part because high-speed modems are more available and more affordable. However, there are also more reasons to use computers to connect to networks—the explosion in Web sites means there is now a critical mass using computers to link to other users (Markus, 1987). So, users can derive a wide variety of benefits from computer connectivity.

The modem also has the potential to change how people use their home computers, as modems help change the home computer from an information processor to a communication medium. Connecting to newsgroups, bulletin boards (BBS), and other sites on the Internet allows users to access information and entertainment, chat with other users online, or send messages to others via e-mail. The explosion in the number of WWW sites, subscribers to online services, and Internet users promises that using computers to communicate may be a major reinvention of home computers ("America Online," 1995; "Ever-Widening Web," 1995; "Most Net Users," 1995).

Perse and Dunn (1995) found in their study of home computer ownership and its relationship to uses of and perceptions about traditional mass media that computer owners were younger, more educated, and earned higher incomes than nonowners. Computer owners also believed that print media were more useful to satisfy needs than video media. Higher levels of home computer connectivity were reflected in seeing home computers useful for learning, for entertainment, for immersion in activity in order to forget one's problems, for companionship, for passing time, and for satisfying a habit. Perse and Dunn observe that the influence of home computer connectivity on perceived utilities of the home computer suggests that there may be some real displacement or disruption effects of traditional media use as more owners use computers to communicate with other people, networks, and information- and entertainment-oriented sites on the Web.

Perse and Dunn found no evidence of computer's displacement or disruption (Krugman, 1985) effects on media use. Instead, their findings suggested an "early adopter" effect (Reagan, 1987; Rogers, 1983, 1986). Because of the expense and technical expertise require to acquire and operate computers, their use may be concentrated for a while in higher education and income groups. Home computer connectivity was strongly related to perceptions about the utility of different media. Computer owners who chose computers for learning, entertainment, and social purposes were significantly more "connected," or more likely to own modems and use their home machines for communication.

Finally, Perse and Dunn (1995) found that computer connectivity was associated with selecting the computer to pass time (to keep busy) and out of habit. In fact, computers were mentioned by home computer owners to keep busy more than any other reason. Pass time and habitual uses are signals of *ritualistic* media use—media use that does not focus on gratifications offered by any specific content, but instead focuses on gratifications offered by the medium itself (Rubin, 1984).

The Online Audience

Different studies of the size of the Internet audience show disparate results and are difficult to reconcile. For example, CommerceNet/Neilsen Internet Demographic Survey (CNIDS) reported that 37 million people 16 years and older in the U.S. and Canada have access to the Internet, 24 million of these people use the Internet, 18 million use the WWW, and 2.5 million of these Web users have purchased offerings over the Internet (CommerceNet Consortium, 1995; CommerceNet/Nielsen 1995).

By contrast, O' Reilly found 5.8 million adults use the Internet (O'Reilly & Associates/ Trish Information Services, 1995), FIND/SVP (1996) estimated that 8.4 million adults and 1.1 million children use the Internet, while Times Mirror (1995) estimated that 25 million adult Americans are on online.

On one item the surveys do agree: The Internet is approximately doubling in size each year, and has been doing since 1990. In other words, each year there are as many new people on the Internet as all the people on the Internet the year before. In addition, the people using the Internet are an attractive market. The typical online family, according to NPD Group, Inc., has a 34-year-old head of household (the average age of a head of household in the United States is 40); with a median income of $54,440 (77% above the national average); and is likely to have a college education (56% are graduates; "Online Profile," 1995). These demographic characteristics are predictive of their use of the Internet. For example, previous research suggests that current Internet use is related to gender, education, income, race, occupation, and even geographic region, with some of the general conclusions being that males are more likely than females to use the Net, people with higher socioeconomic status are more likely to use the Net, and Whites are more likely to use the Net (see, for example, Gupta, 1996; Times Mirror, 1995; Walsh, 1996; Yankelovich Partners, 1996).

Less is known about the audience for the World Wide Web. The most extensive study of the Web audience is the SRI VALS 2 1996 study of the audience for the WWW. The results revealed two Web audiences. The first is the group that drives most of the media coverage and stereotypes of Web users, the "upstream" audience. Comprising 50% of the current Web population, this well-documented group is the upscale, technically oriented academics and professionals who ride on a variety of institutional subsidies. Yet because this group comprises only 10% of the U.S. population, their behaviors and characteristics are of limited usefulness in understanding the future of the Web.

The second Web audience comprises a diverse set of groups that SRI VALS 2 called the Web's "other half." Accounting for the other 90% of U.S. society, these groups are where Internet growth will increasingly need to take place if the medium is to go "mainstream." Among the SRI survey's findings of the Web's "other half" are:

• The other-half gender split—64% male and 36% female—is significantly more balanced than the upstream group's split of 77% and 23%. (The gender split for the overall sample is 70% male and 30% female, a figure that did not change across the 4-month sample period.)

• Many information-intensive consumers in the U.S. population are in the other-half population. These particular other-half consumers report the highest degree of frustration with the Web of any population segment. Although they drive much of the consumer-information industry in other media, they as a group have yet to find the Web particularly valuable.

• The "information have-nots"—those groups not on the Web at all—are "excluded" not because of low income but because of limited education. Although income for the Web audience is somewhat upscale (a median yearly income of $40,000), it includes a substantial number of low-income users (28% have yearly incomes of less than $20,000). The same cannot be said of education, which basically has a high-end-only distribution: 97% of the upstream audience and 89% of the other-half audience reports at least some college education, including the low-income respondents. Thus, education is a major factor of Internet participation. This finding suggests that proposals to empower "information have-nots" with subsidies for Internet access (such has been suggested by U.S. Speaker of the House Newt Gingrich) may not have the desired outcome of increased Internet use.

Pricing

Paramount among the factors that would maximize the size of the initial subscriber household base is the cost of service: The extent to which the pricing of the online service is competitive with existing services. If the price of the service is affordable and perceived to have value for the consumer, then the customer will buy it.

Of course, the price charged by an online service needs to exceed the costs of providing those services. In addition to normal management costs, there are four other types of costs associated with online services:

1. *Bandwidth costs* (Frame Relay, ATM, etc.). These costs represent approximately 30% to 40% of total costs.
2. *Network management* (address assignment, routing, etc.). Network management is mostly considered a sunk cost, but can vary depending on the situation. The management costs may vary depending on the routing technology that the reseller uses.
3. *Customer support* (e.g., marketing, etc.). Customer support costs can vary. Internet Service Providers (ISPs) may try to seek out certain types of customers to limit costs—those who know what they are doing so they won't be constantly calling the ISP's support services. The ISP's marketing strategy determines the types of customers that it will have.
4. *Content acquisition.* AOL, Prodigy, Compuserve, and other ISPs acquire information, which costs money, and resell it.

Many small and medium commercial online service providers start off with flat-rate pricing (i.e., nonmetered pricing). One benefit of such a scheme is that customers are happy with it because it is simple and easy to understand, and they are not inhibited from using the system. Another benefit is that it is easy to implement billing systems for flat-rate schemes.

A major drawback of flat-rate pricing, however, is that there are no incentives for customers to make efficient use of bandwidth. Also, because everyone pays the same flat fee, the service provider cannot assign a higher priority to those customers who are willing to pay more. Finally, there is an issue of equity in that the small volume users actually subsidize the big volume users of the network.

The other option as a service provider is to use usage-sensitive pricing. The advantage of usage sensitive pricing is that it makes for more efficient use of the bandwidth. The drawback is that consumers do not like it.

Until October 1996, major online services such as AOL and Compuserve had a combination of flat rate (e.g., $19.95 per month) and usage-sensitive ($5.95 per hour) pricing. These pricing schemes are simple to understand and implement, although sophisticated enough that users have incentives to act in the most efficient manner. For example, AOL had pricing plans: $9.95 for 5 free hours, plus $2.95 for each additional hour; or $19.95 for 20 free hours, plus $2.95 for each additional hour. Most ISPs, including AT&T, MCI, and Sprint, now charge $19.95 per month for unlimited Net access. AOL could charge the same amount or even slightly less and still make it a profitable strategy, the sources said.

In October 1996, in response to a competitive challenge from the MSN, AOL implemented a new pricing scheme intended to reduce the customer turnover, or "churn." The plan also sought to focus users on AOL's advantages over other ISPs such as its proprietary content, and continue to grow its associated online advertising revenue.

But the success of the flat-rate pricing counts on customers choosing to pay extra for the proprietary content—a likely prospect, according to customer surveys. AOL is a leader in offering a wide variety of proprietary information such as online news, weather, sports, local city guides, and chat rooms to a mass audience on the Net. The proprietary content also gives AOL a bigger stream of advertising revenue than the ISPs, which makes a flat-rate pricing strategy less risky.

Intraindustry Competitive Households

The focus here is on one ISP versus another ISP, such as AOL versus Compuserve. The relationship among online service firms not only influences the survival of one firm versus another, but can also impact the fate of the entire industry. Among the factors that would maximize the share of the intraindustry competitive households for the ISP firm are:

1. *Size of total initial subscriber base.* The size of the total initial subscriber base, in turn, determines the size of each firm's subscriber base and ultimately the number of ISPs that can compete and survive in the industry.

2. *Similarity of service.* Assuming a total initial subscriber base big enough to sustain more than one ISP, the extent to which the scope and content of each firm's information service differs from all other ISPs determines the viability of all these services. The capability of a firm with a nationwide service to find specific niches unserved by other firms and cater to many of those niches would maximize the firm's intraindustry competitive ability. Among the important service attributes to be considered are the types of content, and the ease of use of the service.

3. *Firm behavior.* The 1995 entry of Microsoft into the online services industry has drawn the scrutiny of competitors and of the government concerning predatory business practices. Microsoft's online service, which is bundled with its Windows '95 software system, has already made agreements with NBC to provide content (AOL, who originally had that contract, protested loudly). Microsoft intends to use this content to gain an edge over the competition. Considering that 80% of the world's personal computers use the Microsoft operating system, this could mean a potential instant market of millions of computer users—hence the reason NBC was so willing to get in on the bargain (NBC is not alone—Disney was also in talks with Microsoft for the same reason). Microsoft has also decided to help finance the new Stephen Spielberg, Jeffrey Katzenberg, and David Geffen venture into movie production (Dreamworks SKG). The rationale for this is obvious: the possible revenues from the game rights and merchandise available for CD-ROM production is a small but almost guaranteed revenue source.

4. *Extensive financial resources.* As is the case with any new technology being introduced to the consumer market, the extent to which a firm or its parent companies can sustain initial losses and be patient enough to remain in the industry until weaker firms have withdrawn will determine the viability of that firm and ultimately the online service industry. As a result of financial resources, Microsoft is a formidable competitor of AOL's; Compuserve and Prodigy are much more vulnerable.

When economic and technological issues come to the table, it is also important to look at cultural and political issues. Recently there has been a phenomena called "domainism" that has shown up on the Internet. For example, when AOL ventured onto the Internet, the resulting fray was enough to warrant attention from magazines such as *Time* and *Newsweek*. The original problem was a relatively simple one: An initial bug in the AOL software caused each message from a member to be duplicated eight times. The software was quickly fixed, but the battle lines had been drawn. Within a matter of weeks, the AOL presence on the Internet was an unwelcome one. Subtle differences in the framework of communication on both sides had formulated different cultures on both sides. AOL, with its easy-to-use, icon-driven (and billable) system had bred users who had come to expect near-instant gratification. Their conversations reflected this: AOL jargon infiltrated many distribution lists, further separating them from the resident veteran "Internetters." AOL solicitations for sexual conversation partners were no-nonsense, stemming from the pragmatic problem of having to pay for access time, which left very little time for seduction (time being money).

Internetters, for their part, had been encultured entirely different. A sprawling, nondimensional entity like the Internet refuses to be tamed by any one convenient software program, making the act of seeking information an integral part of the experience. Many Internet users received their access without charge, paid for by either their place of work or by their university's subscription. The lack of financial constraints in obtaining information led to a "netiquette" that advocated "lurking," or reading messages without contributing a response, at least until a new user could get a grip on the specific environment of a newsgroup or distribution list.

The two groups clashed instantly. The brash bluntness of AOL conflicted greatly with the more laidback society of the Internet. Flames shot from one group to the other, prejudices arose, bigoted attitudes abounded. As a unit, the members of both groups unified against the other.

Simply because someone has AOL in their e-mail address, people might assume certain characteristics about them (e.g., they are stupid or ignorant). Now your domain is the equivalent of your skin color (something you cannot hide). Domainism devalues people based upon their domain, similar to racism. When people on the Net stereotype, it is a good example to those who would normally act differently.

Assuming no problems in technology, the viability of the information or entertainment provider is determined by: (a) the presence of a large-enough subscriber base to justify the investment of at least one provider; (b) the absence of excessive and predatory barriers to entry created by the alternative media (such as the cable or phone industries); (c) the absence of extreme and predatory behavior among firms in the online services industry; and (d) the degree to which the enterprise can sustain at least preliminary losses.

THE ONLINE ADVERTISING INDUSTRY

Online advertising expenditures reached $54.7 million in 1995, with about 80% of that on the WWW. Marketers spent an estimated $12.4 million to advertise on the Web in the last quarter of 1995 (Williamson, 1995b). The top spender among the advertisers was AT&T with an estimated $567,000 for the quarter. Netscape Communications, second in ad spending at $556,000, was also the leading advertising site, taking in an estimated $1.8 million for the period.

In September 1995, the online advertising community took notice when eight major marketers, including Pizza Hut, Visa, AT&T, Microsoft, Levi-Strauss and Lincoln-Mercury, signed deals to advertise on ESPN's SportsZone site at rates that are the highest in the industry. The advertisers agreed to pay quarterly fees of $100,000 to place electronic ads on SportsZone. At the same time, some media buyers demanded value-added deals and effective audience measurement before agreeing to the prices new media are asking (Williamson, 1995a). In response, some online sites, like that for Conde Nast's *Conde Nast Traveler*, created special content areas to draw advertisers in.

Other findings showed that the top 10 advertisers accounted for 26% of all Web ad spending, whereas the top 10 sites accepting advertising accounted for 75% of ad revenue. Expenditures are expected to grow to $1.1 billion in 1997 and $5 billion by 2000 (Williamson, 1996a).

Marketing expenditures on the WWW grew from "science fiction for most marketers," in the words of one ad exec, to a medium that "made interactivity tangible and gave the marketing world somewhere to invest" (Taylor & Askey, 1996). Online marketing, once put together practically on the fly with funds siphoned from other marketing areas, is now a big budget item with companies pouring hundreds of thousands and even millions of dollars into new media budgets. Taylor and Askey observed that it remains to be seen "if the 1996 new media budgets are part of an inexorable trend, or whether the hype about interactivity will eventually give way to a much slower emergence of the discipline as a viable advertising medium."

Every major advertiser and advertising agency knows interactive media will fit into their future business plans, but few know exactly *how*. Critics charge that defining online advertising is like "lassoing Jell-O." Traditional advertising agencies are both competing and combining with upstart multimedia production companies in the scramble to succeed in the emerging world of interactive advertising. "It's pretty competitive out there right now," says John Houston of Westport-based Modem Media. "Traditional agencies are spawning interactive groups and multimedia production companies are aspiring to be marketers … and everyone's trying to get that winning combination needed to serve advertisers well" (cited in Cleland, 1995).

The current "hot" new medium for interactive advertising is the WWW. Ad agencies such as Chiat/Day, Winkler McManus, Liggett-Stashower, and Fallon McElligott began establishing a presence on the Web in 1995 as a way of attracting new clients and demonstrating their ability to create interactive campaigns (Wells, 1995). Smaller agencies began to see the Web as a way to compete with larger agencies. "On the Internet, everyone has the same voice," says Sigward Moser, president of Communication House International in New York, "meaning I can compete with a major global agency because everyone has the same possibility and access" (Wells, 1995).

Marketers of products ranging from clothing to banks are drawn to the Web by promising demographics and the low cost of getting started Advertising on the Web, however, is a "terra incognita for advertisers and consumers alike" where "the old rules are turned upside down" and "the consumer is in control and must actively seek out the message" (Kuntz, 1995). At this point, entertainment and service, instead of sales pitches and straight product information, is what keeps consumers coming back to commercial sites on the Web.

Companies that have dominated their fields for years are scrambling to adapt to the new electronic environment. At the same time, newer companies are challenging their dominance, making up for their own lack of a track record with technological know-how the large companies may not have. For example:

• Burrelle's, the New Jersey-based news clipping service, is casting its eye on the Internet as public relations agencies turn to firms like Cyberscan and Ewatch to monitor newsgroups and mailing lists the way Burrelle's and others monitor newspapers and magazines.

• Electronic coupon services Coupons Online and CouponNet are breaking new ground in online coupon distribution while traditional distributors like Val-Pak and Vlassis Inserts explore the Web (Fawcett, 1995).

• Established advertising agencies are both competing with and cooperating with younger upstarts like Modem Media and Organic Online in developing Web sites for large and small marketers (Cleland, 1995a).

• And in the financial services realm, the mad rush to find a system for secure online transactions has brought together such venerable institutions as Bank of America, Wells Fargo, MasterCard and Visa with the likes of Netscape Communications, First Virtual Holdings, and a wide range of others.

• The Web has seen a number of innovations as an advertising medium. A pair of interactive game sites on the WWW are trying to lure consumers with cash and other prizes and marketers with the opportunity to reach demographically defined audiences (Hodges, 1996b). The sites, Interactive Imagination's "Riddler" and Sandbox's "Cyberhunt," offer consumers clues in exchange for personal and demographic information. That information, in turn, is used to present marketers with a statistical profile of the audience.

• Representatives from Microsoft, Prodigy, Time Warner, c/net, InfoSeek, Juno Online Services, Starwave, and Softbank Interactive formed a nonprofit industry organization, the Internet Advertising Council, to instruct the advertising industry on interactive media and Internet marketing opportunities and establish committees to deal with industry standards (Taylor, 1996a; Taylor, 1996c). In addition, the Ad Council has started to place pro bono advertising for nonprofit organizations in traditional media, has now begun to do so on the Web ("Ad Council," 1996).

• There's even at least one advertising "virtual association": A group of advertising agency professional planners calling themselves "The Account Planning Group-U.S." has set up a home page (Goldman, 1995).

• One of the indications of the seriousness of advertisers regarding interactive media is the degree to which Nielsen and Arbitron, the biggest names in media measurement, are at work on methods to quantify and qualify use of interactive media, including online services (Krantz, 1995; Mandese, 1995). Nielsen and Arbitron are sharing space with newcomers like I/Pro and the Delahaye Group in developing online audience measurement techniques (Cleland, 1995; Taylor, 1995). Effective measurement of online interaction is often noted as a missing ingredient in the development of advertising on the Net.

With these innovations, and with many startup companies emerging, some will succeed and some will fail. The survivors, whoever they are, will continue to provide traditional business services in new and different ways and will be a vital part of the world of online commerce. Their success will be determined by how much the advertisers understand about the size and composition of their audience.

Problems in Audience Measurement

A major problem facing AOL and other online services is the lack of clarity underlying the efficacy of interactive advertising. Consequently, most advertisers have been slow to jump on the online bandwagon, devoting slightly less than 1% of their annual ad budgets to online ventures this year, with most of that money coming from advertisers' research and design budgets ("Online advertising," 1995).

Market researchers have yet to reach consensus on how to count the number of people on the Internet (Johnson, 1996), leaving marketing and media executives in a quandary as they try to plan their online strategies. Marx (1996) observed that the quality and quantity of information available about online audiences has come a long way, but the kind of detailed demographic information marketers want has yet to emerge. "Part of the problem," said Johnson, "is too much data from too many sources: No company, Nielsen included, is yet the 'Nielsen' of new media" (p. 58).

As an indication of advertisers' wariness, Proctor & Gamble created a stir in the spring of 1996 when it told Yahoo! it would pay only when a user actually clicked to P&G's own Web site from the Yahoo! ad. Most companies pay based on the number of "eyes" that view their ad, similar to the way TV and print advertising is priced. "People think Yahoo! has put a stake in the heart of the industry," by agreeing to P&G's terms, says a VP at Lycos, which turned P&G down. WebTrack Information Services says only about 1% to 2% of Web ads are compelling enough for viewers to want to investigate further ("P&G Steps in," 1996; Taylor, 1996a; Williamson, 1996c; "Yahoo! caves," 1996).

Tapping the enormous potential of the Internet as a commercial medium and market is proving to be challenging. Computer-mediated environments like the WWW are not well understood and possess unique characteristics which distinguish them in significant ways from traditional, "terrestrial" markets of opportunity (Carveth, 1996; Hoffman & Novak, 1996; Hoffman, Novak, & Chatterjee, 1995). For example, Hoffman and Novak (1995) argued that the estimates of Internet use reported in the CNIDS (Commercenet Consortium, 1995; CommerceNet/Nielsen 1995), were inflated. Trade and popular press reports notwithstanding (Sandberg 1995; Sussman 1995), Hoffman and Novak estimated that 28.8 million people in the United States 16 years and over have access to the Internet, 16.4 million people use the Internet, 11.5 million people use the Web, and 1.5 million people have used the Web to purchase something. An analysis of the 11.5 million Web users revealed four user segments. The "hard core"—1.8 million individuals or 16.1% of Web users—use the Web frequently and last accessed the Web in the past 24 hours. "Regular" Web users, 2.4 million individuals (20.8%), use the Web frequently and last used it in the past week. There are almost twice as many occasional Web users as regular Web users. The 4.2 million (36.7%) Occasional users use the Web less frequently than regular and hard core users and last used the Web a month or more ago. The "infrequent" Web use segment is comprised of the 3.0 million individuals (26.4%) who almost never use the Web and last used it anywhere from the past 24 hours to more than a month ago.

As Hoffman et al. (1995) noted, the business community lacks solid data and information on which to base investment and marketing decisions. Many of the strategic issues surrounding the commercialization of the Internet have been clouded in hype and misinformation. Getting the numbers right can make the difference between good decisions and faulty ones.

Some members of the advertising industry are experimenting with ways to reach out based on relationships and targeting instead of simple numbers and audience and delivery. HotWired, for example, is trying banners that change depending on a visitor's browser or domain name. An experimental site called Firefly from Agents Inc. offers tips on music, movies, and books, accompanied by ad banners that vary according to where the user goes in the site and the demographic profile based on other users who have followed a similar online pattern (Williamson, 1996b, 1996c).

The media are looking not just for numbers but for the right kind of numbers to attract advertisers to new media. "Right now, the galaxies of numbers being spun out in cyberspace repel rather than attract many advertisers" (Fitzgerald, 1996, p. 26). Toward that end, the Audit Bureau of Circulations, is aiming to duplicate the print model of third-party verification with a new Web auditing service. NPD Group's PC Meter service tracks online activity from the user's, rather than the Web site's point of view (Cleland, 1995a). PC Meter follows activity from inside the user's PC.

The online audience measurement firm I/PRO and Internet directory provider Yahoo! are discussing a new service that would rank Web sites by the amount of traffic they generate. The service, which would be akin to the familiar Nielsen rankings of weekly television shows, would initially be based on users who access sites via the Yahoo directory.

C/net, the Computer Network cable TV channel, has introduced its own software to track audiences for advertisers on its home page. The software, which allows advertisers to track traffic to their own sites from C/net and elsewhere, is being offered as a free 1-month trial to charter subscribers on the TV network and its Web site. C/net's system uses a new unit called a confirmed advertisement delivery (CAD), based on the number of times an ad is viewed, to measure online activity and set ad prices (Hodges, 1995a).

Keyword-based advertising sponsorships are becoming more popular on Internet search services, in which the ad that appears depends on the search terms entered by the user (Hodges, 1996a). A searcher entering the word "printer" in the Lycos search form, for example, could see an ad for a printer manufacturer appear together with his or her search results. Keyword-based ads are offered by such search services as Lycos, Yahoo! and Infoseek, according to the article, with advertising rates available on a monthly or "impression" basis (calculated based on the number of times a page with a particular ad is called up).

It remains to be seen, if the 1997 new media budgets are part of an inexorable trend, or whether the hype about interactivity will eventually give way to a much slower emergence of the Web as a viable advertising medium.

ONLINE SALES

Electronic commerce covers a wide range of electronic transactions, from buying software online to purchasing stock electronically. Although electronic commerce is not exclusive to the Internet, it is predicted that the growth of the Internet will make the Internet segment a huge growth market for electronic commerce. Online sales are proving popular with a wide range of businesses, large and small, from florists and supermarkets to mutual funds and major airlines. For example, ESPNet SportsZone, one of the most popular of all Web sites, announced plans to add online sales of licensed pro sports merchandise to its advertising and subscription operations. United Media syndicate, led by the popular Dilbert Zone, has reportedly achieved ad sales of over $200,000 and merchandise sales of about $250,000 since Fall 1995. The overall forecast for the electronic-commerce market ranges from $500 billion into the $1 trillion range by the year 2000.

One subset of the burgeoning electronic-commerce market is what's referred to as *digital cash, electronic money* (e-money) or *electronic cash* (e-cash). These terms all more or less represent the same thing. They refer to forms of electronic cash, in contrast to more traditional forms of payment, such as cash itself and standard credit cards.

A study by Killen Associates (1996) forecasts that by the year 2000, consumers, businesses, governments, and educational institutions worldwide will use electronic cash for 9 billion payment transactions. By 2005, transactions in the evolving electronic commerce market will escalate to almost 30 billion. Growth of this magnitude will impact (a) all companies who provide payment services and products, ATMs, credit cards, debit cards, script, and so forth and (b) how businesses conduct business. E-cash is viewed as a better and cheaper way to process transactions. In addition, e-cash leads to new and more convenient products and services for businesses and consumers.

Although demand will be there for e-cash, and clearly it will be a growth sector, it is not clear whether the technology and the acceptance of the technology will progress as fast as some are predicting. As a whole, consumers seem to like the things to which they are accustomed. Cash is still the preferred method of payment, with 54% preferring to use cash. Major credit cards follow at 39%, and 23% prefer to use checks (Killen Associates, 1996). Thus, the credit card segment, especially MasterCard and Visa, may become the preferred form of payment for buying goods electronically online. People are used to credit cards. It could be argued that e-cash is just another form of cash, and because 54% of people prefer cash, they may prefer e-cash to credit cards. However, e-cash still is not cash, and people are a lot more comfortable with MasterCard and Visa than the unknown. That may change, but it will take some time.

A key need of electronic commerce is the security of financial transactions. Information security is a fundamental building block of online commerce. Without information security, information technologies cannot realize their full potential. Many envisioned information services will only be realized if service providers are compensated for the services they wish to offer. An electronic payment service must have a secure, reliable, and efficient system design. Specifically, the system must be flexible to support many different payment mechanisms, scalable to support multiple independent accounting services, efficient to avoid long bottlenecks, and unobtrusive so that users will not be constantly interrupted.

One serious problem to overcome is network security. In May 1996, computer science researchers at Princeton University uncovered a flaw in the 3.0 beta version of Netscape Navigator software that supports Sun's Java programming language. Programmers with malicious intent could write destructive software "viruses" that could use the security flaw to invade computers using Netscape to surf the Internet. Netscape acknowledged the problem and promised to release a fix for the bug ("New Bug," 1996). Despite the flaw, the U.S. government approved Netscape Communications' plan to distribute its 128-bit encryption software via the Internet in July 1996, as long as it was sent only to U.S. citizens ("U.S. Gov't Approves," 1996). Netscape says its 128-bit encryption software requires 309 septillion more times computing power to break the encryption code than its 40-bit version.

THE FUTURE: CONTENT AND CONVERGENCE

Today, four different industries are attempting to provide the same service with different operational models: (a) the "established" online industry, which includes parent companies such as IBM and Sears (Prodigy), H.& R. Block (Compuserve), and GE (GEnie) that has around 5 million users spread among them; (b) the RBOCs, chiefly among them, NYNEX and Bell Atlantic; c) the cable industry (Time-Warner and TCI both have test runs of both interactive cable and videotex services, Time-Warner in conjunction with NYNEX in one area); and d) the computer industry (such as Microsoft's connections with NBC, Disney, etc.)

Thus, it could be said that Cyberspace is in its high growth stage. Unfortunately, because of its ancillary commercial nature, much of the information currently on the Internet is of extremely low quality. Even for companies that have unlimited funds and ambition, there is not a lot of quality prepackaged information from which to choose. At this point, as the marginal cost of producing and distributing high quality information drops, cyberspace will change dramatically.

The changes facing cyberspace will transform its current users. For example, in 1997, AOL ranked as the biggest online service in the world. AOL can and will use their subscriber base to competitive advantage. Yet, keeping subscribers has been increasingly hard for AOL. The enhancements to both the service and the interface are positive moves. For example, with the addition of the Microsoft's Internet Explorer, AOL will have arguably the best Web browser of the major online services. The compression technology AOL uses makes using the Web with a 14.4-Kbps modem almost twice as fast on AOL as with some other Web browsers. But these features by themselves probably won't be enough. Over time, the increased popularity of the Web and the Internet in general has diminished AOL's once-strong value proposition, or at least the general perception of it.

In October 1996, AOL launched series of marketing initiatives aimed at growing its subscriber base. AOL billed itself as "The Internet and a Whole Lot More." (One of the initial ads uses the music from the futuristic cartoon, "The Jetsons"). It also promoted personalization capabilities and community strengths, and will continue to focus on member satisfaction and loyalty as well as safety and reliability. AOL's strategy is that by remaking itself, it will maintain its leadership position in the dynamic online market.

As a part of the marketing initiatives, the new AOL ads were not just about getting the AOL brand name out there. The advertisements sought to differentiate AOL from the other online services and Internet providers. Plus, AOL sent a videotape to each member that outlines the services on AOL, in an effort to get existing customers excited about the service. The tape package also will contain disk and CD-ROM versions of the AOL software, as well as a kit to give a friend, so that he or she can sign up fro AOL. AOL believes that via its packaging, it can accelerate growth from 6.5 million members to 10 million members by summer 1997.

In terms of pricing, AOL's not a good deal for the heavy user. For new users and for users who plan on being online 20 hours or less, AOL is still a good deal. While it is true that most AOL subscribers fall into the category of 20 hours or less a month, the Internet and the Web are an increasingly big problem for AOL.

For one thing, the online services no longer have many content exclusives. Most of the newspapers and magazines hosted online can also be found on the Web. Although all access services have some costs associated with them, the perception of cost is different with AOL. Flat-fee Internet accounts can be had for as little as $10 a month for unlimited Internet access. A consumer can use Netscape or Internet Explorer (the future browser of AOL) to his ir her heart's content without fear of running up a whopping bill.

AOL still has a value proposition to sell: organizing the vast information available on the Net. AOL has the organization the Internet itself lacks. AOL has built a strong foundation in communications tools. Messaging and chat on AOL is considered easier and better than what is offered on competitive services. Some might argue that the benefits of AOL justify the costs, but this is becoming a more difficult argument, one that AOL plans to address that with the new marketing push.

One of AOL's objectives is not only to get people signed up, but to get them using the service more. For the average consumer, that is where the problems lie. AOL may be easier to use and have a better interface, but, when customers spend more than $20 per month, many are going to have trouble justifying the cost of using AOL. To counter this, AOL had to consider lowering its monthly fee, offering flat-fee pricing, cutting the hourly rate (to about $1) or using various combinations of these price changes.

In the past, AOL has always stayed competitive by cutting prices at just the right time. But the competition is no longer Prodigy or CompuServe, but MSN which announced on October 16, 1996, that it was offering unlimited Internet access for $19.95 per month. Consequently, AOL matched MSN's price and service—unlimited access for $19.95 per month. In doing so, AOL ran into some major problems.

First, if customers wanted to keep the old pricing structure, they could if they notified AOL. Otherwise, the new price became the default price.

Second, the new price structure, and the aggressive advertising campaign, drew more customers to AOL than projected. That, in combination with increased usage of AOL by its customers (especially in the AOL chat rooms), placed a serious strain on its service. AOL's 8 million customers found they had long delays in being able to dial up the service.[2] Although AOL has since invested more than $150 million to upgrade its capacity, its reputation took a serious beating. In October 1997, AOL acquired CompuServe's subscribers. The motivation for that acquisition was said to be Compuserve's underutilized server capacity.

In retrospect, although price reductions may have been necessary for AOL to compete for the heavier users of online services, those users still make up a small percentage of the market. It is not inconceivable that AOL will abandon flat-rate pricing, perhaps substituting it with combinations into service classes (Basic, Plus, Premium) through which customers can choose based on cost/service quality tradeoffs.

---

[2] In January 1997, Compuserve broke an ad during the Super Bowl mocking AOL's service problems, urging customers to switch services by calling 1-888-NOT-BUSY.

The biggest challenge facing online media is *content*. Many of the first group of firms setting up shop on the Web have merely created electronic versions of their traditional materials—marketing brochures, catalogs—for perusal. For example, athletic footwear maker Reebok has found a new use for some of its television commercials: making them available for downloading on its Web site ("Reebok launches," 1996). Several of the 30-second "This Is My Planet" ads featuring star athletes like Shaquille O'Neal and Emmitt Smith have been put on the Web as part of the company's aim of establishing a dialog with younger people.

Internet pioneer Vinton Cerf, in discussing the impact of the Internet on sales, advertising, and customer service, noted businesses have to "start learning to think in computer terms. It doesn't mean having to program computers, it just means having to start thinking of a computer as a telecommunications tool, not simply as a desktop publisher or a word processor" ("Cerfin' the Net," 1995, p. R18).

Today's businesses have figured out that there is value in interactive media such as the WWW. However, they have yet to figure out what sort of message the medium can best deliver. So far, they've mostly tried to transform messages from print and television to the new medium of the Web. MCI ran into this exact problem. Its Gramercy Press page attempted to please those Web users who seek out entertainment, while simultaneously attempting to capture business-minded users with its overt promotional appeal and product information. Separately, each of these appeals can be effective. Combined they muddle the intent of the entire site (Carveth, 1996; Hunt, 1995).

Businesses can tout their messages are interactive. However, if there is nothing new about the message (being recycled from older, more traditional media), then all that is left is interactivity for the sake of interactivity. Most people would rather point and click through the Web to establish contacts with companies who share their interests and provide them with useful information.

Negroponte (1995) observed that developers of new media technology have been concentrating on the *display* or *retrieval* aspects of communication, rather than concentrating on content. For example, in 1997 the computer press has touted the potential of "push technology." In push technology, a "push service," such as PointCast, receives documents from various publishing sources. Then, according to a preestablished schedule, the server then consults a preference profile for each user, selects the appropriate content from its repository, and then downloads it to the user. This process saves the user time by providing customized information. Yet, this process only addresses how information is obtained, not the quality of the information. Negroponte argued that to be successful, interactive media content will not merely reflect the intelligences of the producers of media content, but the consumers of media content as well. Thus, the best content presented on the Web will reflect that users will act on the content (active use), rather than being acted on (passive use).

Convergence

In June 1997, Microsoft announced that was was investing $1 billion in Comcast Corp., the fourth-largest cable-TV MSO in the nation, in return for an 11.5% stake in the company. The deal gives Microsoft an opportunity to deliver high-speed online access via personal computers and cable modems. The deal also provides Microsoft a method for providing high-speed access for WebTV, which the company bought 2 months previously for $425 million. Finally, the deal gives Microsoft the opportunity to get in front of Comcast's 11 million subscribers.

The deal illustrates the current trend to convergence in the new media. There's been a long-standing debate about whether the TV or the PC will reign supreme when it comes to interactivity. The trial studies to date on interactive TV suggest people consumers have no preference.

In 1997, personal computer sales to first-time buyers saw its growth rate slow, a major concern to Microsoft. In response, the company is (a) creating content so compelling that more people will be inclined to buy PCs (and Microsoft software); and (b) attempting to reach consumers even if they do not buy PCs.

In April 1997, Microsoft proposed a standard for digital television that would allow it to work on either a PC or a TV. The company hopes to be able to develop an operating system for this flexible standard. In that way, the company will be covered. In addition, historically distributors of media content have done well financially, so for Microsoft, this seems to be an excellent investment. For Comcast, the money represents extra cash to pour into infrastructure (installing high-bandwidth fiber optics). Comcast also gets a major partner for all that is computer and Internet-related.

Deals such as that between Microsoft and Comcast will become the norm as technologies converge to offer consumers the best quality and variety of online services.

CONCLUSION

Social change relies on *individual* change. Consumers of videotex were not transformed by the new technology in the *predicted* manner. Companies must avoid treating consumer disinterest in long-predicted services as a problem in implementation, and to see it as evidence that people may be more interested in doing new things with a new medium. Visionary thinking about technology is problematic when it simply repeats traditionally futuristic views of a changed society, especially since these visions have not been borne out in the past.

As evidence, a September 1996 study by Yankelovich Partners predicts that the number of consumers who jump online by the end of 1997 will fall by 20% unless PC and online subscription prices drop and content developers produce more informative, user-friendly sites (Aguilar, 1996; Walsh, 1996).

Although between May 1994 and May 1995 the number of online service users doubled, 1996 growth slowed because, as Yankelovich partner Walker Smith noted, "People can't find what they're looking for, and they are unsatisfied with reliability." Churn—consumers switching online and Internet service providers—is also becoming a major problem. Finally, the study found the average number of hours spent online in 1996 was 12, down from 16 in 1995. For services which make more income the longer users are online, this could mean a significant revenue reduction.

According to Smith, the numbers will rise only if content developers produce more compelling sites. "The long-term viability of the medium is driven by the ability to provide people with something beyond a novelty. Otherwise it will be like a pet rock or something you get tired of and put on the shelf." The difference here is that a pet rock cost only a few dollars. Losing the economic battle in online communication services could cost billions.

FURTHER READING

McKnight, L., & Bailey, J. (Eds.). (1997). *Internet Economics*. Cambridge, MA: MIT Press.
Negroponte, N. (1995). *Being digital*. New York: Knopf.
Stoll, C. (1995). *Silicon snake oil: Second thoughts on the information highway*. New York: Doubleday.

REFERENCES

Ad Council breaks first Web advertising. (1996, April 1). *Advertising Age*, p. 38.
Aguilar, R. (1996). *Is the Net worth it?* Available at http://www.ws.com/News/.
America Online shows fast-track growth. (1995, January 1). *Washington Post*, p. D1.
Carveth, R. (1996, Spring). Communication via interactive media: Communication in a new key? *New Jersey Journal of Communication*, 71–81.
Carveth, R., & Metz, J. (1996, Spring). Frederick Jackson Turner and the democratization of the electronic frontier. *The American Sociologist*, pp. 72–90.
Cerfin' the Net. (1995, March). *Sales & Marketing Management*, p. R18.
Cleland, K. (1995a, March 13). Fear creates strange bedfellows. *Advertising Age*, p. S16.
Cleland, K. (1995b, March 20). Online offers truly receptive promotion target. *Advertising Age*, p. 18.
CommerceNet/Consortium. (1995). *CommerceNet/Nielsen Internet Demographic Study*. Excerpts from the questions.
CommerceNet/Nielsen (1995, October 30). *The CommerceNet/Nielsen Internet Demographic Survey, Executive Summary*. CommerceNet Consortium/Nielsen Media Research.
Dickerson, M. L., & Gentry, J. W. (1983). Characteristics of adopters and non-adopters of home computers. *Journal of Consumer Research, 10*, 225–235.
Ever-widening Web. (1995, February 27). *Business Week*, p. 78.
Fahey, A. (1989a, May 29). Prodigy opens videotex to outside creative work. *Advertising Age*, p. 31.
Fahey, A. (1989b, October 23). Prodigy sets trade, consumer ads. *Advertising Age,* p. 16.
Fahey, A. (1990, January 20). Carmakers plug into PCs. *Advertising Age*, p. 54.
Fawcett, A. W. (1995, June 5). Trading scissors for modems. *Advertising Age*, p. 14.
FIND/SVP (1996). *The American Internet user survey: New survey highlights*.
Fitzgerald, M. (1996, March 16). Auditing the Web. *Editor & Publisher*, 26.

Goldman, D. (1995, June 5). The virtues of going virtual. *Adweek* (Eastern Edition), 2.

Gore, A. (1991). Infrastructure for the global village. *Scientific American, 265*(3), 150–153.

Grover, V., & Sabherwal, R. (1989, June). Poor performance of videotex systems. *Journal of Systems Management,* 31–36.

Gupta, S. (1996). *The third WWW consumer survey.* A Hermes Project, in collaboration with GVU Center's 3rd WWW User Survey.

Hanson, G. (1992, January 27). Making waves via computers. *Insight,* 6–11, 32–33.

Hawkins, D. (1991, March). Videotex markets, applications, and systems. *Online,* 97–100.

Hodges, J. (1995, September 4). C/net offers Web traffic tracking, *Advertising Age,* p. 15.

Hodges, J. (1996a, January 15). Words hold the key to Web ad packages. *Advertising Age,* p. 38.

Hodges, J. (1996b, March 11). Marketers play Web games as serious business, *Advertising Age,* p. 16.

Hoffman, D., & Novak, T. (1996, July). Marketing in hypermedia computer-mediated environments: Conceptual foundations. *Journal of Marketing.*

Hoffman, D., Novak, T., & Chatterjee, P. (1995, December). Commercial scenarios for the Web: Opportunities and challenges. *Journal of Computer-Mediated Communication, 1*(3).

Hunt, K. (1995, May 1). Gramercy Press on the Web: MCI's ambiguous adventure in advertising. *Computer-Mediated Communication Magazine, 2*(5), 12–24.

Johnson, B. (1996, February 5). Counting eyeballs on the Net, *Advertising Age,* p. 29.

Killan Associates. *E-Cash payments: Impact and opportunity.* Available at http://www.killen.com/studies/study.ecash.fwd.html

Krantz, M. (1995, April 10). Keeping an eye on I/Pro. *Mediaweek,* p. 12.

Krugman, D. M. (1985). Evaluating the audience of the new media. *Journal of Advertising, 14,* 21–27.

Kuntz, M. (1995, April 17) Burma Shave signs on the I-way. *Business Week,* p. 102.

Maital, S. (1991, November). Why the French do it better. *Across the Board,* pp. 7–9.

Major, M. (1990, November 12). Videotex never really left, but it's not all there. *Marketing News,* 2–3.

Mandese, J. (1995, March 20). "Clickstreams" in cyberspace. *Advertising Age,* p. 18.

Markus, M. L. (1987). Toward a "critical mass" theory of interactive media. *Communication Research, 14,* 491–511.

Marx, W. (1996, February 26). "Light years ahead" but still confusing. *Advertising Age,* p. S8.

Most Web users aren't consumers. (1995, February). *Online Access,* p. 15.

Negroponte, N. (1995). *Being digital.* New York: Vintage Books.

New bug found in Netscape's security. (1996, May 18). *The New York Times,* p. 17.

O'Reilly & Associates/Trish Information Services. (1995). *Defining the Internet Opportunity.*

Ogilvy & Mather Direct. (1994). *The techno-savvy consumer.* Available at: http://www.img.om.com/img/hp012000.html

Online advertising still considered experimental. (1995, March 7). *USA Today,* p. B1.

Online profile. (1995, January 11). *Investor's Business Daily,* p. A4.

P&G steps in. (1996, April 29). *Advertising Age,* p. 28.

Perse, E., & Dunn, D. (1995, August). *The utility of home computers: Implications of multimedia and connectivity.* Paper presented at the annual conference of the Association for Education in Journalism and Mass Communication.

Reagan, J. (1987). Classifying adopters and nonadopters of four technologies using political activity, media use and demographic variables. *Telematics and Infomatics, 4,* 3–16.

Reebok launches TV ad on World Wide Web site. (1996, January 11). *Women's Wear Daily,* p. 7.

Rogers, E. M. (1983). *Diffusion of innovations* (3rd ed.). New York: Free Press.

Rogers, E. M. (1985). The diffusion of home computers among households in Silicon Valley. *Marriage and Family Review, 8,* 89–100.

Rogers, E. M. (1986). *Communication technology: The new media in society.* New York: Free Press.

Rubin, A. M. (1984). Ritualized and instrumental television viewing. *Journal of Communication, 34*(3), 67–77.

Sandberg, J. (1995, October 30). Internet's popularity in North America appears to be soaring. *The Wall Street Journal*, p. B1.

Sussman, V. (1995, November 13). Gold rush in cyberspace. *U.S. News & World Report*, pp. 72–74,77–80.

Taylor, C. (1995, September 11). Yahoo and I/PRO explore ranking of Web sites. *Adweek* (Eastern Edition), p. 38.

Taylor, C. (1996a, March 25). Ziff, 'Click to rep Net ads. *Mediaweek*, p. 6.

Taylor, C. (1996b, April 22). P&G talks tough on Web. *Mediaweek*, p. 6.

Taylor, C., & Askey, L. (1996, January 15). After the year of the Web. *Adweek* (Eastern Edition), p. 27.

Times Mirror. (1995, October 16). *Technology in the American household: Americans going online.* Times Mirror Center for the People and the Press

Truet, B., & Hermann, M. (1989, July 10). A skeptic's view of videotex. *Telephony*, pp. 26–27.

U.S. gov't approves online encryption tool distribution. (1996, July 16).*The Wall Street Journal*, p. B2.

Vitalari, N. P., Venkatesh, A., & Gronhaug, K. (1985). Computing in the home: Shifts in the time allocation patterns of households. *Communications of the ACM*, pp. 512–522.

Vonder Haar, S. (1995, September 25). Not so fast: Study on PC market. *Inter@ctive Week*, p. 16.

Walsh, M. (1996). The 01/05/96 Snapshot, Internet Info. *The Yankelovich Cybercitizen Report.* New York: Yankelovich Partners, Inc.

Web profits unlikely till 2000. (1996, July 3) *Investor's Business Daily*, p. A5.

Wells, M. (1995, March 13). Pitching business the virtual way. *Advertising Age*, p. S18.

Williamson, D. (1995a, October 2). Score one for ESPN, Starwave. *Advertising Age*, p. 34.

Williamson, D. (1995b, December 11). Web ad spending pegged at $12.4M. *Advertising Age*, p. 8.

Williamson, D. (1996a, January 22). Marketers link up to tune of $54.7 million. *Advertising Age*, p. 28.

Williamson, D. (1996b, April 1). Breaking free from boring banners. *Advertising Age*, p. 37.

Williamson, D. (1996c, April 8). Smart agents build brains into Net ads. *Advertising Age*, p. 26.

Yankelovich Partners. (1996). *Cybercitizen II.* Available at: http://www.yankelovich.com/cyber_ii/CY-BER_II.HTML

Ziegler, B. (1995, Feb. 6). Share of homes with PCs rises to 31% in poll. *The Wall Street Journal*, p. B5.

Appendix A: Media Accounting Practices

COST AND MANAGEMENT ACCOUNTING

Cost and management accounting is the branch of the profession that focuses on the accumulation of cost records and their application in managerial decision making. Cost and management accounting serves two purposes. First, it accumulates the necessary cost information for drawing up accurate balance sheets and income statements. Second, it uses "relevant" cost data and other information in providing guidance for managerial decision making.

Just as "managerial" economics focuses on the application of economic concepts and data for assisting in decision making, so managerial accounting involves the application of accounting data and other information for decision making by managers. Much of the data and information accumulated for purposes of making managerial decisions as outlined here is cost accounting data. Reflecting the significant differences between financial and cost and management accounting, there are separate professional associations. The predominant professional association in management accounting is the National Association of Accountants (NAA).

FINANCIAL ACCOUNTING

Financial accounting looks at issues associated with balance sheets and income statements. Financial accounting has a primarily stewardship role—it reports on how management has used the funds entrusted to the business by owners (shareholders). The separation of ownership and management is a primary factor in generating the need for audited financial statements. Nonowner managers are the agents of stockholders (owners, principals) and, as in all agency relationships, prudent principals will monitor their agents. For this reason, auditing costs are considered an agency costs of large business organizations (such as the publicly owned corporation) where managers own only a small part of the firm. The extent of management ownership in media firms varies extensively. In some cases (e.g., Time Warner), the percentage is quite low. In others (e.g., Dow Jones), the percentage owned by managers is substantial.

BALANCE SHEET

The balance sheet reports the financial condition at a point in time and is a statement of levels (stocks). The income statement reports the financial performance over an interval of time (most frequently, a year) and is a statement of flows.

The balance sheet has two sides (see Table 1). On the left hand side are uses of funds and on the right, sources. Uses are assets and sources can be liabilities (debt) or equity. The overall structure is depicted below.

Reflecting this structure and logic, the "balance sheet equation" is expressed as:

$A = L + E$

where:

A = assets,

L = liabilities (debt), and

E = equity.

When reading, analyzing, and interpreting the financial statements of a firm it is particularly important to realize that the asset values reported in the statements are not necessarily even close to current market values. For example, land bought in 1920 for $1,000 is said to have a "historical cost" of ~1,000. Generally, historical cost remains unchanged for long periods if an asset is not sold. Assets appear in the books at historical cost—the cost at the time of acquisition. The historical cost of $1,000 could appear in financial statements in the 1990s at that figure even if its current value is $1 million. "Book values" may not even approximate current market values. Only if assets decrease materially in value from their original

TABLE 1
Major Components of the Balance Sheet

Balance Sheet Structure	
Assets	*Sources*
Current Assets	Current Liabilities
Cash	Bank Loans—Short Term
Accounts Receivable	Accounts Payable
Inventory	Accrued Payable
Investments	Term Liabilities
Financial Investments	Bank Loans—Long-Term Bonds & Debentures
Fixed Assets	Equity
Plant, Equipment	Par (stated) Value
At Historical Cost	Paid-in-surplus (Over par)
Less Accumulated Depreciation	Retained Earnings

("historical") cost are financial accountants required to change the historical cost in the balance sheet.

Land is a special example of an asset in that it is generally considered to not depreciate—decline in v value and have a finite useable life span. In the case of assets that do depreciate, there is substantial judgment as to just how long an asset will last. For example, if an asset costs $2,000, how much of it should be considered "used up" in the first years of its life the second, and so on? The Internal Revenue Service (IRS) guidelines for depreciation are not necessarily adopted for the firm's published financial statements. Firms actually do keep two sets of books— one for the IRS and one for published financial statements.

Balance sheet figures for assets are book values—historical cost minus cumulative depreciation (from the date of acquisition to the date of the balance sheet). Many assets transpire to be fully written off (i.e., all their historical cost is now depreciated) before their useful life expires. This results in useful assets that have no (or perhaps a token) value reported in the balance sheet. It is clear that a meaningful interpretation of the reality represented by a balance sheet must be considered within the context of accounting conventions and the particular circumstances of a firm (e.g.. the age of its assets). The "analysis and interpretation" of financial statements (which is the work of financial analysts) is thus a necessary process in order to fully understand just what reality is reflected in the financial statements.

In the normal ongoing pattern of a viable business, liability values on the balance sheet closely approximate actual amounts owing. Only in circumstances of extreme financial distress do firrns come to terms with their creditors for less than full repayment.

It follows that the dollar figure for the ''equity'' component of the balance sheet does not typically reflect the market value of the firm's shares. Although liabilities figures in the balance sheet are close to market values, assets figures typically are not. Because equity is what remains after liabilities are subtracted from assets (E = A – L), book equity is typically very different from the aggregate market value of the firm's shares. Of course, firms are typically "ongoing" (the "going concern" postulate) and assets are not usually sold en masse. Accounting conventions mean that the financial statements for sequential accounting periods (years) are generally comparable and objectively report on management's stewardship of funds invested in the firm. But regardless, the important factor to emphasize is that assets and equity in the balance sheet are not market values, or even necessarily closely related thereto. This is why it is necessary to consider these concepts as distinct when analyzing a media firm for purposes such as potential purchase or for spinning off assets.

The financial accounting profession has faced considerable criticism for the historical orientation of figures in the balance sheet. The profession is fully aware of the characteristics and criticisms of accounting data. Attempts to become more "realistic" often introduce unacceptable repercussions. Given the stewardship nature of financial accounting, "objectivity" is a highly regarded postulate. Because long term assets are seldom sold, measuring "market value" involves appraisals and other judgments. With appraisals, some objectivity is forsaken and the potential for "exaggerated" figures is a violation of another principle of financial accounting—conservatism. Nevertheless, the profession has attempted to balance realism and objectivity.

INCOME STATEMENTS

The income statement accumulates all revenues and expenses during an accounting period and the difference is the profit or loss. The income statement is actually a part of the equity component of the balance sheet. Equity is the residual claimant—it gets what is left after expenses are paid out of revenues. If inventory that has total expenses of $40 associated with its acquisition and sale is sold for $ 55, the in Come statement would show a profit of S 15. Equity has been increased by $15. And if this was the only transaction in an accounting interval, then equity is increased by $15 during that time.

By defining an accounting period to be sufficiently short, each transaction could be considered in this manner. However, such an approach is practically inefficient, and the process is as follows: All revenues and all expenses for an accounting period are separately accumulated. At the end of an accounting period (typically a year, but it can be a short as a day), total expenses are subtracted from total revenues, and the residual is the profit for the period (loss if expenses exceed revenues). The profit is then transferred from the income statement to the equity portion of the balance sheet, and increases the retained earnings component. Conversely, a loss decreases equity (via its effect on retained earnings). Income statements have the structure shown here:

(1)   Revenues (e.g., Sales)
(2) Minus Cost of Goods Sold manufactured
(3)   =   Gross Profit

Less other expenses:
(4) Selling & Distribution
(5) General & Administrative (including depreciation)
(6) Financial (Interest)
(7)   =   Net Profit Before Taxes (NPBT)
(8) Minus Taxes on the NPBT
(9)   =   Net Profit After Taxes (NPAT)

Typically, some of the Net Profit After Tax (NPAT) is paid to stockholders as dividends and the balance remains as an increase in Equity (retained earnings).

The sales revenues (Row 1) in the income statement are typically "market values"—they are measured in a market transaction, the sale. Expense determination is more complex. Expenses are "expired costs" and the identification of just which costs (outlays) have expired is often complex.

Consider the following example of inventory expense: A publisher has two batches of a book in stock. Block A consists of 50 books and they cost $5 each to produce. Block B also consists of 50 books, and because of a new contract with the printing firm, block B books cost $6 each. The firm sells 50 books in the current accounting period. What is the Cost of Goods (inventory) Sold (COGS)? Under a First-In First-Out (FIFO) inventory expense system the inventory expenses associated with Block A will be considered to have flowed through, and the answer is $250 (50 times $5). In contrast, if a Last-In First-Out (LIFO) inventory expense system is employed, the COGS is $300 (50 times $6).

The materiality of this difference can be considerable. And note that if $6 is considered to best represent current cost levels for income (profit) determination and LIFO is used, then the cost of the books remaining (in the balance sheet under inventory) is "artificially" low. The balance sheet will show inventory at $250, compared with $300 if FIFO is employed. There is a direct trade-off with the choice of inventory cost-flow method—the choice of one method over the other will make the income statement profit figure "better" and the balance sheet valuation of remaining inventory "worse," or vice versa. In time of inflation, use of LIFO provides a more accurate income/profit figure, but the balance sheet inventory figure becomes increasingly outmoded (if a certain minimum level of inventory is always kept on hand).

Appendix B: Financial Management

INVESTMENT DECISIONS

Current Asset Management

Assets are partitioned into two primary categories—current assets and fixed assets. With current assets, the key decisions relate to day-to-day management, including frequent decisions regarding the level and efficient management of cash, inventory, and receivables. Because these decisions are recurring, the use of financial models that employ standardized techniques of analysis is typical. These models often have their origin in management science, the application of mathematical techniques to management problems. The importance of physical inventory varies across the respective media industries. For book publishers, inventory decisions are important, and the size of press runs for particular titles is a significant issue. In contrast, broadcast media have relatively little physical inventory and this is a minor decision area.

Fixed Asset Management—Capital Budgeting

In contrast to the day-to-day focus in the management of current assets. with fixed assets financial management is not involved on an ongoing basis. With fixed assets, the day-to-day management is the responsibility of operations management. Financial management becomes involved Periodically to contribute toward making major decisions regarding the acquisition or disposal of divisions/units/plants. The decision techniques require the comparison of costs with expected benefits. Because the stream of expected benefits occurs over a future time horizon, the interest factor ("Time Value of Money") must be taken into account. As noted in the consideration of valuation in chapter 5, the cost/benefit analysis is structured as follows:

Net benefits = (value of expected benefits) – (cost)

"Net benefits" are defined as the value, in today's dollars, of the present value (i.e., taking interest into account) of the incremental benefits minus the cost of purchasing those cash flows. The incremental benefits are the increase in after-tax cash flows resulting from potential adoption of the project. "Cash flow" is important for the ongoing operations of firms as well as incremental analysis for capital project evaluation. For a given ongoing firm, cash flow is approximately equal to the NPAT plus expenses not requiring cash outlay (i.e., predominantly depreciation). Cash flow is considered by many to be a more significant metric of firm capability than profit figures. For example, the cash flow figure is a more reliable estimate of a firm's ability to meet interest obligations than is the NPAT. Many firms incurring accounting losses have positive cash flows. Another subtlety relates to the use of cash flows generated. A firm could have a sound ability to generate cash flow but if that cash is invested unwisely (e.g., in many overdue accounts receivable) then the overall funds flow may indicate problems. These issues are brought together in the Funds Flow Statement which accompanies the balance sheet and income statement in financial statements and published accounts.

Formally, the calculation of the Net benefits ("Net Present Value/ NPV") is as follows:

$$NPV = \text{Present Value (of incremental benefits)} - \text{cost}$$

Net present value calculations can become somewhat complex. They are considered further in chapter 5. The calculation of incremental cash flows and their present value representation are examined in courses in financial management and both financial and cost and management accounting. The capability to undertake capital budgeting analysis requires data from operations (production, marketing, and distribution) awes well as from other line (e.g., accounting, research and development legal environment) functional areas.

The important insights are that a capital investment decision in incurring present, generally known costs in order to purchase an uncertain stream of future incremental cash flows. When the development or construction of a new project extends over a protracted time period, the initial cost of creating the Fox network has generally been incurred over a lengthy interval, as management clearly knew at the time of initiation.

The expected future cash flows must be estimated (a potentially complex undertaking) and relevant interest rates taken into account to arrive at the value today of the anticipated flows. If the benefits in dollars equivalent to today's (i.e., discounted in the present value calculations) exceed the cost (already in today's dollars), then quantitatively the project is acceptable. Of course, quantitative analysis is only part of the total decision analysis. Particularly in the management of media properties, qualitative factors are important in coming to final decisions.

Financial accounting and financial management are related disciplines that at the same time have substantial differences. They have quite different functions and this often requires different perspectives in the practice of each. As a reflection of the important differences between financial and accounting perspectives, recall that capital budgeting in financial management considers the "benefits" from a project to be the incremental after-tax cash flows (ATCFs), not incremental profits. The use of ATCFs rather than (incremental) profits is not a criticism of positive cash flows. accounting data. Rather, it would be a misuse of accounting data to apply it in this analysis. An important factor is that for accounting, depreciation is an expense (part of general and administrative) to be deducted before calculating profit. In capital budgeting analysis, the cost of acquiring an asset is taken into account directly by subtracting the cost at acquisition, rather than allocating that expense over the life of the project (or as allowed by the IRS), as accounting is required to do.

Capital budgeting decisions can be focused on new assets and increasing the size of the firm or reducing the set of assets employed and shrinking the firm. Much of the restructuring activity that occurred in the media industries during the 1980s resulted from a capital-budgeting analysis of existing products/divisions/units. Many firms found that for various reasons, some existing operations were worth more sold than they could generate as part of the firm. There was a net benefit to selling some operations rather than continuing to operate them. This awareness is the analysis behind much of the sell-off activity that has been widespread in recent years. The reasons why a buyer is prepared to pay for a division than it is worth to the present owner firm are varied. The important point at this juncture is to note that capital budgeting tools and techniques are the mechanism by which such restructuring decisions are made. To evaluate whether an asset should be sold, the formulation is as follows:

NPV = Sale price attainable—PV (expected cash flows if retained)

A variation of this formulation is also used for abandonment decisions. For example, if a magazine is incurring ongoing losses and negative cash flows (and there is no buyer for the title), then the cost of abandonment may be less than the cost of keeping operations going. However, abandonment costs can be substantial. If severance payments or pension expenses will be incurred, large sums may be involved. This gives rise to some aggressive and innovative strategies. For example, some commentators considered the overall management goal in the 1990 New York Daily News confrontation be a shutdown (abandonment) of the operation employing strategies whereby approximately $150 million in severance pay could be avoided. Not surprisingly, this is an emotive issue and is vociferously debated.

FINANCING DECISIONS

Acquiring Needed Funds

When the set of desirable (i.e., "positive NPV") projects has been determined, the manner of financing must be determined. The primary questions are how much debt, how much equity, and, within debt, how much is short term (typically 90-day bank loans or, for large companies, commercial paper) and how much long term (from bonds)? These are complex decisions and the review here should be supplemented by additional study of capital structure by those working in media financial management.

One of the primary relationships in finance is that between expected return and risk. The economic norm is that as risk increases, expected return increases. The media industry is typically a high-risk industry. Few can predict with any certainty whether, say, a film will be a "blockbuster" or a "dud." Few are prepared to invest in corporate stocks with the same expected return as on treasury bills. Of course, the distinction between expected return and actual return is critical. Those who invested in gold at $800 an ounce in 1981 clearly did not expected that it would sell for less than $400 an ounce within 2 years.

Media firms employ a variety of capital structures. As a generalization, the more physical, tangible assets (such as distribution and broadcast facilities) a firm has, the larger the absolute amount (and proportion) of debt it can obtain. Lenders understandably prefer to have tangible readily saleable assets constituting security for their loans/investments. In contrast, some publishing firms with relatively few tangible assets employ relatively little debt. The limited availability of debt in these circumstances reflects the nature of their assets.

On the other hand, in some media industries, while there are relatively few physical assets, the operations can be such that there are predictable profits and cash flows. Media assets with predictable cash flows have demonstrated an ability to attract lenders and have the opportunity to have high debt levels. An example is cable systems. The escalating prices paid for such systems in the late 1980s were often significantly financed by the use of debt. The focus on predictable cash flows as a basis for supporting debt led to many media properties being (acquired in leveraged buyouts (LBOs) in the late 1980s. Particularly for deals put together since 1986, many of the projections for cash flows transpired to have been unduly optimistic. The high level of debt (up to 80% of total asset valuation) has proven to be too much burden for even sound media properties as advertising revenues declined in 1989–1990. Several media firms with high levels of debt in their capital structures failed in 1990. Prominent examples include Gillett Holdings and Ingersoll Newspapers.

When assets are valued at multiples of operating income and cash flows that transpire to be optimistic relative to what is realized, then high levels of debt in capital structures greatly exacerbate the financial pressures. Media LBOs and other restructurings of the 1980s have in many instances transpired to have loaded unmanageable levels of debt servicing responsibilities on the operating cash flows generated.

The general consensus in finance is that there does exist an optimal level of debt (and equity) in the capital structure of firms. However, this optimal level is not easy to identify. It reflects the nature of assets owned by the firm and the structure of ownership (for example, whether the shares are closely held or is it a public company with shares traded on the stock exchanges.) A logical corollary is that the optimal capital structure will change as the asset composition and ownership structure change, in addition to the changes dictated by varying conditions in the financial markets, both domestic and international.

DISTRIBUTION DECISIONS

Operating income refers to what is available after all expenses *other than* interest, taxes and dividends have been met. It is the income derived from operating the firm's assets. This is also known as "Earnings Before Interest and Taxes" (EBIT). In terms of the earlier accounting consideration of the income statement, EBIT can be represented as shown here.

OPERATING INCOME AND EBIT-DISTRIBUTION

(1) Revenues (e.g. Sales)

(2) Minus Cost of Goods Sold/Manufactured

(3) = Gross Profit

Less other expenses:

(4) Selling & Distribution

(5) General & Administrative

( ) = Operating Income   = EBIT:

DISTRIBUTE   *TO*

(6) Financial (Interest, = I)   −I: Distributed to Lenders

(7) = Net Profit Before Taxes   NPBT:

(8) Minus Taxes (T) on the NPBT   -T: Distributed to Govt

(9) = Net Profit After Taxes   NPAT: Available for Stockholders (Pay out or retain)

The distribution decisions technically involve three categories of recipients. However, two of the three decisions provide few degrees of freedom. The payment of interest (I) to lenders provides little freedom of choice unless the strategic considerations of financial distress have come to be relevant. Financial distress here is defined as circumstances where the possibility of default has evolved. The degrees of financial distress vary from a mild condition of cash flow problems through severe insolvency. Hopefully, a firm can meet its interest obligations and will do so. Once financial distress becomes sufficiently developed for the nonpayment of interest to be a serious consideration, then a range of strategic alternatives come into consideration, including bankruptcy.

The payment of tax (T) to the Treasury is also a constrained set of distribution decisions. Firms employ many techniques to legally reduce and/or defer tax payments, but the prevailing tax code and adherence to legal requirements means that the distribution of part of NPBT to the Treasury is largely determined by tax legislation.

The third distribution decision does provide some flexibility in decision making. NPAT is available for two uses—the payment of dividends and retention of profits in the form of increased Retained Earnings in the Equity portion of the balance sheet.

Rate of Return

The rate of return (ROR) is a primary metric in finance. It is a generally simple concept, and can be introduced by way of a numerical example. If a security was purchased a year ago for $100, today it is worth $110, and the security paid a $5 dividend throughout the year, then an intuitively appealing (and correct) rate of return is 15% over the year. Formally:

$$ROR = \frac{PRICE_{end} - PRICE_{beginning}}{PRICE_{beginning}} + \frac{INCOME_{during}}{PRICE_{beginning}}$$

$$= \frac{110 - 100}{100} + \frac{5}{100} = \frac{15}{100} = 15\%$$

or

ROR = Capital Gain component of ROR + Income component of ROR

If a firm does not pay a dividend and invests the foregone dividend in profitable projects, then the stock price at the end of the period may be at least sufficiently higher to offset the lack of a dividend in the ROR equation. If the ROR on the investment project financed with the foregone dividend is greater than the ROR available to stockholders from their other investment opportunities, then the stockholders will prefer the firm pays no dividends. This is why many firms in the early years of their existence, when they have rapid growth and good investment opportunities, do not pay any dividend. Given the ROR on firm's investment opportunities, stockholders are happy with that distribution decision. Of course, for some investors who need dividend income to meet their cash outflows (e.g., retired individuals), there is a preference for regular dividends. The result is a pattern of dividend "clienteles." Investors who are looking to maximize returns and do not need ongoing dividend income may be indifferent regarding dividends and often invest in new and/or high growth firms. Other investors need the dividend income and gravitate to firms with histories of regular and stable dividend payments.

Glossary

Above the line: A term used in motion picture and television budgets that refers to the artistic expenses of a production. Above the line workers include producers, directors, writers, actors; other above the line expenses include the purchase of rights to a story or script.

Acquisition: The purchase of operating assets or stock of one company by another firm. Distinct from a merger or consolidation in that the selling company typically continues to exist following the transaction.

Amortization: Accounting procedure that gradually reduces the cost value of a limited life or intangible asset through periodic charges to income.

Archives: Archives are organizations that collect and store material of historic and cultural significance. In the case of motion picture and television archives the Library of Congress has taken the lead in encouraging legislation that facilitates the development and maintenance of public archives for these media.

Asset: Anything having commercial or exchange value that is owned by a business, institution, or individual.

Balance sheet: Financial report also called statement of condition or financial position showing the status of a company's assets, liabilities and owner's equity on a given date.

Barriers to entry: Real or imagined costs that act to prevent firms from entering a particular industry.

Barter syndication: Barter is a form of syndication in which the cost of programs to stations and cable program services is reduced in return for reserving several commercial availabilities within the program for use by the provider of the program.

Below the line: A term used in budgeting and planning motion picture and television production. Below the line workers include such specialists as set carpenters, camera operators, grips, gaffers, sound mixers, and other technicians required by a production. Below the line expenses include costs of film, lease of production equipment and other facilities.

Blind bidding: An unethical and illegal practice in the distribution of motion pictures, it requires theater operators to bid on productions that they were not allowed to preview prior to their bid.

Block booking: An unethical and illegal practice in the distribution of motion pictures it requires theater operators to commit to presentation of a set or "block" of productions of unknown value in order to show one or more productions of unquestioned value.

Bond: Any interest-bearing or discounted government or corporate security that obligates the issuer to pay a specified sum of money at specified times and to repay the principal amount of the loan at maturity.

Book value: (1) Value at which an asset is carried on the balance sheet. For example, a piece of manufacturing equipment is put on the books at its cost when purchased. Its value is then reduced each year as depreciation is charged to income. (2) Net asset value of a company's securities calculated as total assets minus intangible assets minus current and long-term liabilities and any equity issues that have a prior claim.

Capital expenditure: Outlay of money to acquire or improve capital assets such as buildings and machinery.

Capital structure: Corporation's financial framework, including long-term debt, preferred stock, and net worth. It is distinct from financial structure in that it includes additional sources of capital such as short-debt, accounts payable, and other liabilities.

Capital asset pricing model: Sophisticated model of the relationship between expected risk and expected return. It says that the return on an asset or security is equal to the risk-free return such as that on a short-term Treasury security plus a risk premium.

Capitalization ratio: Analysis of a company's capital structure showing what percentage is debt, preferred stock, common stock, and other equity.

Cartel: A formal or informal arrangement of companies that attempt to eliminate competition between themselves by agreeing to common prices, quality standards, advertising and the like.

Cash flow: In a larger financial sense an analysis of all the changes that affect the cash account in a given accounting period. In investments, refers to the cash generated from operations and may be defined as EBIT, EBITDA, Free Cash Flow, or other variations of net income plus non cash expenses. The sum of retained earnings and depreciation provision made by firms. As an indicator of revenue remaining after all direct expenses have been deducted, it is the source of internally generated long-term funds available to the firm.

Common stock: Units of ownership of a public corporation. Owners typically are entitled to vote on the selection of directors and other important matters as well as to receive dividends on their holdings. In the event that a corporation is liquidated, the claims of secured and unsecured creditors and owners of bonds and preferred stock take precedence over the claims of those who own common stock.

Comparable sales: Those firms, which are comparable in size, location, and profitability, that have been sold lately. As they are like the firm under consideration, they should have similar values.

Comparative advantage: The situation that exists when market forces allocate a nation's resources to those industries where it is relatively most productive, especially in terms of keeping costs low.

Competition: Rivalry of buyers and sellers with and among themselves in a market. The term also refers to a market structure in which many buyers and sellers of the product compete.

Competitive advantage: The situation that exists when a nation or firm holds an industrial advantage over others. Competitive advantage considers not only the costs of production, product quality, product features, but new product innovation as well.

Concentration of market power: A situation where the top firms in an industry collectively control the vast majority of industry sales or assets. It is usually measured by the cumulative market shares of the four to eight largest firms.

Concentration ratio: The proportion of industry sales concentrated within selected numbers of firms, typically 4, 8, and 20.

Concentration: The degree to which the largest companies in the same product and geographic market control the economic activities of that market.

Concept: In the planning and preparation of a broadcast program or cereals a concept is a brief statement of the main idea. It is particularly useful in research to determine the value of program proposals.

Conglomerate: A large corporation composed of companies in a variety of businesses.

Consent decree: A negotiated settlement of an antitrust case before a judgment is rendered. No admission of guilt is implied by such a settlement nor may it be the foundation for assessing damages to injured parties.

Consolidation: A type of merger in which both companies cease to exist after the transaction and an entirely new corporation is formed that retains the assets and liabilities of both companies.

Creamskimming: To take the most desirable and valuable part of a business, akin to skimming cream off the top of milk bottles prior to pasteurization.

Default: Failure of a debtor to make interest or principal payments or to meet some other provision of a bond indenture.

Deficit financing: A situation where the costs of production (including normal profits) are not fully covered by payments, forcing producers to either sacrifice normal profits or cross-subsidize operations from revenues derived in other areas.

Depreciation: Amortization of fixed assets, such as plant or equipment, so as to allocate the cost over their depreciable life.

Distribution deal: A financial arrangement for the production of a broadcast program or series or of a motion picture. A distribution deal commits the producer to making the finished production available to a stipulated channel of distribution, such as network broadcast, cable program service, or videocassette. In return, the distribution channel benefitting from these arrangements provides a part of the financing of the production.

Duopolies: Market structures in which there are two sellers of a product.

EBITDA: Earnings before depreciation, amortization, interest, and taxes are paid.

Economies of scale: Declining levels of average cost accompanying greater expansion of product output and optimal use of plant and equipment. Cost advantages associated with the increasing size of firms.

Equity: Ownership of a company arising from purchasing shares or stock or building the enterprise from scratch.

Excess profits: Profit over and above normal profits.

Exclusivity: A provision of syndication contracts that guarantees that a program purchased by a station or cable program service will not also be available to its competitors within the same national runs covered by the contract.

Expected value: Precisely the mean value of the distribution function. It provides an estimate of average value when the true value is unknown.

Externalities: Factors that can influence the value of goods, or affect an exchange, but that are not ordinarily considered as part of the market for that good. An example might be the desire of a purchaser to gain the prestige of being a publisher.

Fair market value: The expected value of a property under normal conditions. What the typical buyer, or seller, would price a property at.

Financial interest in syndication: A set of federal rules that limit the ownership of programs presented first by a broadcast network. In general, the network on which the program or series is first presented in prime time may participate in ownership only under very restricted conditions such as foreign distribution.

First-run (original) syndication: These are programs and series produced especially for the syndication.

Fixed costs: Costs that do not vary when output is increased or decreased.

"Frame of mind" value: The dimensions of reputation, familiarity, and popularity bestowed upon a production by patronage of an audience.

Free cash flow: Earnings after interest and taxes minus capital expenditures plus depreciation and amortization.

Goodwill: In acquisition accounting, going concern value in excess of book value.

Gross domestic product: The sum total of all goods and services produced in the United States in 1 year.

Highly leverage transaction (HLT): A merger or acquisition predicated on the use of borrowed funds to finance a portion of the transaction resulting in a company that has substantially more debt than is typical for the industry. See also leveraged buyout.

Holding company: Organizational entities that form umbrella structures linking independent advertising agencies.

Income forecasting method: A procedure used by accountants and management of broadcast stations and cable program services to estimate the value of a proposed purchase from syndication. It can also be used to estimate the worth of programs or series already under contract from syndication.

Independent producer: A producer of motion pictures or television programs who operates a production business separate from a motionpicture studio, network. program service, or distribution organization.

Investment bank: A firm acting as an agent that serves as an intermediary between an issuer of securities and the investing public. Additional services include client advisement and the provision of broker-dealer security trading.

Joint operating agreement: A business relationship allowed under law that provides newspapers with an exemption to antitrust law. Under a joint operating agreement two separately owned newspapers combine business operations while maintaining separate news and editorial operations.

Junk bond: Bond with a speculative grade credit rating from Standard & Poor's and Moody's rating services.

Lead-in index: A value calculated from audience measurements that reflects the demonstrated ability of a television program to capture and/or enlarge the audience of the program that immediately precedes it in the broadcast schedule. It is calculated in this fashion:

Leverage: Debt in relation to equity in a firm's capital structure.

Leveraged buyout: Takeover of a company using borrowed funds. Most often, the target company's assets serve as security for the loans taken out by the acquiring firm, which repays the loans from the cash flow of the acquired company.

Limited series: A production intended for presentation on one or more of a small number of days. A limited series may include from two to any number of episodes but is usually not planned for presentation on a once a week basis or for periods of time greater than a few weeks.

Marketing concept: A core principle emphasizing the centrality of consumer need satisfaction in marketing products and services.

Media conglomerate: A corporation that deals in several (seemingly unrelated) media business.

Merger: A combination of two companies either through a pooling of interests, where the accounts are combined; a purchase, where the amount paid over and above the acquired company's book value is carried on the books of the purchaser as goodwill; or a consolidation, where a new company is formed to acquire the net assets of the combining companies. A legal process whereby two or more firms consolidated into one corporation.

Monopolistic competition: The condition that exists in a market where there are many sellers but the products cluster and within each genre of product sellers compete to differentiate their products. A market structure in which a number of competing sellers of similar, but differentiated, products exist.

Monopoly: A market structure in which a single seller of a product exists and controls the market, often resulting in restraint of free trade.

Monopsony: A monopoly from the buyer's (rather than the seller's) perspective.

Multiples: A "quick and dirty" way of estimating fair market value, based on a multiple of some indicator of firm size or profitability.

Multiplex: A movie theater complex with several auditory with a common lobby.

National Association of Television Program Executives (NATPE): A professional association of television program directors and program managers. The annual meeting of the association has become the principal meeting at which programs and series for syndication are bought and sold.

National run (also simply called "run"): The presentation of a motion picture or television program or series to a national audience one time. The audience is deemed "national" in industry practice if presented once in any city. The second presentation in any city begins a second national run.

Natural monopolies: Monopolies that occur not because of acts of competitors but because scale economies and other factors make a single producer most efficient and drive others from the market.

Network: The simultaneous transmission of a program by two or more stations or systems, interconnected by wire or satellites; it also refers to organizations that provide a continuous flow of such programs to prearranged groups of stations or systems that are affiliates.

Normal profits: The rate of return on invested capital for entrepreneurs that provides sufficient compensation to them to invest their scarce time and funds in the enterprise rather than switch to another one; also referred to as the opportunity cost of entrepreneurship.

Off-network series: A television series originally presented on network television in prime time that has subsequently become available for syndication.

Oligopoly: A market structure composed of a few very large and powerful firms that control an industry. The higher the market concentration, the stronger/tighter the oligopoly. A market structure in which competition exists among a small number of sellers of similar products.

Operating profits: That profit which would be earned if no resources were diverted to expansion or reinvestment (retained earnings). The same as EBIT.

Opportunity cost: The economic value of the next best alternative to what one is currently doing.

Package: A collection of films or programs that are sold as a unit in syndication.

Pay-in-kind securities: Fixed income securities, typically bonds, that meet interest payments through the issuance of like securities in the principal amount of the payment in lieu of a cash payment. Similar to a common stock paying a dividend in common stock.

Present value: Value today of a future payment or stream of payments, discounted at some appropriate compound interest or discount rate. For example, the present value of $100 to be received 10 years from now is about $38.55, using a discount rate equal to 10% compounded annually.

Price discrimination: A market situation in which sellers find it possible and profitable to separate two or more markets for its product or service and charge a different price in each of the markets. In the movie business the first market is the theaters (or theatrical window) and the others (cable TV, home video, and over-the-air TV) are referred to as the ancillary markets.

Price/earnings ratio (P/E): The price of a stock divided by the earnings of the company.

Prime time: Hours of peak viewing for a broadcast network or station or cable program service. Although other hours may be designated as prime by a broadcaster, practice has become uniform that in the Eastern and Pacific time zones, for example. prime time on weekdays is from 7 p.m. until 11 p.m. local time.

Prime-time access rule (PTAR): A rule adopted by the FCC in 1971, PTAR provides that the commercial television networks may not program for their affiliates more than three of the week night block of 4 prime-time hours. In addition, in the top 50 television markets local network affiliates may not schedule off-network programming in the daily hour of prime time that they program.

Prime-time alternative: Prime-time alternatives are purchased by independent television stations hoping to attract audience from affiliates during prime time, by network affiliates that intend to preempt network programs with less audience appeal and by cable channels wishing to win audiences from broadcast television stations during prime time.

Private placement: The sale of securities directly to a limited number of institutional investors. A private placement need not be registered with the S.E.C.

Product differentiation: The process whereby a company differentiates itself or its products from those of its competitors.

Publishing: For the purposes of this book, the term **publishing** referred specifically to the book industry; consumer and business periodicals; electronic databases and CD-ROM products; and miscellaneous publishing (e.g., directories, annuals, newsletters, loose-leaf reporting services, etc.).

Pure competition: A marketplace characterized by four conditions: (a) homogeneity of product, (b) smallness of each buyer or seller to the market, (c) absence of artificial restraints, and (d) mobility of resources.

Reality-based programs and series: Television programs or series comprised of material from reality, such as biography, history, nature, science, or extraordinary experiences of ordinary citizens.

Re-release: A motion picture term, it refers to presentations of a motion picture several years after initial release of a theatrical film.

Residuals: Payments to above-the-line workers in motion pictures and television for second and subsequent presentation of the production(s) to which they contributed.

Rough: A relatively crude or unfinished version of a program or series. Roughs are used to give potential purchasers and investors an audiovisual impression of a finished program or series.

Scale economies: Cast savings that result when long-run average costs decline as output and plant size increase.

Self-sufficiency: The condition in which a firm is totally reliant on itself for its supply of inputs into the production or distribution process. Widespread self-sufficiency indicates significant vertical integration.

Shared monopoly: When a cartel arrangement is so stable and successful that the several firms operate in unison as if a single monopolist controlled the industry.

Significantly viewed cable-imported television signal: A television station presented in the market of a local over-the-air television station by cable If the imported station duplicates some programs of the local telecaster, cable is usually required to black out or not present, the program on the imported signal that duplicates the local outlet. If, however, audience measurement within the market indicates that there is a consistently significant audience for the imported station's signal within the counties covered by the local station, then a local station may not use FCC rules to protect its programs against duplicated programming from the "significantly viewed" station.

Speculative presentations: Presentations prepared by advertising agencies in order to attract new business clients.

Stages of production: Product is said to flow through several stages from its earliest origins as raw material through various manufacturing, distribution, and wholesaling levels until its final appearance as a retail consumer product. Each successive stage adds complexity and value to the product.

Strip (strip scheduling): A practice in scheduling television programs in which the programmer schedules the same program at the same time on Consecutive days.

Studio: A motion picture business which produces theatrical films and/or television programs and series. Studios develop and maintain a lot (outdoor sites for shooting films and television), property and setting shops and warehouses, film processing laboratories, film and related equipment.

Superstation: An independent TV station sent via satellite to distant cable markets.

Supplier: A firm which provides programs or series to a television network, cable program service, or syndication.

Syndicated research services: Companies that collect information on media audiences and product usage that is sold to advertisers, advertising agencies, and the media.

Syndication exclusivity (syndex): Rules reinstituted in January 1991 requiring cable systems to black out or substitute other programs for, syndicated programs brought into the local market by cable from distant television stations. The syndics blackout is required only for those syndicated programs under exclusive syndication to a local television station in the cable system's area and after application to the cable system by the local broadcast station involved.

Syndication: The sale of rights to present broadcast programs or series or motion pictures to individual television stations and cable program services.

Syndicator: A firm offering television programs or series or cable program services for syndication.

Tax shelter: Methods used by investors to legally avoid or reduce tax liabilities. Legal shelters include the use of depreciation of assets such as plant and equipment and the amortization of goodwill as operating expenses.

Up-front money: Funds provided to a producer in advance of production of television programs or series.

Use of proceeds: A statement made by an issuing company in an offering prospectus as to how the capital being raised is to be spent.

Utility: A basic concept of economic value, based on the notion that goods are desired because they are somehow useful. Utility is derived as an indicator of "usefulness."

Variable costs: Costs that vary as the amount of output increases. Labor and materials are commonly variable costs.

Vertical integration: The situation where a company occupies adjacent stages of production in an industry, thereby removing this stage either partially or wholly from access by outside companies (depending on the level of self-sufficiency).

Zero coupon security: Security that makes no periodic interest payments but instead is sold at a deep discount from its face value. The buyer of such a bond receives the rate of return by the gradual appreciation of the security that is redeemed at face value on a specified maturity date.

Author Index

Subject Index